THE GREAT
CHRISTIAN DOCTRINES

EDITED BY
JAMES HASTINGS, D.D.

THE DOCTRINE OF FAITH

THE
CHRISTIAN DOCTRINE
OF
FAITH

EDITED BY
JAMES HASTINGS, D.D.

WIPF & STOCK · Eugene, Oregon

Wipf and Stock Publishers
199 W 8th Ave, Suite 3
Eugene, OR 97401

The Christian Doctrine of Faith
By Hastings, James
ISBN 13: 978-1-5326-1873-4
Publication date 3/9/2017
Previously published by T. & T. Clark, 1919

PREFACE.

THIS is not a theological treatise on the one hand, nor on the other is it a volume of sermons. Like its predecessor, the volume on Prayer, it has a distinct office to fulfil, an office that in the judgment of the editor is of immense importance. For between the professor's lecture-room and the preacher's study there is a great gulf fixed. In the lecture-room the lectures on systematic theology are laboriously entered into notebooks, which are useful for the exit examinations. But when the active work of the ministry begins, and so many sermons have to be prepared every week, the cupboard into which those notebooks have been stowed away is left undisturbed. The preacher begins to spin his sermons out of his own brains, with the assistance of such popular books as happen to be at his hand.

This volume aims at bridging that gulf. It is a study of the doctrine of Faith so arranged that each chapter can be taken by itself and made the basis of a sermon or lecture; but, if read right through, offers an account of that doctrine which is sufficiently complete, and sufficiently systematic, to enable the preacher to grasp the subject in its entirety and to feel that he has made it his own.

The great question for the preacher, young preacher and old preacher alike, is *materials*. All the great sermons are full of matter. Take up a volume of Robertson's, of Liddon's, of Watkinson's, of Paterson's, of Macgregor's, of Jowett's—every sermon is full of matter, lit up at every turn with illustration or example.

PREFACE

The editor has command of a large library and has used it freely. Let the preacher take this volume for a winter's course in the Bible Class, the Prayer Meeting, or the Church; let him read each chapter till he knows its ideas and their order; then let him speak his message, quoting the illustrations as he finds that they appeal to him, and quoting them accurately, or substituting other illustrations of his own. In that way the volume on Prayer has been used by men who have written to the editor to say that it has been the means of restoring the Bible Class and the Prayer Meeting to something of their old interest and influence.

JAMES HASTINGS.

CONTENTS.

		PAGE
I. INTRODUCTION	. . . . . .	1
1. THE IMPORTANCE OF FAITH .	. . . .	6
2. THE NECESSITY OF FAITH .	. . . .	15
3. THE HEROISM OF FAITH	. . . . .	21
II. FAITH IN ONE'S SELF	. . . . .	27
1. THE VALUE OF FAITH IN ONE'S SELF	. . .	33
2. ITS PERILS	. . . . . .	38
3. ITS FOUNDATION	. . . . .	44
III. FAITH IN MEN	. . . . . .	57
1. APPRECIATION .	. . . . .	61
2. TRUSTFULNESS .	. . . . .	70
IV. THE RANGE OF FAITH .	. . . .	79
1. IN DAILY LIFE	. . . . .	85
2. IN SCIENCE	. . . . . .	91
3. IN SOCIETY	. . . . . .	98
4. FAITH IN RELIGIOUS LIFE	. . . .	102
V. FAITH IN GOD	. . . . . .	109
1. PURPOSE	. . . . . .	112
2. PROVIDENCE	. . . . . .	118
3. ACCEPTANCE	. . . . . .	124
4. ACTION .	. . . . . .	127
VI. THE VENTURE OF FAITH	. . . .	133
1. SIGHT .	. . . . . .	136
2. KNOWLEDGE	. . . . . .	141
3. RISK	. . . .	144
4. WORTH .	. . . . . .	148

CONTENTS

		PAGE
VII.	FAITH IN JESUS	151
	1. A Recognition	157
	2. An Energy	161
	3. A Relationship	164
VIII.	FAITH IN CHRIST AS SAVIOUR	175
	1. Assent	180
	2. Appropriation	185
	3. Repentance	190
IX.	DEGREES OF FAITH	195
	1. Little Faith	204
	2. Great Faith	212
X.	THE GROWTH OF FAITH	219
	1. The Consciousness of Progress	222
	2. The Encouragement of Progress	227
	3. The Signs of Progress	234
XI.	THE FIGHT OF FAITH	237
	1. The Enemy	244
	2. The Purpose	248
	3. The Method	252
XII.	THE FULL ASSURANCE OF FAITH—(PART I.)	261
	1. The Word	266
	2. The Conditions of Assurance	269
XIII.	THE FULL ASSURANCE OF FAITH—(PART II.)	277
	1. The Object of Assurance	279
	2. The Necessity of Assurance	288
	3. The Value of Full Assurance	295
XIV.	THE FOUNDATION OF FAITH	301
	1. The Church	306
	2. The Bible	311
	3. Argument or Intuition	319
	4. Experience	324

CONTENTS

	PAGE
XV. THE CONFIRMATION OF FAITH	331
1. The Testimony of Others	333
2. Its Fruits	337
3. The Witness of the Spirit	343
XVI. JUSTIFICATION BY FAITH	351
1. The Necessity	354
2. The Meaning	357
3. The Channel	367
4. The Blessings	372
XVII. SANCTIFICATION BY FAITH	381
1. Faith Justifying and Sanctifying	385
2. New Life	388
3. Growth	393
XVIII. PERSONALITY IN FAITH	401
1. The Person of Christ	407
2. Our Own Personality	411

I.
INTRODUCTION.

LITERATURE.

Ainsworth, P. C., *The Threshold Grace.*
Allan, A., *The Advent of the Father* (1907).
Barry, A., *Do We Believe?* (1908).
Connell, A., *The Endless Quest* (1914).
Erskine, T., *An Essay on Faith* (1823).
Everett, C. C., *Theism and the Christian Faith* (1909).
Friedländer, M., *The Jewish Religion* (1900).
Green, T. H., *The Witness of God and Faith* (1889).
Hare, J. C., *The Victory of Faith* (1874).
Hatch, W. H. P., *The Pauline Idea of Faith* (1917).
Herrmann, W., *Faith and Morals* (1904).
Hill, R. A. P., *The Interregnum* (1913).
Holdsworth, W. W., *The Life of Faith* (1911).
Holland, H. S., in *Lux Mundi* (1890).
    „   „   in *The Faith of Centuries* (1897).
Hunter, J., *De Profundis Clamavi* (1908).
Ladd, G. T., *The Philosophy of Religion*, i. (1906).
Lidgett, J. S., *Apostolic Ministry* (1909).
Lodge, O., in *Science and Religion* (1914).
Lucas, B., *Christ for India* (1910).
Macgregor, W. M., *Some of God's Ministries* (1910).
Moulton, J. H., *Religions and Religion* (1913).
Murray, A., *Why do you not Believe?* (1894).
Newman, J. H., *Lectures on the Doctrine of Justification* (1874).
Parry, R. St. J., *The General Epistle of St. James* (1903).
Porter, N., *Yale College Sermons* (1888).
Romanes, G. J., *Thoughts on Religion* (1896).
Sidgwick, A., *School Homilies*, i. (1915).
Stowell, J. H., *Faith and Reality* (1913).
Temple, W., *Repton School Sermons* (1913).
Thomas, W. H. G., *The Work of the Ministry* (1911).
Varley, H., *Faith and Form* (1908).
Wace, H., *The Foundations of Faith* (1881).
Watson, J., *The Doctrines of Grace* (1900).
Welldon, J. E. C., *The School of Faith* (1904).
Constructive Quarterly, ii. (1914), 111 (W. A. Curtis), 138 (P. Green).
Expositor, 4th Ser., ix. (1894) 381 (J. Watson).
London Quarterly Review, April 1907, p. 193 (G. G. Findlay).

INTRODUCTION.

1. "NOT long ago," says Mr. Henry Varley, "an acquaintance of mine, a busy, hard-working tradesman, almost one of the last men I should have thought of as having time to ponder the high matters of theology, Christian and church-goer though he is, told me how urgently needful he deemed it that the preachers of the present day should give their congregations plain and simple guidance on the great questions of Christian doctrine. 'For,' said he, 'there are lots of us who, like myself, are now quite in a fog as to what we are warranted in believing and what we are not.'"[1]

We propose to make an effort to meet that reasonable desire, choosing for our study the Christian doctrine of Faith. We choose the doctrine of Faith, not because it is the easiest of all doctrines to make "plain and simple," but because it is the most fundamental. If the doctrine of Faith is well studied, all the other doctrines of Christianity will be found to group themselves round it and become more easily understood. And not only is faith fundamental in doctrine, it is fundamental also in practice. If we give ourselves sincerely to an understanding of the nature of faith, we shall not be likely to hold ourselves back from the exercise of it. And what is it but just the exercise of faith that brings us into the enjoyment of God's favour, confers upon us the privileges of sonship, and fits us for the inheritance of the saints in light?

¶ Faith is the discovery of an inherent sonship, which, though already sealed to it, already in action, nevertheless cannot but withhold its more rich and splendid energies until this discovery is made; and which discloses them only according to the progressive clearness and force with which the process of discovery advances. The history of faith is the history of this gradual

[1] H. Varley, *Faith and Form*, 9.

disclosure, this growing capacity to recognise and receive, until the rudimentary omen of God's fatherhood in the rudest savage who draws, by clumsy fetich or weird incantation, upon a power outside himself, closes its long story in the absolute recognition, the perfect and entire receptivity, of that Son of man, who can do nothing of Himself, "but what He seeth the Father do," and, for that very reason, can do everything: for whatsoever "the Father doeth, the Son doeth also."[1]

2. In this introductory chapter we shall consider (1) the Importance of Faith, (2) its Necessity, and (3) its Heroism.

But, first of all, it may be well to give two axioms or things that must be taken for granted.

(1) The first is that neither Faith nor any other Christian doctrine can be explained in such a way as to compel one to *believe* it. There must always remain some margin of mystery. And rightly. What value would doctrine have for life and conduct if it left no opportunity for choice, if there were no element of venture in it?

¶ When we set out to make a venture of faith, we must be prepared to answer to many questions, I don't know. And this answer is not in any way evasive or poor-spirited; it is the very ABC of common sense. Of course we don't know. What is there that we do know? We see an inch or two in front of us, and no more—"'Tis but a part we see, and not the whole"—and if any one thinks that he does know why things are what they are, the only place for him is a lunatic asylum. Across the shield of faith runs the motto Ignoramus: that is to say, We don't know. Why do the moths fly into candle-flames? Ignoramus. Why do the shipwrecks and earthquakes and epidemic diseases afflict mankind? Ignoramus. Why was the world ever made at all? Ignoramus. We don't know. We are not so made as to know. We are here not to know everything, but to be something.[2]

(2) The second axiom is that the doctrine of Faith cannot be set forth so persuasively as to compel one to *practise* it. Again there must remain the liberty of choice. And this also is inevitable and right. For faith is a relation to God, and is peculiar to every individual. It is a personal intimacy with God; it is the

[1] H. S. Holland, in *Lux Mundi* (ed. C. Gore), 11.
[2] S. Paget, *Essays for Boys and Girls*, 20.

INTRODUCTION 5

contact of the soul with God; it is the friendship between God and man. Faith means that these two have learned somehow to know one another, and to trust one another, and to love one another. Now what proofs and what evidences are you to give for a friendship you have formed—a friendship with another man? Can you tell the grounds why you trust him, why you have singled him out and said, "This is my friend"? Could you explain to another person perfectly what reasons you have had for holding on by that man's word? Can you tell another why you love him? And friendship is the note of faith; faith in God is friendship with God. Faith is the meeting, the mingling, of spirit with spirit, when the soul touches God, and, touching Him, knows Him and believes. And every soul touches God for itself, and touches God at a separate spot; forms a special intimacy of its own with God—an intimacy of friendship and love which belongs to it alone in all the world; so that it alone knows God from that place where it is, having that character which it has—knows Him individually with that peculiar intensity which it can share with no other, for with no other can it share its own personal identity. So the faith of each soul has a separate story of its own—the story of how it found its God, learned to know Him and to trust Him more and more, and at last to surrender to Him and then to love Him.

¶ If you ask me the grounds for my faith, how can I tell it you? I should have to tell you the whole of my spiritual history, if I were to give you the story and the grounds and the evidences of my faith. How can I deliver that up to you? What words could convey it? Why, I cannot tell it myself to myself—the story of how I came to believe in God through Jesus Christ—the story of the organic growth of my life—the story, the long troubled story, of how the Holy Spirit toiled within my soul to succour it, and to recover and to cleanse it, and to warn it, and to revive it, and to quicken it, and to turn it towards my God. That long story would go far back to the earliest memories of life, of my mother—to childhood's habits, customs, associations; to youth, with impulses, instincts, aspirations, sins, falls, temptations, recoveries, stumblings, risings—all the growth of the faculties and capacities—all the brimming tide of life coming upward, now stained and tainted, and then purified and absolved: all that is the story of my faith. Thousands and thousands of prayers, and of entreaties, and of cries—all the eucharists and absolutions—all the good instincts and impulses that are felt coming and going like the wind under the impulse of the Spirit, who is Himself the wind —imaginations, movements far out of my control, stirrings, voices, calls, friends, companions, and the Church and the Saints—they all belong to the story of how it was that I believed in Jesus Christ. How can I tell it? How say what has happened? Yet that is belief, that is faith; and the whole of that will have to be told in order to tell why I believe.[1]

I.

The Importance of Faith.

"Oh for faith!" cries Thomas Carlyle. "Truly the greatest 'God-announcing miracle' always is faith, and now more than ever. I often look on my mother (nearly the only genuine Believer I know of) with a kind of sacred admiration. Know the worth of Belief. Alas! canst thou acquire none?"[2]

Those who *have* acquired some are as emphatic in assigning it a momentous influence in life. Percy Ainsworth was a thinker who might have matched Carlyle had he lived longer. Yet he lived long enough to show how much fairer are the fruits of believing than of unbelieving thought. He says: "Faith is not an act, but an attitude; not an event, but a principle; not a last resource, but the first and abiding necessity. It is the constant factor in life's spiritual reckonings. It is the ever-applicable and the ever-necessary. It is always in the high and lasting fitness of things. There are words that belong to hours or even moments, words that win their meaning from the newly created situation. But faith is not such a word. It stands for something inclusive and imperial. It is one of the few timeless words in earth's vocabulary. For the deep roots of it and the wide range of it there is nothing like unto it in the whole sweep of things spiritual."[3]

¶ Among the words of wisdom of *A Student in Arms*, another believing thinker who was taken away in early manhood, is this

---

[1] H. S. Holland, in *The Faith of Centuries*, 62.
[2] *Thomas Carlyle: First Forty Years*, ii. 330.
[3] P. C. Ainsworth, *The Threshold Grace*, 21.

sentence: "Faith is an effective force whose measure has never yet been taken."[1]

1. *Faith is the condition of life.*—Bishop Westcott has rightly affirmed that faith is "the absolute condition of all life, of all action, of all thought which goes beyond the limitations of our own minds," and has further declared that "we live by faith however we live." We are born into a world of which, to the end of our days, we know singularly little. The more our science develops the greater becomes the mystery of our existence. As in the moral life those who have risen highest are most conscious of their weakness, so in the intellectual life those who have thought most are most impressed by the completeness of our ignorance. We cannot live at all without putting faith in something which we can never prove to be worthy of our trust. We cannot prove that the sun will rise to-morrow, but we confidently make plans for to-morrow and for all our future lives. We cannot prove the truth of any of our moral judgments, but we confidently approve and condemn and form our own ideals and aspirations. We cannot prove the honesty of any man, but we confidently trust people to do what they are paid to do. We cannot prove that God is loving, yet we try at least to put our lives in His hands.

¶ Besides that it is that by which we live—as of Christ it is said, who is our life—so we may say of faith, in a different sense, it is our life. As Paul says, to me to live is Christ; so we may say, to us to live is to believe.[2]

> Within the soul a faculty abides,
> That with interpositions, which would hide
> And darken, so can deal that they become
> Contingencies of pomp; and serve to exalt
> Her native brightness. As the ample moon,
> In the deep stillness of a summer even
> Rising behind a thick and lofty grove,
> Burns, like an unconsuming fire of light,
> In the green trees; and, kindling on all sides
> Their leafy umbrage, turns the dusky veil
> Into a substance glorious as her own,
> Yea, with her own incorporated, by power

---

[1] *The Spectator*, Nov. 25, 1916.
[2] Matthew Henry, *Works*, 99.

Capacious and serene. Like power abides
In man's celestial spirit; virtue thus
Sets forth and magnifies herself; thus feeds
A calm, a beautiful, and silent fire,
From the encumbrances of mortal life,
From error, disappointment—nay, from guilt;
And sometimes, so relenting justice wills,
From palpable oppressions of despair.[1]

2. *Faith is the condition of progress.*—Faith is the condition of progress both in the individual life and in the life of the world.

(1) *In the individual life.*—Faith is from the first our best guide along all the lines of human thought; and at the same time it is itself gradually perfected as we pursue them. As the intellect seeks to advance from the things and beings that are visible to the knowledge of the great laws by which they are governed, and through these to the great ultimate cause from which they proceed, the conception of a supreme will and a supreme design and purpose inherent in that cause, and implying in it a true Personality, which is the instructive conclusion of faith, is seen by the most advanced philosophy to be the only conception meeting all the facts and establishing itself by scientific investigation. By that philosophy some cruder aspects of faith may be corrected, and some superstitious excrescences may be removed; but the faith itself is rationalized, and so deepened. Faith, we may say, anticipates reason, and is perfected by reason.

So again it is in regard to the continual advance of the moral sense through all the laws and institutions by which our ordinary life is governed towards some ultimate and eternal basis of righteousness. That basis cannot be a merely impersonal and abstract law; for we know that, even in our lower experience, such law cannot perfectly express the righteousness which adapts itself to all conditions, and to all characters. There is a truth in the old proverb, *Summum jus summa injuria*, which even in human government has to be met by the prerogative of suspension and dispensation in the work of the law-giving authority. The supreme righteousness can be conceived as a will of perfect wisdom as well as perfect righteousness — in other words, a

[1] Wordsworth, "The Excursion" bk. iv.

supreme, infinite Personality. Such is the instinctive conclusion of faith, acknowledging all unchanging moral commandments to be the utterances of the Divine Voice, and expressions of the Divine Nature. Such, also, is the maturest conclusion of that which commends itself to us as a thoughtful philosophy, but which our Lord reveals to us as a witness of the Divine Spirit " to the world of sin, and righteousness, and judgment."

So, once more, it is in regard to the profound capacity of affection, the first to awake in our nature and the last to die out, if indeed it can ever die. It draws the soul in all its faculties towards earthly objects through all the network of ties by which mankind is bound together. Yet the attachment to these, both by its reality and by its experience of their imperfection, is an education of the soul to some higher and ultimate development. What shall our supreme object be? The instinct of faith in God makes unhesitating answer, which satisfies the cravings of that earliest and most childlike simplicity which our Lord declared to be a condition of entrance into His Kingdom. But that same answer, rationalized (so to speak) to a full maturity, is the conclusion of the profoundest psychology, and the fullest spiritual experience. For there is no ultimate love, except that of the whole mind, and heart, and strength; and this can be given only to a Personality, infinite and eternal. There is a deep truth in St. Augustine's famous saying that God has made the heart for Himself, and it is restless and disquieted till it finds Him. So "faith spiritualizes love and is perfected in love." In all the aspects of our higher nature faith proves itself a true law of humanity in the abstract. It is no wonder that it manifests itself in many forms through the whole concrete humanity.

¶ If we are honest with ourselves, we shall admit that something best called Faith—a prevailing conviction of our presence to God and His to us, of His gracious mind towards us, working in and with and through us, of our duty to our fellow-men as our brethren in Him—has been the source of whatever has been best in us and in our deeds. If we have enough experience and sympathy to interpret fairly the life of the world around us, we shall admit that faith of this sort is the salt of the earth. Through it, below the surface of circumstances and custom, humanity is being renewed day by day, and unless our heart is sealed by selfishness and sophistry, though we may not consciously share in the process, there will be men and times that make us reverentially feel its reality. Who can hear an argumentative and unrhetorical Christian minister appeal to his people to cleanse their hearts and to help each other as sons of God in Christ, without feeling that he touches the deepest and strongest spring of noble conduct in mankind?[1]

> Thou canst not prove the Nameless, O my son,
> Nor canst thou prove the world thou movest in,
> Thou canst not prove that thou art body alone,
> Nor canst thou prove that thou art spirit alone,
> Nor canst thou prove that thou art both in one:
> Thou canst not prove thou art immortal, no
> Nor yet that thou art mortal—nay my son,
> Thou canst not prove that I, who speak with thee,
> Am not thyself in converse with thyself,
> For nothing worthy proving can be proven,
> Nor yet disproven: wherefore thou be wise,
> Cleave ever to the sunnier side of doubt,
> And cling to Faith beyond the forms of Faith!
> She reels not in the storm of warring words,
> She brightens at the clash of "Yes" and "No,"
> She sees the Best that glimmers thro' the Worst,
> She feels the Sun is hid but for a night,
> She spies the summer thro' the winter bud,
> She tastes the fruit before the blossom falls,
> She hears the lark within the songless egg,
> She finds the fountain where they wail'd "Mirage"![2]

(2) *In the life of the world.*—Faith is also the secret of the world's progress. He whose creation is filled with the working of a spirit of progress, and who rejoices to see His creatures at their best, gives faith the crown. One of the Greek Fathers says nobly, "When the Lord of all power, the Master of angels, the Maker of heaven itself, was asked for His name, leaving others aside He answered, 'I am the God of Abraham and of Isaac and of Jacob.'" Who are these that He should bear their name? Men who betrayed His cause, and dishonoured His name, and who blundered often; but then, they trusted Him, and there is nothing so dear or admirable in His sight as that. Through almost four thousand years it has been the will of God to be

---

[1] T. H. Green, *The Witness of God and Faith*, 64.
[2] Tennyson, *The Ancient Sage*.

INTRODUCTION

commended to the hearts of His creatures by the names of men who trusted.

All honour to those heroic souls whose fidelity never wavered, who, denying themselves, took up the Cross, and followed the gleam of the ideal they had seen, even though a Gethsemane of agony and a Calvary of suffering lay before them. Scorning all offers of compromise with wrong, exhibiting unswerving devotion to the truth, they chose the path of suffering that they might free their children from the chains with which they themselves were bound, and conferred upon them those rights and privileges which they saw only as ideals. The progress of humanity upward has rarely been a gentle gradient along which it could be borne with little effort. Deep chasms have had to be filled and huge boulders have had to be blasted ere the gentle ascent along which the main body is carried so smoothly was rendered possible. The chasm over which we pass to-day is filled with the bodies of those heroes of the race who laid down their lives that we might pass over. The boulders which have been blasted have exacted their toll of noble lives who sacrificed themselves that we might mount upward.[1]

Count me o'er earth's chosen heroes,—they were souls that stood alone,
While the men they agonised for hurled the contumelious stone,
Stood serene, and down the future saw the golden beam incline
To the side of perfect justice, mastered by their faith divine,
By one man's plain truth to manhood and to God's supreme design.

By the light of burning heretics Christ's bleeding feet I track,
Toiling up new Calvaries ever with the Cross that turns not back,
And these mounts of anguish number how each generation learned
One new word of that grand *Credo* which in prophet-hearts hath burned
Since the first man stood God-conquered with his face to heaven upturned.[2]

[1] B. Lucas, *Christ for India*, 422.
[2] Lowell, *The Present Crisis*.

12 CHRISTIAN DOCTRINE OF FAITH

¶ *Belief*, said one the other night, has done immense evil: witness Knipperdolling and the Anabaptists, etc. "True," rejoined I, with vehemence, almost with fury (Proh pudor!), "true belief has done some evil in the world; but it has done all the good that was ever done in it; from the time when Moses saw the Burning Bush and *believed* it to be God appointing him deliverer of His people, down to the last act of belief that you and I executed. Good never came from aught else."[1]

3. *The supreme place of faith in Christianity.*—Faith occupies, in the Christian religion, not only a conspicuous but a commanding place. The great inheritance that has come down to us is largely a history of faith—its trials, its patience, its eclipses, its victories. The great epic of the religious life which is now being written in the books that shall be opened will place on record for ever the adventures of faith. The Song of Moses and the Lamb, the final oratorio of Creation, will be woven round the splendid and innumerable heroisms of faith. There is not a book in the Bible which does not, from one angle or another, contribute its own ray to the halo that gathers round the brow of faith. The truth is that in Christianity faith is so ever-present, as the living link which binds into one the ages of religious progress, that one almost seems to see it, a symbolic and gracious figure, threading its way from Genesis to Revelation. And the Bible is secure for ever of the affection of all noble souls, because it is the veritable and romantic story of this fair daughter of the King, who by His grace rises from beggary to splendour. "Without faith," Jesus said, "it is impossible to please God." It is also certain that without it we are bankrupt of good; we are off the shining track of His Kingdom.

¶ One of the first things which must needs strike every reader of the New Testament, even the most thoughtless and careless, is the perpetual mention that is made of Faith, the great and paramount importance attached to Faith. Faith is there spoken of as the foundation, the source and the principle of everything that can be excellent and praiseworthy in man—as the power by which all manner of signs and wonders are to be wrought—as the golden key by which alone the treasures of heaven are to be unlocked—as the unshakable indestructible rock on which the Christian Church is to be built. When our Lord came down from the

[1] *Thomas Carlyle: First Forty Years*, ii. 331.

mount, where the glory of the Godhead shone through its earthly tabernacle during the fervour of His prayer, and where His spirit was refreshed by talking with Moses and Elias on the great work He was about to accomplish—when, after this brief interval of heavenly communion, He returned to the earth, and was met by that woeful spectacle of its misery and helplessness, physical and moral, the child who was sore vexed by the evil spirit, and whom His disciples could not heal—and when, the cure having been wrought instantaneously by His omnipotent word, He was asked by His disciples why they had been unable to effect it—He replied, Because of your unbelief. And then, having thus taught them what was the cause of their weakness, He tried to revive and renew their hearts by telling them how they might gain strength, and how great strength they might gain: Verily I say to you, if ye have Faith as a grain of mustard seed, ye shall say to this mountain, Remove hence to yonder place; and it shall remove; and nothing shall be impossible to you; thus encouraging them by declaring the infinite power that lies in the very least Faith, if it be but genuine and living. In like manner, when the wonder of the disciples is excited by the withering of the fig-tree, He calls away their thoughts from the particular outward effect, to the principle by which such effects, and far greater, may be produced: Verily I say to you, if ye have Faith, and doubt not, ye shall not only do this which is done to the fig-tree, but also, if ye shall say to this mountain, Be thou removed, and be thou cast into the sea, it shall be done. Passing on from the Gospels to the Epistles, we find the power and workings of Faith still more frequently urged, and still more emphatically dwelt on. The most inattentive reader can hardly fail to observe how the justifying character of Faith, in its absolute exclusive primacy, forms the central point of St. Paul's preaching. And we hear the Apostle of Love joining his voice with that of him who is more especially the Apostle of Faith, and proclaiming that this, and this alone, is the victory which overcometh the world, even our Faith.[1]

(1) CHRIST.—In the Synoptic Gospels faith is the spring of discipleship and its mature confession a disciple's supreme act; it is the condition of healing and miracle and effective prayer and salvation. Christ is constantly looking for it. The men He chose and called were singled out for their possession of it, in some cases perhaps for little else. To the centurion, concerning whom He exclaimed, "Verily I say unto you, I have not found so great faith,

---

[1] J. C. Hare, *The Victory of Faith*, iii. 3.

no, not in Israel," He says, "As thou hast believed, so be it done unto thee." To an afflicted woman He says, "Thy faith hath saved thee." To a distracted father He says, "If thou canst believe, all things are possible to him that believeth," and receives the answer, "Lord, I believe; help thou mine unbelief." Again, in different mood and with other outlook, He asks: "Howbeit when the Son of Man cometh, shall he find faith on the earth?" Such is the power of faith, in His judgment, that a single grain of it, no bigger than a mustard seed, will enable its possessor to "move mountains."

A striking illustration of the manner in which Christ regarded faith is afforded by those occasions on which His wonder is said to have been evoked. In Him that emotion was called forth by causes very different from those by which it is ordinarily aroused among men. That which occasioned wonder to the Jews, and to our Lord's followers, was the exhibition of His power over nature. The disciples on one occasion marvelled, and said, "What manner of man is this, that even the winds and the sea obey him!" It is still this characteristic in our Lord that chiefly excites wonder, as is proved by the common use of the word "miracle." That word is exclusively applied to deeds of physical power, as though the only thing that could affect the mass of men with astonishment were that which is visible and startling to the senses. But with our Lord it is the very reverse. He never speaks as if there were anything strange or unnatural in the miracles He performs. He refers to them, indeed, as "mighty works," or rather as exertions of power, and as intended to impress us with a sense alike of His power and of His goodness. But to Himself they appear perfectly natural and simple. There is a conspicuous absence of all effort about them. His wonderful cures, His raising of the dead, His miraculous appearances to His disciples, all are performed with the quietness and ease which are characteristic of an irresistible force. Any display of effort is a revelation of weakness; but our Lord "speaks and it is done," He "commands and it stands fast." It was by the phenomena of the moral world that His astonishment was occasioned—by its vast capacities on the one hand, and its terrible incapacities on the other. On the one hand, He marvelled at the faith manifested in the appeal of the centurion, who bade Him speak the word only and his servant should be healed; and He expressed a similar admiration at a like display of faith in the Canaanitish woman. On the other hand, when, in His own country, among His own kin, and in His own house, He found Himself without honour, so that He could not do any mighty work, save that He laid His hands upon a few sick folk and healed them, we are told that He "marvelled because of their unbelief." The faith of which men are capable on the one hand, and the unbelief of which they are capable on the other—these are the only two things that are said to have evoked the wonder of the Lord Jesus. These, to His eye, were the only two real marvels exhibited during His ministry.

¶ Jesus' mind was continually fixed on Faith; the word was ever on His lips. It was the recurring decimal of His thinking, the keynote of His preaching.[1]

(2) THE APOSTLES.—In the Acts of the Apostles so essential a feature of Christianity is faith that it actually embodies itself as an objective reality which is called the Faith. Of St. Paul's Epistles faith is so truly the keynote—especially of the great Epistle to the Romans—that Luther conceived himself to be right in representing the Pauline Theology as almost identifying Christianity with the doctrine of Justification by Faith. So, too, the author of the Epistle to the Hebrews insists upon faith in his famous eleventh chapter as "the substance" (or "assurance") of "things hoped for," the "evidence" (or "proof") of "things not seen," and indeed as the vital principle of the spiritual life.

II.

THE NECESSITY OF FAITH.

Faith is more than important, it is necessary. It is necessary both in temporal things and in the things of the Spirit.

1. *Its necessity in temporal matters.*—The more man advances in culture, the more true will it be, and the more evident, that faith is essential to his perfection and his success.

(1) Faith widens and quickens and regulates man's intellectual

[1] John Watson, in *The Expositor*, 4th Ser., ix. 383.

activity. Faith, as an intellectual conviction, assents to the truth. Faith, therefore, cannot exist without some activity of the intellect. This does not mean that faith involves a high degree of intellectual activity or discipline, least of all that it is in any sense a substitute for the training of the scholar or the discipline of experience. But it does mean that it invariably excites to thought, and that its natural tendency is to quicken the intellectual life. Multitudes have found in the beginning of the life of faith the beginnings of intellectual activity.

(2) Faith includes a very large element of feeling. Faith in the Christian sense is pre-eminently emotional, for the reason that it is fixed directly upon a Person who is at once the most perfect and the most unpretending, the loftiest and the lowliest, the mildest and the sternest, the most forgiving and the most uncompromising, the most ideal and the most real, the most divine and the most human. Abstractions and ideals may rouse and satisfy the intellect, but the heart demands a Person. Every Christian household can furnish some living example of an inmate who has been transformed to sweeter love and mellowed self-control by faith in the personal Christ, such as otherwise could never have been attained. Christian burial-places scattered by thousands all over the earth are watched by the loving eye of God, in which reposes the dust of myriads of meek and loving souls who would never have been formed to the loving tempers and governed appetites and conquered pride for which their memory is blessed, except by faith in this personal Christ. More than that, personal faith in Christ trains and stimulates to the finest and most perfect culture, whether in manners, literature, or art. There can be no question that the best achievements in art and literature have been the offspring of such a faith.

¶ I had two delightful hours this afternoon alone with Michael Angelo and Raphael, in the Sistine Chapel and the Vatican. I left the place fully persuaded that the two men were superhuman, unrivalled, and for ever unapproachable. The study of their works ends in the conviction that the painters implicitly believed in the divine truth of the themes they illustrated—nothing else, notwithstanding their God-gifted genius, could have inspired them; and difficult as it is to believe that Raphael really took it for granted that saints, armed with long swords, appeared in the sky at a moment when fortune was going against one of the popes in battle, and so turned the tables on his enemies, I think the assumption must be allowed.[1]

(3) It is by faith that man stands strongly and wisely in duty. Here the old question returns, If a man has faith in duty, what need is there also of faith in a person, who can only exemplify and enforce duty? Because a person who exemplifies duty is more attractive and powerful than any abstract law of duty; because duty is not a cold, unsocial, loveless impulse, but is personal, sympathetic, and social; because love is not the love of goodness in the abstract, but the love of goodness as impersonated; because duty looks up to whatever is higher than itself, and prompts to reverence and worship—the goodness which is grander and greater than itself—and in its own nature delights in faith and loyalty. Duty, therefore, is, by the necessity of its nature, inspired by examples of goodness, and delights in the law of the perfect and reigning God. Duty is not duty if it does not blossom into faith. No man can be loyal to conscience who is not also loyal to the loving and living Jesus.

(4) Faith is necessary to men's happiness. Without faith in God men are miserable. Some men are not conscious of the cause of this misery: this, however, does not prevent the fact of their being miserable. For the most part they conceal the fact as well as possible from themselves, by occupying their minds with society, sport, frivolity of all kinds, or, if intellectually disposed, with science, art, literature, business.

¶ It has been my lot to know not a few of the famous men of our generation, and I have always observed that there is no lasting happiness without faith. All "moral" satisfactions soon pall by custom, and as soon as one end of distinction is reached, another is pined for. There is no finality to rest in, while disease and death are always standing in the background. Custom may even blind men to their own misery, so far as not to make them realize what is wanting; yet the want is there.

> La vie est vaine:
> Un peu d'amour,
> Un peu de haine . . .
> Et puis—bon jour!

[1] W. P. Frith, *My Autobiography and Reminiscences*, 315.

La vie est brève :
Un peu d'espoir,
Un peu de rêve . . .
Et puis—bon soir !

The above is a terse and true criticism of this life without hope of a future one. Is it satisfactory ? But Christian faith, as a matter of fact, changes it entirely.

> The night has a thousand eyes,
>   And the day but one;
> Yet the light of a whole world dies
>   With the setting sun.
>
> The mind has a thousand eyes,
>   And the heart but one;
> Yet the light of a whole life dies
>   When love is done.

Love is known to be all this. How great, then, is Christianity, as being the religion of love, and causing men to believe both in the cause of love's supremacy and the infinity of God's love to man.[1]

2. *Its necessity in the things of the Spirit.*—The great gifts of salvation are ascribed to faith. For instance, the forgiveness of sins :—" Whom God hath set forth to be a propitiation through faith in his blood, to declare his righteousness for the remission of sins that are past." The presence of the Spirit :—" That we might receive the promise of the Spirit through faith." Sanctification :—" Purifying their hearts by faith." Perseverance :—" Who are kept by the power of God through faith." The resurrection of the body :—" He that believeth in me, though he were dead, yet shall he live." Eternal life :—" That whosoever believeth in him, should not perish, but have eternal life." The Body and Blood of Christ :—" I am the bread of life ; he that cometh to me shall never hunger, and he that believeth on me shall never thirst." Or, as all God's ineffable gifts may be compendiously stated in one word, justification :—" That he might be just, and the justifier of him which believeth in Jesus."

Faith is the necessary condition of, and instrument in, our justification, because it is the one thing without which God can

---
[1] G. J. Romanes, *Thoughts on Religion*, 153.

do nothing. God can do everything for man except outrage his free will. To destroy that would be to destroy his very nature as a spiritual being. It is quite impossible to exaggerate this inability of God, this limitation of His Omnipotence. He could destroy man; He could re-create him; He could, if He willed, so alter his nature as to make him a mere machine. He cannot, without a total destruction of him as man, and as a free creature, outrage his free will. If man will not respond to God's gracious overtures God can do nothing. Hence man's faith, the response of his whole nature Godward in knowledge, will, and love, is an absolutely necessary pre-requisite for God's action. It is not of course pretended that faith must be perfect and complete before God can work. A perfect faith would be possible for none but a perfect man. And faith grows, each element in it helping the more perfect growth of the other elements. But a response there must be in man before God can work.

Faith is so essential and characteristic an element of the Christian life that Paul frequently speaks of Christians as believers without specifying the nature or object of their faith—a fact which shows that Christianity, however it may have been conceived and presented at other periods of its history, was for the Apostle a religion based on faith. In like manner the verb *to believe* means to be a Christian, or, in the aorist, to become a Christian, no less than thirteen times in the letters of Paul. Thus, for example, he writes to the brethren in Rome, "For now is our salvation nearer than when we became Christians."

¶ Faith is the EYE of the soul, by which we look unto Christ, as the poor stung Israelites did to the brazen serpent, lifted up upon the pole, and thereby receive a cure from him; but, as Paul saith in another case, 1 Co 12^{14}, the body is not one member but many, so faith is not one member but many. If the whole body were an eye, where were the hearing? verse 17. So if faith were our eye only, and nothing else, what should we do for other instruments of spiritual life and motion? Behold, therefore, how faith besides being our eye, is our FOOT, by which we come to Christ; an expression often used in Scripture, *e.g.* Mt 11^{28}. Come unto me, that is, believe in me. Jn 6^{37}. "Him that cometh unto me," that is, that believeth in me, "I will in no wise cast out." By unbelief we depart from the living God, He 3^{12}. By faith we come to him by Christ, *ib.* 7^{25}. And without him there is no coming, for he is the way, the true, and living, and only way; all that are out of him are out of the way.

It is our HAND also, by which we receive him, Jn 1^{12}. "To as many as received him, to them gave he power to become the sons of God, even to them that believe on his name"; where believing is the same with receiving. In the gospel, God offers him to us, freely and graciously, to be our Prince and Saviour, to be "the Lord our righteousness," to redeem us from iniquity, and to purify us to himself. When we do heartily, by faith, close with that offer, and accept of him to be ours, he becomes ours: we have union with him, relation to him, and benefit by him. But then, there is another act of faith put forth at the same time by another hand, which is the giving act, whereby we give ourselves to him to be his, to love him, and serve him, and live to him. "O Lord," saith David, "I am thy servant, truly I am thy servant," Ps 116^{16}. "They gave their own selves unto the Lord," 2 Co 8^5. Without this our receiving is not right. There is a faith that is one-handed, receives, but gives not; this will not save. They that come to Christ for rest, and receive Christ, must take his yoke upon them, and learn of him.

It is the MOUTH of the soul, by which we feed upon him, and are nourished by him. Jn 6. "Except ye eat his flesh, and drink his blood," that is, believe in him, as it is there explained, ye cannot be saved. And this of all the rest doth in the most lively manner represent to us what it is to believe. To believe, is when a poor soul, being made sensible of its lost and undone condition by sin, doth earnestly desire, as they do that are hungry, and thirsty, after a Saviour. Oh for a righteousness, wherein to appear before God! Oh for a pardon for what is past! Oh for grace and strength to do so no more! And hearing, by the report of the gospel, and believing that report, that all this, and a great deal more, is to be had in Christ; the next request is—Oh for that Christ! Oh, that that Christ might be mine! Why, he is thine, man, if thou wilt accept of him! Accept of him! Lord, I accept of him. Then feed upon him, "His flesh is meat indeed, his blood is drink indeed." Oh, taste and see that he is gracious. How sweet are his promises! What inward refreshment doth the soul find by his suffering and dying to redeem, and save! How is it thereby strengthened, as by bread, and made glad, as by wine! We must and do each of us eat for ourselves, and drink for ourselves. My eating will not refresh another, nor strengthen another; neither will my believing. The just shall live by his faith, his own faith. Other creatures die to make food for our bodies, and to maintain natural life; but then we must take them, and eat them, and digest them, and having done so, they turn into nourishment to us, and so become ours, that they and we cannot be parted again. It is so in believing. Christ died to make food for our souls; and not thereby to maintain only, but to give spiritual life, which other food doth not to the body. But then we must take him, and eat him, and digest him, that is, make a particular application of him to ourselves, and, having done so, nothing shall, nothing can, separate us from him. Oh that unto us it might be more and more given, thus to believe![1]

> I wonder less at God's respect
> For man, a minim jot in time and space,
> Than at the soaring faith of His elect,
> That gift of gifts, the comfort of His grace.[2]

III.

THE HEROISM OF FAITH.

Do we realize how heroic faith is? Believing men are of God's kindred; faith belongs to the upper side of our being. A man may be sober, thrifty, punctual, kindly, and yet have a nature without a spark. There are qualities of character which Nietzsche describes as belonging to cows and Englishmen, and in obituary notices these are insisted on sometimes as if they were paramount. But salvation comes not from the earth, not with sobriety, and good-temper, and diligence, estimable as such virtues are. We are solidly planted here amongst the material things, with much to suggest that nothing else is looked for from us; and when truth or duty beckons from afar, we are tempted to say, "It is far off, it is not for us." It is not easy to believe; so hard is it that, when Jesus one day met with it in perfection, we are told that He marvelled. And when He looked abroad on the hindrances which stand in its way, He said, "When the Son of man comes, shall he find any faith left in the earth?" Faith is a martial virtue, whose business it is to resist the powers of earth. It is the voice of our greatness, and through it there come the heavenly gifts. It is nothing in itself, but it lays hold on God

---

[1] Matthew Henry, *Works*. 101.
[2] Robert Bridges, "The Growth of Love."

who has all things; and thus forgiveness, and the power by which a better life is lived, and the courage by which men stand alone, and the hidden gifts of the heart of Christ are all granted to faith.

True religion, and Christianity as its fulfilment, always raises human life to the heroic. There is nothing commonplace in its history. If it find men apparently commonplace to begin with, the first effect of true religion is to reveal and call forth unsuspected possibilities of greatness within those who yield themselves to its influence. This holds good, not only of the past, but of the present. Religion is not a mere adornment, convenience, or means of enjoyment. If it is to be any or all of these, it must be infinitely more. It is a consecration, which summons all human powers to the complete unselfishness and unworldliness of Divine and human service. The criticisms passed upon the Christian Church from outside in the present day may often be ill-informed and unfair. In their substance and tendency, however, they are abundantly justified from the New Testament itself. Those who profess to be partakers of the Divine nature and to enjoy the boundless resources of God in Christ are thereby enabled and expected to display a greatness of character and aims that is beyond the reach of other men.

¶ To such readers as have reflected, what can be called reflecting, on man's life, and happily discovered, in contradiction to much Profit-and-Loss Philosophy, speculative and practical, that Soul is *not* synonymous with Stomach; who understand, therefore, in our Friend's words, "that, for man's well-being, Faith is properly the one thing needful; how, with it, Martyrs, otherwise weak, can cheerfully endure the shame and the cross; and without it, Worldlings puke-up their sick existence, by suicide, in the midst of luxury": to such it will be clear that, for a pure moral nature, the loss of his religious Belief was the loss of everything.[1]

1. Jesus is the supreme example, the fulfilment, we dare to say the Hero, of faith. His Divinity is manifested in perfect and typical humanity. We have been told of late that we must choose between believing on the Lord Jesus Christ as the supreme object of faith, and treating Him as the first subject of faith. In such teaching the Epistle to the Hebrews seems to be overlooked. Our author seems to know nothing of this contrast. He brings

[1] Thomas Carlyle, *Sartor Resartus*, 111.

together both alternatives in a more glorious whole. If the first chapter of the Epistle sets forth the glory of the Eternal Son, who is "the effulgence of God's glory and the very image of his substance," the second shows us Jesus "made a little lower than the angels." In His humility the Captain of our Salvation is "made perfect through sufferings." He "suffers, being tempted." Nay, "though he was a son, yet learned he obedience by the things which he suffered." Indeed the writer expressly puts in His mouth the confession, "I will put my trust in him." The Deity and Redeemership of Jesus is not incompatible with His incarnate life of faith. Indeed, such faith is the essential mark of His filial nature. Without it He would have been not more, but less, than man. Moreover, according to the writer, without it He would have lacked an essential qualification for His High-priestly office. The glory of the Eternal Son is seen not in His freedom from faith, but in His perfect embodiment of it. The mark of His Divinity is in His sinlessness, and His sinlessness is the triumph of an unbroken faith.

2. And the disciples of Jesus were heroic in proportion to their faith. Virgil said of the winning crew in his famous boat-race, "They can, because they believe they can!" His words are almost identical with words we find in the text—"Whosoever shall say unto this mountain, Be thou taken up and cast into the sea; and shall not doubt in his heart, but shall believe that what he saith cometh to pass; he shall have it." The trouble with many of us is that we do not fully believe that we can do what we are bidden do by the All-wise Master of our life. We are more or less ignorant of our own power—of the hidden spiritual forces of our own nature. We are afraid of great ventures because we under-estimate ourselves. We need more of that self-confidence which in its last analysis is confidence in God—the God who worketh in us to will and to do. In the disciples of Christ we see what faith in God could do for average men, such men as we find in the streets, dull in mind, timid in spirit, weak in will. The whole-hearted committal of themselves to the work of God made them conscious of undreamt-of power, and made them capable of achieving what they never thought possible; changed them from ordinary and commonplace men into heroes and

martyrs whom we remember for ever. Forgetting themselves, and determined to bring in the Kingdom of God, they went forward, and the enthusiasm of their faith operated in the very way their Master said; it enabled them to surmount formidable difficulties, to break down mountainous obstacles, to subdue seeming impossibilities, to overcome a hostile world. And from those days to these all the greatest things that have been done for God and man have been done by men full of the energy of faith. The men of faith have achieved what is impossible to other men. For with God, in union with Him, all things are possible in the way of obedience and service. It is to this power of faith, which connects our life with the spiritual resources of the universe, that God has entrusted the redemption and progress of the world —the Kingdom of Heaven upon earth.

¶ Let us not be slandered from our duty by false accusations against us, nor frightened from it by menaces of destruction to the government, nor of dungeons to ourselves. Let us have faith that right makes might, and in that faith let us to the end do our duty as we understand it.[1]

3. The heroism of faith is found in lowly as readily as in exalted stations. The heroic quality is the true concern, not the heroic stage. The great recital of the deeds of faith in the Epistle to the Hebrews contains some well-known names, but it ends by summing up the victories and achievements of multitudes of men and women unknown to earthly fame. Even in the case of the better known, it was their faith that lifted them out of obscurity. For the most part, however, their greatness was not perceived by their fellows. Indeed, this is precisely the distinction of their faith, that it enabled them to live great lives, to brave great dangers, and to make great sacrifices, not only without the incitements of worldly fame and applause, but under influences exactly contrary to these.

Now that we have seen something of the greatness of Faith, let us not forget that Christ is greater than faith in Him. It is a warning that is needed (and with it this Introduction to the Doctrine of Faith may very properly come to an end). "How

[1] Abraham Lincoln.

strongly," says Maurice, "have I been convinced lately that we spend half our time in thinking of faith, hope, and love, instead of in believing, hoping, and loving! How utterly we forget that the very meaning of the words implies that we should forget ourselves and themselves (the acts, I mean) in the objects to which they refer. For are there not some persons who preach Faith instead of preaching Christ?"[1]

¶ The exaltation of Faith out of its own place of a handmaid awakened Dr. Duncan's jealousy. He said that "some men's Trinity consisted of the Father, and the Son, and Faith"; and he frequently repeated the following anecdote, with the names and circumstances. "At a Highland communion in a meeting for 'speaking to the question,' on a Friday evening, the subject selected was Faith. One after another of the 'men' spoke in glowing terms of the power and the triumphs of Faith, and each speaker exalted it more than the one before him. At last their esteemed minister, jealous for the honour of the Lord Jesus Christ, stood up and said, 'I ask, was Faith crucified for you; or were ye baptized in the name of Faith?'"[2]

[1] *The Life of Frederick Denison Maurice*, i. 139.
[2] A. Moody Stuart, *Recollections of the late John Duncan, LL.D.*, 124.

II.

FAITH IN ONE'S SELF.

LITERATURE.

Burroughs, E. A., *Faith and Power* (1914).
Cornaby, W. A., *In Touch with Reality* (1906).
Diggle, J. W., *The Foundations of Duty* (1913).
Faithfull, R. C., *My Place in the World* (1910).
Holmes, E., *The Nemesis of Docility* (1916).
Horton, R. F., *The Springs of Joy* (1915).
Jowett, J. H., *The Transfigured Church* (1910).
Lock, W., *The Bible and Christian Life* (1905).
Lorimer, G. C., *Messages of To-Day* (1896).
Lynch, T. T., *Sermons for My Curates* (1871).
Macaulay, A. B., *The Word of the Cross*.
Mackennal, A., *The Life of Christian Consecration* (1877).
Maclaren, A., *Last Sheaves* (1903).
Maxson, H. D., *Sermons of Religion and Life* (1893).
Meyer, F. B., *The Present Tenses of the Blessed Life*.
Morison, J., *Sheaves of Ministry* (1890).
Murray, A., *Let us draw Nigh* (1895).
Murray, W. H., *The Fruits of the Spirit* (1879).
Paget, F., *Faculties and Difficulties for Belief and Disbelief* (1889).
Pulsford, J., *Loyalty to Christ*, ii.
Shepherd, E., *Ambrose Shepherd, D.D.: A Memoir and Sermons* (1915).
Simcox, W. H., *The Cessation of Prophecy* (1891).
Simpson, J. G., *Christus Crucifixus* (1909).
Smith, J. H., *Healing Leaves* (1875).
Whiting, L., *The World Beautiful* (1914).
Contemporary Review, xcvii. (1910) 302 (J. G. James).
Experience, xxx. (1911) 140 (J. A. Clapperton).
Holborn Review, lvi. (1914) 337 (A. Hird).
Present Day Papers, iii. (1900) 63 (H. B. Binns).

Faith in One's Self.

In every department of human activity, faith in our own ability to do a thing, no matter what, is almost necessary to our doing it at all, and at all events to our doing it well. To acquire this faith in himself is indeed with every man half the battle of life. Some men never do gain it. They are always so diffident and distrustful of themselves that they are incapable of a really vigorous effort: and life, accordingly, to them, is little other than an important struggle and a disastrous defeat. The very imagination that one cannot do a thing is almost certain either to deter from the attempt or to make it a failure. On the contrary, feel that you *can*, and the simple feeling is of itself almost certain to ensure success. It is so in ordinary life, and it is so in the Christian life. It is just because of this morbid self-distrust, this miserable sickly feeling, *I can't*, that many persons who might be useful in the Church and in the world, who might be ministering angels to the really weak and incapable, remain inactive and useless, and fritter away their lives in merely dreaming about doing good. Whereas it is by the sound, healthy feeling, *I can*, that all the good that is done is really effected.

Most important, therefore, is it that this faith should be acquired. It may be all very right to preach about man's weakness and nothingness in himself, but it will never do to confine ourselves to that. That is only one half of the truth. It is only the dark side of the shield, and we must look at its bright side. We are living under the gospel. Christ's own words are addressed to us, and "they are spirit, and they are life." Christ's own Spirit is given to us, and it is not a "spirit of fear" and timidity, "but of power, and of love, and of a sound mind," so that we may be "always confident," not arrogant, self-conceited, self-righteous, or rash; but consciously able to do anything and to suffer anything to which in the course of Divine providence we may be called.

A man may so grow up to the stature of "a perfect man" in Christ, he may live in such intimate and habitual communion with Him, as to become conscious of the strength of Christ within him, bracing, nerving, energizing his spirit; so that no danger shall daunt, no trouble disturb him, but he shall go calmly and confidently forth, and mountains of difficulty shall vanish at his bidding. Such a man was St. Paul; and such too may we ourselves be. We ought, all of us, to be able in all humility and thankfulness, but at the same time with all confidence, to say, as he said, "I can do all things through Christ which strengtheneth me."

1. Bacon has a poor opinion of "boldness," as he calls self-confidence. He says: "Question was asked of Demosthenes, what was the chief part of an orator? he answered, Action: what next?—Action: what next again?—Action. He said it that knew it best, and had by nature himself no advantage in that he commended. A strange thing, that that part of an orator which is but superficial, and rather the virtue of a player, should be placed so high above those other noble parts of invention, elocution, and the rest; nay almost alone, as if it were all in all. But the reason is plain. There is in human nature generally more of the fool than of the wise; and therefore those faculties by which the foolish part of men's minds is taken are most potent. Wonderful-like is the case of boldness in civil business; what first?—boldness; what second and third?—boldness: and yet boldness is a child of ignorance and baseness, far inferior to other parts: but, nevertheless, it doth fascinate, and bind hand and foot those that are either shallow in judgment or weak in courage, which are the greatest part; yea, and prevaileth with wise men at weak times."[1] Yet Bacon himself was a conspicuous example of self-confidence, as we shall see later.

¶ *Modesty* has a natural tendency to conceal a man's talents, as *impudence* displays them to the utmost, and has been the only cause why many have risen in the world, under all the disadvantages of low birth and little merit. Such indolence and

[1] *The Moral and Historical Works of Lord Bacon,* 31.

incapacity is there in the generality of mankind, that they are apt to receive a man for whatever he has a mind to put himself off for; and admit his overbearing airs as proofs of that merit which he assumes to himself. A decent assurance seems to be the natural attendant of virtue; and few men can distinguish impudence from it: As, on the other hand, diffidence, being the natural result of vice and folly, has drawn disgrace upon modesty, which in outward appearance so nearly resembles it.[1]

¶ Nothing so fascinates mankind as to see a man equal to every fortune, unshaken by reverses, indifferent to personal abuse, maintaining a long combat against apparently hopeless odds with the sharpest weapons and a smiling face. His followers fancy he must have hidden resources of wisdom as well as of courage. When some of his predictions come true, and the turning tide of popular feeling begins to bear them toward power, they believe that he has been all along right and the rest of the world wrong. When victory at last settles on his crest, even his enemies can hardly help applauding a reward which seems so amply earned. It was by this quality, more perhaps than by anything else, by this serene surface with fathomless depths below, that Lord Beaconsfield laid his spell upon the imagination of observers in Continental Europe, and received at his death a sort of canonisation from a large section of the English people.[2]

2. A Spanish philosopher of the same time as Bacon rates the value of self-confidence highly. "In great crises," says Balthasar Gracian,[3] "there is no better companion than a bold heart, and if it becomes weak it must be strengthened from the neighbouring parts. Worries die away before a man who asserts himself. One must not surrender to misfortune, or else it would become intolerable. Many men do not help themselves in their troubles, and double their weight by not knowing how to bear them. He that knows himself knows how to strengthen his weakness, and the wise man conquers everything, even the stars in their courses."

¶ A man who believes in himself will attain results and conquer difficulties far beyond the power and scope of characters in which we should have seen much more promise of effectiveness. He will, to take the very lowest estimate of his life, be outwardly

---

[1] Hume, *Essays, Moral, Political, and Literary*, ii. 380.
[2] Viscount Bryce, *Studies in Contemporary Biography*, 65.
[3] *The Art of Worldly Wisdom*, 100.

successful: he will do what he wishes and intends to do: he will make other people believe in him and work for him: difficulties will disappear because he will not see them, and distant ends will come within his reach because he never doubts that they are so.[1]

3. It is better that a man, and especially a young man, should have too high than too low an opinion of his own merit and usefulness. For the world will not be backward in bringing him down to his true level, while it will never trouble to raise him up to it. If you value yourself, your labour, your time, your talents too highly, the world may for a time receive you at your own valuation, until, in disgust at being deceived, it forces you to take an account of your worth that is no truer, inasmuch as it will err from defect as much as it had before erred in excess. But if you value yourself too low, the world will not correct you, it will take you at your own valuation, and will allow you to feel that you are of little use, so that you will let many opportunities of doing good, of helping others, of improving and strengthening your own character slip by. The Scotsman's prayer, "Gie' us a guid conceit o' wursells," might be offered up with great advantage by some of us.

> There is nothing, I hold, in the way of work
>   That a human being may not achieve
> If he does not falter, or shrink or shirk,
>   And more than all, if he will *believe*.
>
> Believe in himself and the power behind
>   That stands like an aid on a dual ground,
>   With hope for the spirit and oil for the wound,
> Ready to strengthen the arm or mind.
>
> When the motive is right and the will is strong
>   There are no limits to human power;
> For that great force back of us moves along
>   And takes us with it, in trial's hour.
>
> And whatever the height you yearn to climb,
>   Tho' it never was trod by the foot of man,
>   And no matter how steep—I say you *can*,
> If you will be patient—and use your time.[2]

---

[1] F. Paget, *Faculties and Difficulties for Belief and Disbelief*, 261.
[2] Ella Wheeler Wilcox, *Maurine and Other Poems*, 209.

FAITH IN ONE'S SELF

I.

THE VALUE OF FAITH IN ONE'S SELF.

1. The men who do great deeds, who leave a mark behind them, who bend stubborn circumstances to their will, who influence other men (bearing into their hearts the passions or the policy which they have themselves conceived), are always the men who have a firm faith in their own judgment, and a resolute conviction that they will achieve what they have set themselves to do: so that they are not always explaining and apologizing and qualifying and standing on the defensive, but rather going straight forward and fearlessly calling upon others to follow them.

We may have seen, perhaps, in the great world, the almost irresistible power of those who have this faith in themselves, who never doubt that they are aiming at the one right aim. And in the narrower world of our home or private life, we may know how easily we accept the advice, or even welcome and rest and delight in the control of one who is not afraid to bear the responsibility of a positive decision, who can venture largely by faith in himself.

¶ Thomas Chalmers had faith in God—faith in human nature —faith, if we may say so, in his own instincts—in his ideas of men and things—*in himself*; and the result was, that unhesitating bearing up and steering right onward—" never bating one jot of heart or hope "—so characteristic of him. He had " the substance of things hoped for." He had " the evidence of things not seen."[1]

¶ It was continually interesting to note the differences between my two comrades [Millais and Collins], one fated to win honours, whatever the obstructions might be; the other, spite of original gifts and of strenuous yearnings, doomed to be turned back on the threshold of success by want of courageous confidence.[2]

¶ I believe (although I admit I have no utterance from him as foundation for my belief) that from the very beginning of his political work Roosevelt kept before him the idea of becoming

---

[1] John Brown, *Horæ Subsecivæ*, ii. 127.
[2] W. Holman Hunt, *Pre-Raphaelitism and the Pre-Raphaelite Brotherhood*, i. 299.

President, and he had the large measure of self-confidence which is one of the most essential factors towards political success. This self-confidence, an admirable quality in itself, needs, however, in order not to interfere with a good development of character and with the foundations of judgment, to be kept in control. An exuberance of assured opinions is natural enough in a man of a certain temperament and at an age which may still be classed as sophomoric. As a man grows older and his responsibilities increase, he ought, in order to maintain a wise relation with his fellow-men, to keep his self-confidence under lock and key, so to speak, bringing it to the open only at critical moments.[1]

2. A man's faith in himself will give him a strange power and energy for work: he will set himself great tasks and bear great labour and privation, if this is—as probably in some form it will be—necessary: for he will feel that his life is a great thing to be ordered and lived on a large scale, with aims that are worth all the more self-denial because he is sure that he will attain them.

¶ The young have naturally more faith than the old, more faith in themselves, because they have no experience of their limitations; more faith in the world, because they are at liberty, according to their fancy or their ideal. This is wisely ordered in both respects, for how shall a man act if he has no faith in himself? and how should he attempt to do anything for the world if he thought the world was not worthy of his exertions? So much for faith as a spur to action.[2]

¶ Responsibility may be defined as a man's ability to respond, but our use of the ability is our own, and it cannot be forced. God coerces no man, though He allures by the ceaseless play of a love that *will* not let us go. That we do not always respond is due to our lack of sensitiveness to the lure; we have not the length of vision which sees the end of splendour to which it fain would draw us. Archdeacon Wilberforce found the root of all sin to consist in ignorance of our highest good.

> " Know this, oh man, sole root of sin in thee
> Is not to *know* thy own divinity."

The quotation was ever on his lips.[3]

---

[1] G. H. Putnam, *Memories of a Publisher*, 139.
[2] John Stuart Blackie, *Day-Book*, 99.
[3] C. E. Woods, *Archdeacon Wilberforce: His Ideals and Teaching*, 83.

3. The man who has faith in himself, if he is a good man, will resolutely put away all mean and little ways of self-indulgence; he will not be always rewarding himself for everything he does; he will be truthful and outspoken, since falsehood and dissimulation are the refuge of men who are uncertain or ashamed of themselves: and he will lift his life and thoughts above all that may degrade or hinder or enfeeble him. Even a little faith in himself can wonderfully raise and strengthen a man: even as there is no more hopeless temper than to have mean or base or grumbling thoughts about that which God has made us and given us.

¶ There is a class of people who are comparatively valueless to the world because of a certain morbidness which they are pleased to call sensitiveness. In reality it is nothing of the sort. It is self-love—a refined variety of it, to be sure, but none the less is it the result of a selfishly subjective state, in which they look in and not out, and down and not up, and fail to lend a hand—not from any real unkindness or unwillingness, but simply because they are looking in, and looking down, and do not see the opportunity. They will tell you they are "so lonely" and "so blue" and "so unhappy" and so exceedingly "misunderstood." Well, perhaps they are misunderstood and undervalued. Often it is true; often they are persons of fine susceptibilities (which they mistake for fine sympathies), and perhaps under different circumstances would reveal qualities of a higher kind than those they manifest. Environment is a very determining influence, and there are probably few of us who might not have been much worthier and much happier persons under circumstances quite different from the existing ones. To have been born to inherited wealth and culture and its extended opportunities would certainly seem to be a factor in advance over that of being born in a log cabin, and learning to read by the light of a pine-knot. As a matter of actual record, however, the history of great lives puts a premium on the hardships and the pine-knot.[1]

  Reckless of danger, loss, and shame,
   In the free, fearless faith of youth,
  Forward through good and evil fame
   To battle in the cause of truth.

[1] Lilian Whiting, *The World Beautiful*, 15.

> Go, hope to bear, through toil and pain,
>   Her standard on to victory,
> And from the very strife to gain
>   Strength to dispense with sympathy.
>
> Truth must prevail. Meanwhile endure.
> Of worldly peace let worldlings boast.
> Amid the storms of life, be sure
> The loftiest spirits suffer most.

4. The man who has faith in himself will exercise his will and overcome. Now every man has some will, enough to constitute his responsibility, and will, like any other gift or power, can be cultivated. An act of will means more will. No man knows how much will he has until he wills to put forth his will for all it is worth. Let him fortify his will by thought and watchfulness, let him bring to it the mighty re-enforcement of prayer, let him regard it as a sacred trust to be consecrated to the highest ends, let him thus guard against undue depression when it seems to fail him, and he will be daily heartened to find what surprises of achievement there are at the heart of a power which is always there, if we will believe it. It is in the cultivation of the will that, of all places, we must say, and have the courage of our word:

> Boldness has genius, power, and magic in it,
> Only engage, and then the mind grows heated;
> Begin, and then the work will be completed.

¶ Men, in fast increasing numbers, have virtually arrived at the conclusion that fate, by whatever name it may be called, is our grim, but real deity, working through the two principal forces of heredity and surroundings. The past not only in ourselves, but in the line of which we come, determines our future; and *where* we are is practically *what* we are, and what we must be. I am confronted at almost every turn of my ministry with this doctrine, which empties life of its sacredness, and gives the lie to everything that makes this human world of ours grand and glorious. It has become an atmosphere, and men breathe it who never try to phrase it. These men would be the last to claim any merit in this; and it might be unjust to charge them with wilful folly. They are, as a rule, the average people about us, who do not trouble with such questions as "Is life worth living?" They simply accept the fact that they have an existence to be got through as best they can. When we try to reason with them about responsibility, they tell us that they were not consulted about their coming into the world; that they had no choice as to parentage, or in the circumstances they found here of place, home, and surroundings; and, deprived of a choice compared with which no other is worth the name, it is too late in the day to talk about responsibility. "Every man," says one who is now held to speak with authority, "is the product of his times, and the instrument"—mark the term—"the instrument of his circumstances." And there is just enough in all this to make the essential lie at the heart of it the more deadly. Its inevitable effect is to destroy man's faith in himself.[1]

5. Finally, the man who has faith in himself will (again, if he is a good man) love himself and that truly. The duty of self-love is clearly and definitely set forth in the second great commandment of the gospel. In Christ's own words, that commandment runs thus: "Thou shalt love thy neighbour as thyself." "As thyself." These are the crucial words of this commandment. It is obvious, therefore, that until we have learnt what "self" means we cannot know what "neighbour" means; and until we have practised the duty of true self-love we cannot know how best to practise the duty of true love towards our neighbour. We must learn how we ought to love ourselves aright before we can learn to love aright our neighbours as we ought; seeing that Christ Himself has constituted self-love as the safe and just standard of our love to others. Our duty to ourselves is the only true measure of our duty to our fellow-men. It is not until we understand what we owe, and ought to do, to ourselves that we can clearly see what we owe, and ought to do, to our fellow-men. Not only for our own sake, therefore, but for the sake of our neighbours, it is of supreme importance to ponder in our hearts and carry out in our conduct this great duty of self-love—a duty which, while never allowing us to forget, but always insisting that in fear and trembling we remember, the depravity of our nature and the dangers of that depravity, yet insists also that we should never forget, but always remember in wonder and love and awe, the divinity of our nature and the possibilities of that divinity.

[1] *Ambrose Shepherd, D.D.: A Memoir and Sermons*, 93.

It is our paramount duty to look at, and love, ourselves comprehensively, and look at, and love, ourselves whòle.

In fulfilling this duty we shall be preserved from the peril of allowing the lustful schism of any part in us to destroy the happy union of the whole. Self-love is love of the soul and love of the body, and each in its proper place. Sometimes the metaphor is used that the soul is a precious gem contained in the casket of the body. But such a metaphor falls far short of the truth; a casket may be battered, defiled, spoilt; yet open it and you shall find the gem, perfect, pure, and inviolate. Not so with the soul and body; if self-indulgence, or sloth, or unworthy deeds, abuse and stain the body, you cannot throw the body aside and find anywhere a soul pure and untouched; a truer analogy of the relation between soul and body would be that between the electric light and the wire along which it flashes: if the wire is spoilt or cut, the light can only shine more dimly or 'not shine at all. A body well disciplined, kept in strict control, wakeful, alert, ready for action, will lend its own strength to the soul; the soul, free from defiling memories, free from embarrassing entanglements of the body, will gain an assured confidence to act on the side of all that is right. We must test the powers of our own body, we must know its functions: we must treat it as the great ally of our soul, and then we shall feel that interaction of soul and body which Browning has expressed so well and which he has put into the mouth of a Jewish Rabbi:

> Let us not always say
> "*Spite of* this flesh to-day
> I strove, made head, gained ground upon the whole!"
> As the bird wings and sings,
> Let us cry "All good things
> Are ours, nor soul helps flesh more, now, than flesh helps soul!"

II.

Its Perils.

Faith in one's self lies perilously near to some of the most hindering and ruinous defects of character: to conceit, to presump-

FAITH IN ONE'S SELF

tion, to obstinacy, to neglect of other men's thoughts and feelings, to loss of sensitiveness and gentleness and delicacy, to a deficient sense of humour: all 'these are close about it, threatening to assimilate it to themselves, or to mix themselves with it.

¶ Self-confidence is apt to address itself to an imaginary dulness in others; as people who are well-off speak in a cajoling tone to the poor, and those who are in the prime of life raise their voice and talk artificially to seniors, hastily conceiving them to be deaf and rather imbecile.[1]

> Selfishness has swept the house,
> Vanity has garnished it,
> With desires furnished it.
> Not a crumb to feed a mouse
> Have they left of household bread,
>   Duty, honour, charity.
> "Food for common mortals," said Vanity.[2]

1. The most obvious peril is *selfishness*. Standing alone, consciously or unconsciously without any knowledge of God, uninfluenced by any thought of a future life, without any intelligent conception of the responsibility we all have for those among whom we live, a man becomes to himself the centre of thought, almost of worship; his wishes, his wants, his success—these are the sole motive forces within him; and in the full strong belief in his own capacity to push his way—not sensitive enough, or finely strung enough, to contemplate the possibility of mistake or failure in himself—he goes forward, regardless of what may happen to any with whom he comes in contact, utterly indifferent as to who may fall or who may suffer, provided only he may succeed. And so, step by step, the strong pushing man grows into the hard selfish man of the world, who, making great boast of his own capacities and powers, forces his way right on to the prize he means to grasp. Of course, the refinements of cultured life do something to conceal such a character under a decent varnish of consideration for others; good taste and the laws of society require certain courtesies from us in dealing with each other, and he is

---

[1] George Eliot, *Daniel Deronda*.
[2] Margaret L. Woods, *Poems*, 148.

too shrewd and too alive to his own interests not to comply with these demands.

2. The selfishness of the self-confident is sure to show itself in *harsh judgment*. Carlyle is a notable example. His biographer does his character less than justice; but in representing him as scornful of weaker intellects and weaker wills than his own, and in his scorn using too freely that biting tongue of his, Froude must, it is feared, be acquitted of unfairness.

¶ Carlyle's existence hitherto had been a prolonged battle; a man does not carry himself in such conflicts so wisely and warily that he can come out of them unscathed; and Carlyle carried scars from his wounds both on his mind and on his temper. He had stood aloof from parties; he had fought his way *alone*. He was fierce and uncompromising. To those who saw but the outside of him he appeared scornful, imperious, and arrogant. He was stern in his judgment of others. The sins of passion he could pardon, but the sins of insincerity, or half-sincerity, he could never pardon. He would not condescend to the conventional politenesses which remove the friction between man and man. He called things by their right names, and in a dialect edged with sarcasm. Thus he was often harsh when he ought to have been merciful; he was contemptuous where he had no right to despise; and in his estimate of motives and actions was often unjust and mistaken. He, too, who was so severe with others had weaknesses of his own of which he was unconscious in the excess of his self-confidence. He was proud—one may say savagely proud. It was a noble determination in him that he would depend upon himself alone; but he would not only accept no obligation, but he resented the offer of help to himself or to anyone belonging to him as if it had been an insult.[1]

3. Another peril is *persecution*. When those who, in their confidence, pass judgment harshly on others, have the power to persecute, they are only too ready to use that power.

¶ The edict of Nantes was recalled on the 17th November 1685. The elder Le Tellier, dying aet. 83, some days later, sang a *Nunc dimittis*. Long before, many churches had been destroyed, 141 in 1663 alone, Roman clergy authorised to force their way to the dying, children of seven allowed to change their religion and

[1] *Thomas Carlyle: First Forty Years*, 471.

claim a pension from their parents; singing of psalms was forbidden in the open air or in the churches while a procession went by; funerals were restricted to the twilight; dragoons quartered on the Protestants with orders to push them to the last extremity, to live very licentiously. Louvois has enriched our language with two words, the verb "to dragoon," the substantive "dragoonade." By the edict all churches were destroyed; all pastors banished with one fortnight's grace under pain of the galleys; lay emigration entirely forbidden; all children, from five to sixteen years of age, to be taken from their parents and brought up as Catholics; death to all pastors found in the country; men who helped them to be sentenced to the galleys, women to prison for life; death to all holding assemblies or any exercise of religion; all who in sickness refused the sacraments, on recovery to be sent to the galleys or prison for life, in case of death, their bodies to be cast out unburied; in either case their estates confiscated; books of religion, Bibles, prayerbooks, psalters, to be burnt; all offices and professions, down to that of midwife, closed to professors of the *religion prétendue réformée*; the marriages of Protestants were declared void, their children illegitimate. I mention only one torture out of many, the invention of Foucault, very effective in procuring conversions: the torturers by relays keeping sleep from the victims' eyelids. This Foucault was, I grieve to say, a scholar, and, by a strange irony of fate, first discovered Lactantius "On the death of persecutors." All these and countless other penalties, more grievous than death, were summarily inflicted without due form of trial. In one year, though France was kept like a dungeon girt by troops and ships, 9000 sailors, 12,000 soldiers, 600 officers had emigrated, including the best general of his age, Schomberg. Switzerland, the Low Countries, Germany, England, America, the Cape, all gained by the loss of the flower of the French industry and learning. Berlin, till then not half the size of our present Cambridge, made rapid strides. In London there were thirty-one churches of French Protestants. The present Lord Mayor, the Bishop Designate of Worcester, our Junior Missioner at Walworth, are all of emigrant blood.[1]

4. But the self-confident man runs another risk, more personal, more subtle, and more hurtful. He runs the risk of *presumption*. We are careful to distinguish between the serene courage which best deals with danger and the foolhardiness which courts disaster. The collier descending underground with his safety-lamp has our

[1] J. E. B. Mayor, *Sermons*, 138.

sympathy whilst he walks warily; but when he forces his lamp to light his pipe, we only despise and condemn. The line of demarcation between wise conduct in the presence of danger and recklessness is generally clear. Sensible men cherish the habit of awareness; they watch over their health and safety, make the margin between themselves and loss as wide as possible, keep well within the lines chalked out by experience, and risk nothing without adequate cause. On the contrary, the foolish presume on their cleverness; they confide in luck, graze the rock, swim the river just above the falls, their supreme piquant entertainment being "a narrow shave." We see examples of both types alike in daily and in moral life.

(1) In ordinary life, when men run serious risks something of consequence stands to be won. Whenever one goes forth with a shroud under his arm to attempt any enterprise, he has, as a rule, an adequate prize in view, or at least thinks that he has. Alfred Nobel, the famous inventor of explosives, lived for years dealing with the most dangerous substances and making experiments fraught with peril. He was ever handling terrible compounds like nitro-glycerine, gunpowder, dynamite, blasting glycerine, guncotton, blasting gelatine, cordite, and any hour might have been blown to atoms. He habitually faced death in its most terrible forms. But this hazardous life was redeemed by a great purpose. The brave experimentalist sought to solve important problems, and to equip the engineer with forces that might the sooner establish the pathway of civilization. He who in a daredevil spirit sports with gunpowder, cordite, or dynamite is a fool.

(2) To dabble with any forbidden thing in the moral life is inexcusable folly; for it does not, and it cannot, bring any advantage whatever. The wounds received in the service of sin carry no honour; the ventures made at the bidding of vicious caprice yield no profit; the forbidden precipices we climb with bleeding feet only render our folly the more conspicuous and our punishment the more complete. "What fruit then had ye at that time in the things whereof ye are now ashamed? for the end of those things is death." What fools we are! How incurable is our folly! Shall we never learn that there is nothing worth having beyond the hedge? Everything good for the body; everything in nature, art, science, literature, adventure, that gives intellectual

entertainment and delight; whatever society bestows of love and joy; the world, genius, life, the affluence of the present, the splendour of hope, all are ours within the lines of reason and righteousness; yet in very wantonness we break bounds and trespass on ground where we stand to lose everything! To put our great life into pawn at the bidding of arrogant recklessness is the supreme infatuation.

¶ The wife of the celebrated physician, Sir William Priestley, was a strenuous advocate of the theories of Pasteur, and in her book entitled *The Story of a Lifetime* she describes a dinner given at her house to enable Mr. Chamberlain to meet some of Pasteur's disciples and to become acquainted with his methods. "On entering the drawing-room after dinner, Mr. Chamberlain had the felicity of finding himself, for the first time in his life, in a veritable museum of living disease. On every side were glass tubes, with nothing between himself and a variety of contagious diseases but cotton-wool stoppers. Standing in the presence of this awe-inspiring world, Chamberlain was not afraid." No, these gentlemen were not afraid; they gaily talked and laughed, although meeting in a veritable museum of horrors, amid tubes containing flourishing families of disease, plates smeared with gelatine containing microbes of various kinds, and microscopes through which could be seen the bacilli when taken fresh from the blood of disease-stricken men or animals. Only a frail particle of cotton-wool separated them from the ghastliest plagues; yet it was enough. This narrative is a parable of our moral situation and peril. The world in which perforce we dwell and act is a museum of living disease; everything is infested with contagion; we are threatened by a thousand deaths: yet are we perfectly secure. The ethereal defences by which God renders His sincere children immune are sufficient. We may live in perfect confidence and peace, enjoying without a disturbing thought all the pleasant things life has to give. The God of our salvation can seal "the pit of the abyss" with an electron, render a bubble a fortress, hedge us in with a gossamer; or, to drop the imagery, the altogether invisible and intangible action of divine grace will secure the absolute safety of all who are pure in heart, even though Pandemonium seethe around them. "Surely he shall deliver thee from the snare of the fowler, and from the noisome pestilence. Thou shalt not be afraid for the terror by night; nor for the arrow that flieth by day; nor for the pestilence that walketh in darkness; nor for the destruction that wasteth at noonday. A thousand shall fall at thy side, and ten thousand at thy right hand; but it shall not come nigh thee. There shall no evil befall thee, neither shall any plague come nigh thy dwelling."[1]

III.

Its Foundation.

We have seen that to have faith in one's self is to have power, but that it has its dangers. How are we to have the power and escape the peril? The answer is, by seeing to it that we have a good foundation for our faith.

1. A man may be self-confident by *temperament*. Is that a good foundation?

(1) If by temperament a man is an optimist, that is certainly better than if he were by temperament a pessimist. It is better for himself; it is better also for the world. Nothing can well be more distressing to one's self or more depressing to others than a disposition to look always on the dark side of things. An extreme example is that of Marie Bashkirtseff, who was born at Poltava in the Ukraine in 1860, the daughter of General Bashkirtseff, a wealthy landed proprietor, and who died in 1884, before she had completed her twenty-fourth year. Here is one of the entries in her Journal:

"I am profoundly disgusted with myself. I hate everything I have done, written, and said. I detest myself, because I have fulfilled none of my hopes. I have deceived myself; I am stupid; I have no tact—and have never had any. Show me one really clever thing I have said—one wise thing I have done. Nothing but folly! I thought I was witty; I am absurd. I thought myself brave; and I am timid. I thought I had talent; and I don't know what I have done with it. And, with all that, the pretension of being able to write charmingly. Ah! my Emperor! you may possibly take all I have been saying for wit; it looks like it, but it isn't. I am clever enough to judge myself truly, which makes me seem modest, and I know not what besides. I hate myself!"[2]

(2) On the other hand a temperamental self-confidence, if

---

[1] W. L. Watkinson, *The Fatal Barter*, 142.
[2] *The Journal of Marie Bashkirtseff*, i. 350.

FAITH IN ONE'S SELF

more comfortable, may exceed all reason or reality, and end in disaster. Perhaps the most conspicuous case is Lord Bacon's. This is what Dr. E. A. Abbott says of Bacon:

"If throughout his life, if even in his private prayers, he habitually used the language of conscious and superior virtue, he was not thereby imposing upon others more than he imposed upon himself; however he might occasionally dissemble and justify dissembling, he never deserved to be called a hypocrite, for he was thoroughly persuaded of his own general rectitude, and even in his deepest disgrace and dejection he still retained his self-esteem. Yet to many readers, after perusing the following pages, Bacon's retention of self-esteem will appear nothing less than portentous. To describe it as bordering on insanity would be unpardonable, for Bacon's nature was eminently sane; but it would be nearer the mark to say that from his restless, perfervid mother, who is said on reasonable grounds to have been 'frantic' for some years before her death, Bacon inherited some abnormal characteristics, one of which took the shape of an excessive and even monstrous self-confidence. But for this, Bacon's *Apology* would have been more humble and more accurate; but for this, the *Novum Organum* would never have existed; it was the secret alike of his great strength and great weakness; it nerved him to superhuman enterprises, and blinded him to his own most obvious faults."[1]

> Beware of too sublime a sense
> Of your own worth and consequence!
> The man who dreams himself so great,
> And his importance of such weight,
> That all around, in all that's done,
> Must move and act for him alone,
> Will learn, in school of tribulation,
> The folly of his expectation.[2]

2. Without being temperamentally an optimist or even an egotist, one may believe in one's *destiny*. Is that a good foundation for faith?

(1) There is no doubt that a sense of "calling" is a mighty incentive to heroic deeds. In the old days of paganism success thus gained would be credited to the gods.

---

[1] E. A. Abbott, *Francis Bacon*, xvii.   [2] W. Cowper.

The career of Timoleon, as described by Plutarch, is perhaps the most remarkable instance of unchequered success ever recorded. Though unskilled in strategy, he undertook to lead a small Corinthian force for the liberation of Sicily from the tyrant Dionysius and the Carthaginians. In respect to material force the enterprise seemed desperate; but the omens were highly favourable. During the ceremonies at Corinth which preceded his departure, a crown of victory, detached from some decorations, fell down upon his head; and a light as from heaven guided his ships towards Rhegium. By skill and address he slipped across the strait, evading the Carthaginian galleys. Victory crowned his daring rush against their troops, whom he took unawares. The Greek cities, startled by these signs of divine favour, espoused his cause; and he succeeded in capturing the citadel of Syracuse and Dionysius himself. A plot to murder Timoleon was foiled by an avenger of blood striking down the very man who was about to take the hero's life. All these events (says Plutarch) "made the people reverence and protect Timoleon as a sacred person sent by heaven to revenge and redeem Sicily." He himself before the crowning battle against the Carthaginians gave a happy turn to what seemed an evil omen with a skill like that displayed by William the Conqueror at the landing in Pevensey Bay. Finally, after giving liberty and just government to Sicily, Timoleon thanked the gods for the favour which they had vouchsafed, and erected a shrine in his house to Good Fortune, ascribing all his successes to her. Clearly these uninterrupted triumphs were in large measure the outcome of the belief in the special favour accorded to him by the gods.

(2) But if the "high calling of God" is no more to a man than good luck, however it may be enforced by resolute effort, it is sure enough to end in disaster at the last. Napoleon, a child of the Mediterranean, brought up among a primitive people, half hunters, half fishermen, realized the force of superstition. Perhaps at one time he was imbued by it; for he retained the custom of crossing himself on the receipt of good news. He early rejected revealed religion, but he retained his belief in good luck, much as Frederick the Great did. He knew that soldiers, peasants, and many of a higher station as well, worshipped good fortune, the shadow of all primitive cults. It is therefore highly probable that

FAITH IN ONE'S SELF

his appeals to his star, or fortune, or destiny, were designed to enlist on his side the crude but potent conceptions which have always counted for so much among the Mediterranean peoples, nerving the Greeks to do more than their best for Alexander the Great, Epaminondas, and Timoleon. Some generals are lucky, others unlucky. Napoleon determined to be among the lucky ones, and set himself to conquer Fortune by claiming that she was already on his side.[1]

¶ Let me tell you a saying that is given in that lovely book, *Christ's Folk in the Apennines*. The cholera was raging in the district, and there was a peasant woman, Marina, a very beautiful woman of 25, with her two little children, who in the demand and the need of the dying patients offered herself to nurse them. She went into the dangerous atmosphere and nursed them with her own hands, and with great tenderness and skill; people protested against it, and said, " Why should you expose your life for those who are not connected with you at all ? " Her answer was, " The poor things must not be neglected, and I am as fit to do it as anyone." Then she said to her friends who spoke to her about it: " You see, when you have a call everything is easy."[2]

3. Will it do to rely upon our *gifts*?

The word is promising. If we recognize our ability to do this or that as a gift of God, it is not likely that we shall use it foolishly. But how often does the word "gift" retain its true meaning for us? It may express no more than the conscious possession of certain powers—even if it expresses so much. And it is not powers that we must rely upon but power. Powers we have. Not only are they the prime cause of our weakness, however, but often the more a man has the worse off in this matter he is. How often has a man been prevented from finding and living by the power of God through possessing such "riches" and " powers " of his own as, say, social position, or personal charm, or artistic temperament, or quickness of brain, or distinction in games? The greater our "powers," the greater our need of " power," if only because we are the more likely to be blind to our own weakness.

---

[1] J. Holland Rose, *The Personality of Napoleon*, 202.
[2] R. F. Horton, *The Springs of Joy*, 178.

¶ Has it ever struck you that, in the material universe, "power" is never originated by man, but always given to him? Man has to find the power and to apply it, but it is *there* quite apart from him. An electrical "power-station" is not a place where power is created, but a place where power *already found* in one form is converted into another and applied to certain uses afterwards. And then look at the machinery to which it is applied. It has "powers"—it is designed to do certain things, and can do them. But when? Only while it uses, or rather *is used by*, the power laid on. *Then* you get your light, or motion, or heat. Your machine has "received power," and "in" that power it can "do all things" which it was made to do. But if the power be cut off, the engine stops, and the light goes out; in spite of its "powers" the machine stands "powerless."[1]

4. What is the best foundation? One word will answer the question—*sonship*. That is the best and the only foundation for faith in one's self.

¶ When it was said in the presence of John Smith, who was an under-master at Harrow School, and whose life was, as far as we ever can say it of any human life, a perfect and saintly one, that someone had a very difficult task before him, he exclaimed in astonishment, "Difficult? Difficult? Why, he is a Christian."[2]

(1) To be a Christian—that is the foundation. Says St. Paul, "I can do all things through Christ which strengtheneth me" (Phil. iv. 13). By "all things" he means all that he desires, as a Christian, to do. He means also all that, as a Christian, he has to suffer. Just as in a great factory where all the power is generated at one spot, perhaps by one engine, and is all conveyed and distributed to each part so that every wheel is turned, every hammer is lifted, every implement is employed in a perfect harmony and with complete efficiency, the power distributed according to the direction, so it is to be understood that an individual life placed in Christ is in the line of power, and exactly what is wanted is supplied. But the difference is, this is not a factory, nor is it a machine; it is a Divine Person whose omnipotence moves the universe.

(2) Now to be a Christian, to possess sonship, there is necessary

---

[1] E. A. Burroughs, *Faith and Power*, 6.
[2] R. F. Horton, *The Springs of Joy*, 166.

FAITH IN ONE'S SELF

first of all the recognition of two things standing over against one another—the grace of God and the faith of man. "Grace" is simply a convenient term for "all the ways in which God comes in to the help of our lives." And over against it stands "faith," which similarly covers "all the ways in which we appropriate the help of God." The terms are correlatives; neither, strictly, can be conceived of without the other.

A small boat is in the bay and wants to cross to the other side. The power which is to help it across is all there in the wind; but when is that power effectual? Only when those on board give it the means of communicating itself to the boat, by hoisting a sail. True, the sails are powerless without the wind, but so is the wind useless till a sail is held up for it to fill and drive. Faith is the continual readiness to count upon the presence and to claim the help of a God who is such as we see Him in Christ. It is the stretching out of the hand, the hoisting of the sail. And, because God *is there*, faith succeeds; and, succeeding, confirms itself. The experiment passes into an experience: an attitude results from the act. Not, however, the attitude of mere passive adherence, but the *active* dependence of friend upon Friend, the faith which is not only made active but kept in activity through love.

(3) The first effect of the hoisting of the sail is forgiveness. For the very central element in our "weakness" is the strange fact we call sin. There is no more serious handicap to a man than a guilty conscience, and even those who do not themselves feel the burden of their past, yet know its weakening effects. To have chosen wrongly many times is almost tantamount to selling your free-will, and compelling yourselves to choose the same way again. Thus, the grace of God appears, first and foremost, as *forgiveness*—that is the first way a man needs God's help in his life. He requires to be "justified by faith" in order that he may "have peace toward God." But then, when that is provided, and the handicap removed, there is still need of help for the course before him, and that need may be summed up as the need of *power*, the thing which we find we have not in ourselves.

(4) And with peace of conscience (or before it) there comes the sense of sonship. This is the central fact. It is reconciliation to and harmony with God; it is heirship of God, joint-heirship

with Jesus Christ; it is the assurance of God's love to us—
"Behold, what manner of love the Father hath bestowed upon us,
that we should be called the sons of God." Everything Christ
said and did had the grand intention of quickening man's nobler
nature to the realisation that, in spite of all the demons that
possess him, of the insanity that maddens him, of the sin that
encumbers him, he is yet a son of God. What man is yet to be,
he has not now the faculties to know; but even now, in his fallen
condition and ruined state, he can claim the great prerogative of
sonship to God. Wherever Christ went and taught He developed
in men the consciousness of this stupendous fact of their Divine
relationship to God. He quickened it in publicans, sinners, and
harlots. He sealed it by His rising from the dead and the out-
pouring of His Spirit, and wheresoever He quickened it two results
followed: first, a prostrate sense of utter unworthiness; and,
secondly, an unspeakable thankfulness for God's mercy and love
in making men His sons.

¶ There are two stages in religious experience; there is the
fear and horror of sin, in which passion clutches at the skirts of
an unknown and awful Deity; but there is another and more
blessed state into which we may come: I mean the victorious
faith, peace and fellowship of the Sons of God. For those who
enter into that communion there is no devil, no Power of Evil, no
duality in the worlds of God.[1]

¶ I have faith in the hereafter because I have faith in myself.
I pray God that I may ever be humble, and think of myself as a
child should who feels that he owes everything—being, guidance,
support—to his Father. But may He keep me from that false
humility which imposes a sense of self-degradation, that pulls His
dignity downward as it sinks. I am proud of the Father in me;
and because I am His child I dare not write myself downward
below a certain height of being. I feel that eternity is mine
because I inherit it through Him. I feel that immortality is mine
because His Spirit begot me, and out of His loins death cannot
come. And so I say to those who say, "there is no life beyond,
there is no world to come: to the grave we go, and in the grave
we stop for ever and ever"—very well, take that for your faith.
Faith in vacuity; faith in nothingness; have that for your faith.
But I have that in me,—faculties, powers, beginnings of powers,
thought and awakenings of thought, fruit, blossoms, buds, germs,

[1] H. B. Binns, in *Present Day Papers*, iii. 69.

FAITH IN ONE'S SELF

beginning of germs, that point with the prophecy of indestructible life to ages ahead, as theirs.[1]

> Here where the loves of others close
> The vision of my heart begins.
> The wisdom that within us grows
> Is absolution for our sins.
>
> We took forbidden fruit and ate
> Far in the garden of His mind.
> The ancient prophecies of hate
> We proved untrue, for He was kind.
>
> He does not love the bended knees,
> The soul made wormlike in His sight,
> Within whose heaven are hierarchies
> And solar kings and lords of light.
>
> Who come before Him with the pride
> The Children of the King should bear,
> They will not be by Him denied,
> His light will make their darkness fair.
>
> To be afar from Him is death
> Yet all things find their fount in Him:
> And nearing to the sunrise breath
> Shine jewelled like the seraphim.[2]

(5) We are made sons of God by the Cross of Christ. But when St. Paul says, "I can do all things through Christ which strengtheneth me," it is clear that he is thinking of Christ not as He died on Calvary but as He is alive now and for ever. It is undeniable that he recognized Jesus Christ as living and accessible; that he lived in direct, intimate, habitual communion with Him: and that the strength by which he was enabled to do and to suffer was strength imparted to him immediately by Christ, without whom he could do nothing. It was not by his own native force of resolution, not by his own courage and fortitude, constitutional or acquired; nor was it from any *past* supply of gracious influence which he had received, that he was enabled to go on confronting

---

[1] W. H. Murray, *The Fruits of the Spirit*, 75.
[2] A. E., *Collected Poems*, 247.

danger and enduring affliction, maintaining a calm contented mind in the midst of privation and difficulty; but only by a continual supply of strength directly from Christ Himself.

Look, for example, at the account which he gives of his mysterious rapture into Paradise. Lest he should be exalted above measure by the abundance of the revelations, there was given him "a thorn in the flesh"—some grievous infirmity, or some sharp, constant, humiliating affliction—which he describes as "the messenger of Satan to buffet" him. And "for this thing," he says, "I besought the Lord thrice." Earnestly and repeatedly, he prayed to Christ Himself, "that it might depart from me; and he said unto me, my grace is sufficient for thee: for my strength is made perfect in weakness. Most gladly, therefore," he continues, "will I rather glory in my infirmities, that the power of Christ may rest upon me."

Here, then, we find him not only communing directly with Christ, and receiving from Him the assurance of such a constant supply of spiritual strength immediately from Himself as should enable him to bear up under the infirmity with which he was still to be harassed, but also welcoming his affliction, as the means of his enjoying larger communications of Christ's gracious influences than he would otherwise have been privileged with. And "therefore," he goes on to say, "therefore I take pleasure in infirmities, in reproaches, in necessities, in persecutions, in distresses for Christ's sake; for when I am weak then am I strong": when I am the most sensible of my own utter insufficiency and impotence, then am I strongest in the strength which Christ immediately imparts. In a similar manner he writes to Timothy—"At my first answer no man stood with me, but all men forsook me. Notwithstanding the Lord stood with me, and strengthened me"—filling him with a courage and a fortitude no human countenance could have inspired—"and I was delivered out of the mouth of the lion." So again he says to the Galatians, "I am crucified with Christ: nevertheless I live; yet not I, but Christ liveth in me": liveth in me by the energy of His own spirit animating and sustaining me. All these, and other similar passages clearly show that Paul lived in personal and habitual communion with Christ, and that when he speaks of Christ strengthening him, his language must be accepted in its strict and literal meaning.

Now, where Christ is self cannot be. The entrance of the love of Christ drives out the love of self. There is "the expulsive power of a new affection," of which Chalmers spoke. Truly, if there is no God-life in us, we cannot think too meanly of ourselves. But if He, and not nature, is the Root of our life, we cannot think too much of ourselves. Therefore our Divine Teacher and Lord counsels us to repudiate our recent, carnally-generated selfhood; and to love, and lay up wealth in Heaven for our Divine identity. "If any man come to me, and hate not his own life, he cannot be my disciple." In other words, if he will hold to his earthborn selfhood, he cannot inherit his Divine selfhood. "He that loveth his life shall lose it; and he that hateth his life in this world shall keep it unto life eternal." The ground which Christ takes on our behalf is absolute, and not debatable. We cannot follow Him up the high path of our return to our God-born humanity and blessedness, unless we conclude once and for ever that our nature-born selfhood is unworthy of us.

And as self is driven out there enter *love* and *service*. The religion of Jesus, says John Pulsford, is sublimely simple; it is insusceptible of wranglings and independent of all ecclesiastical systems. If the two great loves prevail in us, no moral darkness can ever blind our eyes, nor any death touch our central life. Children in the house of their father and mother quietly assume their birthright, and all the rights and privileges of their home. So do the angels of Heaven; and the men and women of the earth, as much as angels, when they know who they are, whence they came, and whither they are going. By leading us into ourselves Jesus awakens in us self-reverence and quenchless affections; and the recognition in all men of the same God-derived nature as in ourselves makes us sacred to each other as members of one Divine Household.

¶ There is a sound of altercation among the little ones; cries of "I want!" are heard. Whereupon mother enters and exclaims: "That is never my Charlie!—snatching and shouting like this! I don't know that rude boy! Send him away, and let me see my loving little Charlie back again!" She repudiates the grasp-the-whole-world self of her little boy, and teaches him to do the same, in order that his higher self may be reinstated.

And before long, as her efforts are rewarded, there is a different cry heard. It is still "I want," but the I is that of a higher self, which says: "I want to kiss you, mother." The selfish little grasper has disappeared: the submissive little son has come back. The two are mutually exclusive. To realize the one is to repudiate the other.[1]

¶ How wild are our wishes, how frantic our schemes of happiness when we first enter on the world! Our hearts encircled in the delusions of vanity and self-love, we think the Universe was made for us alone; we glory in the strength of our gifts, in the pride of our place; and forget that the fairest ornament of our being is "the quality of mercy," the still, meek, humble Love that dwells in the inmost shrine of our nature, and cannot come to light till Selfishness in all its cunning forms is banished out of us, till affliction and neglect and disappointment have sternly taught us that self is a foundation of sand, that we, even the mighty *we*, are a poor and feeble and most unimportant fraction in the general sum of existence. Fools writhe and wriggle and rebel at this; their life is a little waspish battle against all mankind for refusing to take part with them; and their little dole of reputation and sensation, wasting more and more into a shred, is annihilated at the end of a few beggarly years, and they leave the Earth without ever feeling that the spirit of man is a child of Heaven, and has thoughts and aims in which self and its interests are lost from the eye, as the Eagle is swallowed up in the brightness of the sun, to which it soars.[2]

¶ The apostles were impressed with the fact that they were builders, that their work was constructive, that a world purpose was being effected through their ministry. The eye of St. Paul never left, if we may so put it, the map of the great Empire which he was to claim for Christ. "Fear not, Paul, thou must also see Rome." His conversion meant the conviction of an imperial, nay, a universal apostolate committed to him and making constant demands not only upon an intensity to which all things were possible but upon a statesmanship, an economy of opportunity, a husbandry of power, which could trust in God and keep its powder dry. He is never carried away by the impetuous impulse, though the imperious claim of the gospel never lets him rest. He is master of himself and therefore commands the situation. There is no tactless anxiety for the salvation of souls. He knows how to become all things to all men in the strenuous

---

[1] W. A. Cornaby, *In Touch with Reality*, 142.
[2] Carlyle, in *The Love Letters of Thomas Carlyle and Jane Welsh*, ii. 158.

effort to save some. He knows how to abound as well as how to suffer loss. His life is confined in no narrow channel. For him truth, beauty, excellence, as these things are understood by the cultivated intelligence, retained their interest and meaning. The evangelist has not ceased to be the critic, the observer, and the gentleman. What strikes the mind in contemplating the career of St. Paul is not so much "Here is a man who has made the great renunciation," but "Here is the man of power." His missionary journeys rival in interest the travel of Odysseus. They impress us by the fulness of their experience rather than by the greatness of their self-sacrifice. The strong man delights in dangers, in hairbreadth escapes, in critical situations. The adventurous lad who first hears the celebrated catalogue of Pauline perils hardly pities the man who encountered them. These are all in the day's work of him who would earn the reward of efficiency. The strong man, who disdains crucifixion, shrinks from no suffering:

"I sought where-so the wind blew keenest. There I learned to dwell
Where no man dwells, on lonesome, ice-born fell,
And unlearned man and God and curse and prayer,
Became a ghost, haunting the glaciers bare." [1]

[1] Canon J. G. Simpson, *Christus Crucifixus*, 29.

III.

FAITH IN MEN.

LITERATURE.

Alexander, A., *The Glory in the Grey* (1914).
Boyd, A. K. H., *Landscapes, Churches and Moralities* (1874).
Cabot, R. C., *What Men Live By* (1915).
Connell, A., *The Endless Quest* (1914).
Farrar, F. W., *Social and Present-Day Questions* (1903).
Finlayson, T. C., *Essays, Addresses and Lyrical Translations* (1893).
Hutton, R. H., *Aspects of Religious and Scientific Thought* (1899).
Jefferson, C. E., *The Building of the Church* (1910).
Kelman, J., *Honour Towards God* (1903).
Major, H. D. A., *The Gospel of Freedom* (1912).
Maxson, H. D., *Sermons of Religion and Life* (1893).
Paget, F., *Faculties and Difficulties for Belief and Disbelief* (1889).
Porter, N., *Yale College Sermons* (1888).
Potter, H. C., *Sermons of the City* (1880).
Smith, W. C., *Sermons* (1909).
Temple, W., *Repton School Sermons* (1913).
Watkinson, W. L., *Frugality in the Spiritual Life* (1908).
Modern Essays (reprinted from Leading Articles in "The Times") (1915).

FAITH IN MEN.

1. THE Prayer-book version of Ps. cxvi. 10 may not be the most accurate version (it is a difficult verse to translate), but it is full of suggestion: "I believe, and therefore will I speak; but I was sore troubled: I said in my haste, All men are liars." The Psalm is the cry of a man torn by doubts, but not conquered by them. It is the voice of one who has been down into the deep waters and for a time has lost his footing. "The snares of death compassed me round about: and the pains of hell gat hold upon me. . . . O Lord, I beseech thee, deliver my soul. I shall find trouble and heaviness, and I will call upon the name of the Lord." And then, as the clouds begin to break, and the light begins to dawn, "Gracious is the Lord, and righteous: yea, our God is merciful: the Lord preserveth the simple: I was in misery, and he helped me. Turn again then unto thy rest, O my soul." Come back, O tempest-tost wanderer, seeking peace and shivering in the dismal sense of loneliness and doubt, "turn again unto thy rest, for the Lord hath rewarded me. And why? thou hast delivered my soul from death: mine eyes from tears, and my feet from falling!" And then, as the whole consciousness of the man wakes up out of the hideous dream of distrust and despair in which he has been walking, he breaks forth into that sublime assertion of his faith and trust, "I will walk before the Lord, in the land of the living. I believed, and therefore will I speak; but I was sore troubled: I said in my haste, All men are liars!"

In discovering God the Psalmist discovered man. It is always so. "I have found," says James Smetham,[1] "the Art of Finding how to get thought out of books, out of men, out of

[1] *Letters of James Smetham*, 88.

things. I have learned the art of Appreciation. I am nearer to my kind. And I have learned—blessed knowledge !—the philosophy of Life, as it respects me and mine. Eureka! I have found Him of whom Moses and the prophets did write; I have found how He comes to man's soul, how He dwells, rules, guides, consoles, how He suffices. I have found the Way, the Truth, the Life." He puts the discovery of man first, but with him as with us all the discovery of God's faithfulness came first, then the discovery of the truthfulness of men.

2. Faith in the personal Christ is essential to faith in man. It is significantly said of the Master that He knew what was in man, and yet He loved man, and even trusted man. It is esteemed in these days the highest achievement, if not the necessary completion, of a man's training, that he should learn to distrust men in order that he may manage men. The world of business and, to a large extent, the world of science and letters, of politics and professional life, is divided into two classes—the sharp and critical and hard men, and the so-called weak and confiding men whom the world treads down with its iron heel, or passes by with supercilious neglect. The sharp men make it a rule to criticize and distrust everybody: the confiding men learn, by being often deceived, in their turn to distrust and to hate. The tendency of our times is to idolize sharpness and criticism, and to sacrifice at their altar the generosities and charities and graces of life, as also the Divine sweetness of that charity which believeth all things, and endureth all things. There is no force that will fill the heart of an individual with courage and self-reliance on the one hand, and with sweetness and light on the other, that will bind man to man in the noble magnanimity of a wise but generous faith, except a living faith in the living Christ.

¶ Faith in man is a duty as well as faith in God; in fact, our general conduct every day in our intercourse with our fellow-beings depends at every turn on our faith in our fellow-beings. When that faith ceases, society ceases with it, and a rule not of men with moral natures, but of tigers and foxes in the guise of men, commences with it.[1]

[1] *The Day-Book of John Stuart Blackie*, 116.

¶ There are a few quiet places in England that are in a national sense holy ground, and one of these is Stoke Poges Churchyard, among whose yews and graves Gray wrote the beautiful "Elegy." It is a point for pilgrimage; though the pilgrim must not allow himself to be shown round. A place in which to sit and rest and be calm, and not one in which to use the eyes "to botanise," as it were, upon a mother's grave. There once sat the poet Gray and forgot that he was Gray, and spoke for England—let the rich earth speak for him.

> Perhaps in this neglected spot is laid
>   Some heart once pregnant with celestial fire;
> Hands, that the rod of empire might have swayed,
>   Or waked to ecstasy the living lyre.

The great faith in the human being, above all in the English human being, is what that poem breathes. It is written to anonymous England, to the Hampdens, Cromwells, Miltons, hidden under the common life and ordinary aspect of the people who never come to the front. All that is noble in the annals of England has been done not simply by accidental people that the race threw up, but by the race itself, by "the happy breed" of England.[1]

I.

APPRECIATION.

"Somebody said that when Thoreau died there was no one left to appreciate the vast silence of the American forest. And when Grant died we felt that there was no one left to appreciate the little triumphs of little men. The talent that none else observed, the success that none else remarked, found warm commendation from him. Those shrewd observing eyes kindled to praise and to encourage, and there is no one left so kindly and so deft now that he is gone. I remember hearing him say: 'The gifts of fragrance that the wise men brought to Jesus would make sweet the road they came. Deliciously the myrrh would smell even through its wrappings; there would be a trail of perfume from east to west.' That was just Grant's life—a trail of perfume from east to west—a life of kindnesses."

That is said of a Scottish minister whose influence (which was

[1] Stephen Graham, *Priest of the Ideal*, 296.

very notable) was greatly due to the gift of appreciation—Alexander Duncan Grant of Greenock. It is one of the most precious gifts that God gives to His ministers. And it is bestowed sometimes on others besides priests and prophets. There is an entry in *Amiel's Journal* for 22nd April 1878 which, in spite of a touch of condescension, goes far to redeem that book from the sin of self-regard. This is the entry: "Letter from my cousin Julia. These kind old relations find it very difficult to understand a man's life, especially a student's life. The hermits of reverie are scared by the busy world, and feel themselves out of place in action. But after all, we do not change at seventy, and a good, pious old lady, half-blind and living in a village, can no longer extend her point of view, nor form any idea of existences which have no relation with her own.

"What is the link by which these souls, shut in and encompassed as they are by the details of daily life, lay hold on the ideal? The link of religious aspiration. Faith is the plank which saves them. They know the meaning of the higher life; their soul is athirst for Heaven. Their opinions are defective, but their moral experience is great; their intellect is full of darkness, but their soul is full of light. We scarcely know how to talk to them about the things of earth, but they are ripe and mature in the things of the heart. If they cannot understand us, it is for us to make advances to them, to speak their language, to enter into their range of ideas, their modes of feeling. We must approach them on their noble side, and, that we may show them the more respect, induce them to open to us the casket of their most treasured thoughts. There is always some grain of gold at the bottom of every honourable old age. Let it be our business to give it an opportunity of showing itself to affectionate eyes."[1]

Look at man in himself; look at him as he makes himself by yielding to and aiding the fraud and malice of the devil, and hardly any language is too bitter to describe his baseness and degradation; but look at him in the light of revelation, look at him under the triple overarching rainbow of faith and hope and love, look at him ransomed and ennobled into a filial relationship with God, and you will see at once where men have learned their high faith in themselves, and who has taught them to speak of

[1] *Amiel's Journal* (tr. Mrs. Humphry Ward), 249.

man in such noble accents. They learned them from St. Paul: "And such were some of you: but ye are washed, but ye are sanctified, but ye are justified in the name of the Lord Jesus, and by the Spirit of our God." They learned them from St. Peter: "But ye are a chosen generation, a royal priesthood, an holy nation, a peculiar people; that ye should show forth the praises of him who hath called you out of darkness into his marvellous light." They learned them from St. John: "Beloved, now are we the sons of God, and it doth not yet appear what we shall be: but we know that, when he shall appear, we shall be like him; for we shall see him as he is." They learned them most of all from Christ Himself: "I say not unto you, that I will pray the Father for you; for the Father himself loveth you, because ye have loved me, and have believed that I came out from God."

Oh for the gift of vision, that we might behold the teeming marvels and delights of this fair earth, whose most modest shapes are rich in bloom and beauty! Oh for the gift of faith and love, that we might interpret truly the events of life, and find in each a theme for delectable song! Oh for the heavenly charity which can recognize in our brethren patience, kindness, and heroism, where a niggling intellect can see nothing but imperfection and failure! Oh that we might behold with open face the goodness of God in Jesus Christ, and live in the spirit of adoring wonder and loving consecration! If we do not grow in grace, let us turn over a new leaf; let us try the focus of appreciation instead of that of criticism; let us be freer to see the beautiful, to appreciate the good, to praise the high; and if only we are humble, sympathetic, and pure, the glory and joy of life will stand freshly revealed in everything, the law of praise will be on our lips, and in the genial glow we shall grow as flowers and palms in the sun.

> Love greatens and glorifies all things,
> Till God is aglow to the loving heart,
> In what was mere earth before.[1]

1. There can hardly be a happier or more fruitful and wonder-working life than his in whose company men are always stirred to brightness and unselfishness just because he always believes that they are purer and better than they are: by whose trustful

[1] Browning.

expectation they are reminded of what they once desired and hoped to be, so that the long-forgotten ideal seems again to come within their reach, and they live, if only for a while, by a light which they never thought to see again. For thus this quickening and enlightening power of faith in our fellow-men changes the whole air and aspect of a life; and he who is thus trustful and hopeful draws out in one man the timid and hidden germ of good, and engenders in another the grace and warmth which his faith presumes—and the dullest heart is startled into sympathy with the charity which believeth all things, and hopeth all things: so that everywhere this faith is greeted by the brightness which itself calls out, as the sun is welcomed by the glad colours which sleep until he comes.

There is a scene in the life of St. Paul which is not without eminent meaning. Near the close of his ministry he writes a letter, which has been preserved, to his pupil and companion, the youthful Timothy. What a ring it has, from its first word to its last, of brotherly confidence and trust! He is soon to be put to death and he knows it; he has been deserted by all but one of his fellow-labourers, and he knows that; he has made as yet but the smallest impression upon that huge mass of imperial heathenism which has bound him a prisoner in Rome; but none of these things has shaken his faith in the Master whom he serves or in that son in the ministry to whom he writes. When he called to mind, as he says, the unfeigned faith which dwelt in those who had borne and nurtured Timothy—and he adds with exquisite tenderness, " I am persuaded is in thee also "—he had no doubt, no, not for an instant, concerning this absent fellow-labourer. He was old, he was deserted, he was a prisoner, and yet what is the tone of his letter? Does he write a stinging satire upon the faithlessness of men? Does he caution Timothy against sacrificing himself to impetuous hopes, and tell him that after all zeal is well enough, but that it may better be tempered by an habitual distrust and suspicion, especially of one's fellow-men? On the contrary, were there ever words of such hopeful import, of such serene confidence, of such tender and undiminished trustfulness as he speaks to this untried young man? Now, St. Paul was not a novice or an innocent. He was in the largest and worthiest sense a man of the times. He knew society in the forum and in the

market-place quite as intimately as he knew it in the temple or
the synagogue. He knew the sins of his age and his race, and the
shames and falsehoods that had stained even believing communities and Christian churches, like those of Corinth or of Ephesus.
But these sad experiences had not made of him a cynic in society
or a pessimist in religion. He knew enough to know how, underneath its falsehoods and unrealities, the nature that is not true
loathes its falseness and longs and aches to be free from it. He
knew that if men were to be won to love truth and goodness, it
must be by appealing to that instinct, or impulse, or aspiration in
them which could own and respond to such an appeal, and not by
denying its existence. And what he knew he taught and preached
and lived, until that mass of corrupt and perishing heathenism to
which he went, wakened at last out of its hopeless lethargy,
owned the message of hope, and the image of redeeming love and
life which he held up before its eyes.

¶ My dear friend and teacher, Lowell, right as he is in almost
everything, is for once wrong in these lines, though with a noble
wrongness:—

> Disappointment's dry and bitter root,
> Envy's harsh berries, and the choking pool
> Of the world's scorn, are the right mother-milk
> To the tough hearts that pioneer their kind.

They are *not* so; love and trust are the only mother-milk of
any man's soul. So far as he is hated and mistrusted, his powers
are destroyed. Do not think that with impunity you can follow
the eyeless fool, and shout with the shouting charlatan; and that
the men you thrust aside with gibe and blow are thus sneered
and crushed into the best service they can do you. I have told
you they *will* not serve you for pay. They *cannot* serve you for
scorn. Even from Balaam, money-lover though he be, no useful
prophecy is to be had for silver or gold. From Elisha, saviour of
life though he be, no saving of life—even of children's, who
"know no better"—is to be got by the cry, Go up, thou bald-head.
No man can serve you either for purse or curse; neither kind of
pay will answer. No *pay* is, indeed, receivable by any true man;
but *power* is receivable by man, in the love and faith you give him.
So far only as you give him these can he serve you; that is the
meaning of the question which his Master asks always, "Believest
thou that I am able?" And from every one of his servants—to

the end of time—if you give them the Capernaum measure of faith, you shall have from them Capernaum measure of works, and no more.

Do you think that I am irreverently comparing great and small things? The system of the world is entirely one; small things and great are alike part of one mighty whole. As the flower is gnawed by frost, so every human heart is gnawed by faithlessness. And as surely—as irrevocably—as the fruit-bud falls before the east wind, so fails the power of the kindest human heart, if you meet it with poison.[1]

> I wish that I might tell you what you are
> To me—you seem so fine and strong and true,
> So bold, and yet so gentle, so apart
> From petty strivings that confuse men's minds.
> I wish that I might make you understand
> How your clean, brave young life has made me brave,
> How I am cheered and strengthened and upheld
> When I consider that the world holds you
> A hero; in a world of false ideals
> Your truth, your worth, has blazed its own brave way.
> Yes, I would have you know this, know how dear
> My heart holds what you stand for, for I fear
> You might do something that you might not do,
> My dream's embodiment, if you but knew.

2. How rarely do we recognize the value of appreciation—except when we receive it ourselves. We are startled sometimes into incredulity when we hear of a great man accepting appreciation thankfully. Mr. A. C. Benson represents Father Payne as saying: "There's that odd story of Robert Browning, that, when he received an ovation at Oxford, and someone said to him, 'I suppose you don't care about all this,' he said, 'It is what I have waited for all my life!' I wonder if he *did* say it! I think he must have done, because it is exactly the sort of thing that one is supposed not to say." Yet in the same book Mr. Benson approves of the well-known incident in Johnson's life which is very similar: "I remember his telling me a story of Dr. Johnson, how in the course of his last illness, when he could not open his letters, he asked Boswell to read them for him. Boswell opened a letter from some person in the North of England, of a complimentary

---
[1] Ruskin, *Modern Painters*, v., pt. ix., ch. xii.

FAITH IN MEN

kind, and thinking it would fatigue Dr. Johnson to have it read aloud, merely observed that it was highly in his praise. Dr. Johnson at once desired it to be read to him, and said with great earnestness, ' *The applause of a single human being is of great consequence.*' Father Payne added that it was one of Johnson's finest sayings, and had no touch of vanity or self-satisfaction in it, but the vital stuff of humanity. That I believe to be profoundly true: and that is the spirit in which I have set all this down." [1]

¶ To the friends, and to the friends of the friends, whose work Ruskin had occasion to praise, the lectures in Oxford on *The Art of England* gave the liveliest pleasure. Mr. Holman Hunt wrote to Ruskin expressing in the most generous terms the help which he had derived from the praises of his friend. The lecture on Mr. Hunt's "Triumph of the Innocents" gave fresh confidence to the artist's patrons, and encouraged the artist himself to persevere with the completion both of the original design and of the second version painted from it. Upon the work of Burne-Jones Ruskin did not say within the necessary limits of time all that he had hoped; but the appreciation, as it stood, even in a compressed report in the *Pall Mall Gazette*, greatly pleased the artist's friends. "A spirit moves me," wrote Mr. Swinburne to his friend in the "palace of painting," "to write a line to you, not of congratulation (which would be indeed an absurd impertinence), on the admirable words which I have just read in this evening's paper's report of Ruskin's second Oxford lecture, but to tell you how glad I was to read them. If I may venture to say as much without presumption, I never did till now read anything in praise of your work, that seemed to me really and perfectly apt and adequate. I do envy Ruskin the authority and the eloquence which give such weight and effect to his praise. It is just what I 'see in a glass darkly' that he brings out and lights up with the very best words possible; while we others (who cannot draw), like Shakespeare, have eyes for wonder but lack tongues to praise." [2]

¶ It is said of Edward Irving that he went about making men noble by thinking them so. Mrs. Oliphant says: "He had so much celestial light in his eyes that he unconsciously assigned to every one whom he addressed a standing ground in some degree equal to his own. He addressed ordinary individuals as if they were heroes and princes; charged a candidate for the ministry to be at once an apostle, a gentleman, and a scholar; made poor

---
[1] A. C. Benson, *Father Payne.*
[2] E. T. Cook, *The Life of Ruskin,* ii. 469.

astonished women in tiny London apartments feel themselves ladies in the light of his courtesy; and unconsciously elevated every man he talked with into the ideal man he ought to have been." [1]

> Believe in me, at once you bid
> Myself believe that, since one soul has disengaged
> Mine from the shows of things, so much is fact: I waged
> No foolish warfare, then, with shades, myself a shade,
> Here in the world—may hope my pains will be repaid! [2]

3. If we can show a man that we have faith in him we do more for him than incite him to do his best, and we do more than rouse in him feelings of gratitude. Such faith is often the very means of his recovery. Read the parable of the prodigal son, of the lost piece of money, of one sheep that went astray. Read Christ's encounter with Matthew, with the rich young man, with the woman that was a sinner; do you find falling from those pure and perfect lips anything of the distrust, the scorn, the faithlessness in human nature that falls too often from our most imperfect lips? Christ's was not that charity which thinks lightly of evil, but rather that charity which is slow to believe in it; and when He deals with men in sin—with those whose guilt was indisputably clear—this was the supreme thought that animated Him: that such an one had fallen from his real nature and could not be at peace with himself; that there must be a better soul behind, where God's long-suffering love would find a hearing yet; and that, anyhow, through whatever suffering and discipline, there was a possibility that the vilest and guiltiest of those to whom He came might be won back to truth and purity and God.

¶ Those who trust us educate us. [3]

¶ Scott had hardly been a week in possession of his new domains, before he made acquaintance with a character much better suited to his purpose than James Hogg ever could have been. I mean honest Thomas Purdie, his faithful servant—his affectionately devoted humble friend from this time until death parted them. Tom was first brought before him, in his capacity of Sheriff, on a charge of poaching, when the poor fellow gave such a touching account of his circumstances—a wife, and I know

---

[1] J. Lewis, *The Mystic Secret*, 79.   [2] Browning, "Fifine at the Fair."
[3] George Eliot, *Daniel Deronda*.

not how many children depending on his exertions—work scarce and grouse abundant—and all this with a mixture of odd sly humour—that the Sheriff's heart was moved. Tom escaped the penalty of the law—was taken into employment as shepherd, and showed such zeal, activity, and shrewdness in that capacity, that Scott never had any occasion to repent of the step he soon afterwards took, in promoting him to the position which had been originally offered to James Hogg.[1]

¶ There is a hero in every man, a Christ in every man. See one there. Choose your meeting-ground with your fellow-man. Do not meet him on his plain side but on his least plain most beautiful side. Worship the Christ in him. Give your vote and your allegiance and your faith to the man who has a tender heart and a hand of power, one who from the fount of love can produce the miracle of life. But what is the miracle of life? It is the interpretation of dull fact into bright sense, the transformation of barren metal into gold, the ray of sunshine through the poor window, the picking up of the despised piece of creation whether human being, animal, flower, or thing, and putting it where it gives glory to God.[2]

4. No doubt there is praise and praise. And the test which will enable us to distinguish between a flatterer and an encourager, between just appreciation and excessive and hurtful praise, is not one that can easily be expressed in words. It lies partly in the character of the speaker. An honest, sincere, and hearty friend, who is simply speaking the truth in love, may generally be trusted, even though we know well enough that our friends often think too highly of us. On the other hand, there is an untoward race of people who are afflicted with a positive disease of smooth-speaking, people who seem to be always bidding for intimacy and affection—a craving which is a token of self-indulgence rather than of love. The test, however, lies partly in the hearer. There are some who can not only stand praise, but who are better for it. It braces them for fresh endeavour, and inspires them to be worthy of the good opinion with which their friends have honoured them. Others are so vain, so silly, so unused to self-examination, that praise intoxicates them. For want of independent self-examination many a pleasant character has

[1] J. G. Lockhart, *Memoirs of the Life of Sir Walter Scott, Bart.*, ii. 192.
[2] Stephen Graham, *Priest of the Ideal*, 340.

been disfigured and destroyed in this way, through its very virtues.

¶ J. M. Barrie has said, "The praise that comes of love does not make us vain, but humble rather." In a magazine recently I saw a distinction drawn between what were called "plus" and "minus" people. Did you ever think that there are people whose most fitting symbol is a "minus" sign? They never add to your happiness or your hopes or your faith either in your self or anybody else. Rather they take away from these. When they leave your company, you feel that you are somehow poorer than you were in your own esteem, and in your belief in others. These are the "minus" people. But there are others, thank God, of a different sort. They never come to us but they add to our store of all the best things far beyond their thought or intention. They believe in us, and so help us to do better. They draw out the best side of us, and sometimes that side surprises even ourselves. They radiate courage and hope and faith. Their praise humbles us, yet leaves us tingling with desire to be more worthy of it. I ask you, Is it not better to be "plus" than "minus"?[1]

¶ Letters constantly came to him, telling him—it almost seems in exaggerated strain—how much he had done. These letters were to him like the staying up of Moses's arms when he engaged in prayer. A friend recalls his words: "Do not be chary of appreciation. Hearts are unconsciously hungry for it. There is little danger, especially with us in this cold New England region, that appreciation shall be given too abundantly."[2]

II.

TRUSTFULNESS.

The Rev. W. A. Crokat, one of Bishop John Wordsworth's chaplains, writes of him: "One of the things that made the deepest impression at the time was his absolute trust in a man when he once accepted him into his confidence. It was such as would make any man ashamed even to seem to come short of it. Trust in money matters, and trust in confidential matters where

---

[1] A. Alexander, *The Glory in the Grey*, 76.
[2] A. V. G. Allen, *Phillips Brooks*, 578.

others were concerned, seemed at times almost greater than they ought to be. But it arose so evidently from the simple goodness of the Bishop's heart; his sense of the greatness of the work entrusted to himself was so real, and his wish that others younger than himself should take their full share in their more limited sphere was so strong, that one's own ideals of work were unconsciously raised to a higher level." [1]

1. Such trustfulness is the mark not only of a good but also of a great man. It is the secret of secrets in the successful career of Lord Roberts of Kandahar. One memorable instance of it may be quoted from his autobiography. Who can tell what troubles it prevented, even what disasters it averted, in the years to come? It is very probable for one thing that the history of the Mutiny would have been different had Roberts pursued a different policy at this time.

"Of the many subjects discussed and measures adopted during this, the last year of Lord Dufferin's Viceroyalty, I think the scheme for utilizing the armies of Native States, as an auxiliary force for the service of the Empire, was the most important both from a political and military point of view. The idea was, in the first instance, propounded by Lord Lytton, who appointed a committee to consider the pros and cons of the question. I was a member of that committee, but at that time I, in common with many others, was doubtful as to the wisdom of encouraging a high state of efficiency amongst the troops of independent States; the excellent work, however, done by the Native Contingent I had with me in Kuram, and the genuine desire of all ranks to be allowed to serve side by side with our own soldiers, together with the unmistakable spirit of loyalty displayed by Native Rulers when war with Russia was imminent in 1885, convinced me that the time had arrived for us to prove to the people of India that we had faith in their loyalty, and in their recognition of the fact that their concern in the defence of the Empire was at least as great as ours, and that we looked to them to take their part in strengthening our rule and in keeping out all intruders." [2]

[1] E. W. Watson, *Life of Bishop John Wordsworth*, 184.
[2] Lord Roberts, *Forty-One Years in India*, 523.

72 CHRISTIAN DOCTRINE OF FAITH

¶ "To the best of my belief, therefore, I was the first European who had ever been seen in the Vizeeree Thull; yet my full confidence in the honour of Swahn Khan, who undertook to guide me, may be gathered from the circumstance that I took with me only five-and-twenty horsemen, and those at his request, in case of any casual opposition from tribes over whom the Vizeeree had no control. I pause upon this apparently trifling incident, for no foolish vanity of my own, but for the benefit of others; for hoping, as I earnestly do, that many a young soldier glancing over these pages will gather heart and encouragement for the stormy lot before him, I desire above all things to put into his hand the staff of confidence in his fellow-man.

> Candid, and generous, and just,
> Boys care but little whom they trust—
> An error soon corrected;
> For who but learns in riper years,
> That man, when smoothest he appears,
> Is most to be suspected?

is a verse very pointed and clever, but quite unworthy of 'The Ode to Friendship,' and inculcating a creed which would make a sharper or a monk of whoever should adopt it. The man who cannot trust others is, by his own showing, untrustworthy himself. Suspicious of all, depending on himself for everything, from the conception to the deed, the ground-plan to the chimney-pot, he will fail for want of the heads of Hydra and the hands of Briareus. If there is any lesson that I have learnt from life, it is that human nature, black or white, is better than we think it; and he who reads these pages to a close will see how much faith I have had occasion to place in the rudest and wildest of their species, how nobly it was deserved, and how useless I should have been without it."[1]

2. Does trust in one's fellow-men pay? It does not always win, certainly. We may find ourselves the victims of misplaced confidence. But if we have kept within us a living soul and a healthy mind, it will be better worth our while to have failed than to have lost these in our so-called success. "There is a spring of year-long blessedness in the very nature of faith itself. The most brilliant and unshadowed life that can be lived under the sun, if it lack trust, has a scathing anathema in it." So says a

---

[1] H. B. Edwardes, *A Year on the Punjab Frontier*, quoted by Ruskin, *Works*, xxxi. 411.

wise and good writer of our times, and he says the truth. Those who are always protecting themselves by low views of human nature forget that there is nothing so dangerous as to sink into a miserably minded man who disbelieves in the world he has to live in, and distrusts the men he has to deal with. This is to escape the risk of battle only to fall into the certainty of disease; it is to choose to be a spiritual neurotic rather than a wounded soldier.

(1) It is sometimes the best policy.

¶ I have mentioned Sâdik Mahommed Khan. He was a servant of the Maharajah, appointed to do duty with the Nâzim of Mooltân, and, when the rebellion broke out, was drawing pay from both. . . . Moolraj expected him to side with him, but, though unable to escape, on account of his house and family, he refused to set his seal to the oath of rebellion on the Korân, and the very day that I arrived before Mooltân, Sâdik and his father took their hawks on their wrists, and, under pretence of hunting, issued forth from the city and joined me. It is an incident illustrative of those strange uncertain times that, two days afterwards, he was my faithful henchman at Suddoosâm, and, being well mounted, was often the only man by my side.

Had he been a traitor, he might have killed me at any moment. But I heard his story, believed it, trusted him, and was rewarded by invaluable service throughout the rest of the rebellion.

Yet it was as hard to trust in those days as it was necessary.

The very moment before this battle of Suddoosâm I was dipping my head into a pail of water, preparatory to putting on a thick turban, so as to keep my brains cool as long as possible in the sun, when Sâdik Mahommed's own uncle insisted on speaking to me.

Lifting my dripping head out of the pail, I listened to the old man's solemn warnings to be on my guard; "for," said he, "all these men, like my nephew, who have come over from the enemy are here by Moolraj's orders and consent. You are drawn into a trap. Half your soldiers are friends, and half are foes, and, like rice and split peas, they are all mixed up in one dish. If there is not some treachery in this day's fight, my name is not Sûrbulund Khan!"

The idea was not pleasant, and I soused my head under water again, desperately; but soon came up, wrung out the water, clapped a turban over my wet hair, and thanked the old gentleman for his information, which was too late to be useful, mounted my horse, and—never found out any of the traitors from that day to this![1]

(2) Even if not always best as a matter of policy, it is right to take the highest view of things. And when we come to consider the actual risks, even as regards outward success, we find them not so great as they appeared. Between man and man there are two ways of dealing. Every man has both good and evil in him, and the question for all who would influence the conduct of others is which of these two they shall take to be the real truth of the man's character, which represents most accurately his real self. It is a question of leverage. Are we to appeal for leverage to a man's worst or to his best? Those who take the former course try to get him upward into right conduct by suspicious watchfulness, by bullying and threatening him into goodness, by hard and cold commandments. To do this is to appeal to the worst that is in him, to his fear and cowardice and subserviency. It may succeed. In some desperate cases it may be the only way. But in the vast majority of cases it is the wrong way, and it will fail to produce anything but a mechanical and slavish character. On such terms no man will ever do his best. To do his best a man needs to be trusted.

Every one desires, deep down in his soul, to be good and true. We do, in the hearts of us, love the best things best. Until you remember that, and count upon it for leverage, you will never get any one to put spirit and enthusiasm into his work. As a rule people will do pretty much what they feel is expected of them. He who is thoroughly discouraged, who sees his work going down the stream, and feels that nobody sees any good in him, will never be anything better than a failure and a disappointment. But set tasks for such a man, within his range. Judge him competent, and let him find to his surprise that somebody believes in him, and he will be a new creature. Every man is shy about his best self. Often that best is buried deep below the fragments of broken attempts at manhood. He hardly dares to take his best self seriously. He will not speak about his most worthy things.

[1] *Life and Letters of Major-General Sir Herbert B. Edwardes*, i. 130.

Those who trust him do him the incalculable service of impressing upon him the reality of his best. Let him but grasp that fact, and there is nothing too high to hope for him.

Now, in our dealings with our fellow-men which is the better working hypothesis: to assume with David, in his haste, that all men are liars, or to prefer to believe that on the whole all men are not liars? Which will best serve to redeem the fallen, and steady the tempted, and inspire the timid? Give your brother man your confidence. Provoke him to love and to good works by the good which you look to see in him. And you that are fathers and mothers ennoble the child whom you are training by appealing to that which is noble in him. Amid all his faults and waywardness, strive to love him with an unextinguishable hope and trust.

¶ In those early days Jerry McAuley set an inestimable value upon every token of trust in him. He had been so long hunted and dogged and accustomed to the thought that he was an outcast and outlaw whom nobody would trust out of sight with the value of a cent, that it was a new and sweet experience to him *to be trusted*. What a moral invigorator a little timely confidence and reliance on his honour was to him, and may be to others in like circumstances, as illustrated in one or two incidents, was often referred to in his public testimonies. He used to say, after telling what a miserable wretch, and moral and physical wreck he was before Jesus picked him up, "Just look at me now [holding open his coat and making a comical gesture of looking himself over], I have everything a man could wear. I have plenty to eat, a good home and good clothes, and *I am respected and trusted.* Think of Jerry McAuley, the biggest bum that used to hang out around this ward, turned into a respectable citizen. Why, a few years ago, if a man with five dollars in his pocket met me coming down the street, he'd cross over on the other side, and lucky for him too; but now I go down town, walk into a big banking-house, take an armchair, put up one leg over the other, *and talk with the boss* as big as life; and they don't set any detectives to watch me either, or send for a policeman to run me out. This is what Jesus has done for me—made a man of me; and He will do it for you too if you will let Him."[1]

¶ Sir George Henschel tells a story of Mr. Harry Brewster, an American artist, who made his home in Paris and in Rome.

---

[1] R. M. Offord, *Jerry McAuley*, 165.

"He was both philosopher and poet, and not only *was* both but *lived* both." This is the story:

"In the large households of Italy, particularly, I think, in Rome, it is not unusual for a family to have a major-domo, that is to say, a sort of superior cook-housekeeper who, besides his salary, gets a certain sum per month to 'run the house' on. Brewster's establishment in that splendid old 'Palazzo Antici Mattei' in Rome was founded on that system. His was the good luck of having a major-domo who not only gave him every satisfaction as such, but whom he also esteemed as a man, and who, in his turn, seemed greatly and almost affectionately attached to his master. It was therefore a great shock to Brewster when one day, in examining the books which were brought to him at regular intervals for that purpose, he seemed to detect some irregularities in the keeping of the accounts. At first he ascribed it to a probable oversight on his own part, and, loath to believe in the possibility of dishonesty on that of the trusted servant, waited for the next occasion, and again the next, until, alas, he could no longer reject the proofs in his hands. There was no doubt the man had for some time past deliberately and systematically deceived and robbed him. Having grown to be sincerely fond of the man, the discovery caused Brewster pain amounting to a real grief. This he carried about with him for several days, unable to decide on the course that would appear the best to be taken in a matter which affected him very deeply. At last his mind was made up. Seated before the writing-table in his study, the proofs of the man's guilt spread before him, he rang the bell and asked for the major-domo to be sent to him. The man entered, visibly turning pale at the sight of his master's serious face, and evidently divining the reason for this unwonted summons. There was an ominous silence in the lofty room as the two men faced each other, until Brewster broke it by quietly telling his servant how great a grief it was to him to have found that for some months past he had been cheated by him . . . that he could only assume the salary he had been paying him had been insufficient, and that from that day on he would double it. . . . That was all. Doubtless a risky thing to do; one which might, in nine cases out of ten, have proved an utter failure. But Brewster knew the sort of nature he had to deal with. There were no words of response from the servant. Prostrating himself before his master and kissing his hands, he silently sobbed until Brewster bade him get up. The man then left the room as one in a daze—not only a better, but a good man for the rest of his life."[1]

[1] G. Henschel, *Musings and Memories of a Musician*, 381.

(3) It is God's way. The policy of God has been to save men by trusting them. His method of salvation has been to commit to the unworthy an incomparable gift and a great task—the gift of Christ and the task of Life. And, after all is said, surely God knows best, and He has chosen to take this risk. How long will it be till we learn that the foolishness of God is wiser than men? "The Eternal also is wise," to quote with a difference a famous passage, "you and I are not the only wise ones."

But the policy of God may be judged by its own history. Looking down the long vista of the past, the eye falls upon the Cross of Jesus Christ, standing erect above the wreckage of two thousand years. Why is the Cross, that symbol of apparent failure, still conspicuous, while most of the successes which took the eyes of men are forgotten? Christ was God's great trust to man, the paramount act of confidence, and the Cross is the frightful monument of man's broken faith. Yet that supreme betrayal has awakened the world's conscience, and brought back the noblest spirits of all those two thousand years in shame and penitence to the feet of the Crucified. That Cross has settled for ever the question of the wisdom of God's policy of trust in man. It was the supreme trust and the supreme betrayal, and round it are gathered an innumerable company of men whom it has made trustworthy.

Because of Thy strong faith, I kept the track
Whose sharp-set stones my strength had wellnigh spent;
I could not meet Thy eyes if I turned back:
    So on I went.

Because Thou wouldst not yield belief in me,
The threatening crags that rose my way to bar
I conquered inch by crumbling inch—to see
    The goal afar.

And though I struggle toward it through hard years,
Or flinch, or falter blindly, yet within,
"You can," unwavering my spirit hears:
    And I shall win.[1]

(4) And it is the way of Christ. When He "ate and drank

[1] W. T. A. Barber, *The Morning of Life*, 31.

with publicans and sinners," He saw the possibilities of goodness and of blessedness that lay beneath all the vice and misery. He had His word of stern severity for the respectable, self-righteous Pharisee; but you never find Christ railing bitterly or scornfully against mankind. For the fallen He had a heart to pity and a hand to help. His love detected the elements of goodness that lay smouldering in the ashes. They tell us that "love is blind"; but be sure that hatred or even indifference is far blinder. Love may sometimes be blind to faults, but it has a quick eye for excellences. It has a quick eye, too, for the possibilities of character, for the ideal that lies within the actual, for the perfect statue that may yet be chiselled out of the marble. You cannot see *the best* that is in any man or woman until you look through the eyes of love. And therefore, if at any time we begin to feel the chill of the cynical mood creeping over us, let us place ourselves anew by the side of Christ, and try to feel a little of what He feels as He looks down on our weak, struggling, tempted, sorrowing humanity.

¶ Carlyle was in gloomy humour and finding fault with everything, therefore Sterling defended with equal universality. At last Carlyle shook his head and pronounced, "Woe to them that are at ease in Zion." Sterling was reminded of a poem which Goethe has translated, which introduces the carcase of a dead dog, which one after another approaches, expressing disgust at the smell, the appearance, etc.; at last Christ passes, looks on it, and says, "What beautiful white teeth it has!"[1]

[1] *Caroline Fox: Her Journals and Letters*, i. 322.

IV.

THE RANGE OF FAITH.

LITERATURE.

Archibald, M. G., *Sundays at the Royal Military College* (1912).
Arnold, T., *Sermons*, ii. (1878).
Barry, A., *Do We Believe?* (1908).
Bowman, A. H., *Christian Thought and Hindu Philosophy*, i. (1917).
Bowne, B. P., *Studies in Theism* (1880).
Brown, W. A., *Christian Theology in Outline* (1907).
Burroughs, E. A., in *The Faith and the War* (1915).
Chandler, A., in *The Faith of Centuries* (1897).
Clarke, J. F., *Common-Sense in Religion* (1888).
Cuckson, J., *Faith and Fellowship* (1897).
Diggle, J. W., *Religious Doubt* (1895).
Douglas, L., *Christus Futurus* (1907).
Fairchild, H. P., *Outline of Applied Sociology* (1916).
Gardner, P., *Modernity and the Churches* (1909).
Hare, J. C., *The Victory of Faith* (1874).
Harker, J. A., in *Science and Religion* (1914).
Harris, C., *Pro Fide* (1914).
Herman, E., *Christianity in the New Age* (1919).
Hicks, W. J., in *After-War Problems* (1917).
Hyde, W. D., *Jesus' Way* (1903).
Inge, W. R., *The Philosophy of Plotinus* (1918).
James, J. G., *The Coming Age of Faith* (1912).
Jefferson, C. E., *Things Fundamental* (1904).
Jones, E. G., *Faith and Verification* (1907).
Kelman, J., in *Ideals of Science and Faith* (1904).
Mackenzie, J. S., *Elements of Constructive Philosophy* (1917).
Mackenzie, W. D., *The Final Faith* (1910).
Oliver, F. W., *Ordeal by Battle* (1915).
Orr, J., *Ritschlianism* (1903).
Parkhurst, C. H., *The Pattern in the Mount* (1890).
Sidgwick, A., *School Homilies*, i. (1915).
Spens, W., *Belief and Practice* (1915).
Stalker, J., *The Ethic of Jesus* (1909).
Stowell, J. H., *Faith and Reality* (1913).
Strong, T. B., in *The Meaning of the Creed* (1917).
Tarrant, W. G., in *Things New and Old* (1910).
Ward, J., *The Realm of Ends* (1911).
   „   „ *Psychological Principles* (1918).
Westcott, B. F., *The Historic Faith* (1883).
   „   „ *The Incarnation and Common Life* (1893).
Winterbotham, R., *Sermons* (1900).

THE RANGE OF FAITH.

1. THERE are a few words in the English language which are associated chiefly with God and the things of God. One of these words is "faith." But unlike such words as, say, "grace" and "salvation," "faith" has also a purely human meaning and use. And this serves to remind us that, when they entered the New Testament, all such terms were terms of common life. The early Christian writers did not use theological language. To have done so would have entirely defeated their object. They used language which *became* theological, partly because they used it, partly because it so well expressed the ideas they had to convey.

¶ The reading of most of the Epistles in the New Testament is a difficult task for young students. The subjects with which they deal are to a great extent abstract—things of the mind. Words such as justification, grace, glory, and even faith, convey no very clear idea to a beginner. A proper name or a bit of narrative is welcomed as a relief.

This is very natural. The real value of the Epistles can only emerge when more of life has been experienced; and yet it ought to be interesting at any period of life to know what were the thoughts of such men as Peter, Paul, and John about the meaning of the facts which they spent their lives in telling to men all over their world. We shall be more apt to realize the living interest of the Epistles if we recollect that the men who wrote them were not trained from an early age to use a certain kind of language, but were for the most part making for themselves the vocabulary which they used.

The abstract words of which I spoke—grace, justification, and the rest—were not, as now, smooth stones from the brook, worn down by constant attrition, but were rather blocks freshly hewn from the quarry. By their first readers these letters were most anxiously looked for; every word was of importance; and they would determine the line of action and mould the daily life of a whole community. Moreover, on these documents, next to the reports of our Lord's own life and teaching, the foundation of the whole enormous structure of Christian theology has been raised. They have ruled the lines along which millions of Christian lives have moved. The Gospels are the most important books in the world, and the Epistles are only less important than the Gospels. "Une espérance immense a traversé la terre." The Epistles are among the first books written to show what effect this hope ought to have upon the lives of ordinary men and women.

A beginner may perhaps have some notion of this: but I am sure that it will be good for him to remind himself of it, and to insist upon attaching some definite meaning to the words he reads. It is not to be expected that he will get as much out of them at an early stage of his career as will come in after years; but at least, in setting out upon the study of these writings, he should start with the conviction that the writer whose work he is to read had a very clear idea of what he meant; that his words were addressed to simple people; that the meaning of them can be attained in a measure by the simple as well as by the clever of our own days; and that it is well worth attaining.[1]

2. Not only has faith a *human* meaning and use. "Almost every forward step in the progress of life could be formulated as an act of faith—an act not warranted by knowledge—on the part of the pioneer who first made it. There was little, for example, in all that the wisest fish could know, to justify the belief that there was more scope for existence on the earth than in the water, or to show that persistent endeavours to live on land would issue in the transformation of his swim-bladder into lungs. And before a bird had cleaved the air there was surely little, in all that the most daring of saurian speculators could see or surmise concerning that untrodden element, to warrant him in risking his neck in order to satisfy his longing to soar; although, when he did try, his forelimbs were transformed to wings at length, and his dim prevision of a bird became incarnate in himself. So put, these instances will seem largely fanciful, I am well aware—too Lamarckian even for Lamarck. Still they serve to bring out the one fact, namely, that when we regard the development of living forms as a continuous whole, we are forced to recognize, as immanent and operative

---

[1] M. R. James. *Second Peter and Jude* (Cambridge Greek Testament). p. ix.

throughout it, a sort of unscientific trustfulness, that from the very first seems to have been engrained in all living things. This trustfulness—might I say ?—is comparable to the faith of Abraham, who, 'when he was called to go out into a place which he should after receive for an inheritance, obeyed; and he went out, not knowing whither he went.' No doubt with perfect knowledge all this would be otherwise; but the point is that with limited knowledge such as ours there is always 'room for faith,' and always need for it: here the maxim holds, 'Nothing venture nothing have.' We trust and try first, not understanding till afterwards: our attitude in short is not unlike that of Anselm's famous *Credo ut intelligam.*" [1]

"It is in unconscious obedience to law not bound by physical dimensions that all life works. This obedience is not of understanding, but of faith. How else do the daisy's petals close at night, or when the shadow of the rain-cloud threatens? How have the long white florets of its aureole learned their gift of service, whereby, in renouncing their privilege to carry anthers and pollen for the perfecting of their seeds, they have gained power of service to become manifest in increase of beauty? How has the daisy's cousin, the blue cornflower, learned an even greater serviceableness and beauty in her blue outer florets? These are quite sterile, but give the conspicuous beauty to the flower, rather than the lilac-hued central florets which are creationally perfect. The large blue trumpets proclaim the inherent dignity of service; and the surrender of personal privilege to make such service possible shines forth in beauty. The pot of very precious ointment is quite ordinary property to the lilies of the field, which, especially in so far as they do not toil and spin, eclipse in beauty the laboured self-conscious art of us Solomons. They also serve who only stand and wait, and they know not how the light within shines from their blind faces. The faith of the daisy and the cornflower and the wild guelder-rose is the faith of the Woman with the precious ointment. Such faith and its beauty are alike unselfconscious; but they are the very means of surviving the disaster which comes to a morality built upon utility and commerce and prudence.

"Or how does the lark know with the first breath of spring

[1] James Ward, *The Realm of Ends*, 415.

that he need no longer fear, but may rise into the empyrean and scatter his praise over the sleepy earth? What profits it him, beyond his new understanding of the faith which kept him alive through his tragic migrations? Now he can lavish the wealth of song, now he can sacrifice his physical strength fearlessly before his Maker! For has he not found love again and the service of his mate, and the sharing with her of hope? It is all faith; and a faith that must be glorified in prodigal song, despite the cost and the disappointments of wintry spring. What is it inspires the missel-thrush, as he swings on the leafless apple-tree, thrusting his open beak into the teeth of the sleet-laden north-east wind, and carols of the coming spring with all his mirth?

> 'Love again, song again, nest again, young again,'
>   Never a prophet so crazy!
> And hardly a daisy as yet, little friend,
>   See, there is hardly a daisy."[1]

3. To return to faith in human life. We use freely and constantly such expressions as faith in a principle, faith in an enterprise, faith in a remedy, faith in a person—in a teacher, perhaps, or leader, or doctor, or lawyer, or friend. With equal naturalness we use the word "faith" with reference to a guide of our bodies up a difficult mountain, or through a dangerous illness, and to a guide of our minds through their problems on the way to a satisfying answer. To the word "faith" so used one dominant notion always attaches, namely, confidence, reliance, trust.

Men could have no business dealings with one another without an element of mutual trust and confidence. Before we approach our fellow-man at all we must trust him in some measure. You believe that the man with whom you are about to open an account is, in the first place, a real man; even if you have never seen him, you believe that he exists, indeed you *must* believe that he exists, or you would not trouble to write to him. And, in the second place, you believe that he is, or at least may be, ready to open business relations with you; on the mere chance of this you are prepared to go to considerable trouble and expense beforehand; if you thought there was no such chance, you would never dream of incurring trouble in vain. It is still more so in offering your

[1] G. Macdonald, *The Child's Inheritance*, 244.

friendship to any one. Every such relation is built on a firm, deep foundation of mutual trust and confidence.

It is the glory of friendship and of love that they make large drafts on the bank of faith, which are drawn willingly and gladly, and which are as gladly honoured and returned. We feel, indeed, that the chief benefit of human friendship is the fact that it gives faith in one another so large and perpetual an exercise. It is my joy that my friend trusts me implicitly, ventures his credit on my faithfulness, my devotion, my willingness to help him in any possible way, that I do the same by him. Nay, even more than this: we value friendship chiefly because it is so stimulative of a further faith that enriches the soul, and quickens its noblest qualities into life and vigour.

¶ Who can fail to see the value even of natural faith if, as Professor Herzog says, "All personal relations in human life rest on faith. I can respect no one unless I believe him possessed of some excellencies of nature and character. I can love no one unless I believe him possessed of some affinity to me, naturally in the blood, or spiritually in the mind. In human life faith is the connecting link between man and man. Thereby it becomes the latent source from which all individual development springs, mental and spiritual. Man was made for faith, and it is faith that makes the man. He who has lost his power of faith, his faculty of belief, is dead. But in no respect is this more true than in man's relation to God."[1]

I.

IN DAILY LIFE.

All human relationships are founded upon trust. It is the first power that helps men to rise above barbarism, and it is the basis and groundwork of the latest and most finished civilization. It is equally indispensable in all departments of life, and it is equally universal in all relations between men. The child from his earliest years trusts his father and his mother; and as soon as he can think at all, as soon as the beginnings appear of any of those powers and feelings which distinguish us from beasts, so soon does the parent also begin to trust the child. Trust is

[1] H. W. Webb-Peploe, in *Church Congress Report*, 1890, p. 214.

the basis of all trade, beyond the most barbarous form of barter. It is the pillar of all free government, of all law, of all liberty: for what, without the trust of the people, is the statesman, or the judge, or the representative? It is the very life of friendship; without confidence the lowest form of human love is not worthy of so sacred a name.

¶ A child is told by his parents to be careful and tidy; he is threatened with punishment if he is not so; he is promised some little reward if he is. The parents are not present; the punishment and the reward are not actually before the eyes of the child, while the temptation is; that is to say, he feels that it is a trouble to put his things together, and that at the very moment when he sees something which he wishes to be doing immediately. Now, if he thinks more of the future reward and punishment than of the present trouble and pleasure; if he cares more for his parents, whom he may not see for an hour or two, than for the plaything which lies before his eyes; if he accordingly puts his things together, and is careful and tidy, then this child has, after his humble measure, acted by faith; he has gained some experience of that principle which, if he is a follower of Jesus, must be the guide of his life till that hour when all earthly things shall pass away.[1]

1. We all believe in the stability of the outward world, and walk by that faith. We all go to bed at night, and fall asleep—which is just like dying—believing that we shall wake in the morning, and that there will be a morning to wake in. We expect to find our house and furniture and family to-morrow just as they were to-day. We shall sit down to breakfast to-morrow believing that it will feed us and not poison us. We shall go to our business expecting to find people to deal with, and work to do, as we found them yesterday. We all repose, in perfect security, on this firm faith in the stability of the universe. We walk by it, live by it, are saved by it.

¶ What a vast interval there is between that knowledge of the laws of Nature, of their principles, connexion, and operation, towards which Science is gradually ascending, and that simple confident unquestioning faith in the laws of Nature, which is necessary to the very subsistence of man as man. Think for a moment how much faith is implied in the labours of the husbandman. How many causes must work together, in order that

[1] T. Arnold, *Sermons*, ii. 2.

his desire may be accomplished! He must have an undoubting assurance that, according to the covenant made with Noah, "seed-time and harvest, and cold and heat, and summer and winter, and day and night shall not cease." In this assurance he plies his daily task, "plodding on cheerfully" through many difficulties and discouragements, confident that, after moons have waxed and waned, the seed he sows will spring up, and will fill the golden ear, and be reaped in the joyful harvest, and be stowed in the foodful garner, and that men and women and children will receive the sustenance of their life from it. Such power has a living practical faith in the laws of Nature. Its effect, even in this one mode of its manifestation, has been that the chief part of the earth has been constrained to bring forth food for the use of man, and that millions upon millions of human beings have been fed for hundreds of generations. And surely our faith in the certainty and stability of the laws of the spiritual world ought to be no less strong—nay, far stronger. For while Nature and her laws may be changed as a vesture—being nothing more than the vesture wherein God, in this nook of time and space, is pleased to array His will—the laws of the spiritual world can never change or fail. Heaven and earth shall pass away; but not one jot or tittle of them. On them therefore we should rely, never doubting that, when we go forth to sow our seed of whatsoever kind in God's spiritual field, He will bless our labours with His increase, and in His own good time will make the seed spring up and will ripen it for His heavenly harvest.[1]

> There is no unbelief;
> Whoever plants a seed beneath the sod
> And waits to see it push away the clod,
>   He trusts in God.
>
> Whoever says when clouds are in the sky,
> Be patient, heart, light breaketh by and by,
>   Trusts the Most High.
>
> Whoever sees, 'neath field of winter snow,
> The silent harvest of the future grow,
>   God's power must know.
>
> Whoever lies down on his couch to sleep,
> Content to lock each sense in slumber deep,
>   Knows God will keep.

[1] J. C. Hare, *The Victory of Faith*, 112.

Whoever says, To-morrow, The Unknown,
The Future, trusts that power alone,
He dares disown.

There is no unbelief;
And day by day and night, unconsciously,
The heart lives by that faith the lips deny,
God knoweth why.[1]

2. As we pass from what is visible—the forces of the material world—to what is invisible—purpose and love and character—faith comes by her own, and is the indispensable guide of life. There are, no doubt, in the workings of societies, especially such workings as come into the field of political economy, some uniformities which are almost as much to be trusted as those of the physical world. Gresham's law that, when purer and more debased coins circulate together in a country, the worse will have a tendency to drive the better out of circulation, acts almost with the regularity of a law of nature. But when it is a question of individuals and of private conduct, experience loses its cogency, since we never know with scientific certainty what course of action any man or woman will take. And then we have to trust to faith.

(1) How little of the knowledge which we possess rests on evidence which we have personally or scientifically investigated; how much depends on the testimony of others. How few (if any) of the acts which we perform do not involve dependence. Suppose I post a letter, I commit it to agencies and arrangements which are to me invisible, of many of which I know nothing, and over which I have no control. My confidence that the letter will reach its destination can be described as nothing else than an act of faith. So it is with all transactions relating to the unseen, the distant, and the future, that is, with all that lies beyond my direct and immediate experience. Yet, while thus trusting to the good faith of others, and the arrangements of society, have I not the best and most rational grounds for so acting? Here is a case of the simplest order, which shows that whatever faith is, it is not necessarily an acting without sufficient grounds, or in opposition to reason.

[1] Edward Bulwer Lytton.

¶ After all, what *do* we know without trusting others? We know that we are in a certain state of health, in a certain place, have been alive for a certain number of years, have certain principles and likings, have certain persons around us, and perhaps have in our lives travelled to certain places at a distance. But what do we know more? Are there not towns (we will say) within fifty or sixty miles of us which we have never seen, and which, nevertheless, we fully believe to be as we have heard them described? To extend our view;—we know that land stretches in every direction of us, a certain number of miles, and then there is sea on all sides; that we are in an island. But who has *seen* the land all around, and has proved for himself that the fact is so? What, then, convinces us of it? The *report of others*—this trust, this faith in testimony which when religion is concerned, then, and only then, the proud and sinful would fain call irrational.[1]

(2) What, then, is it we do when we put faith in a fellow-creature? Is it not this—that we accept him as he offers himself to us, and act accordingly? Thus, a teacher of any science puts himself forward as an adept in his particular department; and those who wish to acquire that science, if they believe in him, wait on his prelections and accept with confidence the information he conveys.

¶ Faith is the one thing that can establish on any firm foundation, or endow with any beauty and nobility, the close relations between the teacher and the taught. If you who learn cannot have trust in the power, or at least the sincere endeavour, of us who teach, to find out the truth and to show it you, to cherish the good and repress the bad in you, to do you instant and full justice, and to guide you right, then you know that a school is a mockery and an abomination, and all our rules will only make confusion worse confounded. And on the other hand, if we cannot put trust in you, trust that you will strive after that steady energy without which no manliness can be, trust that you will be honest in your dealings and truthful in your words, trust also that you will try to be helpful to each other, to be jealous of the ancient honour of this place, and to leave your society better than you found it; if this trust, with due allowance made, of course, for weaknesses and failing and temptation, cannot find some reality to rest upon, cannot be better than a vision or a dream, then all our traditions and pride in our school and daily

[1] J. H. Newman, *Parochial and Plain Sermons*, i. 194.

boasts are all as nothing, and it were better for us that we had never been brought together here.[1]

3. Our faith in any of our friends or colleagues is based upon our experience of his past behaviour, or on our reading of his character. It goes, however, beyond the experience, for if we trusted people only in matters in which we had known them to take the right course, we could not live an ordinary human life.

We constantly believe and act upon impressions which we could not put into words without seeming ridiculous, and which we could not ignore without being irrational. The merchant, or captain, knows well that one course is better than another, but he would often be sadly puzzled to justify his opinion by anything but the favourable result. Such action and judgment partake of the nature of instinct. They are the total outcome of our past experience; and, although the reasoning element has almost entirely disappeared, they are, in general, far more trustworthy than our laboured calculations. The reasons for trusting or distrusting persons, also, are seldom susceptible of formulation; and that, too, in cases where the greatest interests are ventured. This is especially the case with personal influence. An impression is made upon us, and we are stirred and moulded by something which we feel but cannot tell. In short, the great bulk of human belief and action rests upon grounds which admit of no satisfactory statement; yet we cannot disallow such grounds of belief and action without declaring life to be illogical and irrational.

4. But if faith rests on past experience it is also a venture into the future. Without the venture there is no faith. There is a sphere in all our lives which seems to be under our direct control, but we soon discover that its range is very limited. We wander hither and thither in the exercise of our prerogative of freedom, but on every hand we soon touch the darkness, and reach the gloomy edge of an ocean where we need a pilot. Many things are put within easy reach of our eyes and hands, more perhaps are given unsolicited and without research; but other things, often the divinest and of deepest consequence to us, are far off. They lie behind concealing veils, and the way to them is over

[1] A. Sidgwick, *School Homilies*, i. 208.

THE RANGE OF FAITH

dark, untrodden spaces, and across many a desolate bog and morass. If life were unprogressive, or limited in its scope, if it were a mere round of daily routine, a thinking of familiar thoughts, and a doing of ordinary things, this necessity for treading in the dark, and trusting where we cannot trace, would not exist. There would be no occasion for faith. But when we yield to an upward and onward impulse life becomes a good deal of a venture. When we attempt some entirely new thing, or even try to lift an old thing to a new pitch of excellence—then we walk by faith and not by sight. We enter many a struggle the issues of which are by no means obvious. We often gaze into darkness for a light that will not shine, or that comes only in fitful and transitory gleams. We strike invisible barriers which refuse to yield, and plunge into bold ventures without seeing exactly where we are to emerge.

¶ Not only do we reckon on the stability of the world and the continuity of its laws. We tend to believe that there is a more perfect order in the universe as a whole than that which has been in the past definitely discovered. The anticipations of nature and forecasts of human history depend on this kind of faith. Having found, for instance, that there are various ways in which progress has been brought about by human effort, we have a tendency to believe that we may advance to a kind of perfection of which we have no experience, that the difficulties with which we have to contend will be finally eliminated, that

> somehow good
> Will be the final goal of ill.

Such a view may lead us in the end to a sublime optimism such as that which was held by Browning:—

> God's in His heaven;
> All's right with the world.[1]

II.

In Science.

1. Science and religion are by many supposed to be opposed, if not incompatible; the scientific and the theological tempers are

[1] J. S. Mackenzie, *Elements of Constructive Philosophy*, 134.

considered to be poles apart. And yet deep down in the scientist's mind there is a profound element of belief or faith. When he approaches a scientific mystery, or sets about making a discovery in the realms of matter, or devotes himself to the perfecting of an invention, there is one thing he feels sure of beforehand—that there is such a thing as truth, and that it is accessible to him who goes about studying it in the right way. The universe, he feels, is a harmonious, self-consistent, rational order; of this he never for a moment has any doubt; if he has any doubt it is about himself, and whether he is investigating its laws in the right way; if he is, then he knows that at last he will arrive at the truth he is seeking. Now this is faith, and it is faith in its purest form as a postulate, it is something taken for granted as the basis of all inquiry, and without which no scientist would for a moment think of wasting his time in inquiring about anything.

Fundamentally the advance of science and the advance of religion rest upon precisely the same basis, and that basis is faith. We cannot make the least advance in science until we have learned to *believe*—to believe certainly and without the smallest hesitation — in certain fundamental truths outside ourselves. That is why for so many centuries science made no real advance. It was not ignorance, or stupidity, or want of apparatus, that stood in the way; it was want of faith. Men had not learned to believe devoutly in the stability, the orderliness, the reasonableness, the unchangeableness, of nature and her laws. They thought that the forces which ruled in the outward universe were capricious, incalculable. They were so confused by the tangle of shifting phenomena in the midst of which they lived that they altogether failed to grasp the uniformity of law—certain and simple as it really is—which lies behind this tangle. It was *faith* that saved science, it is *faith* by which science lives; faith which is not, of course, identical with religious faith, but which is fundamental and closely akin to it. All science, like all religion, rests for ever upon certain assumptions which are absolutely incapable of proof, which are absolutely essential to progress.

¶ By faith we believe in our personality and in the fundamental deliverances of conscience; by faith we believe in memory and its correspondences with our personality; by faith we believe in a transcendence of thought, and in intelligence without consciousness; by faith we believe in the existence of an external world, and in the correspondence between its phenomena and the impression which they make upon our minds; by faith we believe in the genera and species and the extension of growth to the whole universe; and some of those agnostics loudest in their scorn of faith receive on its authority doctrines which would strain to breaking the faith of the firmest believer. By what unparalleled acts of faith do men believe that matter contains the power and potency of things; that the phenomena of the universe have their source and cause in an immaterial, uncreated, impersonal, and inscrutable force. But more wonderful still is the act of faith upon which rests the doctrine of the spontaneous generation of life. At the present day it has been demonstrated, as far as demonstration is possible, that life comes only from life. The unqualified acceptance of this law would necessitate the acceptance of the doctrine of life by creative action. But this would be impossible to an advanced man of science, and so by an act of faith he declares that once upon a time the world was in a condition in which life originated *de novo*; but that that condition speedily disappeared, and has never returned. Not only, then, has a tremendous act of faith been found when required to get rid of a disagreeable doctrine, but the eternity and inviolability of a law of nature has been readily sacrificed for the same end. I have occasionally heard something of the economics of theologians, but what are they to these?[1]

2. No fact is more familiar to the student of history than the long rivalry and conflict between science and religion. Yet it is not, *prima facie*, apparent either that this is a necessary or that it will be a permanent state of matters. On the contrary, one is impressed by the great number of interests, methods, and ideals which they have in common. Each of them aims at the discovery, the unification, and the orderly presentation of human knowledge. Each ultimately rests on faith, inasmuch as each is forced back upon convictions which are beyond the possibility of further analysis or proof. Every one asserts this of religion, but it is not always remembered that it is equally true of science. The reality of an external world, the connexion of cause and effect, the reliability of the inquirer's powers of observation and reasoning, are fundamental elements in knowledge of the same kind as the ultimate data of religion. Even the methods of their advance are

[1] Sir Andrew Clark, in *Church Congress Report*, 1890, p. 223.

common to the two, for although the deductive method is usually associated with religion, it is often used by science; and all living religious faith is continually verifying and correcting its beliefs by experience, using just those methods of hypothesis and experiment which inductive science uses. Many ideals also—ideals of civilization, culture, and philanthropy—they hold in common, where either is properly understood.

¶ Science and religion are no more separate—far less opposed—than are the animal and the vegetable kingdoms. A man and an oak are extremely different. But go down to the lowest forms of animal and vegetable life, and you do not know which is which; they are not yet differentiated. So it is with science and religion—fundamentally they are altogether alike, for the life and soul of each is faith; and the essential note of faith is the consciousness of being able to *rely* upon a something outside ourselves which will not alter, will not deceive, will not mock us, will not leave us in the lurch. You may call this something outside ourselves which is reliable "the uniformity of nature," or "the goodness of God." To my mind there is no difference in what is meant. And the effect upon the soul of man is the same. He has got his feet upon the rock; in science, or in religion, he can run and not be weary, he can walk and not faint.[1]

3. Before science can proceed to investigate a single question, she must make a number of pure acts of faith. She must make, for example, (1) an act of faith in the trustworthiness of human reason—*i.e.* in its ability to lead the inquirer to true conclusions; (2) an act of faith in the trustworthiness of human memory, for unless memory is trustworthy it is impossible either to amass facts or to construct a chain of arguments; (3) an act of faith in the trustworthiness of the senses, for unless the senses can be trusted knowledge of the external world is impossible; (4) an act of faith in a number of unprovable principles, generally summed up in the phrase "the uniformity of nature." All these propositions are assented to by acts of faith of the most absolute kind. They are not only not proved by science, but never can be proved.

Even so decided an agnostic as Professor Huxley says: "The ground of every one of our actions, and the validity of all our reasonings, rest upon *the great act of faith* which leads us to take

[1] R. Winterbotham, *Sermons*, 410.

the experience of the past as a safe guide in our dealings with the present and the future. From the nature of ratiocination [reasoning], it is obvious that the axioms on which it is based cannot be proved by ratiocination." And again: "[The laws of Universal Causation and of the Uniformity of Nature] are neither self-evident, nor are they, strictly speaking, demonstrable. . . . If there is anything in this world which I do firmly believe in, it is the universal validity of the law of causation; but that universality cannot be proved by any amount of evidence, let alone that which comes to us through the senses."

¶ Not many years ago it might with justice have been said that the attitude of some leaders of scientific thought was strongly antagonistic to acceptance of many of the miracles, more particularly those which appeared to involve conflict with their preconceived ideas. But let us examine for a moment what should be the attitude of a scientific man to the apparent miracles of his own science. The position has been well stated by a former President of the American Chemical Society, as follows:—
"He who would carry out successful scientific research must exercise belief, based on suitable evidence outside personal experience, otherwise known as faith. This will require no great mental effort on the part of the student of the physical sciences. He has to apply the very highest orders of faith to the fundamental principles of these sciences. What is more, reliance on the dicta and data of investigators whose very names may be unknown to him lies at the foundation of physical science, and without this faith in authority the structure would fall to the ground; not the blind faith of the Middle Ages, but a rational belief in the concurrent testimony of individuals who have recorded the results of their experiments and whose observations and whose statements can be verified." [1]

4. As we look at the great men of science, we see that faith is the very breath of their life. They *believe* that there is some great rational law which connects and explains what are now mere disjointed items of truth. Their ideas as to the nature of that law are crude and unsatisfactory at first. Their theory will not work; it does not explain things; the facts reject it; the tight-shut doors of truth do not fly open at their talisman. But they do not despair; their faith does not fail: they recast their

[1] J. A. Harker, in *Science and Religion*, 90.

hypothesis, modify, alter, enrich it. Again and again they manipulate their blocks with a clearer and more luminous picture before them, until at last the stubborn facts group and relate themselves; the ideal of the mind is realized before the eyes; the magic formula which induces order has been pronounced, and faith has given birth to new knowledge.

¶ Darwin believed in the kinship and common origin of species now quite separate and distinct, and set himself to find the law of their derivation. If their parentage was the same, how is it that the members of the family diverge so widely in after-ages? "Variation through natural selection" is the answer, the hypothesis of faith, which by vast and patient labour is shown to fit and explain the most alien and discordant facts. It was only by unconquerable faith in system and order, and in the ultimate connectedness of things, that the greatest discovery of our age was won.[1]

5. However much the truth may be overlooked, physical science is occupied with the invisible. It is the revelation of the invisible. That with which the student of nature deals is not the phenomenon, the appearance, but the fact which he is led to infer from it. He constructs the universe with atoms which no eye has seen or ever can see, and we rejoice in the vision of unimagined order which is laid open to us. He detects the presence of movements of exquisite sensibility in the inorganic masses which seem to us to be dead matter, and we rejoice in the presence of a life immeasurably vaster than we had known. He carries backward the lessons which he reads to-day, and "the everlasting hills" unfold a record of progress which enlarges and ennobles our conception of the Divine counsel and of the Divine working. He carries these forward, and in doing so He teaches us with solemn emphasis that the earthly order which we can trace and follow is a limited episode in the order of existence, of which the end can be fixed in the scale of years. *By faith not by sight* is, in a word, the phrase which must be written over the most splendid achievements of the physicist.

¶ When Leverrier (and Adams in England) discovered the planet Neptune by pure calculation, he was able to predict the precise time and place in the heavens when this planet could be

[1] A. Chandler, in *The Faith of Centuries*, 3.

THE RANGE OF FAITH

seen. But as yet no eye had seen it. Up to this point, no one would question that belief in the existence of Neptune was, even for the discoverer, an act of faith. But when the telescope was actually pointed to the heavens, and the new planet was identified in the very spot which had been indicated, faith was changed to sight.[1]

6. The demonstration of by far the greater part of scientific hypotheses consists simply in showing that the facts are unintelligible upon any other assumption. No one ever saw an atom, and no one ever will. But the phenomena of matter are inexplicable except upon the atomic theory, and this fact is its only proof. No one ever saw the ether, but we cannot comprehend heat and light without assuming it. To show this is to verify the theory. No one was present when the earth was fluid. We verify such an assumption only by showing that the present state of the earth is incomprehensible without it. The hypothesis of a spiritual author of nature is verified in the same way; and if it can be shown that the physical universe is unintelligible without this assumption, and that from every side we are led down to this ultimate affirmation, then the hypothesis of an intelligent Creator has just the same kind of verification as the bulk of scientific theories have.

¶ The assumption that all space, or all at least of which we have any cognizance, must be imagined to be completely filled with a supposed medium of which our senses give us no information, already makes, we might reasonably say, a severe demand on our credulity; and indeed there are, or at least have been, minds to which the demand appeared to be so great as to cause the rejection of that theory of light. And when we provisionally assume the existence of an ether, and use it as a working hypothesis in our further investigations, we find ourselves obliged to admit properties of this supposed ether so utterly different from what we should have imagined beforehand, through our previous experience, that we are half staggered. . . . How the ether can at the same time behave as an elastic solid in resisting the gliding of one portion over another, and yet like a fluid in letting bodies freely pass through it, is a mystery which we do not understand. Nevertheless, we are obliged to suppose that so it is.[2]

[1] J. Orr, *Ritschlianism: Expository and Critical Essays*, 252.
[2] Sir George Stokes, *Natural Theology*, 20.

III.

IN SOCIETY.

1. Society is founded on faith. This becomes clearer as civilization becomes more complex, and the mutual interactions of men more intricate, more potent in their influence. Men depend on one another for kinds of conduct which cannot be regulated by law or controlled by courts of justice. Standards of honour are erected by common consent which become powerful over the selfishness and greed and meanness of individual members of society. These often exercise a sway far beyond that of formal legislation. But it is evident that their fulfilment is secured by faith. In all business affairs men have to lean on one another for promptitude and honesty. In the deeper relations of family and friendship faith is the very soul of reality. Thus we can have no true love, no frank intercourse, no purity of motive, and no sincere sacrifice except as we are bound together by this golden chain of personal trust. The very fact that we realize this more openly and intelligently than was possible in past ages is proof that the social order is becoming more truly ethical, that its most sacred and solid boons are known and confessed to be the fruit of that free movement of conscience and heart which is the very atmosphere of the great principle of faith.

¶ Professor Giddings remarks that good faith is an essential of co-operation, and in fact the whole social structure is built upon the assumption that men will conform. Organized life in society would be impossible if the great majority of men did not conform. An examination of almost any incident of one's daily routine will reveal how completely and unreservedly we count on the reliability of others—of men in general. We are constantly placing our welfare, our health, our very lives in the power of other individuals whom we may not know, may not see, may not even ever have heard of. One goes into a restaurant and orders a meal. The viands may not be wholly to his taste, but at least he expects them to be clean and wholesome, and it never enters his head that the cook may be an expert poisoner, working with diabolical ingenuity to see how many lives he may undermine in the course of his career. One buys a ticket for a railroad journey. Unless there has happened to be a succession of recent accidents, he has no thought of special danger. At any rate, he unconsciously takes it for granted that every individual connected with the running of that railroad, from the superintendent and train-dispatcher to the switchman and section hand, is devoting himself single-heartedly to seeing that that train reaches its destination safely. One goes into a haberdashery and buys a hat. He asks to have it charged and delivered. When the bill comes, he pays it with a cheque. In this simple, everyday transaction, there is a complicated chain of confidences, expectations, and dependences. If there were failure anywhere along the line, the fundamentals of business life would be weakened.[1]

2. This faith is, of course, modified, and often painfully modified, by our experience of men's frailties and imperfections; as we grow older we have to make more and more allowance for these drawbacks; unquestioning and unlimited confidence is the privilege of childhood, which soon passes away when the fresh morning of life gives place to the burden and heat of the day. But yet, with all this allowance, we have still to accept it as the social basis of our existence; if it is lost, or even overshadowed by a cynical scepticism, life is hardly worth living; for isolation is impotence, and want of sympathy leads to want of insight. In fact credit, although not unlimited credit, is the condition of all the undertakings—as of commercial, so also of social, political, and religious life. Humanity must grow as a whole, and mutual faith is the one bond of unity.

What we ought to feel is that it needs specific evidence of untrustworthiness to justify suspicion, rather than that it needs specific evidence of trustworthiness to justify belief. We do not, even in ordinary cases of well-grounded confidence, believe because we have calculated the probabilities, and find a great balance in favour of the testimony we are weighing, but we accept that testimony at once, so long as there are no strong warnings of its positive untrustworthiness. It is, in any wholesome state of society, unbelief on all matters involving personal testimony for which we need explicit evidence rather than belief. The instincts and affections are the true basis of trust. On all matters of personal confidence, recourse is had to an intellectual estimate of probabilities, only when there is some warning of experience given us to distrust those instincts and affections—*i.e.* that they are in

[1] H. P. Fairchild, *Outline of Applied Sociology*, 20.

danger of being abused. The initiative lies properly with those who would sap confidence; and unless that initiative be taken, trust once established, whether by a long experience of trustworthiness or by the far more rapid process of personal affinities and insights, remains legitimately in possession of the field.

¶ How do we gain the sustaining, invigorating thoughts of patriotism, of friendship, of love? How scantly the appearance in itself justifies the devotion which we feel for country, for friend, for father or wife or child. We see a little, and the soul uses in faith what it sees as the vantage ground for its own generous activity. It turns itself from nothing and it interprets, it transforms, all things. It dares to regard the strifes and the selfishnesses of classes and parties, and to look through them to that common enthusiasm which lies still and deep, drawn from long ages and ready for service in time of need. It dares to take account of the weaknesses and imperfections and faults of those by whose fellowship it is strong. It dares to acknowledge the misunderstandings, the coldnesses, the failures of sympathy, the frailties of self-will, which cloud the sunshine of the family. It dares, in a word, to rest on faith and not on sight: to realize not by any creative energy but by a true power of divination that to which the appearance most imperfectly witnesses.[1]

3. A corrupt society is, above all things, marked by two characteristics—a universal habit of questioning all that is said, and an equally universal habit of saying what is not true. On the contrary, in a healthy society like that of England, habits of trust and of truth equally support each other; and it has now become, for instance, a principle of education that the best way to evoke truthfulness in boys is uniformly to believe them, even when appearances are against them.

¶ Over and above the properties of which we have knowledge there are qualities in every man concerning which

> We have but faith; we cannot know;
> For knowledge is of things we see.

It is only that element in personality which appears to act spontaneously in which we can have faith, that element in whose actions we descry an inner unity upon diverse occasions where outward unity is impossible. In the story of Gethsemane, when

[1] B. F. Westcott, *The Incarnation and Common Life*, 367.

THE RANGE OF FAITH

Jesus says to the sleeping three, "The spirit is willing, but the flesh is weak," He evinces faith in hidden elements of character, hidden in the past under selfish rivalries and claims for reward, and now under the desertion and denial He had Himself prophesied as at hand. Yet by action based on such estimate of His followers, He, humanly speaking, conquered the civilized world.[1]

¶ Bishop Blomfield, a great classic, took it into his head to teach mathematics, which bored his pupils not a little. They were struggling through a proposition in Euclid, when one of the Sheridans, who was amongst them, said to his tutor, "Pray, sir, may I ask whether Euclid was a good man?" "What do you mean?" said the other. "I mean," replied Sheridan, "was he a good, honourable, truthful person?" "Oh yes!" said Blomfield; "I never heard anything to the contrary." "Then, sir," rejoined the other, "don't you think we might take his word for this proposition?"[2]

4. But, over and above this belief in humanity at large, and far more important in the education of mind and character, is the faith which we place in human personalities greater and higher than our own. For mankind has its natural leaders, whom the mass of men are rightly inclined to follow, with a loyalty generally strong, and sometimes even pathetic in its intensity. Those leaders it recognizes sometimes as invested with an authority of station and position; sometimes as endowed with exceptional gifts of ability, knowledge, learning, and character, giving them a natural ascendancy over their fellow-men; sometimes as having, or appearing to have, a mission and inspiration from above. It is by trust in such leaders that the forward steps in human progress are actually made by mankind as a whole. It is even startling to think how much of our actual knowledge, and of the rules which guide our conduct day by day, is due, not to our own discovery or origination, but to what we have made our own by trust in those whom we believe to be greater, wiser, better, than ourselves.

¶ No soul is desolate as long as there is a human being for whom it can feel trust and reverence. Romola's trust in Savonarola was something like a rope suspended securely by her path, making her step elastic while she grasped it; if it were

---

[1] L. Douglas, *Christus Futurus*, 34.
[2] M. E. Grant Duff, *Notes from a Diary*, ii. 55.

suddenly removed, no firmness of the ground she trod could save her from staggering, or perhaps from falling.¹

¶ A story is told of two English soldiers in the South African War of 1899–1902. They were toiling through the night, over the trackless veld, on one of Lord Roberts's great strategic marches. "What is the use of it?" said one of the two, wellnigh worn out, stumbling on in the twilight over the rough and endless plain. "Never mind," said the other; "come along; Roberts knows." This was precisely Faith. Its foothold was firmly set on the man's experience of his chief's capacity and power. From that foothold it reached boldly out into the unknown, and trusted the chief's hidden plan without a murmur.²

IV.

Faith in Religious Life.

1. While faith underlies all life it finds its most characteristic exercise in spiritual things. Spiritual things are in a peculiar sense unseen and eternal. Other things pass, as it were, from earth out of sight, out of time; but these come to us from that loftier, sightless, timeless order to which they properly belong. None the less they belong also to us. As we were made to live in relation to the visible, we were made to live also in relation to the invisible. We are made to seek God, made to seek the One, made to seek unity in the many parts of our own personal nature, unity in our relations to the great world in which we are placed, unity in our relations to Him in whom we are. Religion is the striving, however imperfectly, partially, even unconsciously, after this unity; and it is by faith that we are enabled to make the effort to gain it. In this aspect, to borrow the image of the patriarch's dream, faith is as the ladder joining earth and heaven on which the angels of God find footing as they fulfil their ministries of love.

2. Faith in its religious sense is of the same kind as faith in common life. It is distinguishable only by its *special object* and its *moral intensity*. Take first its object. The special object of faith is God, Christ, or the Gospel.

¹ George Eliot, *Romola*.   ² H. C. G. Moule, *Faith*, 14.

(1) GOD.—There is faith in oneself, and such faith is by no means unaccompanied with power. No one can read the life of Napoleon Bonaparte, from his obscure early days in Corsica to the brilliant days when he strode across Europe like a Colossus, without being impressed with the amazing energy which attached to an audacious self-confidence. He fought for no principle, he had no ideals, he was allured by no constant and noble ambition. His confidence was not in a cause, but in himself, and his confidence generated a marvellous strength. But there is a faith and confidence higher than this, and endowed with a corresponding larger dynamic and resource. There is a faith in principles, in causes, in the tenacity of truth, in the indestructibility of virtue, in the invincibility of the righteous order of the world. Such faith is uninfluenced by bribes, undismayed by majorities, untroubled by threats and frowns: it tightly holds to the truth, and confidently waits its day. But still higher is the plane to which we can rise in the ascending gradient of faith. There is a faith in the living God, a faith in His love and goodwill, a confidence in His blessed presence and companionship, an assurance that we are one with Him in the sacred inheritance, and that in Him we are partakers of all the mighty ministries of grace. That is the sublimest of all faiths, and it carries with it the most tremendous of all energies, for it has behind it the omnipotence of God.

¶ Up to the time of Moses, all the worthies named as having true faith, as Abel, Enoch, Noah, Abraham, Isaac, Jacob and Joseph, had none of our Scriptures to originate and strengthen their confidence. They had the ever-living God, and they trusted Him with simple confidence. No Jesus had revealed to them, as to us, the very heart and face of God, as suffering in and for men, yet Almighty to effect the objects of love. At best, clouds and darkness were to them the habitation of His throne. Yet their faith in God, if simple and elementary, was firm; and if, in the darkness, they regarded Him as partial, such limitation of faith is not commended: only that confidence in His power and goodness on which, spite of all appearance to the contrary, they relied for themselves and for their posterity. "Abraham," said our Lord, "rejoiced to see my day, and he saw it, and was glad." What was the vision of the day of the Lord which gladdened the heart of the patriarch? Just this promise: "In thee, and in thy seed, shall all the nations of the earth be blessed." The faith of Abraham, as the faith of Paul and of Jesus, had respect to others rather than to himself; and to himself in others as a natural and spiritual posterity. He had what our Lord urges all disciples to have—" the faith of God." That substantial certainty, which is eternal and unchangeable in Him—that He will, can and must, in the perfect freedom of consent of the creature, bring all to His home and heart.[1]

(2) CHRIST.—" The life which I now live in the flesh I live by the faith of *the Son of God, who loved me, and gave himself for me.*" The apostle refers to Jesus who is the true object of Christian faith. But it is to Jesus not as a mere man, not even like the loveliest of the lovely, or the grandest of the grand among men, or the holiest of the holy, like the apostle himself, for instance, or like the apostle of love, the apostle John. Oh no. It is Jesus as *the Son of God,* Jesus as of one essential nature with the great Father; not merely as one in moral character, but as one in ideal nature, so that He is Divine, and thus able, for instance, to rise again from the dead and to ascend into glory, and able also to save to the uttermost even the chief of sinners who listen to His voice as He says, " Come unto me," and so put their trust in Him. It is Jesus as that Son of God in whom we see the express image of the Father.

Our faith passes through these stages which Christian thought has delighted to mark. *Credit Christum*; it believes that He is what He reveals Himself to be—true Son of Man and Son of God above all created being. *Credit Christo*; it believes the promises of Christ, as Abraham against all apparent possibility believed the word of God, and by these promises it marks and lights the way from this world to the next. *Credit in Christum*; it throws the whole soul on His salvation, resting on His atonement for remission of sin and on His grace for redemption from bondage of evil, and there finds the unity with God which is the life eternal. In each and all of its stages it has access through Him to the bosom of our Father in heaven, and so the spiritual life is " hid with Christ in God."

¶ We hear statements about Christ—statements made by those we love; statements made by those who speak from their own experience of what He can be and do for the soul; state-

---

[1] J. W. Farquhar, *The Gospel of Divine Humanity,* 83.

ments which, though they surpass our thoughts, are not inconsistent with—nay, they coincide with—our highest intuitions and ideals. We accept these statements as true. If we take trouble to investigate we find them corroborated by historical records of indisputable accuracy; and specially by the inimitable description given of His character by the four Evangelists.

We form the highest estimate possible of Christ. In our soul's secret place we enshrine and bow before Him. We recognize Him as Son of God, the Word Incarnate, the Saviour of men, the Lord of Love, the King of the Ages.

We commit to Him the sin and shame of our past for forgiveness and cleansing; the trials and temptations of the present; the keeping of our souls for all the future.

We believe that He is absolutely trustworthy. He promised to take all the burdens that the weary and heavy-laden would cast on Him, and when we transfer all our sins, sorrows, anxieties, perplexities, and difficulties to His hands, we are certain that He accepts them and undertakes. He promised that He would forgive all our sins and treat us as though we had never sinned; that He would cleanse us from the love and power of sin; that He would turn our darkest night into day, and we are absolutely sure that He cannot fail. He is Yea and Amen to the Divine promises. Immediately we realize that the whole burden is now on His shoulders, the peace that passes understanding descends to the door of our heart.

The floodgates are opened then, and within our innermost being arises a fountain of eternal love, fed from Himself; we yield ourselves to Him for the execution of His purposes and for strengthening by His power. We abide in Him and He in us; and we can do all things in Him who strengthens us.[1]

(3) THE GOSPEL.—"Jesus came into Galilee, preaching the gospel of God, and saying, The time is fulfilled, and the kingdom of God is at hand: repent ye, and *believe in the gospel.*" What is the gospel which we are called to believe in? It is the gospel, or "good news," of redemption through Jesus Christ. And by His words at the Last Supper, "This is my blood of the covenant which is shed for many unto remission of sins," our Lord made His death the culmination of His mission, and marked this event for the future as the object of saving faith.

Paul the apostle declares to us explicitly "the gospel." He says to the Corinthians, "Brethren, I declare unto you *the gospel*

[1] F. B. Meyer, *The Soul's Wrestle with Doubt*, 6.

which I preached unto you, which also ye have received, and wherein ye stand; by which also ye are saved, if ye keep in memory (or hold fast) what I preached unto you, unless ye have believed in vain," *and this is impossible, unless it be false that Christ rose from the dead*; "for I delivered unto you first of all that which I also received, *how that Christ died for our sins according to the scriptures; and that he was buried, and that he rose again the third day according to the scriptures.*" The gospel, then, is this—" Christ died *for our sins*, and was buried, and rose again."

¶ The true knowledge of Christ consists in receiving him as he is offered by the Father, namely, as invested with his Gospel. For, as he is appointed as the end of our faith, so we cannot directly tend towards him except under the guidance of the Gospel. Therein are certainly unfolded to us treasures of grace. Did these continue shut, Christ would profit us little. Hence Paul makes faith the inseparable attendant of doctrine in these words, "Ye have not so learned Christ; if so be that ye have heard him, and have been taught by him, as the truth is in Jesus" (Eph. iv. 20, 21).[1]

3. But religious faith differs from the faith of man in man or in nature not only in its object, but also in its intensity or assurance. Everything in life is done by faith. Fathers educate their children, young men and maidens marry, tradesmen enter into business, in faith that their objects will be fulfilled. There is, however, this important difference between secular and religious faith, that the former has always an element of uncertainty in it; whereas it is the unspeakable advantage of a true religious faith to be absolute, to have no shadow whatever of uncertainty about its object. I rise in the morning, intending to reach a certain place, and so set out in the reasonable faith that I shall arrive at my destination. But I may miss the train, or, finding it, there may be a fatal accident. I may lend money, or give credit on what seems evidence of good security, but my creditor may fail or abscond. That on which faith rests being temporal, not substance itself, but a symbol of substance, must always have an element of uncertainty. Yet it would be very foolish and unprofitable not to have faith in any one or any thing because we cannot be certain that all will prosper as we believe

[1] Calvin, *Institutes of the Christian Religion*, ii. 100.

THE RANGE OF FAITH

and hope. While in every temporal affair the pious mind has always a *Deo volente* expressed or understood, there ought to be no such reservation for true faith. I may not say, "God willing I shall be saved, or my brother shall finally be brought to know and to love God," for God wills, and can will, nothing less. He is "not willing that any should perish"; He "willeth that all men should be saved, and come to the knowledge of the truth"; "This is the will of God, even your sanctification." Any doubt in such matters comes from feebleness of faith. If we introduce the time element, as in praying that such an one may be converted this day or year, then the event becomes temporal, and subject to temporal contingency under the Divine will. Faith in relation to eternal ends being based on substance, and thus demonstrably evident, is without the possibility of flaw or failure.

¶ Faith is indeed the energy of our whole nature directed to the highest form of being. Faith gives stability to our view of the universe. As soon as we pass outside ourselves, beyond deductions from the limitations of our own minds, we rest on Faith. By Faith we are convinced that our impressions of things without are not dreams or delusions, but for us true representations of our environment. By Faith we are convinced that the signs of permanence, order, progress, which we observe in nature are true. By Faith we are convinced that fellowship is possible with our fellow-men and with God.[1]

[1] B. F. Westcott, *The Historic Faith*, 176.

V.

Faith in God.

LITERATURE.

Ainsworth, P. C., *The Pilgrim Church*.
Albright, M. C., in *Present Day Papers*, i. (1898).
Barry, A., *Sermons Preached at Westminster Abbey* (1884).
Beeching, H. C., *The Apostles' Creed* (1905).
Brooks, P., *The Light of the World* (1891).
Charles, R. H., *Forgiveness* (1887).
Clow, W. M., *The Evangel of the Strait Gate* (1916).
Connell, A., *The Endless Quest* (1914).
D'Arcy, C. F., *God and Freedom in Human Experience* (1915).
Dods, M., *Footsteps in the Path of Life* (1909).
Drummond, R. J., *The Relation of the Apostolic Teaching to the Teaching of Christ* (1900).
Eaton, T. T., *Faith and the Faith* (1900).
Erskine, T., *The Spiritual Order* (1876).
Everett, C. C., *Theism and the Christian Faith* (1909).
Ferries, G., *The Growth of Christian Faith* (1905).
Gardner, P., *Modernity and the Churches* (1909).
Holland, H. S., *Fibres of Faith* (1910).
Hunter, J., *De Profundis Clamavi* (1908).
Inge, W. R., *Faith* (1909).
Jowett, J. H., *The Transfigured Church* (1910).
Ker, J., *Sermons*, i. (1885).
Lilley, A. L., *The Religion of Life* (1910).
Meyer, F. B., *The Soul's Wrestle with Doubt* (1905).
Mills, B. F., *God's World* (1891).
Moule, H. C. G., *Thoughts on the Spiritual Life* (1889).
Moulton, J. H., *The Christian Religion in the Study and the Street* (1919).
Paget, F., *Faculties and Difficulties for Belief and Disbelief* (1889).
Peake, A. S., *The Heroes and Martyrs of Faith* (1909).
Pierson, A. T., *Foundation Truths*.
Sears, A. L., *The Drama of the Spiritual Life* (1915).
Shepherd, E., *Ambrose Shepherd* (1915).
Sorley, W. R., *Moral Values and the Idea of God* (1918).
Storr, V. F., *Development and Divine Purpose* (1906).
Thom, J. H., *Laws of Life after the Mind of Christ*, i. (1910).
Van Dyke, H., *Manhood, Faith and Courage* (1906).
Waggett, P. N., *Our Profession* (1912).
Westcott, B. F., *The Historic Faith* (1883).
Wilberforce, B., *The Power that Worketh in Us* (1910).
Williams, T. R., *Belief and Life* (1898).
Woods, H. G., *Christianity and War* (1916).

FAITH IN GOD.

1. THE faith which Jesus said men must have before they could do apparently impossible things was faith in God (Mark xi. 22, 23). He had been speaking to His discouraged disciples about faith and what faith can do in the way of overcoming and removing hindrances. To add emphasis to what He had been saying He pointed perhaps to the hill on which the Temple stood, and assured them that if only they had faith enough they could remove that mountain. Let them have faith in God, let them summon up all their spiritual forces, and any mountain of wrong thoughts and ways which obstructed and resisted their progress would disappear and their path would become straight and plain before them. It was a work which must have appeared impossible, beyond all human ingenuity and power; and with man unrelated and alone it was impossible, but not with God—for all things are possible with God; that is, to man with God, working in the line of the will of God and strengthened by His Spirit.

2. What, then, is it to have faith in God? How would this faith affect our way of thinking and acting? By what change in our life can it lead us to the marvellous strength and fruitfulness which is promised by Christ?

That is the question which we are now to attempt to answer.

But let us notice, first of all, the word *in*. Though very small, it is an emphatic word. We speak of believing *in* God—not merely believing certain truths about Him, not merely believing that there is such a Being, but something much deeper and more important than this; to believe in God is so to believe in Him as to make the belief the ground of all we do, the measure of all we think and say. I may easily believe a fact which is told me, and yet the belief may have no influence upon my conduct; there may be facts in science which are of this kind, there may be abundance of facts in newspapers or in books of the same kind, facts which are asserted on good authority, which therefore I admit to be true and probably never think about again. And this is just the kind of belief concerning God, which we ought *not* to have; it is perhaps worse than that belief which is spoken of as pertaining to devils, for their belief at least makes them tremble.

How often we say, "I believe in God"! How easily the sentence falls from the lips! But it is one thing to say it, and another thing to live as one who feels God to be the Alone and Everlasting Reality of human life. "I believe in God." Yes, but with what sort of a belief? "Thou believest there is one God," writes St. James with solemn sarcasm; "thou doest well; the devils also believe." Mr. Froude says of Sir Robert Cecil that he believed in God in "a commonplace kind of way." When a man says, "I believe in God," the question is, What is the quality of his belief, and what its influence? Does he hold the belief, or does the belief also hold him? The selfish man who has lost all sense of the eternal necessity for truth and righteousness of life, says, "I believe in God," but his belief is not worth anything. In his business and intercourse with men he lives "without God"; he is ruled and guided, not by the Divine will, but by passion, pride, pleasure, self-interest.

¶ There is a section of Miss Nightingale's *Suggestions for Thought* called "Cassandra." It is the story of a girl's imprisoned life; it is in part autobiographical, and I have quoted from it several times in the course of this work. It ends with the death of the heroine. "Let neither name nor date be placed on her grave, still less the expression of regret or of admiration; but simply the words, *I believe in God.*"[1]

I.

PURPOSE.

1. We believe in God when we believe in a Divine purpose in the world. This is not always believed. In the ancient and the

---

[1] Sir E. T. Cook, *The Life of Florence Nightingale*, i. 490.

FAITH IN GOD

modern world men have believed this, and men have denied it. When we were children we were taught to believe it. The world proved the existence of the Creator, as a watch that of the watchmaker. The design could be read in all the details of the wondrous construction. Now, it is true that the modern scientist and the modern theologian are dissatisfied, and say that the argument in that form is not tenable. The theologian cannot do with a God clean outside his world in that way, and the scientist cannot find that everything fits quite so precisely; but the kernel of the old argument stands, namely, that there is a general order in things, that the whole is the unfolding of a purpose, that we must think of it all as *designed*, must posit a supreme intelligence and will in it, through it, behind it, above it. This to us to-day stands as an essential, fundamental truth.

¶ Unless the universe in which I find myself is a *divine cosmos*, I cannot treat it, either in my thought or in my conduct, as absolutely trustworthy. I cannot trust in the practical permanence of natural law, upon which all science proceeds. The seeming cosmos, trusted in ordinary human life, *may* become finally chaotic instead of cosmic—if all must at last be resolved into Unknowableness; and our intelligence and science *may* dissolve at last in irretrievable confusion. In continuing to live and act, and to interpret any portion of the universe, I must proceed upon the Final Venture—that nature in experience is really the language of God, and that Divine Order is supreme and universal.[1]

> Lord, my weak thought in vain would climb,
>   To search the starry vault profound;
> In vain would wing her flight sublime,
>   To find creation's utmost bound.
>
> But weaker yet that thought must prove
>   To search Thy great eternal plan,—
> Thy sovereign counsels, born of love
>   Long ages ere the world began.
>
> When my dim reason would demand
>   Why that, or this, Thou dost ordain,
> By some vast deep I seem to stand,
>   Whose secrets I must ask in vain.

[1] A. Campbell Fraser, *Biographia Philosophica*, 302.

When doubts disturb my troubled breast,
  And all is dark as night to me,
Here, as on solid rock, I rest,
  That so it seemeth good to Thee.

Be this my joy, that evermore
  Thou rulest all things at Thy will;
Thy sovereign wisdom I' adore,
  And calmly, sweetly, trust Thee still.[1]

2. This belief is not to be reached by reasoning. Somewhere, sooner or later, we are brought to a standstill and are bound to confess that, for the moment at any rate, reasoning can go no farther. Yet we must live and act, we must even try to present to ourselves intellectually the meaning of the world as a system of completely articulated thought. We are convinced that it is such a rational system, and where we cannot know we trust. Unless we are content to be simply sceptical (and an attitude of utter scepticism is self-contradictory, and so impossible for men, either as practical or as speculative beings), we must, and habitually do, adopt, in the last resort, beliefs which reason can never completely justify. They do not contradict reason, but reason cannot explicate in its own terms all their content. Such is our attitude in the case of the argument from design, an argument which carries with it great weight, and which is strengthened when taken in connexion with other arguments for God's existence. Behind the terms of logical inference in which the argument is cast lies the larger conviction, and this will always remain operative despite any explanations which science may give of adaptations in Nature. For we cannot observe adaptations without wondering at them, without seeing in them a significance, without regarding them as expressive of a purpose.

¶ Doubt, yes, doubt be justified—doubt, so it were straightforward and honest. Forms and accessories—these he was willing to let go—though always with respect and care for the weaker brothers and sisters to whom they stood for things of value; but Faith beyond those forms he clung to, faith fearless and triumphant, uprising out of temporary moods of despondency into ever securer conviction of righteous guidance throughout creation and far-seeing divine Purpose at the heart of things.[2]

[1] Ray Palmer.   [2] *Tennyson and His Friends*, 282.

¶ Faith is not a crop which springs out of the world to reward a careless harvester; it is rather the work of a soul which, out of a world which would otherwise seem dead, extracts the answer of confidence in God. Did I speak of the world as if it were empty of meaning? It is alive with meaning, filled with a voice of God. But it is the voice rather of God's question to us than of His answer. It challenges, it provokes the response of faith, and the dark places, the breaks—

> What if the breaks themselves should prove at last
> The most consummate of contrivances
> To train a man's eye, teach him what is faith?
> And so we stumble at truth's very test.[1]

3. The Divine purpose is righteous and it is prophetic.

(1) *It is a righteous purpose.*—The God in whom we believe is a "righteous" God. And by "righteous" we mean a God who can be relied upon to hold to His intention. He will be sure to see His own purpose out. He will bring out judgment unto victory. He is a God who abides one and the same: with a permanent character, and an intelligible resolution. His personal identity secures our confidence in His enduring faithfulness. He has an end in view, and He means to get there. He will not be found wanting: He is not a man that He should repent. He will never go back from His word. Facts and circumstances will change, but through all He will press toward a fixed consummation. So He is revealed in history as "righteous." "The Lord our God is a righteous God."

It follows that men cannot trample under foot the Divine laws of justice and humanity and yet presume upon the Divine favour. If that were possible, it would mean an utter degradation of the nature of God. No amount of patriotism, no amount of self-sacrifice, will justify in God's sight a nation which is daily transgressing His commandments. Only in so far as we feel that we are ready to surrender our will to His can we hope to make good our assurance that He is going before us. Humble obedience, cheerful submission, singleness of purpose, and honesty of heart— these are among the qualities which God requires from those who count upon His protection.

[1] P. N. Waggett.

(2) *It is a prophetic purpose.*—That is to say, the purpose of the "righteous" God develops. It starts from a small beginning, but it looks to the whole wide world. It begins in one selected man; but it proposes to embrace all nations in the counsel, though they be as the stars for multitude. It moves forward, as times and seasons permit. It expands in scope as new possibilities open out. It gathers volume, force, significance: it draws everything on towards a great justifying conclusion—a day of complete manifestation, when the full plan will be disclosed, and God's faithfulness to it verified. God, as history reveals Him, is a God whose manifestation of Himself is progressive: it develops: it grows. This is the key of prophecy.

The prophet is the man who most intimately corresponds with the counsel that is being unrolled: and the prophet interprets what he can detect of the counsel in present working by ever seeing it in the light of what it works for in the end. He is the man who catches sight, in the confused turmoil of actual experience, of symptoms and signals of a purpose that struggles and strains towards a fuller achievement, towards a consummating close. He lifts the stupid, cruel facts of the passing day into the light of the Day of the Lord, in which all days end. And the temper which desperately clings to this far purpose, and relies on the end which shall come in God's good time, and never despairs of the purpose that is even now at work towards the end, and which, through the delays that sicken the heart, and the defects that spoil the joy, and the black nights that hide the light of the Divine desire, still grimly and desperately asserts the certainty of God's faithful achievement, is called "faith."

> One adequate support
> For the calamities of mortal life
> Exists—one only; an assured belief
> That the procession of our fate, howe'er
> Sad or disturbed, is ordered by a Being
> Of infinite benevolence and power;
> Whose everlasting purposes embrace
> All accidents, converting them to good.[1]

4. But this purpose of God in history is a purpose to be achieved through man's co-operation. Man is the subject, the

---

[1] Wordsworth, "The Excursion," bk. iv.

material, the instrument of the purpose. God has a counsel into which He admits men; and that counsel is a counsel on man's own behalf. It is a purpose by which man, in and through the facts of a progressive history, shall himself become what God designs him to be, and has qualified him to become. God's mind is to issue in and through man: and man comes to his full self in corresponding to that Divine mind. This is possible only if God and man are capable of working together with one mind and one will. And the bond between them, therefore, without which intelligent and willing co-operation is impossible, is a moral one.

Christ, come in the flesh, lived a life of faith or trust in His Father. As the Head and Representative of men He trusted in the Father's purpose of deliverance for the race, and in this trust He yielded Himself up to the power of that purpose, so that it was accomplished in Him. And He did this that all men might apprehend the trustworthiness of the Father and the power of a real trust in Him, and might thus be strengthened and encouraged to partake in His trust, that so they might also partake in its results.

The righteousness of God towards man consists in this loving purpose, and the righteousness of man towards God consists in his faith in that purpose, a trust which makes man a fellow-worker with God in carrying it out. The eternal Son came into our world to reveal the Fatherhood of God; none but a Son could have made such a revelation, and none but those who are created in the Son's nature could be capable of comprehending or receiving it. He came to draw and guide the hearts of the children to their Father by revealing the fatherliness of the Father's heart, and He did this by His own unfaltering trust even whilst standing in their place, accepting and enduring that penalty which they had incurred.

(1) The call to this work is a call to the mind of the man, that he should understand what he is about—that he should enter into the mind of God for him. The purpose is an intelligible purpose, and he is to be a rational agent. So the call is personal. Each man, with his own special power of intelligence, is to make the plan his own, and to offer to it his own reasonable contribution. Each, then, is called by name, like Abraham. Each finds

himself alone: mind to co-operate with mind and will with will. Alone, separate, individually—so he finds himself under the stars, with God, in the eye of the everlasting heaven.

(2) Yet he who is called is not called for his own sake. He is called to co-operate, in his representative character, as an embodiment of entire humanity. His value, in his separate individuality, accrues to him solely by virtue of his being a typical expression of that for which he stands. And the purpose in which he is to co-operate, and the end for which he serves, is absolutely universal. So it was with Abraham. In him, in his solitary person, alone under the stars, all the sum of nations over the whole earth was to be blessed. So it is now; as each one of us is smitten by the call. The faith which gives itself to the high duty of co-operation takes in the whole destiny of man. "I believe" means "I, in my own individual and personal freedom, give myself to the work of co-operating with God in the Divine purpose which reaches from end to end of the story of man on earth. By faith, I make a covenant with God: I bind myself to the service of this great hope. By faith, I dedicate myself to this end; and have no other significance or value. My righteousness lies in my steady adherence to this purpose. All sin lies in the disloyalty which betrays it. Goodness is wisdom—the wisdom that sees, understands, adheres to, and never fails to correspond with, the work of God.

II.

Providence.

The purpose of God is pursued in His providence. What He designs to do He sees done. This we know by faith. It is by faith that, in spite of all the appearances to the contrary, we hold fast our belief that the world is not abandoned by Him, but remains the sphere wherein He still acts. Not indeed always with the effortless word, for in the things of the spirit He is limited by the attitude of His creatures whom He has endowed with a measure of independence and free will. And therefore, while in the realm of matter His will moves triumphantly and directly to its end, in the realm of spirit it is often only through

FAITH IN GOD

thwarting and disappointment, by unchosen and unwelcome ways, that He attains His goal. And the Christian watches the vexatious disappointment and agonizing delay, and is tempted to despair. But it is the victory of faith that he believes in God, not simply as the Creator of the universe, but as its ever-active Lord who will, in spite of all suspense and postponement, at last bring all opposition to an end and reign as the unchallenged King of kings.

1. Creation by a good God carries with it the ideas of purpose in creating and providence in bringing this purpose to fulfilment. A God who is Father must have at heart the highest welfare of His children; and one who is Almighty will pursue that welfare till it is secured. This faith in God's providence, to which our hearts thus give in their assent, we as a matter of fact owe—like the rest of our belief in God—to the revelation in the Scriptures, of which the main topic is the gradual working out of God's good purpose in Israel, and through Israel for the world. The Jewish prophets laid their chief stress on Jehovah's *mercy* and *truth*, or, as we should say, His *love* and *faithfulness*. Having promised to bless the world by their means, He brought them out of Egypt, guarded them in the wilderness, subdued before them the land of Canaan, and by judges and kings and prophets trained them in His ways; ever holding out before them some new hope if they would be willing and obedient. From the first, emphasis is laid on the fatherly care and zeal of Jehovah. His very name is said by some scholars to imply the limitlessness of His goodwill to His people: the sense being not "I am that I am," but "I will be what I will be." He was Jehovah, "merciful and gracious, slow to anger, plenteous in goodness and truth."

¶ How exquisitely is God's fatherly lovingkindness to Israel expressed in that ancient song in Deuteronomy xxxii.: "He found him in a desert land, and in a waste howling wilderness; he led him about, he instructed him; he kept him as the apple of his eye. As an eagle stirreth up her nest, fluttereth over her young, spreadeth abroad her wings, taketh them, beareth them on her wings: so the Lord alone did lead him." And the prophets are full of assurances of God's continual love and pity, despite desperate ingratitude on the part of Israel. The evangelical prophet describes God as bearing all the troubles of His people.

"In all their affliction *he* was afflicted, and the angel of his presence saved them: in his love and in his pity he redeemed them; and he bare them, and carried them all the days of old." Without any counting of the cost, the fatherly love of God pursued its purpose.[1]

2. This prophetic revelation of God's Fatherhood has been almost superseded by the revelation in Jesus Christ, who showed on the one hand the utmost that God's love would do and bear to bring man to his goal, while on the other He showed that man found his true life and happiness in responding to that Divine love. But even so, even for us who believe in the Father not so much through the prophets as through the Son, faith still retains its character as a confidence which is less than proof, owing to the experiences that still remain unreconciled. Christ gave us no final solution of the problem how evil can exist in a world which is governed by the fatherly love of almighty power.

¶ The Apostles' Creed was very probably framed to meet the teaching of the heretic Marcion, who in the second century found this very problem of evil his stone of stumbling. Believing that evil was a property of matter, he denied that the supreme God could be the God who created matter, and so he was forced to distinguish the creating God of the Old Testament from the redeeming God of the New Testament. The former he regarded as an inferior deity, just indeed, but not loving, who did His best, but was obliged to punish His creatures for disobedience; the latter was the supreme God who took pity on men and sent His Son to save them. Of course such a theory, which separated righteousness from love, justice from mercy, was no solution of the difficulty, and only made havoc of the Bible, by ignoring the tenderness of the God of the Old Testament and the holiness of the God of the New. Moreover, it destroyed all belief in the providence of God. A God who did not make mankind, and had no purpose in them, but simply took pity on them in a crisis, was entitled to such gratitude as would befit the Good Samaritan in our Lord's parable, but had no claim to obedience, or co-operation, or filial love. And so the Church would have none of Marcion's explanations of the difficulty; but expressed in clear words the truth of which it was sure, despite its difficulties—"I believe in God the *all*-ruling Father."[2]

[1] H. C. Beeching, *The Apostles' Creed*, 31.
[2] *Ibid.* 33.

3. Regarding God's providence two views are held with more or less distinctness: the belief in what is technically defined as special providence, and the belief in that which may be called general providence. The terms are inadequate, but we may use them for convenience. According to the first view every element of life and every event in life is specially adapted to the special needs of each individual, so that if special suffering comes to a man, or special joy, there is the question why this joy or suffering should have come to this particular individual. According to the other view the laws of nature are invariable, and every spirit alike is subject to them. Therefore when this or that experience comes to an individual, he does not ask why the special event should have happened to him, but sees in it one manifestation of the forces by which all men are surrounded. According to the first view, a man's relation to the world is like a bath that has been specially prepared in accordance with the directions of the physician, with just such qualities to the water, and just such temperature, and so on. According to the other view, the relation is like bathing in the ocean, where there is no preparation for the individual, but the same surf beats upon all alike.

It may be asked, where, if we take this latter view, is the possibility of recognizing any providence at all? Where is there any opportunity for faith? The difference, however, between the two views is largely one of detail. There is opportunity for precisely the same sort of faith in the one case as in the other, the faith in an absolute ordering of events. Only according to the second view we assume that the Divine providence has ordained this subjection of man to a system of invariable law as the best method of education for the spiritual life, recognizing that in a world where laws might be suspended, where the action of forces might vary according to every varying need, the soul would lose its strength and vigour.

¶ There are unseen elements which often frustrate our wisest calculations—which raise up the sufferer from the edge of the grave, contradicting the prophecies of the clear-sighted physician, and fulfilling the blind clinging hopes of affection; such unseen elements Mr. Tryan called the Divine Will, and filled up the margin of ignorance which surrounds all our knowledge with the feelings of trust and recognition. Perhaps the profoundest philosophy could hardly fill it up better.[1]

4. However we regard the question of a general and a particular providence, one thing is certain, that without some view of providence the soul cannot rest and religion cannot exist. All that religion demands is the recognition of an infinite spirit of love into relation with which the finite spirit is brought. And every man must by faith make this recognition for himself. When our Lord addresses His disciples, "Wherefore, if God so clothe the grass of the field, which to-day is, and to-morrow is cast into the oven, shall he not much more clothe you, O ye of little faith?" we can have no doubt of the sense in which He employs the word "faith." No one can question that He means by it, that *confidence in God's protection* which their observation of His care for the lowest parts of His creation ought to imprint upon the hearts of every one of His children—who should feel that they are objects of far warmer love and of far tenderer care. A glance at the whole passage will show that it is designed to condemn, in God's children, all that unreasonable solicitude about life and its wants in which they are so prone to indulge—to banish a doubtful mind concerning the supply of our necessities, by the recollection that our heavenly Father knoweth that we (each one of us) have need of these things.

> Here in the country's heart,
>   Where the grass is green,
> Life is the same sweet life
>   As it e'er hath been.
>
> Trust in a God still lives,
>   And the bell at morn
> Floats with a thought of God
>   O'er the rising corn.
>
> God comes down in the rain,
>   And the crop grows tall—
> This is the country faith
>   And the best of all![2]

[1] George Eliot, *Janet's Repentance*.
[2] Norman Gale, *Collected Poems*, 5.

5. But it is one thing to be in God's hands—as we all most surely are; it is another thing to know that this is so. The sense of dependence is easily lost. God does not stamp all His gifts with the broad seal of heaven. The one Divine touch that testifies to the other-world origin of life's commonest bounty is sometimes like the hall-mark on precious metal-work—put where you won't see it unless you look for it.

Do we look out for God's providence? Have we the eye of faith? We have our dull and ignominious times, when nothing seems to prosper with us, when we feel as if everything Divine were remote or unreal, when our prayers have been so long, unanswered that we begin seriously to doubt whether prayer avails. To have an eye for things spiritual makes all the difference at these times. The veil that hides the forces which really rule this world is lifted, and we see things in their true relations. We see the swift couriers of Jehovah incessantly streaming in from all parts of the earth, we see that there is nothing unobserved, and that He to whom this detailed information is present does not wait to be urged or prompted to action, but that with gravity, earnestness, and impassioned tenderness, He interposes at the fitting juncture. While we are thinking that our efforts to set matters right are not observed or regarded by any higher power, there is a grave and comprehensive consideration of our affairs, a sense of responsibility which accepts and discharges the management of all human interests, an efficient activity to which ours is as negligence.

> I know not if or dark or bright
>   Shall be my lot,
> If that wherein my hopes delight
>   Be best or not.
>
> It may be mine to drag for years
>   Toil's heavy chain,
> Or day and night my meat be tears
>   Or bed of pain.
>
> Dear faces may surround my hearth
>   With smiles and glee,
> Or I may dwell alone, and mirth
>   Be strange to me,

> My barque is wafted to the strand
> By breath divine,
> And on the helm there rests a Hand
> Other than mine.
>
> One who has known in storms to sail
> I have on board;
> Above the raging of the gale
> I have my Lord.
>
> He holds me when the billows smite,
> I shall not fall.
> If sharp, 'tis short; if long, 'tis light;
> He tempers all.
>
> Safe to the land! Safe to the land!
> The end is this;
> And then with Him go hand in hand
> Far into bliss.[1]

III.

ACCEPTANCE.

Faith in God is faith in His purpose and in His providence. It is also acceptance of His will.

1. First of all, there is a desire for help from God. For God has a way of letting the sinner or the sufferer wander on and try all other ways of cure, not to tantalize him with shadows, but to lead him through them to the great reality. He lets the prodigal go far away and deep down among the swine and the husks, and make experience of all man's friendships, such as they are in his poor circle, and find them all hollow and heartless, that his Father's house and face may rise glowing before him in the depth of his darkness, and he be driven to know them as never before. So He has suffered us perhaps to wander and exhaust all our strength and hope, sometimes on the world's pleasures, sometimes its moralities, sometimes on its business, sometimes its philosophy, and still to find the burden and the sore and the void,

[1] Dean Alford.

till, wearied in the greatness of the way, toil-worn and travel-sick, we say, "There is no hope," that out of our despair this hope may rise like the morning-star out of black night. All other physicians have been tried, that this question may be stirred—"Is there no balm in Gilead; is there no physician there?"

2. Next, there is confidence in the love and care of God. No doubt there are mysteries in God's providence, and there is a necessity that there should be mysteries; but still the one question remains, "Are the known ways of God so full of goodness that faith in Him for the yet unknown is a claim that He may justly make?" What are these mysteries? So far as they are of a moral nature, with which alone we are concerned, they arise from this—that all earthly experience is for the *education* of our souls, in kinship to God Himself; in the notable words of Christ, that we may come to have life in ourselves. It was mystery that made possible the existence of such a being as Christ—the mystery that goodness should suffer, the mystery that the innocent should seem stricken of God and deserted, the mystery that the righteous should be delivered into the hands of the unrighteous, that power should wait upon sin, and the Holy One of the Father have no place to lay His head. Remove such mysteries and you remove the Cross, you remove the spiritual glory of Christ; and human goodness, without a struggle, without a difficulty, without a temptation, could only be spontaneous movements following natural instincts—that is, it could only be an animal development. We should become only as God's creatures who cannot disobey His will, and cease to be His children who give Him our hearts.

¶ One of the finest incidents recorded in that "tall quarto of 533 pages" in which Robert Stevenson told the story of his operations at the Bell Rock Lighthouse may here be narrated as it is given in *A Family of Engineers*. A great storm had broken upon the rock and the ship *Pharos* riding at her anchor beside it, on September 5, 1807. All the following day it raged with unabated violence, now threatening to tear her from her moorings, now to overwhelm and break her to pieces as she rode. After twenty-seven hours of what to the landsman seemed imminent peril, he made the best of his way aft and saw the tremendous spectacle of the waves. "On deck there was only one solitary individual looking out, to give the alarm in the event of the ship breaking from her moorings . . . and he stood aft the foremast, to which he had lashed himself with a gasket or small rope round his waist, to prevent his falling upon deck or being washed overboard. When the writer looked up, he appeared to smile." The writer goes on to record that he had been much relieved by that "smile of the watch on deck, though literally lashed to the foremast. From this time he felt himself almost perfectly at ease; at any rate he was entirely resigned to the ultimate result." We offer no apology for telling the story as a very perfect allegory of the grandson's faith. His storm also was long and affrighting, and he was not only "entirely resigned to the ultimate result," but indeed "almost perfectly at his ease." The reason was that he too, looking out, had seen a smile upon a certain Face.

> Well roars the storm to those that hear
> A deeper voice across the storm.[1]

> God! Thou art love! I build my faith on that.
> Even as I watch beside Thy tortured child
> Unconscious whose hot tears fall fast by him,
> So doth Thy right hand guide us through the world
> Wherein we stumble. . . .
> I know Thee, who hast kept my path, and made
> Light for me in the darkness, tempering sorrow
> So that it reached me like a solemn joy;
> It were too strange that I should doubt Thy love.[2]

3. Faith is desire for help and includes a glad hope in a God of all goodness, and then a restful acquiescence in His righteous will. It is held to be *righteous*, since man's will is urged to seek righteousness; the pains in nature cease to be an insurmountable obstacle when regard is had to the surest knowledge we possess—knowledge, moreover, which relates to the last and crowning product of the world, namely, the human will. Such faith, as is seen from the circumstances in which it appears, is not a blind, irrational feeling, but a reasonable trust. The highest morality is reasonable; the choice of the highest goodness is wisdom, the fine flower of intelligence, being reason not in the form of abstract knowledge, but as directly applied for the regulation and moulding of life. Hence, as faith in God follows upon that choice, and is

---

[1] J. Kelman, *The Faith of Robert Louis Stevenson*, 266.
[2] Browning, "Paracelsus."

FAITH IN GOD

in intimate connexion with it, faith is not a product of blindness, but has as one of its elements and concomitants the best kind of intellectual activity, the knowledge which is wisdom.

¶ On the next day I addressed a thousand negro children, and when I enquired, "May I send an invitation to the good Abraham Lincoln to come down and visit you?" one thousand little black hands went up with a shout. Alas, we knew not that at that very hour their beloved benefactor was lying cold and silent in the East room at Washington! At Fortress Monroe, on our homeward voyage, the terrible tidings of the President's assassination pierced us like a dagger, on the wharf. Near the Fortress poor negro women had hung pieces of coarse black muslin around every little huckster's tables. "Yes, sah, Fathah Lincum's dead. Dey killed our bes' fren, but God be libben; dey can't kill Him, I's sho ob dat." Her simple childlike faith seemed to reach up and grasp the everlasting arm which had led Lincoln while leading her race "out of the house of bondage."[1]

> Whatso it be, howso it be, Amen.
> Blessed it is, believing, not to see.
> Now God knows all that is; and we shall, then,
> Whatso it be.
>
> God's Will is best for man whose will is free.
> God's Will is better to us, yea, than ten
> Desires whereof He holds and weighs the key.
>
> Amid her household cares He guides the wren,
> He guards the shifty mouse from poverty;
> He knows all wants, allots each where and when,
> Whatso it be.[2]

IV.

Action.

There are three stages in faith in God. There is, first, a conviction of the truth of that to which it is directed. There is, next, a quickening of love by which the conviction is made personal confidence. And then there is a readiness for action corresponding to the conviction.

---

[1] T. Cuyler, *Recollections of a Long Life*, 152.
[2] Christina G. Rossetti, *Poetical Works*, 201.

1. First, there is *a conviction of the truth.*—A voice resounds within the soul and the conviction of things unseen, the assurance of God and His grace, shine out in clear certainty. As Paul says, it is not simply the truth of the word that evokes this faith. The message of God and of His being and power may be borne in upon the mind with conclusive proof. The truth of the gospel may be so clearly perceived and so strongly held that it can be taught with cogent power. It is too easy to describe the form of godliness and to deny its power. A voice must be heard by a finer organ than the outer ear. It must be acknowledged by a higher power than the conscience. It must be a voice within the soul. "With-the heart man believeth unto righteousness." When the spirit of the convicted and contrite man hears the voice of Christ speaking within, then, and not till then, has faith been born. There is a mood, a season, a moral and spiritual condition, in which we believe. Then the voice of Christ calls an appeal, and as we hear He comes in as the guest of the soul.

¶ The electrician sets up on some high bluff by the seashore his wireless installation. He prepares his delicate apparatus so keenly sensitive that it can send its message a thousand miles away, and can catch and interpret every vibration which is set in motion by the touch or even the breath of man. Far beyond the reach of sight a ship is fitted with an attuned instrument. But the apparatus may be out of order, or the operator may be absent from his post, or he may be drowsed in sleep, or he may be engaged in idle talking. The message vibrates and strikes his wires in vain. It is not heard. Another, a mile distant, hears and interprets the word. As he does so, personalities and truths and messages become sure and certain knowledge. They are all beyond the range of sight. But their word has been heard, and faith in them is inevitable.[1]

2. Next, there is *personal confidence.*—"Confidence" is very often used in Scripture with regard to God. But the climax of all the repetitions of it is in 1 John v. 14: "And this is the confidence that we have in him, that, if we ask any thing according to his will, he heareth us; and if we know that he hear us, whatsoever we ask, we know that we have the petitions that we desired of him." That is a sublimely complete exhibition of confidence—

---

[1] W. M. Clow, *The Evangel of the Strait Gate*, 117.

that anything that we ask of Him, whatsoever it be, if it is according to His will, we not only shall have it, but have it already—such confidence in God's promise that we take it to be fulfilled already. It reminds one of what Coleridge says in that terse little couplet of his:

> Faith is an affirmation and an act
> That bids eternal truth be fact.

"Then came the disciples to Jesus apart, and said, Why could not we cast it out? And Jesus said unto them, Because of your unbelief!" There is no uncertainty in the diagnosis. The cause is not complicated. It is single and simple. "Unbelief!" There had been a want of confidence. There was doubt at the very heart of the disciple's effort. There was a cold fear at the very core of his enterprise. He went out with a waving banner, but the flag in his heart was drooping! "Because of your unbelief!" Our Lord is not referring to unbelief in any particular doctrine, but rather to the general attitude and outlook of the soul. There was no strong, definite confidence in the disciple, and such unbelief always ensures paralysis and defeat.

A true faith has sometimes been defined to be not a faith in the unseen merely, or in God or Christ, but a personal assurance of salvation. Such a feeling may be only the veil of sensualism; it may be also the noble confidence of St. Paul. "I am persuaded, that neither death, nor life, nor angels, nor principalities, nor powers, nor things present, nor things to come, nor height, nor depth, nor any other creature, shall be able to separate us from the love of God, which is in Christ Jesus our Lord." It may be an emotion, resting on no other ground than that we believe; or a conviction deeply rooted in our life and character.

¶ Such a vision as St. Paul so securely alleged is the first great acme or topmost peak of faith. It is the excellence of an unwavering certainty, a knowledge that cannot be shaken, a trust that will stand fast though no man helps us to sustain it. How different very often is our modern apologetical effort! Our modern apologetical effort is a running round society to see if we can get some one to keep us in countenance while we believe in Jesus Christ. The other day we were to be daunted by the traces of the origin of species. One day I remember it was seriously suggested that we might be dismayed by a message from one of the stars, that He had not been seen there.[1]

3. Lastly, there is the expression of the *faith in action.*—Things are sometimes said about the life of holy faith, the life of rest upon and in the Son of God, which leave, or seem to leave, no place for spiritual effort and resolve. Yet the Scriptures have very much to say about these latter things. They speak of "girding up the loins of the mind," of "working out salvation," of "being in earnest" (our English Bible renders it "labouring") "to enter into the" heavenly "rest," of "giving diligence to make our calling and election sure," of "watching and being sober," of "keeping under the body and bringing it into subjection," of "labouring fervently in prayer." We may be very sure, then, that this fact of spiritual effort is no accident of the spiritual life, but a large and vital truth in it. It would be strange if it were otherwise. All conscious personal life has much to do with exercise and effort in the course of its healthful development. A life, conscious and personal, which should be a life of mere and pure quiescence, would hardly be a life worth living.

All spiritual interests that are not embodied in action, or do not terminate in fresh growths of character, are only so much waste of spiritual power; for the pulsings of aspiration, the tears of penitence, the bitter outpourings of shocked self-knowledge, are, unless they take some onward step into the infinite of Divine truth and goodness, but the experiences of a self-deceiving heart, and, so far from witnessing to or deepening faith, are smoothing the way to a final and impotent despair. Yes, faith is not a sentiment, but a power divinely practical. It takes religious convictions and carries their influence into every transaction of business, every scheme of pleasure, every phase of a man's public and home life. Faith takes religious feelings and translates them into heroic deeds and unselfish devotions; faith takes aspiration and develops therefrom the nobler growths of character, the higher possibilities open to a child of God.

¶ Maurice once said with something of a caustic tone about Carlyle that he believed in a God who lived until the death of Oliver Cromwell. The gibe was not quite fair to Carlyle, but

[1] P. N. Waggett, *Our Profession*, 28.

emphatically that kind of faith will not do. An expositor has very shrewdly remarked of the woman at the well of Samaria, that in two phrases, "Our fathers worshipped in this mountain," and "When Messias cometh," she betrayed the fact that religion as a vital force was dead in her, and remained only as a dim memory or a distant hope. That will not suffice. We shall soon lose the energy of faith, unless we believe God to be present in the life of every day. It is tedious work calling to a God who has receded out of all intimate relations with our daily life. But if every day begins with the knowledge that the outstanding fact in it is to be the unknown quantity, the Divine interpositions, the incalculable influences, the voices from within, then the quest for a persistent faith will not be so hazardous and impossible a task.[1]

¶ The work of self-discipline, of brotherly kindness, of Christian testimony, the simple homely pieties of life—without these faith will die—it must perish from the earth.[2]

[1] A. Connell, *The Endless Quest*, 8. [2] *Ibid.* 9.

VI.

THE VENTURE OF FAITH.

LITERATURE.

Adam, J. D., *Religion and the Growing Mind* (1912).
Alexander, A. B. D., *The Ethics of St. Paul* (1910).
Barry, A., *Do We Believe?* (1908).
Bramston, J. T., *Fratribus* (1903).
Brooks, P., *The Mystery of Iniquity* (1893).
Burroughs, E. A., *The Valley of Decision* (1917).
Chadwick, S., *Humanity and God* (1904).
Coffin, H. S., *University Sermons* (1914).
Cox, S., *Expositions*, i. (1885).
Fletcher, M. S., *The Psychology of the New Testament* (1912).
Gardner, C., *Vision and Vesture* (1916).
Granger, W., *The Average Man* (1899).
Holdsworth, W. W., *The Life of Faith* (1911).
Illingworth, J. R., *Christian Character* (1904).
Hutton, J. A., *Loyalty the Approach to Faith* (1917).
Jones, R. M., *Studies in Mystical Religion* (1909).
Lynch, T. T., *The Mornington Lecture* (1885).
McGiffert, A. C., *The Rise of Modern Religious Ideas* (1915).
Mackenna, R. W., *The Adventure of Life* (1919).
Moule, H. C. G., *Faith* (1909).
Newman, J. H., *Parochial and Plain Sermons*, iv. (1868).
Skrine, J. H., *The Heart's Counsel* (1899).
  „   „   *What is Faith?* (1907).
Strong, T. B., in *The Meaning of the Creed* (1917).
Walpole, G. H. S., *Life's Chance* (1912).
Ward, J., *Psychological Principles* (1918).
Williams, T. R., *Belief and Life* (1898).
Workman, W. P., *Kingswood Sermons* (1917).
Wyndham, G., *Essays in Romantic Literature* (1919).

The Venture of Faith.

Faith is always a venture. The venture may be made with confidence or with doubt, but it is, and must be, a venture. There is always in it an element of the unseen and unknown. No doubt faith and sight stand in close connexion with each other, and often seem to run over, so to speak, into one another. Faith, in its true and sane sense, cannot live without some foothold on what we may call sight. But faith *in itself* is precisely that which ventures out beyond sight, and moves and works in the dark, in the unseen, in the unknown.

Take for illustration the case of the physician. You are ill, and you send for your doctor, and you give yourself over to his care, because you have faith in him. What does it mean? Your physician is quite visible to your eyes, and his treatment is felt by your body; all this falls under the heading of sight. But your faith in him is that attitude of thought and will which leaps off into what to you is the unknown region of his medical science and training. He knows what you do not know about your disease, and about the proper remedies or reliefs. You know him well enough, as a man, to trust him out of sight, so to speak, with things which you know not but which he knows. Precisely in that region, in what is a dark void to your own understanding, your faith in your physician lives, and moves, and works.

¶ I don't agree with you that anything so vital as Christianity ought to be indisputable—

> You must mix your uncertainty
> With faith, if you would have faith be.

If it is to be anything but *mere* intellectual consent, as if to the fact that the world is round, it must be the attitude of throwing oneself on the things that are highest and best in life, and committing oneself to the most lovable and strongest personality in all history—the attitude of saying "I will take the side of this Man, the most perfect and most heroic who has ever lived; he *cannot* have been mistaken."[1]

> Who am I? Lord, I know not; lead me on.
> The night is dark; no stars are in the skies;
> All hint, all outline of the path is gone,
> And fierce and rough the sullen night winds rise.
> Where only One illumes the night,
> Do pilgrims question of His right?
>
> Dost thou believe that I am very God?
> I know not, Lord, I know not; lead me on.
> This much I know—that where Thy steps have trod
> Some Light still shines as it has always shone.
> Where only One illumes the night,
> Do pilgrims question of His right?
>
> Dost thou believe then that I died for thee?
> I know not, Lord, I know not; lead me on.
> This much, no more in all the world I see,
> Where Thy Light falters every light is gone.
> Where only One illumes the night,
> Do pilgrims question of His right?
>
> Dost thou then love Me, thou that criest so?
> I know not, Lord, I know not; lead me on.
> This much, no more in all the world I know—
> The darkness grows and I am all alone.
> Where only One illumes the night,
> Do pilgrims question of His right?[2]

I.

SIGHT.

It is characteristic of human nature to seek to rise from the visible sphere to that invisible sphere in which it stands alone face to face with the eternal. Thus, in respect of thought, it strives to pass beyond the visible phenomena around us, to the invisible truths which underlie them, and the invisible Cause from

---

[1] *Life and Letters of Maggie Benson*, 303.
[2] Edith Sichel, *New and Old*, 171.

THE VENTURE OF FAITH 137

which they all proceed. In respect of morality, the conscience bears its witness to an invisible and eternal righteousness, which is but imperfectly expressed in the laws and institutions by which the visible life is governed. In respect of beauty—whether the beauty of grandeur or the beauty of perfection—the imagination cannot be content with its visible manifestations; it must endeavour to grasp the ideal principles, which they can but imperfectly embody. In respect of affection, our higher humanity must go beyond that which is sensuous and transitory in love to the spiritual element in it, which cannot fade or pass away. In respect of what we call especially spiritual aspiration, the soul has an inexpressible yearning for the invisible perfection of goodness, which alone can satisfy a nature stamped with a Divine Image. It is therefore natural and even inevitable that, in respect of that personal relation of which faith is the vivid recognition, there should be a corresponding tendency to rise from the visible to the invisible, from the finite to some infinite personality, on which our whole being can absolutely rest.

1. The realm of the invisible into which faith brings us may be a realm of ideas and ideals. The first man in his immaturity deals with things. Man as he grows maturer deals also with ideas. The things are visible and tangible. The ideas no eye has seen, no hand has ever touched. Subtle, elusive, and yet growing to be more real to the mind of the man who truly deals with them than are the bricks of which his house is built, or the iron tool with which he does his work, the great ideas of justice, of beauty, of sublimity, become at once the witnesses and the educators of man's deeper powers which must come out to do their work. The birth of the power of recognizing and dealing with ideas, the birth of ideality, is an epoch in the history of the world or of a man.

¶ In a part of the battle of Neuve Chapelle where things were more than usually muddled, a British subaltern received the order to lead his men out against the trenches opposite. The barbed wire in front of them was obviously intact, and to do anything of the sort seemed to be merely useless suicide. The men, realizing the situation, refused, and were in fact justified by a counter-order a few minutes later. But their officer could not understand their refusal. Again and again he implored them to follow him, and at last, with tears in his eyes, sprang up himself, saying, "If you will not follow me, I'm going alone." He was hardly over the parapet before he fell back, severely wounded. As they carried him off on a stretcher, he was weeping bitterly —not for his own failure or the pain of his wound, but because his men had disgraced themselves by refusing the impossible. That is the only right spirit for the Christian to-day —the spirit which is prepared to attempt the impossible, because the alternative is more unbearable still. But, if the faith of a Christian is not a delusion the whole way through, then for him the impossible does not exist. The Commander he serves under never blunders, and there is no such thing as going forward alone. On the contrary, the faith which is willing to face the impossible is itself the appointed means of achieving it. "This is the victory which has overcome the world, even our faith." "Nothing shall be impossible unto you." [1]

2. The ideal towards which faith leads us is perhaps unattainable here but attainable hereafter. The instinctive expectation of an immortal life beyond the grave, which is found in the humanity of all races and of all ages, always includes some development of this hope of future perfection. In fact, it is in relation to this ultimate expectation that hope itself, in spite of all its disappointments in this earthly sphere, lives on still, as a source of comfort and a spring of energy even to the end. If faith is perfected by love, it is also in another sense perfected by hope. It is not a little remarkable that the so-called definition of faith with which the eleventh chapter of the Epistle to the Hebrews opens, that it is the "assurance of things hoped for, and the discernment of things unseen," is so large and comprehensive as to include all these aspects of that tendency of human nature, which has been described, to rise from the visible to the Invisible, and to cherish the undying hope of a future growth to perfection.

Passage, immediate passage! the blood burns in my veins!
Away, O soul! hoist instantly the anchor!
Cut the hawsers—haul out—shake out every sail!
Have we not stood here like trees in the ground long enough?
Have we not grovell'd here long enough eating and drinking
    like mere brutes?
Have we not darken'd and dazed ourselves with books long
    enough?

[1] E. A. Burroughs, *The Valley of Decision*, 363.

Sail forth—steer for the deep waters only,
Reckless, O soul, exploring, I with thee, and thou with me,
For we are bound where mariner has not yet dared to go,
And we will risk the ship, ourselves and all.

O my brave soul!
O farther, farther sail!
O daring joy, but safe! are they not all the seas of God?
O farther, farther, farther sail![1]

3. The ideal of faith is finally and perfectly only God Himself. It is "seeing him who is invisible." That is to say, it is the consciousness of a Divine Personality, the hope of the fulfilment of His promises, and the rest on communion with Him. This it is which is the essence of all vital religion; and it may be unhesitatingly affirmed that in this sense of the word, religion, in spite of many imperfections, obscurities, and perversions, is in possession of the whole world of humanity, as soon as that humanity emerges from the darkness of mere savagery.

¶ There is a profound truth in St. Paul's celebrated declaration at Athens, that God "made of one blood all the nations who dwell on all the face of the earth, that they should seek him if haply they might feel after him, and find him, though he is not far from any one of us, for in him we live, and move, and have our being." In that great saying we have the truths which the maturest human thought acknowledges more and more—first, that there is a spiritual unity of all humanity in relation to God; next, there is in that humanity a universal consciousness, which feels after Him, and in various measures finds Him; and, lastly, that with this tendency to search after Him is associated the feeling that, in some way, our life lives, moves, and has its being in Him.[2]

4. But it is not enough to "feel after and find" God through faith. What is the nature of the God we find? No experience, however momentous and significant it may be for the person who has it, can settle for everybody else the question: Is there in the universe a God who is personal and all-loving? No empirical experience of any sort can ever answer that question, and to the end of the world men will be called upon to walk by *faith*, to make their venture in the light of what ought to be true, and in the light of what seems to them true, and to live by that faith.

[1] Walt Whitman.   [2] A. Barry, *Do We Believe?* 19.

¶ Faith sees the Divine omnipresence to which materialism is blind; Christian faith further recognizes it as the presence of a Father. For the Fatherhood of God is the fundamental thought of the Sermon on the Mount. "Ye shall be perfect, as your heavenly Father is perfect." "Thy Father which seeth in secret shall recompense thee." "Your Father knoweth what things ye have need of, before ye ask." "After this manner therefore pray ye: Our Father which art in heaven."[1]

5. Faith in God, therefore, is always a venture. We may not discover meaning in the world as we gaze upon it, or as its manifold life unrolls itself before our eyes. It may seem only a complex of blind and conflicting forces. Everything looks like the mere play of chance. Conclusive evidence that the race is growing better, or that there is a moral order of the universe, is difficult to find. But we resolve that the world shall have meaning for us, that it shall be a moral world in which our moral purposes shall be accomplished and our moral ideals realized, and we live our lives under the compulsion of this resolve. This is to have faith in God, and the only kind of faith that is real; not the faith of passive acquiescence or consent, but the creative faith of active purpose and effort.

The world is plastic in our hands. It is not offered to us ready-made and complete with the moral values all there and the spiritual purposes already realized. It is given us to make of it what we will. We may find God in it, if we live by the postulate that He is there, or we may never discover Him if we stand off and wait for Him to reveal Himself. The religious man is he who makes the postulate, who dares to venture faith in God and to live his life thereby. And he has proved his faith who finds it livable, who finds his moral purposes realizable and his reading of the world in moral terms justified. But the venture cannot wait upon the proof; we must believe ere we can know that our belief will vindicate itself as sound.

¶ In the world of startling surprises into which a child is born, he finds little difficulty in imagining the unseen beings of whom he is told, and living in their actual society. The Santa Claus, to whom he posts a Christmas letter in the chimney, is so real that he can readily be induced to think that the wind he hears blowing over

---

[1] J. R. Illingworth, *Christian Character*, 66.

the chimney-top is the swift passing of an airy postman carrying the mail to the kindly patron of good children. The invisible God, to whom he addresses his nightly "Now I lay me down to sleep," and says, "Our Father, which art in heaven," is as sensibly at hand. The pictures children form of God vary with what they are taught and the impressions they receive, but the sense of His actuality they themselves supply. Mrs. Browning's lines in which she describes a child's thought of God put this graphically:

> They say that God lives very high:
> But if you look above the pines
> You cannot see our God; and why?
>
> And if you dig down in the mines
> You never see Him in the gold;
> Though, from Him, all that's glory shines.
>
> God is so good, He wears a fold
> Of heaven and earth across His face—
> Like secrets kept, for love, untold.
>
> But still I feel that His embrace
> Slides down by thrills, through all things made,
> Through sight and sound of every place:
>
> As if my tender mother laid
> On my shut lips her kisses' pressure,
> Half-waking me at night, and said,
> "Who kissed you through the dark, dear guesser?"[1]

II.

KNOWLEDGE.

1. There is always a certain abandon in faith. It is trusting ourselves to the Unseen, to One whom, though invisible and shrouded in mystery, we feel in the depth of our hearts, and apart from all arguments and reasonings, to be absolutely wise and good, with an unlimited right to our allegiance. And Christian faith is the outgoing of our heart's affection and obedience to this invisible God, *as Christ presents Him to us*—that is, as our

[1] H. S. Coffin, *University Sermons*, 177.

Father; it is the endeavour to give ourselves up to Him even as Christ was one in mind and will with the Father who sent Him. Now, this is a thing which concerns a deeper part of our nature than our understanding. Evidences and arguments may bring a man to the brink of faith, but they cannot launch him on its sea. Their province is the solid ground of fact; but that province, after all, is but a little island in the midst of an infinite ocean. If we would pass from its narrow limitations to the largeness of religious life, we must commit ourselves to what to the eye of reason appears an uncertain element; we must trust to be upborne. There is no doubt a deeper reason than reason knows for the act, and in the end it will justify it; but the act itself, whether on the part of child or of sage, is always a step *beyond* knowledge: it is the committing of ourselves to the keeping and the commands of our God and Father.

The desire for exact certainty, for definite evidence in matters of our Christian creed cannot hope to attain to the blessing of willing childlike faith. For, firstly, that evidence is not given us; we cannot prove our faith by logic. The evidence vouchsafed to the doubting apostle of the sight and touch of his Lord's risen body cannot be looked for now; and so if we refuse to believe anything that we cannot logically prove, we can never enter at all into the certainty about spiritual and Divine things which makes the Christian's faith. And again, the very nature of faith, like that of heroism in action, implies a boldness, a venturesomeness which will sacrifice the safe certainty of logical proof, and will go forward boldly into the region of what is beyond all human demonstration, acknowledging that beyond the sphere of human knowledge there lies a world, an infinite world of truth, which we shall hereafter see and understand, but which now we can accept only by a higher method even than reason, by the power of faith, "believing where we cannot prove."

¶ If any one of us, as nowadays so many, goes travelling on through his years without the strength and inspiration of full Christian faith, through tardiness in making up his mind about religion because there is this and that difficulty, worrying perhaps for ever over a chapter in Genesis which will not square with geology (as why need it?), or stumbling at a Gospel incident of which the proof is only of the historical and not the geometric character, let him remember that John believed first, and realized belief afterwards, yet he found his belief was right and had not

THE VENTURE OF FAITH

misled him. There must in faith be a venture; there must be a spring of our nature as a whole to embrace the truth as a whole. Then we shall know in good time the parts which make the whole. But venture we must. Do not then let us go without the blessedness of faith because we are too cold-blooded to make the spring.[1]

¶ One result of this temperamental peculiarity was this, that during the winter of 1908–1909 there were numerous families huddled around Flaxman Island (where, as it turned out, the *Rosie H.* was wintering) with the idea that it was impossible for them to get caribou for food or for clothing, while we went inland to where every one said there was no game, and were able to live well. Our own small party that winter in northern Alaska killed more caribou than all the rest of the Eskimo of the country put together, because we had the faith to go and look for them where the Eskimo "knew" they no longer existed.[2]

2. How is this venture of faith related to reason? Is it reasonable to believe that there is but one God, that that God rules everywhere, and that He is good?

By "reason" is here meant, not the scientific intellect, but the rational nature of man. A thing which cannot be demonstrated may yet be reasonable. The existence of God can never be proved by a certain number of arguments; but faith in God can nevertheless be a reasonable faith. And only the faith which has the sanction of reason can be a true faith. The very ventures of faith are, as it were, directed by reason, and rooted in it.

¶ If all creation is one, my Ruler must be the Ruler of all. This is the faith that crosses the stretches of the unknown, and this is the faith whose roots are deep down in the rational nature of man. In the region of things observed a thousand things *seem* to question it; but it holds me, and I cannot get away from it.

> Yes, in the maddening maze of things,
>   When tossed by storm and flood,
> To one fixed trust my spirit clings;
>   I know that God is good.[3]

¶ Faith is the pioneer section of reason. It is reason without reasoning. But it does not fear reasoning. It invites it to follow, if reason recognizes that faith has its own legitimate place, and if

---

[1] J. H. Skrine, *The Heart's Counsel*, 65.
[2] V. Stefánsson, *My Life with the Eskimo*, 67.
[3] T. R. Williams, *Belief and Life*, 142.

the reasoning powers recognize that they must possess the ability to handle the problems with which they undertake to deal. For it is not brave to go into a current which is too much for one's strength; it may be a form of suicide.[1]

3. If action in general may be called a correspondence with an environment of facts which can be modified by the forces of our will, adventure is that kind of action in which we match ourselves against an environment of facts which are future and therefore unknowable; it is action upon *res adventura*, an operation upon fortune, an encounter with chance and change and danger. To match wit and nerve rightly against the force of uncertainty in human things is good adventuring. To miscalculate the odds and be destroyed or disgraced in consequence is bad adventuring; but also to decline the risks through overestimating the odds is bad. It is failure to wrap up the talent in a napkin for fear of losing it in trade; it is failure to cast oneself down, without warrant of angels, from the pinnacle. The blunderer who cannot come through, and the faint heart who fails even to begin, are ill adventurers both of them. Their response to the *res adventura* is an inadequate one.

¶ Great ventures generally succeed by narrow margins and fail by broad ones. The Prussian campaign was a great one; its successors were to be of even larger dimensions as to conception. When they were successful, it was by an even narrower chance; when disastrous, it was with frightful completeness.[2]

> Glory best is gained
> By daring means to end, ashamed of shame,
> Constant in faith that only good works good,
> While evil yields no fruit but impotence![3]

III.

RISK.

1. Every venture of faith involves the element of risk. Risk is everywhere where faith is concerned. And faith has to be

---
[1] J. D. Adam, *Religion and the Growing Mind*, 58.
[2] W. M. Sloane, *Napoleon Bonaparte: A History*, ii. 434.
[3] Browning, "Aristophanes' Apology."

THE VENTURE OF FAITH

exercised in our relation to everything. The man who will not exercise faith because there is a risk, will not venture anywhere, for there is no such thing in this world as absolute knowledge concerning anything.

In every age it has been the faith that risked that has moved mountains, cast out devils, and healed the nations. That is where faith finds its test and its triumphs; and, alas! that is where faith so often breaks down. We can trust God for receiving; we can trust even for sanctifying grace: but when it comes to risk! When obedience may mean loss of position, loss of money, loss of home, how many there are that shrink back! When faith involves risk of failure, the sorrow of reproach, and the sting of ridicule, what then?

¶ After Bunyan had been a preacher for five or six years, he was seized for pursuing this unlawful calling, and at the end of seven weeks' preliminary imprisonment, he was had up to Bedford, where it was charged, " That he, John Bunyan, labourer (for the Lord, they might have said), hath devilishly and maliciously abstained from coming to church to hear Divine service, and is a common upholder of several unlawful meetings and conventicles," etc. So they determined that against such a devilish and malicious man they would angelically and benevolently do what they might. Conventicles, indeed, instead of churches! Shame on you, John Bunyan, you can listen to the bell-ringing, cannot you, if there is nothing else you can hear at church to your liking. So Judge Keeling says, " Hear our judgment. You must be back to prison; lie there three months. Then if you don't come to church you shall be banished the country, and if you are not gone by the day appointed, or come back, plainly, you must stretch by the neck for it." To this Bunyan answered, " If I am out of prison to-day I shall preach again to-morrow." And as to hanging, he had his thoughts about that, sometimes comfortable, sometimes not. What if he should quake and faint? That was not pleasant to think of. But if he might convert only one soul by his last words, that would make some amends for hanging. But what of his own faith? " I'll leap off, blindfold," said he, " come heaven, come hell, sink or swim. Lord Jesus, if Thou wilt catch me, do; if not, I venture for Thy name." Bold words, yet humble; but he was not to climb up to heaven by way of the hangman's ladder. Sometimes in his solitude he had comfort, great comfort. Taken in the very act of saving sinners, and for no other crime, his Saviour was with him, and he rhymes his experience thus:

> The prison very sweet to me
> Hath been since I came here,
> And so would also hanging be
> If God will there appear.[1]

2. Faith that goes forward triumphs. Seas divide at its touch and mountains move at its word. It spreads tables in the wilderness and turns desert sands into springs of water. Under its influence the weak become strong and the timid lose their fear. It subdues kingdoms, works righteousness, obtains promises, stops the mouths of lions, quenches the power of fire, delivers from the edge of the sword, and turns weaklings into invincible warriors, who put to flight the armies of the alien. By it men sing in the night, worship in caves, and pray in prisons. Nothing can daunt them; nothing can overcome them; nothing can resist them. Exultant, jubilant, triumphant, the men of faith are the hosts of God. He is their Leader, their Captain, their Father, and their Lord.

¶ I toiled on from day to day, my heart almost sinking sometimes, with the sinking of the well, till we reached a depth of about thirty feet. And the phrase, "living water," "living water," kept chiming through my soul like music from God, as I dug and hammered away!

At this depth the earth and coral began to be soaked with damp. I felt that we were nearing water. My soul had a faith that God would open a spring for us; but side by side with this faith was a strange terror that the water would be salt. So perplexing and mixed are even the highest experiences of the soul; the rose-flower of a perfect faith, set round and round with prickly thorns. One evening I said to the old Chief—

"I think that Jehovah God will give us water to-morrow from that hole!"

The Chief said, "No, Missi; you will never see rain coming up from the earth on this island. We wonder what is to be the end of this mad work of yours. We expect daily, if you reach water, to see you drop through into the sea, and the sharks will eat you! That will be the end of it; death to you, and danger to us all."

I still answered, "Come to-morrow. I hope and believe that Jehovah God will send you the rain water up through the earth." At the moment I knew I was risking much, and probably incurring sorrowful consequences, had no water been given; but I had faith

---

[1] T. T. Lynch, *The Mornington Lecture*, 108.

that the Lord was leading me on, and I knew that I sought His glory, not my own.

Next morning, I went down again at daybreak and sank a narrow hole in the centre about two feet deep. The perspiration broke over me with uncontrollable excitement, and I trembled through every limb, when the water rushed up and began to fill the hole. Muddy though it was, I eagerly tasted it, and the little "tinny" dropped from my hand with sheer joy, and I almost fell upon my knees in that muddy bottom to praise the Lord. It was water! It was fresh water! It was living water from Jehovah's well! True, it was a little brackish, but nothing to speak of; and no spring in the desert, cooling the parched lips of a fevered pilgrim, ever appeared more worthy of being called a Well of God than did that water to me![1]

¶ I was glad to row in my College boat, but I declined the beer and port wine, which were at that time considered essential to training. "No," I said, "I will leave the boat, but I will not take drink!" I was strengthened by a firm assurance that I was obeying the commandment of God. Strange to say, five of the eight men followed my example. The Common-room butler, with the licence of an old servant, looked in at our meals and said derisively: "Toast and water! you'll be bumped—no boat can go up on toast and water!" It was that year that our boat rose from the bottom of the river and started on its career which at last put it at the head.[2]

¶ It is to the credit of the world that it has never been without those who readily follow the path of venture and loss. Again and again there are courageous chivalrous spirits who are quite ready to risk all in some high adventure if they may but attain their Ideal of Love. As Tennyson sings—

If I were loved, as I desire to be,
What is there in the great sphere of the earth,
And range of evil between death and birth,
That I should fear,—if I were loved by thee?
All the inner, all the outer world of pain
Clear Love would pierce and cleave, if thou wert mine,
As I have heard that, somewhere in the main,
Fresh-water springs come up through bitter brine.
'Twere joy, not fear, claspt hand-in-hand with thee,
To wait for death—mute—careless of all ills,
Apart upon a mountain.[3]

---

[1] *John G. Paton*, ii. 182. [2] R. F. Horton, *An Autobiography*, 165.
[3] G. H. S. Walpole, *Life's Chance*, 34.

IV.

WORTH.

What is the venture of faith worth?

1. *It gives reality to our hopes.*—Hope sees in its dreams the ladder reaching into heaven. Faith resolutely plants its feet upon the rungs, and takes the risk of their vanishing. Hope sees the horses and chariots of fire round about its Dothan. Faith, strong in these insubstantial defenders, faces the horses and chariots of the King of Syria. Hope believes that this life is not all. Faith takes the risk that Hope is dreaming, and resolves to act upon the assumption that "earth is but a pupil's place." Faith is, and must be, in the first instance, a leap in the dark. It is "the resolute choice to stand or fall by the noblest hypothesis." "To stand or fall"—faith's act always contains this alternative, "to stand or fall." You must say to Christ, "If I perish, I perish on Thy shoulder; if I sink, I sink in Thy vessel; if I die, I die at Thy door"; and you need not think that you are not ready to come to Christ because of your "ifs." Faith is—taking the risk, venturing all on your hopes, going forward in confident assurance that your hopes of the Unseen are true.

¶ At the end of the Kingswood dining-hall there used to be a narrow ledge, nearly five feet from the ground. I have sometimes put a little friend of ours there and asked her to jump down. Then I have watched her, and seen how hope and fear did battle within her eyes—hope of the wild rush through the air and the love that waited at the end, and fear of the yawning gulf below, fear that found words in "Daddy, I shall fall." Then Faith took its great resolve to act as if Hope were truth, there was a sudden avalanche of golden hair, and the little one was safe in her father's arms. There are those here that are even as that child. They stand irresolute before the grand adventure of Faith. They would like to take the leap if they were certain that they would reach the Father's arms; but—but—are there not those who say that the Father is dead, or, at least, that He careth not? They are tired and would fain be at rest; but is there rest anywhere to be found for the sole of their feet? To such I say, "Act as if your hopes were facts, and you shall prove them such. Act as if God were, and you shall see Him as He is."[1]

[1] W. P. Workman. *Kingswood Sermons*. 195.

THE VENTURE OF FAITH

2. *It changes doubt into certainty.*—When we hear that God loves us, and would have us love Him; when we hear that we cannot love the Father whom we have not seen unless we love the brother whom we have seen; when we hear that because He lives we will live also, or that we can be free only as we obey His law, and rule only as we serve, and gain the best things only by loss of things inferior; when we hear that He will render to every man the due recompense of his deeds, and that we ought to live therefore as those who must give account to Him: when, in short, we hear any distinctively Christian or spiritual truth, there is that in us which recognizes its truth and responds to it. We are aware that it is that which is best and highest in us that leaps up to greet it and bear witness to it, to assure us that by grasping these truths we will be laying hold of the most noble and precious realities.

But, while that which is spiritual in us moves toward them and incites us to trust in them, flesh and blood bear the other way. These remind us of how much, and how much that is pleasant and dear to them, we will have to give up if we commit ourselves to the truth and suffer it to mould our life. Possibly these unspiritual powers suborn reason itself, and turn it against us. Reason whispers: "But where is the proof that these things are true? Ask for proof; wait for proof. Do not be in haste. These may be realities; they may be, as you assume, the supreme and only realities. But they are very mysterious, and even a little questionable. Do not commit yourself to them till you can see them more clearly, and see too how to reconcile them with each other and with the common and received opinions of men." And, as we listen, we pause and stand in doubt.

Now that moment is one of the critical moments in our life, one of the moments in which it has to be determined whether we will follow the promptings of the Divine Spirit within our soul, which moves us to risk all for duty, for righteousness, for love, for God; or whether we will at least defer the decision and so make it less likely that we will ever reach it. If we make the venture, if we follow the impulse of that which is deepest and best in us, if we resolve that we will no longer confer with flesh and blood, but yield ourselves to the Spirit that stirs and speaks within us, we emerge from the cold atmosphere of doubt in which all miracles —and above all the great miracle of a radical moral change—are impossible, and rise into that native and genial realm of the spirit in which all things become possible, and all that is spiritual in us ripens and unfolds. The eternal truths which we have seen by faith become ours. We are saved from the thraldom of sense and of the sensible world. We pass out beyond the shows of time to find a higher life in the kingdom of righteousness and joy and peace.

3. *It is the condition of vision.*—Now, "where no vision is the people perish." The most powerful advocate of this fact in modern times, perhaps in all time, is William Blake; and he himself is the best example of the connexion between faith and vision. His latest interpreter uses the word "imagination," but Blake himself would have used "faith" or "wonder." Speaking of Blake's Real Man, Charles Gardner says: "His imagination is vision. Imagination is Eternal. Through imagination he feasts at Messiah's table, drinking the wine of Eternity. Through imagination he enters the great communion of Saints, and with piercing vision detects brothers and sisters among the fallen and outcast. He has passed through the valley of the shadow of Death, and henceforth starts at no shadows, and neither tastes nor sees Death."[1]

> There was a guide
> Invisible, went ever at my side.
> He said, "Poor timid thing, that cannot dare
>   To risk the upper air,
>   The hard ascent
> And stony summits, but would ever go
> Just high enough for beauty and too low
> For desolation, you shall never know,
>   Thus sheltered by the ring
> Of noble dreams and mounting thoughts, the sting
> Of truth, the wide horizons of the real.
>   Turn from the fair,
> Climb, strive, slip, fall upon the pent
>   Of his steep home,
>   Until you come,
>   Breathless and spent,
> To the bare summits that his world reveal."[2]

---

[1] C. Gardner, *Vision and Vesture*, 99.
[2] Evelyn Underhill, *Theophanies*, 59.

VII.

Faith in Jesus.

LITERATURE.

Abbott, E. A., *Johannine Vocabulary* (1905).
Alexander, A. B. D., *Christianity and Ethics* (1914).
Barry, A., *Sermons Preached at Westminster Abbey* (1884).
　„　„ *Do We Believe?* (1908).
Beeching, H. C., *The Apostles' Creed* (1905).
Cairns, D. S., *Christianity in the Modern World* (1906).
Carnegie, W. H., *Democracy and Christian Doctrine* (1914).
Cox, S., *Expositions*, i. (1885).
D'Arcy, C. F., *God and Freedom in Human Experience* (1915).
Davidson, A. B., *Waiting upon God* (1904).
Drummond, R. J., *Faith's Certainties* (1909).
Elmslie, W. A. L., *Studies in Life from Jewish Proverbs* (1917).
Gamble, J., *Christian Faith and Worship* (1912).
Garvie, A. E., *The Master's Comfort and Hope* (1917).
Grist, W. A., *The Historic Christ in the Faith of To-day*.
Herrmann, W., *Faith and Morals* (1904).
Holland, H. S., in *The Faith of Centuries* (1897).
Hughes, H., *Religious Faith* (1896).
Law, R., *The Emotions of Jesus* (1915).
Macgregor, W. M., *Repentance unto Life* (1918).
McIntyre, D. M., *Life in His Name* (1909).
Mackintosh, H. R., *The Doctrine of the Person of Jesus Christ* (1912).
Maclaren, A., *The Holy of Holies* (1890).
　„　„ *The Victor's Crowns*.
Maurice, F. D., *The Epistles of St. John* (1893).
Mozley, J. K., *Ritschlianism* (1909).
Orchard, W. E., *The New Catholicism* (1917).
Robson, G. B., *The Way to Personality* (1916).
Seeberg, R., *The Fundamental Truths of the Christian Religion* (1908).
Selwyn, E. G., *The Teaching of Christ* (1915).
Simpson, P. C., *The Fact of Christ* (1900).
Stalker, J., *The Ethic of Jesus* (1909).
Swete, H. B., *Faith* (1895).
Vaughan, R., *Stones from the Quarry* (1890).
Westcott, B. F., *Peterborough Sermons* (1904).
Williams, C. D., *A Valid Christianity for To-day* (1909).
Williams, T. D., *Belief and Life* (1898).
Expositor, 6th Ser., v. (1902) 287 (G. G. Findlay).
Harvard Theological Review, ii. (1909) 354 (C. H. Hayes).
London Quarterly Review, April 1907, p. 193 (G. G. Findlay).

FAITH IN JESUS.

CHRISTIAN faith is faith in Jesus. We often forget that that name was common, wholly undistinguished, and borne by very many of our Lord's contemporaries. It had been borne by the great soldier whom we know as Joshua; and we know that it was the name of one at least of the disciples of our Master. Its disuse after Him, both by Jew and by Christian, is easily intelligible. But though He bore it with special reference to His work of saving His people from their sins, He shared it, as He shared manhood, with many another of the sons of Abraham. Of course "Jesus" is the name that is usually employed in the Gospels. But when we turn to the Epistles, we find that it is comparatively rare for it to stand alone, and that in almost all the instances of its employment by itself, it brings with it the special note of pointing attention to the manhood of our Lord Jesus.

Who does not feel, for example, that when we read "let us run, with patience the race that is set before us, looking unto Jesus the author and finisher of faith," the fact of our brother Man having trodden the same path, and being the pattern for our patience and perseverance, is tenderly laid upon our hearts? Again, when we read of sympathy as being felt for us by the great High Priest who can be "touched with a feeling of our infirmities, even Jesus," we cannot but recognize that His humanity is pressed upon our thoughts, as securing to us that we have not only the pity of a God, but the compassion of a Man, who knows by experience the bitterness of our sorrows.

In like manner we read sometimes that "*Jesus* died for us," sometimes that "*Christ* died for us"; and, though the two forms of the statement present the same fact, they present it, so to speak, from a different angle of vision, and suggest to us different thoughts.

When Paul, for example, says to us, "If we believe that *Jesus* died and rose again," we cannot but feel that he is pressing on us the thought of the true manhood of that Saviour who, in His death, as in His resurrection, is the Forerunner of them that believe upon Him, and whose death will be the more peaceful, and their rising the more certain, because He, who, "forasmuch as the children are partakers of flesh and blood, likewise took part of the same," has thereby destroyed death, and delivered them from its bondage. Nor with less emphasis and strengthening triumphant force do we read that this same *Jesus*, the Man who bore our nature in its fulness and is kindred to us in flesh and spirit, has risen from the dead, has ascended up on high, and is the Forerunner, who for us, by virtue of His humanity, has entered in thither. Surely the most insensitive ear must catch the music, and the deep significance of the word which says, "We see not yet all things put under him (*i.e.* man). But we see *Jesus* crowned with glory and honour."

So, then, Christian faith first lays hold of that manhood, realizes the suffering and death as those of a true humanity, recognizes that He bore in His nature "all the ills that flesh is heir to," and that His human life is a brother's pattern for ours; that, He having died, death hath no more terrors for, or dominion over, us; and that whither the Man Jesus has gone we sinful men need never fear to enter, or doubt that we shall enter too.

1. When Jesus was on earth He demanded faith in Himself as the condition of receiving blessing from Him. Not only did He demand it, He depended upon it. Even His power of physical healing was limited in this way. He could exercise this power only in proportion to the measure of the faith of the sufferers. In the accounts of miracles of this kind we find the question, "Hast thou faith to be healed?" often asked and generally implied. "According to thy faith be it unto thee," "Thy faith hath saved thee," were words with which He accompanied His acts of healing; while with regard to the inhabitants of one district we are told expressly that "he could do no mighty works there because of their unbelief." We find the same principle asserting itself in an accentuated form when we rise from the level of physical miracles, and consider His method of meeting man's spiritual needs. Here

again we find Him insisting that only those endowed with special qualifications are capable of receiving His teaching, and making it clear that comparatively few were thus endowed in the degree which He required.

2. This fact, which is so strange at first, is understood the moment we see what faith is. God Himself cannot give us what we are unable to receive. We have only to consider that, for the reception of any spiritual gift or power, a hand to take is as necessary as a hand to bestow; that it is inconsistent with the goodness of God or the freedom of man that the gates of the soul should be forced open from without instead of being thrown open from within; and that even the purest light, though it bring health and healing on its wings, cannot be seen until men open their eyes on it. Faith is the eye of the soul. Faith is the hand of the soul. Is there then anything arbitrary or unreasonable in the invariable and imperative demand for faith? Is it not, rather, inevitable that faith should be the constant condition on which both the reception and the exercise of any spiritual power or grace are made to depend? Once admit that faith is the eye by which we discern and the hand by which we grasp the realities of the invisible and spiritual world, and the demand for faith becomes wholly reasonable to us, because it is grounded in the very constitution of our nature. With that admission once made, it would be as rational to complain that we can enter into the ideal world of poetry and art only by an effort of the imagination, as to complain that we can rise into the spiritual realm and possess ourselves of its wealth only by the ventures and endeavour of a living and active faith.

¶ We find that Christ always gave way to men; He receded or advanced according to the temper they showed. He did not cry, nor lift up, nor use compulsion, but invariably gave place before men's free will.[1]

3. Following the Baptist, Jesus set out with the summons, "Repent, and believe the good news," namely, that "the kingdom of God is at hand"; like Moses, He summoned Israel to accept His mission as from God, and showed "signs" to prove this. As His teaching advanced, it appeared that He required an unparalleled

[1] A. B. Davidson, *Waiting upon God*, 176.

faith in *Himself* along with His message, that the Kingdom of God He speaks of centres in His person; that, in fact, *He is* "the word" of God that He brings, *He is* the light and life whose coming He announces, "the bread from heaven" that He has to give to a famished world. For those "who received him," who "believed on his name," faith acquired a scope undreamed of before; it signified the unique attachment which gathered round the person of Jesus—a human trust, in its purity and intensity such as no other man ever awakened, which grew into and identified itself with its possessor's belief in God, transforming the latter in doing so, and which drew the whole being of the believer into the life and will of his Master. When Thomas hails Jesus as "My Lord, and my God!" he "*has believed.*" This process is complete in the mind of the slowest disciple. The two faiths, in God and in Jesus, are now welded inseparably; the Son is known through the Father, and the Father through the Son; and Thomas gives affiance to both in one. As Jesus was step by step exalted towards the Divine, in the same degree God came nearer to these men, and their faith in God became richer in content and firmer in grasp.

If the progress of the disciples towards complete faith in Jesus was gradual, they came in due course to the great conviction that He was the Son of God. The stages of this progress are indicated by the various confessions of faith to which the disciples gave utterance. When Andrew first met with Jesus, he confessed his belief that He would prove to be the Messiah for whom men were hoping. Later, Peter said in the name of the twelve, "We have believed and know that thou art the Holy One of God." After the feeding of the five thousand, and the appearance of the Lord walking upon the sea, the disciples in the boat worshipped Him, saying, "Of a truth thou art the Son of God." And finally, after months of living and working with Him, the conviction to which they had come was voiced in the great confession of faith, spoken by Peter, "Thou art the Christ, the Son of the living God." During these months their knowledge of Him had been deepened and their love for Him strengthened, as His personality exerted its ever-increasing influence upon their minds and hearts, until finally there resulted this climax of faith and this solemn assertion of their full belief in Him as their personal Lord Christ. Thus

FAITH IN JESUS

they began with facts, and their gradual, perhaps unconscious, induction from what they observed led naturally to the most intense spiritual faith.

We find faith in Jesus as it is disclosed in the Gospels to be a Recognition, an Energy, and a Relationship.

I.

A Recognition.

Faith in Jesus is the recognition of His Messiahship, of His power, and of His love.

1. *Faith is the recognition of Jesus as the Messiah.*—The earliest Christian confession, the simplest and sufficient creed, was, Jesus is the Christ. What do we mean by that? We mean, first and plainly, that He is the realization of the dim figure which arose, majestic and enigmatical, through the mists of a partial revelation. We mean that He is, as the word signifies etymologically, "anointed" with the Divine Spirit, for the discharge of all the offices which, in old days, were filled by men who were fitted and designated for them by outward unction—prophet, priest, and king. We mean that He is the substance of which ancient ritual was the shadow. We mean that He is the goal to which all that former partial unveiling of the mind and will of God steadfastly pointed. This, and nothing less, is the meaning of the declaration that Jesus is the Christ; and that belief is the distinguishing mark of the faith which this Hebrew of the Hebrews, writing to Hebrews, declares to be the Christian faith.

¶ I believe that *Jesus* is the Christ. That is to say, I believe that there is a living bond between me, the poor, helpless human creature, and the absolute perfect Being. I believe that His Love has come near to me in a human person, whom I may claim as the brother of me and my race. I believe that Person is the Son of God; that in Him dwelt the fulness of the Godhead bodily. I believe, therefore, that I am related to that Love which created the world, and all that is in it. I may claim affiance in it. Again, I believe that Jesus is the *Christ*. I believe that He is anointed with the Spirit of God to the end that He may bestow that Spirit upon men. I believe that the Spirit in Him was a uniting Spirit, a self-sacrificing Spirit, a Spirit of active, suffering, sympathising Love. I believe that that Spirit is acting upon us, and can work in us the love which is most foreign to our selfishness.[1]

2. *Faith in Jesus is the recognition of His power.*—He elicited by degrees a growing confidence in His power. "Why are ye fearful?" He said to them in the storm on the Sea of Galilee; "have ye not yet faith?"—*i.e.* have you not yet learned confidence in Me? And to St. Peter He said, "O thou of little faith! wherefore didst thou doubt?"—*i.e.* doubt My power to protect you. The words of the leper are: "If thou wilt, thou canst." And the centurion's words are like these: "My servant lieth at home sick of the palsy: speak the word only, and he shall be healed." This was true faith; the conviction, not that Christ certainly would, but that, if He would, at least He could. And that is true faith still. The comfortable assurance, "He has willed to heal me," is one of God's good gifts to those whom He has first healed; but the preliminary condition is only this, "I believe that, if He will, He can."

Faith in Jesus' power is usually faith in His power to work miracles. "This beginning of miracles did Jesus in Cana of Galilee, and manifested forth his glory; and his disciples believed on him" (John ii. 11). Hitherto the disciples of Jesus had followed Him chiefly because of the testimony of John the Baptist. Now, however, they saw that in their new Master which awakened a fresh feeling towards Him. They beheld the miracle, and in or through it they caught a glimpse of the glory of the Lord. They had believed, on the testimony of the Baptist, that He was the Messiah; now they see something of Him which creates faith in Him. "His disciples believed on him."

But it is not said that those who before were unbelieving were overpowered by what they saw and forced into faith; it is said only that those who had already followed Christ cast themselves, so to speak, upon Him with an absolute trust when they recognized the working of His Divine power. The outward event might be disregarded or explained away or cavilled at; the inner meaning was discernible only by the spiritual eye.

[1] F. D. Maurice, *The Epistles of St. John*, 255.

The truth is, that faith does not depend on signs; nor is it in the last resort a matter of argument or philosophic reflection, but a property of the soul itself. The sense of God belongs to us. And even when we have been expecting signs, and cannot see them, we pray to a God above the clouds, whose face is light and whose favour is life. Like the man in the Gospels we say, " I believe; help thou mine unbelief." We may doubt all the arguments for God's existence, declare this unsatisfactory and that untenable, and when every argument fails we find we believe in God still. We feel and know that He is here. "Eternal Father, strong to save," Thy child lives in Thee.

¶ He who believes feels himself surrounded by wonders—faith is always faith in the marvellous—for he feels the nearness of the all-ruling Lord and thereby sees the inflexible things of this world become pliant means in the hand of his God.[1]

3. *Faith in Jesus is the recognition of His love.*—The foundations of faith are not yet laid simply by the fact that the historical appearance of Jesus affects us. There must be added the fact that the same Man who becomes judge and conscience to the person who comes face to face with Him interests Himself in him with a patient and unparalleled love. At the same time that He makes the sinner insecure by the simple power of His personal life He sets him on his feet by His kindness. Therefore those who have been led by Him to feel the bitterness of their plight, yet feel themselves for that very reason drawn to Him. It was thus that He once forgave sinners. He before whose eyes is unfolded the vast misery of mankind, their profound lovelessness and their weakness of will, has yet the calm trust that He can snatch them from the hell which in their own souls they have prepared for themselves, whether for the present or for the future.

The contrast between the faith of wonder and the faith of love is at the same time both touching and teaching. While Jesus was going about doing good, there came to Him a woman, wearied with sin, worn with sorrow. She had shut herself out from human sympathy. There was no whisper left to comfort her, no balm remaining to heal her. Mighty works were reported

---

[1] R. Seeberg, *The Fundamental Truths of the Christian Religion*, 83.

of this Jesus of Nazareth; and multitudes ran after the fame of Him. But she, poor soul, had no heart for wonder. She had worn out and palled each successive excitement. She had no eyes to gaze, for they were hot and dim with weeping. But she had stood with the crowd and had listened, and the dew of gentle words had gathered over the dearth of her heart. From out of the depths of that heart came the yearnings of mighty love. The piercing taunts of the multitude without, the freezing gaze of the assembled Pharisees, were to her as nothing. Full of earnest purpose, she passed by them all; she pressed into the beloved Presence; she bathed the sacred Feet with her tears, she wiped them with her hair; she earned for herself the precious testimony —precious for her, precious for all time—" Her sins, which are many, are forgiven; for she loved much."

¶ There is, in one of the letters of Emily Lawless, a passage which sums up her whole creed—her faith in Christ and in Love and in their power of inspiration:

It has grown upon me more and more to feel that though belief, in the doctrinal sense of the word, becomes yearly more impossible, more obviously human in *all* its innumerable manifestations, on the other hand Love—a clinging to something outside ourselves and not liable to accidents—becomes yearly *more* possible, and seems to me to be the one supreme truth that will some day emerge clearly above all the fog and the jar and tangle of disputing creeds. I do not know what I should do if I had the sole directing of a young ardent nature in such matters, but I feel that what I should do would be to try and get that capacity for love developed, and then let everything else take its chance.

At the lowest the Being that she had learnt to love would be the noblest and tenderest in all history, and as for miracles, the miracle of His turning the bitter waters sweet, and pulling wrecked lives straight, and that not by ones and twos, but by millions upon millions, is quite miracle enough for me. Of course the *advocatus diaboli* will whisper that one is adoring a myth, but one must just *let* him whisper, and once the root of love is well grounded I do not think such whispers matter. The heart is a far more tenacious organ than the head, and not nearly so much at the mercy of those loud winds of Doubt.[1]

[1] Edith Sichel, *New and Old*, 172.

II.

AN ENERGY.

Faith in Jesus is an energy. It requires the effort of spiritual insight and the surrender of personal trust.

1. *Spiritual insight.* — We have seen how faith in Jesus apprehends His majesty and power, and we have seen how it apprehends His love; let us now see how it calls upon spiritual thought and purpose. "The disciples came to the other side and forgot to take bread. And Jesus said unto them, Take heed and beware of the leaven of the Pharisees and Sadducees. And they reasoned among themselves, saying, We took no bread. And Jesus perceiving it said, O ye of little faith, why reason ye among yourselves, because ye have no bread? Do ye not yet perceive, neither remember the five loaves of the five thousand, and how many baskets ye took up? How is it that ye do not perceive that I spake not to you concerning bread? But beware of the leaven of the Pharisees and Sadducees. Then understood they how that he bade them not beware of the leaven of bread, but of the teaching of the Pharisees and Sadducees" (Matt. xvi. 5–12). Only a short time previously Jesus had been engaged in a painful interview with some of the Pharisees and Sadducees, on which interview, and on His general work and spiritual teaching, they might, had they been possessed of more sympathetic insight, have judged that His thoughts were now dwelling, rather than on their omission to provide bread; more especially as this was an omission which they might know it was fully within His power to supply in case of need. But they, being concerned chiefly about things of sense, and having little perception of the spiritual thought of Jesus, attached a carnal signification to the word "leaven," and so were reproached by Him for the smallness of their faith.

Such faith is the result not of sight, but of insight; and insight is faith. "Touch me not," said the risen Christ to the eager Mary. Why? asks St. Bernard. And his answer is: to teach her, and through her all Christ's followers, that in matters of religion, in things of the spirit, it is not on the evidence of the senses they must rest, but on faith, which reads the deeper evidence, goes straight to the inmost soul, penetrates to the inherent congruity of things, and believes because it has met the truth, and can do no other.

> Oh, I am tired out to-day:
> The whole world leans against my door:
> Cities and centuries. I pray,—
> For praying makes me brave once more.
>
> —I should have lived long, long ago,
> Before this age of steel and fire.
> I am not strong enough to throw
> A noose around my soul's desire
> And strangle it, because it cries
> To keep its old, unreasoned place
> In some bright simple Paradise,
> Before a God's too-human face.
>
> I know that in this breathless fray
> I am not fit to fight and cry.
> My soul grows faint and far away
> From blood and shouting, till I fly
> A blinded coward, back, to hide
> My face against the dim old knees
> Of that too-human God, denied
> By these quick crashing centuries.
>
> And there I learn deep secret things:
> Too frail for speech, too strong for doubt:
> How through the dark of demon-wings
> The same still face of God gleams out;
> How through the deadly riotous roar
> The voice of God speaks on. And then
> I trust Him, as one might before
> Faith grew too fond to comfort men.
>
> —I should have lived far, far away
> From this great age of grime and gold:
> For still, I know He hears me pray,—
> That close, too-human God of old![1]

2. *Personal trust.*—It was not in the first instance to a belief in any doctrine of His Person that our Lord called His followers.

[1] Fannie S. Davis, *Myself and I*, 62.

FAITH IN JESUS

He seemed deliberately to avoid statements about Himself; He did not even announce Himself as the Christ; He silenced the evil spirits who recognized Him. He imposed no form of belief upon those who came to Him: His one demand was personal submission, unbounded confidence in the Master, readiness to follow His leading under all circumstances. This was what He meant by "faith," and on this purely personal trust He made all to depend. The apostles carried on this teaching. To believe on the Lord Jesus Christ was the condition of salvation which they constantly offered. They held up before the world not a philosophy or a system of doctrines, but a living Person, upon whom they endeavoured to fix the attention, and for whom they claimed the absolute loyalty, of men.

Upon an attitude of reliance He laid the utmost stress. Now by precept, now by parable, now by the discipline of circumstance, He commended that attitude to His followers as all-pleasing to Himself and all-helpful to their highest good. There was nothing which more delighted Him than to see that attitude taken by the human hearts that turned to Him for the succour of His power, for the bliss and rest of His lovingkindness. If ever anything like an abnormal exercise of faith was visible to His gracious eyes He met it not only with complacency but with a *wondering* pleasure, unspeakably moving as we see it in Him. Whatever the reason, such was the fact; to the Lord Jesus there was in the faith of a human suppliant something which He met with a vivid pleasure and to which His response, at once or after a brief discipline of delay, was always generously large.

¶ In the early years of the Carrubber's Close Mission, a lady came over from Hamburg for the express purpose of attending its meetings. She was engaged to be married to a Swiss missionary, but in the great revival of 1859-60 she discovered that she was no true Christian, and feared that she would only be a hindrance instead of a help to her future husband in his work.

Having heard in Hamburg of the blessing in Edinburgh she resolved to cross over to the latter city in the hope that she too might be blessed.

One of our workers spoke with her night after night, but apparently without any result. One evening on leaving the mission premises it occurred to him to conduct her to her hotel in Princes Street by another and a shorter road. This shorter road led from the foot of Carrubber's Close, the scene of the mission's earlier premises, which were then housed in the old Whitfield Chapel, by a narrow low arched passage, not too well lighted, underneath the North Bridge, and then on to Princes Street. Just as they were underneath the old chapel windows he paused and remarked to her, "Now you have come with me this strange road. You have trusted yourself to me, an entire stranger, in the faith that I shall take you to your hotel. Could you not trust your soul to Jesus?"

"Oh, is that it?" she answered; "if I had a thousand souls, I could trust them all to Jesus." And then she added, "I might have known this at Hamburg." She returned home full of the joy of the Lord.[1]

> I have a life with CHRIST to live,
>   But, ere I live it, must I wait
> Till learning can clear answer give
>   Of this and that book's date?
>
> I have a life in CHRIST to live,
>   I have a death in CHRIST to die;—
> And must I wait, till science give
>   All doubts a full reply?
>
> Nay rather, while the sea of doubt
> Is raging wildly round about,
> Questioning of life and death and sin,
>   Let me but creep within
> Thy fold, O CHRIST, and at Thy feet
>   Take but the lowest seat,
> And hear Thine awful voice repeat
> In gentlest accents, heavenly sweet,
>   Come unto Me, and rest:
>   Believe Me, and be blest.[2]

III.

A RELATIONSHIP.

The relationship is between Jesus and the Father. We notice (1) that faith in Jesus presupposes faith in God; (2) that faith in

---

[1] *William Robertson of the Carrubber's Close Mission*, 128.
[2] J. C. Shairp.

FAITH IN JESUS

God leads to faith in Jesus; (3) that on the other hand faith in Jesus leads to faith in God; (4) that faith in Jesus is faith in Jesus as standing for God; and (5) that faith in Jesus *is* faith in God.

1. *Faith in Jesus presupposes faith in God.* — So Jesus Himself seems to say: "Ye believe in God, believe also in me" (John xiv. 1). The disciples had begun with belief in God. As pious and patriotic Jews they trusted, worshipped, and served Jehovah as the covenant-God of their nation. They accepted, and expected the fulfilment of, the promise of God regarding the Messiah. Even although the fulfilment had not, according to their expectations, corresponded with the promises, yet they had been led by the teaching and influence of Jesus to confess Him as Messiah. Their faith in God had brought them to faith in Him. He had taught them to regard His death as a necessity of the purpose of God; now let them exercise their faith in God in continuing to believe all that He taught them about the will of God regarding Himself. As they had trusted Him as the Messiah sent of God, let them continue their trust even when it was being put to the test of His separation from them. Let them not now abandon their faith in Him, for to that faith they had been led by their faith in God.

Manifestly, every one must believe in God before he can believe in Jesus Christ in any deep sense; for to say that "Jesus is the Son of God" already implies a belief in God. This was clearly true of the Christian converts from among the Jews, who were already worshippers of Jehovah; and it was true also, though to a less extent, of the Greeks, as St. Paul recognized in his famous speech at Athens; and it remains true of the converts from heathendom to-day. In the mind of all men there is some recognition of a Creator Spirit, with whom they are led to identify the Spirit of Jesus. And so the progress of belief is logically from the first article to the second, from belief in God the Father and Creator to belief in Him whom the Father sent. At the same time, the belief in Jesus at once reacts upon the belief in God. The heathen convert, though he may employ the same word for God as before, has very different thoughts about Him; he is taught to believe that the holiness and lovingkindness of Jesus are the holiness and lovingkindness of the Creator God; and even the pious Jew gained a new insight into what these great qualities meant— the mercy and truth which he had always held to be the attributes of Jehovah. The two beliefs therefore go together. I learn to believe, first, in God the Father, who has made me, and all the world; secondly, in God the Son, who has redeemed me, and all mankind.

2. *Faith in God leads to faith in Jesus.*—Listen again to Jesus Himself. On one occasion He spoke to a body of Jews as follows: "If God were your Father, ye would love me: for I came forth and am come from God; for neither have I come of myself, but he sent me. Why do ye not understand my speech? Even because ye cannot hear my word. Ye are of your father the devil, and the lusts of your father it is your will to do. He was a murderer from the beginning, and stood not in the truth, because there is no truth in him. When he speaketh a lie, he speaketh of his own: for he is a liar, and the father thereof. But because I say the truth, ye believe me not. Which of you convicteth me of sin? If I say truth, why do ye not believe me? He that is of God heareth the words of God: for this cause ye hear them not, because ye are not of God" (John viii. 42–47).

There our Lord clearly implies that if the Jews had truly believed in God they would have believed in Himself as soon as He appeared before them. So throughout the apostolic writings those who have real faith in God give evidence of this faith by accepting His revelation of Himself in Christ when it is brought before them. They believe it and they act upon it, and so are numbered among those who have justifying faith in Christ.

Moreover, the belief in Jesus to which one is led from belief in God is a real trust and surrender of heart—just what faith in God is. It is a very low and inadequate interpretation of the words "Ye believe in God, believe also in me," to take them as meaning little more than "Believe in God, believe that He is; believe in Me, believe that I am." But it is scarcely less so to suppose that the mere assent of the understanding to His teaching is all that Christ asks for. By no means; what He invites us to goes a great deal deeper than that. The essence of it is an act of the will and of the heart, not of the understanding at all. A man may believe in Him as an historical person, may accept all that is said about

Him here, and yet not be within sight of the trust in Him which He here speaks of. For the essence of the whole is not the intellectual process of assent to a proposition, but the intensely personal act of yielding up will and heart to a living person. Faith does not grasp a doctrine but a heart. The trust which Christ requires is the bond that unites souls with Him; and the very life of it is entire committal of myself to Him in all my relations and for all my needs, and absolute utter confidence in Him as all-sufficient for everything that I can require. Let us get away from the cold intellectualism of "belief" into the warm atmosphere of "trust," and we shall understand better than by many volumes what are the meaning and the sphere and the power and the blessedness of that faith which Christ requires.

3. *Faith in Jesus leads to faith in God.*—We have seen that our Lord's disciples began with faith in God, and that because they had faith in God they came to have faith in Him. Did this continue to be the order of their faith? Or had Jesus Himself become more surely and fully the object of their faith than God Himself? Had the acquired relation become a more potent influence than the inherited? Was it now easier for them to trust Jesus than God Himself? Had He made God more real, attractive, and authoritative for them than He had been before? If so, then the argument implied in Jesus' call would be this: God's purpose for Me may seem mysterious for you. You may not be able to understand why I should suffer and die; but do not doubt or distrust God, for I do not doubt or distrust. If you still trust Me, trust the God I trust. If you still believe Me the Messiah, believe that even in death God is fulfilling His purpose in the Messiah. This is the more probable view, for Jesus offers Himself to His disciples as the true and living Way to the Father, and affirms that God is seen in Him. He assumes, accordingly, that the teaching and the training of His disciples have not been in vain, but that they have such a faith in Him as can be made the basis of their faith in God as, in spite of all present contrary appearances, ordering all things well for Him. He requires them to trust God's providence even when that involves, as He has Himself taught them, betrayal by one disciple, denial by another, and His separation from them all.

This is the way with the apostles in their writings. One of the first efforts at definition of a Christian is that implied in St. Peter's words: "Ye who through him do believe in God." The faith conveyed by Jesus is no mere abstract truth separable from Himself, as the truth of the law of gravitation is separable from Newton. We are able to understand and use the laws of nature while totally ignorant of those to whose research and genius our knowledge of them is due, but the highest and purest faith in God can be attained in no way but one; it comes through a believing response to the person of Jesus Christ. It is what we see in Jesus that inspires a triumphant certainty of God. All great saints in the past, all who at this hour enjoy the peace of reconciliation and are labouring with buoyant energy at the tasks of the Divine Kingdom, are evidences and illustrations of this. The apostle's two-edged word is only a transcript of experience: "Whosoever denieth the Son, the same hath not the Father: he that confesseth the Son hath the Father also." Apart from Jesus men may know much of God—of His wisdom, His power, His sublimity, even His benevolence; but of His Fatherhood, with all the loving-kindness to the sinful embraced in that great name, they can know nothing.

There can be no doubt as to what is the order of faith for most men to-day. There may be some thinkers who are led to Christianity by way of theism; but most men whose faith is not an inheritance, but an achievement, have come to God because they were first drawn to Christ. Not a few men to-day must begin with the Synoptic Gospels and the human Jesus. As a man studies, meditates on, becomes absorbed in, and comes under the influence of, this literary testimony, the historical reality of Jesus as truest Teacher, best Example, most loving Friend, lays hold of him. As he companions with Jesus, he discovers not only more of His truth and grace, but also more about himself, his sinfulness, weakness, and unworthiness. Slowly yet surely he comes to feel that he needs, and that Jesus is, more than Teacher, Example, Friend; and only one word can express what that is, even Saviour. As Saviour, who leads him not only to self-discovery, but even to self-recovery, He as Lord claims the life that He has saved. But in this contact with Jesus there is an immediate and intimate contact with God. It is God's truth that He teaches, God's grace that He imparts, God's forgiveness that He pronounces. As He lives, moves, and has His being in God as Father, the man who trusts and yields himself to Him as Saviour and Lord finds, and cannot but find, God's Fatherhood for himself in Him. When the believer in Jesus realizes what forgiveness means for himself and what it must mean for God, it is likely that he will begin to see a meaning in the Cross of Jesus which he never saw before. As he continues to live the Christian life, and the Saviour and the Lord comes more near, and becomes more dear to him, the historical reality becomes a spiritual presence, for his dealings in his soul's salvation are not with the dead but with the living; and thus the Resurrection becomes credible. It is true that there is endless variety in Christian experience, and not every man's path to God through Christ will in all details correspond with that which has just been sketched: but more or less the experience described is typical; and it is in some such wise that faith in Jesus leads to faith in God.

¶ There are many things in our records I cannot understand. But one thing for me is certain, whenever I contemplate Him, and especially when I contemplate His cross, I am made conscious within of what to me is God. This is experience; theories can wait. The fact that I believe this all came through a life truly human and natural gives me a different sense of what "human" and "natural" really mean. I have a strong conviction that Jesus would have this effect upon all others if we could let them see Him. I do not want a theory to explain Jesus. I agree rather with the apostolic theology, that He is the clue to myself and the universe and God. If Jesus is not this, that is, if He is not primarily a Gospel, all other discussion is wasted. It is the practical value of Jesus that we want to recover—that would be true theologizing.[1]

4. *Faith in Jesus signifies that Jesus stands for God.*—It is plain in the Gospels that the belief of those who approached Jesus with any degree of faith was, that He stood before them as in some very special sense a Representative of God; that the attributes and purposes of God were in some very special way made manifest in Him. This at least they were persuaded of before they learned from His own lips the most exact truth

[1] W. E. Orchard, *Problems and Perplexities*, 59.

concerning His Nature and His Mission; and it was this persuasion—involving, as of course it did, a subsequent readiness to listen to whatever He might teach them — that sufficiently constituted the faith which He commended.

Jesus was to them at first, perhaps, simply man. But as their knowledge of Him widened, and deepened, and cleared, the very endeavour to understand Him, to make a unity of their thoughts about Him, led them on to conclusions about Him that caused the spirit to thrill with awe and wonder, and yet with joy. They became aware of something mysterious and transcendent in Him, something which was to the human lineaments of the character what the thought is to the word. Behind and through Jesus they discerned *God*, and that vision it is which causes the strange thrill and glow of their later writings.

Consider what this discovery must have meant to these men. They had lived on terms of daily intimacy with Jesus. He knew each of them as a friend, had often named them by name, had intertwined Himself in the most intimate fashion with their lives. The growing conviction that "God was in Christ," which acquired articulate and conscious form only after His death, but which was implicit in the later stages of their human fellowship with Him, must have come with heart-shaking power into their human intimacy. We can imagine what it would be to any one among us if God in articulate thunder named him by name. But such a summons, astounding as it would be, could touch only one moment of his life. It would be a poor thing compared with the discovery that God was incarnate in his dearest friend, for that discovery would teach the soul along the whole range of their common intercourse. That would be an incomparably richer thing than the most beautiful system of religious truth about God and about duty. Above all, it would have an individualizing force about it that would make an altogether new life in God possible to him.

¶ Here is the witness of an educated man, who had long ceased to be a Christian in the conventional usage of the term. He is writing freely to one who had been more than a friend for Christ's sake, and it is fair to give his words, because death is no longer a mystery to him. "Half-unconsciously I hummed the tune rather than the words of the famous hymn [*When I survey the wondrous Cross*]; as I did so there appeared before me, not a vision of Christ's person, but of the meaning of the glorious crown of thorns He wore. The King of Heaven, the Prince of Peace, is a man—He took not upon Him the nature of angels. That would have been easy but futile. It would not have linked Him with us closely enough. So my vision told me. He must needs suffer for us. . . . And if suffering, and forgiveness, and love of our fellows, and general self-forgetfulness be what is required of every one of us, how greatly we all stand in need of His atonement. That was the lasting impression of my vision: but subsidiary, there was another. I felt, for a moment, a sense of divine spectatorship, as if there was but God in the world besides me; and God, all-seeing, all-understanding, with whom no words were necessary."[1]

¶ Throughout the Fourth Gospel we find the true or highest faith represented as that which by a purely spiritual act takes Christ, as the manifestation of God, into the soul without waiting for conviction by sensible signs.[2]

5. *Faith in Jesus is faith in God.*—In the New Testament Jesus stands in the focus of religion; from first to last He is the object of that mingled trust, awe, and love which we call worship. It does not occur to any of the apostolic writers that this is a fact requiring either explanation or apology. We see not a trace of embarrassment; at each point they are speaking directly out of experience and striving to convey the same new sense of Christ to others. It is obvious that the spirit of Jesus dominates their spirits, modifying belief, re-shaping ideals and enthusiasms, making new the soul's environment, transmuting the flow of conscious thought, laying on the will an unseen constraint to that service which is perfect freedom. To this more than human influence they respond with an intensity which has no reserves. They rest on Jesus only for all that can be called salvation. Their monotheism is a passion which repels idolatry as the one unpardonable sin; yet in face of this they put their whole faith in Jesus Christ. Some one has observed that a high Christology has often been accompanied by a weak sense of God, but the implicit censure, however relevant to certain historic sentimentalisms, is inapposite to the New Testament.

Religion, as religion, is theocentric to the core; and the irre-

---

[1] W. A. L. Elmslie, *Studies in Life from Jewish Proverbs*, 277.
[2] T. H. Green, *The Witness of God*, 52.

sistible impulse of which the apostles were conscious to give Jesus the central place in religion was for them the final ethical proof that He could not be lower than the highest Godhead. As source of pardon, as giver of new life, as medium and vehicle of a presence of God beyond which the mind can never go, He conveyed to them the powers of the higher world; and if the traditional concept of the Divine was incapable of making room for the creative and unparalleled content of His person, it must perforce be deepened and widened. It was at least certain that He who made the Father known must have come forth from the Father's life.

This, then, is the all but incredible, but wholly inevitable, conclusion to which we are brought—that Jesus means God. As reason cannot receive Jesus as a demi-god, and as religion cannot regard Him as merely an intermediary revelation, we, who say unalterably that He is more than a man, must go on to say: " and the Word was God."

¶ The faith of the Christian is the old faith of Abraham and Habakkuk, the faith in the Lord Jehovah only now made manifest in a new and completer manner, in a more intimate relation to human life, and with a more winning appeal to the human heart.[1]

¶ The Godhead shines through Christ, but *He* is not a mere transparent medium. It is Himself that He is showing us when He is showing us God. "He that hath seen Me hath seen"—not the light that streams through Me—but "hath seen, in Me, the Father." And because He is Himself Divine and the Divine Revealer, therefore the faith that grasps Him is inseparably one with the faith that grasps God. Men could look upon a Moses, an Isaiah, or a Paul and in them recognize the eradiation of the Divinity that imparted itself through them, but the medium was forgotten in proportion as that which it revealed was beheld. You cannot forget Christ in order to see God more clearly, but to behold Him is to behold God.[2]

¶ The character of Jesus is the character of Almighty God, the holiness of Jesus the holiness of God, the wrath of Jesus the wrath of God, the compassion of Jesus the compassion of God, the Cross of Jesus the revelation of the sorrow and self-sacrificing love with which the sin of man fills the heart of the Eternal.[3]

---

[1] C. Gore, *St. Paul's Epistle to the Romans*, 24.
[2] A. Maclaren, *The Holy of Holies*, 7.   [3] R. Law, *The Emotions of Jesus*, 11.

FAITH IN JESUS

The Spirit of the Age spoke on a certain day:
"Rise up, my child, and cast thy early faith away."
I rose to go; my freedom seemed complete;
In vain! Once more, O Lord, behold me at Thy feet.
Thou art the very life that beats within my heart:
I have no power to choose: from Thee I cannot part.
O Light of all the world that gladdened weary eyes!
Didst Thou to darkness sink, never again to rise?
O Voice more sweet than men had known on earth before!
Has Thy strange music died to silence evermore?
O Death through which we dreamed of gain in utter loss!
Was it indeed defeat, that passion of the Cross?
Then—Brother, Master, King! I take my part with Thee,
And where Thou art, O Lord, there let Thy servant be.

The awful unknown Power that in the darkness lies,
Thou saidst could be revealed through Thee to mortal eyes;
And what though earth and sea His glory do proclaim;
Though in the stars is writ that great and dreadful name—
Yea—hear me, Son of Man—with tears my eyes are dim;
I cannot read the word which draws me close to Him.
I say it after Thee with faltering voice and weak:
"Father of Jesus Christ"—this is the God I seek.
And can it be that Thou mistookst that name divine?
Then let me share Thy dream, my error be like Thine.
On Thee I lean my soul, bewildered, tempest-tost;
If Thou canst fail, for me then everything is lost.
For triumph, for defeat, I lean my soul on Thee:
Yes, where Thou art, O Lord, there let Thy servant be.[1]

---

[1] *The Life of Sir Colin Scott-Moncrieff*, 349.

VIII.

FAITH IN CHRIST AS SAVIOUR.

LITERATURE.

Abbott, E. A., *Philomythus* (1891).
Abbott, L., *The Christian Ministry* (1905).
Adams, J., *The Great Sacrifice* (1915).
Alexander, A. B. D., *The Ethics of St. Paul* (1910).
Beeching, H. C., *The Apostles' Creed* (1905).
Binney, T., *The Practical Power of Faith* (1870).
Burroughs, E. A., *The Faith of Friends* (1918).
    „   „ in *The Faith and the War* (1915).
Cairns, D. S., in *Friends and the War* (1914).
Clow, W. M., *The Secret of the Lord* (1910).
Erskine, T., *An Essay on Faith* (1823).
Fosdick, H. E., *The Meaning of Faith* (1918).
Foster, J. M., *The White Stone* (1901).
Gardner, P., *Modernity and the Churches* (1909).
Harris, G., *Moral Evolution* (1896).
Harris, J. R., *Memoranda Sacra* (1892).
Hatch, W. H. P., *The Pauline Idea of Faith* (1917).
Herrmann, W., *The Communion of the Christian with God* (1906).
Hill, R. A. P., *The Interregnum* (1913).
Hodge, A. A., *A Commentary on the Confession of Faith* (1870).
Hodge, C., *The Way of Life*.
Hughes, H., *Religious Faith* (1896).
Jeffrey, R. T., *The Salvation of the Gospel* (1890).
Kilpatrick, T. B., *New Testament Evangelism* (1911).
Lindsay, T. M., *A History of the Reformation*, i. (1906).
Maclaren, A., *The Victor's Crowns*.
McLeod, M. J., *The Unsearchable Riches* (1911).
Morison, J., *Saving Faith* (1886).
Winterbotham, R., *Sermons* (1900).
Expository Times, ix. (1897–98) 485 (W. Morgan).
Harvard Theological Review, ii. (1909) 354 (C. H. Hayes).
London Quarterly Review, April 1907, p. 193 (G. G. Findlay).

FAITH IN CHRIST AS SAVIOUR.

1. IT is the meaning of the Christian revelation that God was in Christ reconciling the world to Himself; that being infinite in love and sympathy He bears on His heart the sorrow and sin of mankind, and that Christ reveals Him bearing them—reveals the Eternal Passion and Sacrifice. In Christ the Divine Goodness is not only taught, but incarnate. God in Christ is, in truth, Christianity.

How few realize this belief! The average religious man is more Pagan than Christian in his conception of the Divine character and ways. We say we believe in the Deity of Jesus Christ, but do we not miss altogether and fail to realize the vital spiritual truth of the doctrine when we think of the Invisible God as having dispositions toward His creatures and His children that are not Christlike; when we think that God can be less or other than that which the Son reveals Him to be, less than infinite in His compassion and helpfulness, other than the Everlasting Father and Saviour of men? "The love of God in Jesus Christ our Lord" is the heart of the Christian gospel. Do we believe it? It is true that the presence and spirit of Christ in human life quicken and deepen the sense of sin, but it is also true that in the circle of Christ's influence and in His fellowship, the liveliest and deepest sense of sin can never lead to despair. The man who truly believes in Jesus Christ, the Son of God, believes in redeeming mercy and grace; he is delivered from the fear which weakens and the despair which kills; dark regrets and forebodings are no longer his companions; the gloom and anguish and dread have gone out of his soul; he is more than conqueror, " through him that loved us," over all the shadows and spectres of evil which once pursued and vexed him.

2. But, further, Jesus called on the world to "believe the good news" of His coming for redemption. This task, marked out by Old Testament prophecy and laid upon Him at His birth and baptism, from an early period of His ministry our Lord connected with His *death*. The words of Matt. xxvi. 28, pronounced at the Last Supper (which must be vindicated in their integrity as original), make it clear that Jesus regarded His death as the culmination of His service to mankind, and in a very specific sense; He is ready to offer His "blood" to seal "the covenant," under which "forgiveness of sins" will be universally guaranteed. Thus our Lord, having concentrated upon *Himself* the faith of men, giving to faith thereby a new heart and a boundless energy, finally fastens that faith upon *His death*; He marks this event for the future as the object of the *saving* faith, the faith that brings "remission of sins" and covenant-fellowship with God.

St. Paul was the chief exponent of this "word of the cross" which was at the same time "the word of faith"; but St. Peter in his First Epistle, St. John in his First Epistle and Apocalypse—or the Elder John, as some say, of the Apocalypse—and the writer to the Hebrews, each in his own fashion, combines with St. Paul to focus the redeeming work of Jesus in the Cross. According to the whole New Testament, the forgiving grace of God confronts sinful man there as nowhere else; the two come to an understanding through the mediation of Jesus Christ—and "in his blood"! The faith of the gospel is just the hand reached out to accept God's gifts of mercy proffered from the cross of our Lord Jesus Christ.

¶ Spenser's faith (Fidelia), says Ruskin, is spiritual and noble. He quotes these lines—

> She was araied all in lilly white,
> And in her right hand bore a cup of gold,
> With wine and water fild up to the hight,
> In which a Serpent did himselfe enfold,
> That horrour made to all that did behold;
> But she no whitt did chaunge her constant mood:
> And in her other hand she fast did hold
> A booke, that was both signd and seald with blood;
> Wherein darke things were writt, hard to be understood.[1]

---

[1] Ruskin, *The Stones of Venice*, vol. ii. ch. viii.

FAITH IN CHRIST AS SAVIOUR

3. This faith in Christ as Saviour involves Assent and Appropriation—assent to the truths concerning the meaning of His Cross, and appropriation of the salvation found in Him. It has also a vital connexion with Repentance.

¶ That specific act of saving faith which unites to Christ, and is the sole condition and instrument of justification, involves two essential elements:—

(1) Assent to whatever the Scriptures reveal to us as to the person, offices, and work of Christ. (*a*) The Scriptures expressly say that we are justified by that faith of which Christ is the object. Rom. iii. 22, 25; Gal. ii. 16; Phil. iii. 9. (*b*) Rejection of Christ in Scripture is declared to be the ground of reprobation. John iii. 18, 19, viii. 24. Assent includes an intellectual recognition and a cordial embrace of the object at the same time. It is an act of the whole man—intellect, affection, and will—embracing the truth. This special act of faith in Christ, which secures salvation, is constantly paraphrased by such phrases as "coming to Christ," John vi. 35; "looking to him," Isa. xlv. 22; "receiving him," John i. 12; "fleeing to him for refuge," Heb. vi. 18;—all of which manifestly involve an active assent to and cordial embrace, as well as an intellectual recognition of the truth.

(2) The second element included in that act of faith that saves the soul is trust, or implicit reliance upon Christ, and upon Christ alone, for all that is involved in a complete salvation. (*a*) The single condition of salvation demanded in the Scriptures is that we should "believe *in*" or "*on*" Christ Jesus. And salvation is promised absolutely and certainly if this command is obeyed. John vii. 38; Acts x. 43, xvi. 31; Gal. ii. 16. To believe *in* or *on* a person implies trust as well as credence. (*b*) We are constantly said to be saved "by faith *in*" or "*on* Christ." Acts xxvi. 18; Gal. iii. 26; 2 Tim. iii. 15. "Faith is the *substance* of things hoped for." Heb. xi. 1. Trust rests upon the *foundation* upon which expectation is based. Hope reaches forward to the *object* upon which desire and expectation meet. Hope, therefore, rests upon trust, and trust gives birth to hope, and faith must include trust in order to give reality or substance to the things hoped for. (*c*) The same is proved by what are said to be the effects or fruits of faith. By faith the Christian is said to be "persuaded of the promises"; "to obtain them"; "to embrace them"; "to subdue kingdoms"; "to work righteousness"; "to stop the mouths of lions." Heb. xi. All this plainly presupposes that faith is not a bare intellectual conviction of the truth of truths revealed in the

Scriptures, but that it includes a hearty embrace of and a confident reliance upon Christ, His meritorious work and His gracious promises.[1]

¶ The sum of Christianity is—(1) God manifest in Christ, the God of grace, accessible by every Christian man and woman; and (2) unwavering trust in Him who has given Himself to us in Christ Jesus—unwavering, because Christ with His work has undertaken our cause and made it His.[2]

I.

ASSENT.

In its widest sense, faith is an assent to truth upon the exhibition of evidence. It does not seem necessary that this evidence should be of the nature of testimony; for we are commonly and properly said to believe whatever we regard as true. We believe in the existence and attributes of God, though our assent is not founded upon what is strictly called testimony.

1. The testimony that is always valid is that of the Holy Spirit. It is the faith founded on that witness that is the faith commended in the New Testament—a faith which rests upon the manifestation by the Holy Spirit, of the excellence, beauty, and suitableness of the truth. This is what Peter calls the precious faith of God's elect. It arises from a spiritual apprehension of the truth, or from the testimony of the Spirit with and by the truth in our hearts.

Of this faith the Scriptures make frequent mention. Christ said, "I thank thee, O Father, Lord of heaven and earth, that thou hast hid these things from the wise and prudent, and hast revealed them unto babes" (Luke x. 21). The external revelation was made equally to the wise and to the babes. To the latter, however, was granted an inward illumination which enabled them to see the excellence of the truth that commanded their joyful assent. Our Saviour therefore added, "No man knoweth who the Son is, but the Father; and who the Father is, but the Son,

---

[1] A. A. Hodge, *A Commentary on the Confession of Faith*, 206.
[2] T. M. Lindsay, *History of the Reformation*, i. 430.

and he to whom the Son will reveal him." When Peter made his confession of faith in Christ, our Saviour said to him, "Blessed art thou, Simon Bar-jona: for flesh and blood hath not revealed it unto thee, but my Father which is in heaven' (Matt. xvi. 17).

Paul was a persecutor of the Church; but when it pleased God to reveal His Son in him, he at once preached the faith which he before destroyed. He had an external knowledge of Christ before; but this internal revelation he experienced on his way to Damascus, and it effected an instant change in his whole character. There was nothing miraculous or peculiar in the conversion of the apostle, except in the mere incidental circumstances of his case. He speaks of all believers as having the same Divine illumination. "God," he says, "who commanded the light to shine out of darkness, hath shined in our hearts, to give the light of the knowledge of the glory of God in the face of Jesus Christ" (2 Cor. iv. 6). On the other hand, he speaks of those "whose minds the god of this world hath blinded, lest the light of the glorious gospel of Christ, who is the image of God, should shine unto them." In the second chapter of his First Epistle to the Corinthians, he dwells much upon this subject, and teaches not only that the true Divine wisdom of the gospel was undiscoverable by human wisdom, but that when externally revealed, we need the Spirit that we may know the things freely given to us of God. For the natural man receiveth not the things of the Spirit of God, for they are foolishness unto him; neither can he know them, for they are spiritually discerned. Hence the apostle prays for his readers, that the eyes of their understanding (heart) might be opened, that they might know the hope of their calling, the riches of their inheritance, and the greatness of the Divine power of which they were the subjects (Eph. i. 18, 19). And in another place, that they might be "filled with the knowledge of his will in all wisdom and spiritual understanding" (Col. i. 9). By spiritual understanding is meant that insight into the nature of the truth which is the result of the influence of the Spirit upon the heart.

Since faith is founded on this spiritual apprehension, Paul says, he preached not with the enticing words of man's wisdom, because a faith which resulted from such preaching could be at best a rational conviction ; but in the demonstration of the Spirit and of power; that the faith of his hearers might stand, not in the wisdom of men, but in the power of God (1 Cor. ii. 4, 5). Hence faith is said to be one of the fruits of the Spirit, the gift of God, the result of His operation (Eph. ii. 8 ; Col. ii. 12). These representations of the Scriptures accord with the experience of the people of God. They know that their faith is not founded upon. the testimony of others, or exclusively or mainly upon external evidence. They believe because the truth appears to them both true and good, because they feel its power and experience its consolations.

¶ We must do away with the claim that faith, like every other means whereby men seek to come to God, is a human work. Had we to admit the unqualified truth of this claim with regard to the faith of which we speak, then even our faith would be an effort to lay hold on God by human means. But it is just this that we ought expressly to exclude from the communion of the Christian with God. It is well known that in their opponents the Reformers encountered the view that faith is one among many human efforts all equally necessary to union with God. "They think that faith is a thing which it is in their power to have or not to have, like any other natural human work; so when in their heart they arrive at a conclusion and say, 'Verily, the doctrine is right, and therefore I believe it,' then they think that this is faith. Now when they see and feel that no change has thereby taken place in themselves and others, and that works do not follow, and they remain as before in the old nature—then they think that the faith is not enough, but that there must be something more and greater." Thus Luther knew a kind of faith which a man himself begets by bringing himself to assent to doctrines of some sort. Luther calls such a faith worthless, because it gives us nothing.[1]

2. But if faith means assent to truth, it is obvious that its nature and attendants must vary with the nature of the truth believed, and especially with the nature of the evidence upon which our assent is founded. A man may assent to the proposition that the earth moves round its axis, that virtue is good, that sin will be punished, that to him, as a believer, God promises salvation. In all these cases there is assent, and therefore faith,

[1] W. Herrmann, *The Communion of the Christian with God*, 214.

FAITH IN CHRIST AS SAVIOUR

but the state of mind expressed by the term is not always the same.

What are the truths which the Spirit of God commends to our acceptance? They are the truths which are summed up in the gospel.

(1) Now, first of all, the gospel asserts Christ's essential Godhead. Speaking of Him it says, "Who being in the form of God." That was His proper form, the form that properly and naturally belonged to Him as the Eternal Son of the Eternal Father. Yet, though He was in the form of God, and by nature and right the equal of God, He "took upon him the form of a servant." He had to take that. Being in the form of God He could have the form of a servant only by taking it. Hence, as He had covenanted to do a servant's work, He "took upon him the form of a servant," and so was "God manifest in the flesh." Then another Scripture says, "When the fulness of the time was come, God sent forth his Son, made of a woman, made under the law." By natural and Divine prerogative He was the Lawmaker, and thus above the law. But He was made under the law, for, having taken the form of a servant, He must be under the law so as to be in circumstances to give service, to render obedience, and thus "fulfil all righteousness."

(2) By thus taking manhood into God, and thereby blending our nature with His own, Christ became qualified to act as the Substitute of sinners. Under bond of the New Covenant, He had engaged to discharge all our liabilities. Accordingly, in our room He obeyed the law which we had violated, and endured the punishment which we had incurred. He lived to work out for us a righteousness, and He died to save us from the curse of death. Through His doing and dying in our stead the conditioned obedience was rendered to the law, and the requisite atonement was made to God. Hence it comes to pass that we have redemption through His blood, for His blood was the stipulated price of our redemption. "He was made sin for us." Our sins were legally imputed to Him; transferred to His account. "The Lord laid on him the iniquity of us all," and "his own self bore our sins in his own body on the tree." And this transfer of our sin to Him was in order that "we might be made the righteousness of God in him"—that is to say, His righteousness is imputed to us,

just as our sin was imputed to Him, and we are reckoned and treated before the law as righteous, because we are "made the righteousness of God in him." Thus is Christ "the end of the law for righteousness."

3. But faith as assent to truth is never purely intellectual, it always involves a moral act. No doubt, even in the writings of St. Paul, faith sometimes means simply the theoretical acceptance or intellectual conviction of the facts of salvation as in Rom. iv. 25, or in the declaration that God raised up His Son from the dead. But even in such a case there is always a moral element which depends not upon the knowledge of merely historical fact, but upon the personal confidence in God's character and purpose. This confidence is not simply an assent of the mind. "With the heart," says Paul, "man believes." What Paul dreads and protests against in his Epistles both to the Romans and to the Galatians is that proud self-satisfied temper of legalism which assumed that mere theoretic acceptance or verbal assent was enough to make a Christian, the mere mental acknowledgment of the terms of the ancient covenant. He is everywhere contending for a new content of the word "faith" which will exhibit itself in overt practical life.

¶ No one, probably, has ever found his life permanently affected by any truth whereof he has been unable to obtain a *real apprehension*, which, as I have elsewhere shown, is quite a different thing from real *comprehension*. Intellectual assent to truths of faith, founded on what the reason regards as sufficient authority for, at least, experimental assent, must, of course, precede real apprehension of them, as also must action, in a sort experimental, on faith of truths so assented to; but such faith and action have little effective life, and are likely soon to cease, or to become mere formalities, unless they produce some degree of vital *knowledge* or *perception*.[1]

¶ I think it is clear that all religious faith, if it is to be worth anything, must rest finally on choice and be able to maintain itself in face of hostile evidence. The point is beautifully illustrated in one of R. L. Stevenson's "Fables," called "Faith, Half-faith and No-faith-at-all," in which three men, going on a pilgrimage, discuss the grounds of faith. One, a priest, bases his

---

[1] Coventry Patmore, *Principle in Art*, 219.

FAITH IN CHRIST AS SAVIOUR

faith on miracles, another, a "virtuous person," on metaphysics; the third, "an old rover with his axe," says nothing at all. At last one came running and told them all was lost; that the powers of darkness had besieged the Heavenly Mansions, that Odin was to die and evil triumph.

"I have been grossly deceived," cried the virtuous person.

"All is lost now," said the priest.

"I wonder if it is too late to make it up with the devil?" said the virtuous person.

"Oh, I hope not," said the priest, "and at any rate, we can but try. But what are you doing with your axe?" says he to the rover.

"I am off to die with Odin," said the rover.[1]

II.

APPROPRIATION.

1. The gospel, or message of salvation, which is offered to faith is more than a discourse concerning Christ. It is an actual presentation of Christ, a definite offer of Christ; and Christ, with all His saving power, is present by His Spirit in the Word, which preaches Him. The due response to the message, therefore, cannot be merely an intellectual assent to the propositions it contains regarding Christ, even when these are accompanied by æsthetic admiration, or emotional delight. It must consist in a hearty consent to the claims made on behalf of Christ, which indeed He makes for Himself—an owning of Christ, in an individual act of homage, as supreme in the whole realm of human life; a personal acceptance of Him as Saviour and Lord; a trustful commitment of the soul to Him, as the One who alone can redeem from the guilt and power of sin, with all its penalties; a definite choice of Christ, as the highest good and satisfaction of man, as He is also the perfect revelation of God. The usage of Scripture, confirmed by Christian experience, warrants us in giving this religious, soteriological significance to faith. In it God reaches man, and occupies him wholly; and man reaches God, committing himself absolutely to the love crowned on Calvary.

[1] R. A. P. Hill, *The Interregnum*, 10.

¶ I am persuaded that faith in the gospel always is and always must be an appropriating faith, and that there is no true faith in the gospel which is not so. When a man opens his eyes upon the sun, he necessarily appropriates his share of its light, and he cannot look upon the sun without making this appropriation. In like manner no man can look upon the Sun of righteousness, which is the love of God manifested in Christ Jesus, without appropriating his own share of its blessed light. He that believes really in the love of God to the world cannot but believe in the love of God to himself. The general belief and the appropriating belief are not two beliefs, but one—just as the general receiving the light of the sun, and the particular receiving our own share, are not two receivings, but one. God tells me in His Word that "He is in Christ reconciling the world unto Himself, not imputing unto them their trespasses." When this message comes to me, can I put any other interpretation on it than that God is reconciling me, and not imputing my trespasses to me? I think that any person who understands the meaning of these words, and believes them to be the true words of God, must see that they imply forgiveness for himself.[1]

¶ The more I think of the teaching of our Lord concerning faith the more I have the sense that around us there is a sea of power and love and strength and life, and that the thing that we need to learn above all else is to become so receptive that that sea can break in upon us. Is not that the message that we need as we confront the duty that lies before us? Truth is given only to men and women who are facing their duty. As we face the task that we have to do, somehow there comes to us the revelation of God that can help us to do it. If we shun our whole duty our thought of God contracts, and less seems possible to us. As you and I face what lies before us now, let us realize that it may be that we are also face to face with the greatest potentiality of getting to know God that we have ever had in our lives, and our victory depends upon our opening our minds to Him in order that He may come in to flood them with His strength and life.[2]

2. This receptivity of faith is one of the overlooked, or at least under-estimated, facts in Christian experience. The evangelist is quite aware of its truth, and yet he fails to emphasize it. It seems too high and too mystic to the ordinary believer. It leads us into mysteries for which many have no care. Yet it is really as simple

---

[1] T. Erskine, *The Unconditional Freeness of the Gospel*, 62.
[2] D. S. Cairns, in *Friends and the War*, 84.

FAITH IN CHRIST AS SAVIOUR 187

and as natural as most of the tenderer and sweeter and more potent experiences of life.

(1) How much inspiration and courage and hope, and how much healing and vitality, is continually passing from man to man. That is a certainty to which every student who has been intellectually quickened sets his seal. In his formative and plastic youth he came under the influence of some teacher whom he learned to trust, and of whose good-will and eager desire to help he gained assurance. That teacher's word awoke his dull and dormant mind, and quickened his sluggish energies. To be with him, to hear him speak, and to catch the kindling light in his eye was to find that the teacher's virtue was passing into the scholar.

¶ Carlyle has told us that he spent ten absorbing days in reading Gibbon's *Decline and Fall*. At their close the spirit of Gibbon, his zeal for knowledge, his love of large and far-seeing generalizations, and his power of visualizing the scenes of the past, became in some measure the possession of his reader. In simpler and in swifter fashion we know how the spirit of a general on the field of battle will animate and renerve every regiment of his line. In that deeper world of spiritual experience the receptivity of faith comes to the fulness of its power. Most men and women believe in man before they believe in God. Little children gain first an assurance and a conviction of their father's wisdom and their mother's love, and through these they pass to faith in God. The awaking of a young soul, and the rising up within him of zeal and of desire, are usually due to some strong personality in whom he whole-heartedly believes. Faith is a subtle contagion. As he comes into contact with the man or woman he trusts the words spoken sink down into his heart, the prayers uttered become the liturgy of his petitions, the hopes which are his leader's motives make the young disciple's face to shine. There were men and women who felt that McCheyne's spiritual passion passed from him into their souls. There were devout believers who made long and costly journeys that they might be reconsecrated by an hour in Spurgeon's presence. There were students trembling under their temptations who felt that Henry Drummond's influence was the elixir of life to their wills. His unfaltering loyalty and intense purity seemed to run along the chords of their being.[1]

(2) But no man, however wise and however godly, can be to his fellow-man what Christ is to His people. When we trust Him we lay ourselves soul and spirit and body before Him, and

[1] W. M. Clow, *The Secret of the Lord*, 288.

His Divine energy floods our being. We receive because we believe, and we receive according to our faith. We understand how all things are possible to him that believeth. As we trust and open out our nature to Him, we receive new life into our dying souls, new strength into our flagging wills, new vigour into our drooping thoughts, new power into our withered faculties. We can receive new vitality not only into our soul and our spirit, but into our body.

This is the truth which Christian Science has been feeling after, although it has stumbled on its very threshold. It is not God's way to work needless· miracles. It is not His will to prevent our suffering when we break His laws. It is not Christ's way to keep us from dashing our foot against the stone if we fling ourselves from some pinnacle in self-will. It is not God's will to heal all our sorrows and to quench all our pain. God has a message in sorrow and a ministry in pain. Neither sorrow nor pain is evil. It is the sin behind them that burdens God's heart. But it is an uncontestable fact, which even a sceptical science has begun to realize, that a healing and renewing energy from Christ can pass, not only into the soul and the spirit, but into the body of the man who trusts Him. He receives his healing because he believes. Only in the atmosphere of faith can Christ work His miracles of healing. Virtue goes out of Christ into those who touch with faith only the hem of His garment.

> Faith spans up blisse; what sin and death
>   Puts us quite from,
> Lest we should run for't out of breath,
>   Faith brings us home;
> So that I need no more, but say
>   *I do believe,*
> And my most loving Lord straitway
>   Doth answer, *Live!*[1]

3. The receptiveness of faith is like all knowledge of truth and all use of forces. Man does not create any truth. He discovers it, receives it. Man does not add a particle to the power in existence. He adjusts himself to it, appropriates it. Faith, however, is not mere passivity. Faith is the supreme energy of

---
[1] Henry Vaughan, "Faith."

man in self-committal, as he puts himself under the law and spirit of Christ. The action of man in receiving and responding has been minimized almost to nothing, because the faith alone without its object is nothing, as if man's energy, because it is unavailing without the forces of nature, were unessential, whereas those forces are unavailing unless man understands them and directs them to his uses. Intellectual reception is not passive. Instruction, we say, has only to be received. But, to receive it, one must be teachable, attentive, alert. One has only to receive reproof, but, to receive it, he must be humble and repentant. To receive Christ by faith, one must make himself over, in his whole purpose and energy, to the law and leading of Christ. As a strong personality dominates another intellectually, inspiring him with the zeal of knowledge, or influences his character, so Christ dominates His followers through the faith which His perfection and love inspire.

¶ One of the passengers on board the *Atlantic*, which was wrecked off Fisher's Island, was Principal J. R. Andrews of New London. He could not swim but he determined to make a desperate effort to save his life. Binding a life-preserver about him, he stood on the edge of the deck waiting his opportunity, and when he saw a wave moving shoreward, he jumped into the rough breakers and was borne safely to land. He was saved by faith. He accepted the conditions of salvation. Forty perished in a scene where he was saved. In one sense he saved himself; in another sense he depended upon God. It was a combination of personal activity and dependence upon God that resulted in his salvation. If he had not used the life-preserver, he would have perished; if he had not cast himself into the sea, he would have perished. So faith in Christ is reliance upon Him for salvation; but it is also our own making of a new start in life and the showing of our trust by action.[1]

4. But faith is more than reception. It is more than the reception of a personal Saviour. It is appropriation. It is the reception of Christ as one's own " proper " Saviour. For it is not enough for the sinner's peace that he believes that God is gracious. He must believe that God is gracious *to him*. It is not enough that he believes that Christ made atonement for sins. He must believe that Christ made atonement for *his sins*. He

[1] A. H. Strong, *Systematic Theology*, iii. 840.

must find the word *me* in the bosom of the word *world*. The language of his faith must be—" God so loved ' me ' that he gave his only-begotten Son that ' I,' believing in him, should not perish but have everlasting life. The Son of God loved 'me' and gave himself for ' me '." The believer thus realizes his property, or, as it was often called, his "right of propriety," in the grace of the Great Father, and the atoning work of the Great Saviour. He appropriates to himself what God is, and did, and does, in so far as He is exhibited in the gospel—in so far as He is the Father of mercies. He appropriates to himself what Christ did, and does, and is, in so far as He too is exhibited in the gospel—in so far as He is a merciful High Priest and Saviour.

¶ It is at once the privilege and the duty of the sinner to "ply diligently," as Luther used to express it, "the first personal pronoun," and say '*me, me*.

¶ "What avails to believe that God is a Father," asks John Rogers reasonably, "*if I believe him not to be mine?*" What avails to believe "that Christ is a perfect Saviour, who died for man's sins, and rose again for his righteousness, except I believe that *he did these for me*?" What avails to believe in " the forgiveness of sins, and the resurrection to eternal life, except I believe they belong to me?"[1]

¶ How beautiful is that verse, Ps. xxxi. 14, " I have trusted in thee, O Jehovah: I have said, Thou art my God." Those last four words sublimely express appropriation. And if you want to see how the Psalmist understood appropriation, look in Ps. xviii. Nine times he uses the possessive personal pronoun in the singular number—*my*. "I will love Thee, O Lord, my strength." "The Lord is my rock, and my fortress, and my deliverer; my God, my strength, in whom I will trust; my buckler, and the horn of my salvation, and my high tower." That is about as many " mys " as we can get into one verse.[2]

III.

REPENTANCE.

1. What is the link between faith and repentance? True repentance ends in believing, and true faith begins in repentance.

[1] *Doctrine of Faith*, 27.   [2] A. T. Pierson, *Foundation Truths*, 36.

FAITH IN CHRIST AS SAVIOUR

It is quite remarkable that Mark should tell us, in the first chapter of his Gospel narrative, that the Lord Jesus Himself began to preach, saying, "Repent ye, and believe the gospel." Our Lord's primary gospel message was a call to repentance, and faith in the gospel. And these two things are inseparably linked. Paul told the Ephesian elders that his testimony both to Jews and to Greeks was "repentance toward God, and faith toward our Lord Jesus Christ"—another mark of the inseparable link.

¶ McCheyne used to say: "Never get rid of your soul's anxiety except by looking unto the Lord Jesus. If you get rid of your anxiety in any other way, it may never return." A solemn word of warning! To drown anxiety in pleasure, to dull sensibility by the hardening influence of continuance in sin, may lead to the loss of all anxiety, but, alas, because of a petrified spiritual nature. But if you lose it by coming to the Lord Jesus, then you will know what Peter means by the words, "Till the day star arise in your hearts"—not a reference, I take it, to the second coming, but to the rising of the Lord Jesus Christ over the horizon of the believing soul.[1]

2. Our Lord makes repentance and faith the principal conditions of entrance into the Kingdom, and the major stress seems to be placed upon faith. The fact that where the two are named in conjunction repentance stands first is no token that it has a logical priority. The order followed in the Gospel statements may be regarded as the homiletical order. Under certain conditions the preacher may very properly begin with insisting upon the need of repentance. Still in the logical order faith is prior to repentance. It is the positive side of the total transaction of which repentance is the negative. The latter is the turning away from the soiled and imperfect. But no one gains any effective incentive to this turning away except through an appreciative vision of something better. He must perceive and give at least initial assent to a higher ideal in order to motive and strength for parting from the lower. Now this initial assent, or inner movement toward self-committal, is faith begun. The positive force, or motive-power, is thus with faith, and repentance is logically secondary.

In repentance there is a change of mind, heart, and will con-

[1] A. T. Pierson, *Foundation Truths*, 29.

cerning sin; condemnation takes the place of approval, aversion of delight, resistance of indulgence. In Christian repentance sin is judged with the mind of Christ, hated with His heart, and withstood by His will. We must think of God as Father, and man as child, to see the horror and heinousness, shame and curse of sin as disturbing this kinship and kindness, even as Christ saw. We must love goodness and God in some measure as Christ loved to detest and abhor sin as we should. We must be as dependent on and submissive to God in Christ as He was as Son to His Father, if our will is to get the Divine direction of antagonism to sin. In brief, Christ Himself must change our mind, heart, and will concerning sin, if we are to repent. But this means that repentance is impossible without the faith which makes the grace of Christ ours, by which God's truth, love, holiness, take the place of sin in us as guiding principle, constraining motive, and commanding purpose. This grace brings us God's light, love, life, so that we become sharers in the Divine nature.

¶ Sorrow for sin, not simply on account of its evil consequences to the transgressor, but on account of its intrinsic hatefulness as opposed to divine holiness and love, is practically impossible without some confidence in God's mercy. It is the Cross which first makes us truly penitent (cf. John xii. 32, 33). Hence all true preaching of repentance is implicitly a preaching of faith (Matt. iii. 1–12; cf. Acts xix. 4), and repentance toward God involves faith in the Lord Jesus Christ (Acts xx. 21; Luke xv. 10, 24, xix. 8, 9; cf. Gal. iii. 7).[1]

¶ Repentance and faith must go together to complete each other. I compare them to a door and its post. Repentance is the door which shuts out sin, but faith is the post upon which its hinges are fixed. A door without a door-post to hang upon is not a door at all; while a door-post without the door hanging to it is of no value whatever. What God hath joined together let no man put asunder; and these two He has made inseparable—repentance and faith.[2]

3. Since repentance and faith are but different sides or aspects of the same act of turning, faith is as inseparable from repentance as repentance is from faith. That must be an unreal faith where there is no repentance, just as that must be an unreal repentance

---

[1] A. H. Strong, *Systematic Theology*, 835.
[2] C. H. Spurgeon, *Sermons*, No. 2073.

FAITH IN CHRIST AS SAVIOUR

where there is no faith. Yet, because the one aspect of his change is more prominent in the mind of the convert than the other, we are not hastily to conclude that the other is absent. Only that degree of conviction of sin is essential to salvation which carries with it a forsaking of sin and a trustful surrender to Christ.

¶ Never will Christ enter into that soul where the herald of repentance hath not been before Him.[1]

¶ Old Mr. Dodd, one of the quaintest of the Puritans, was called by some people "Old Mr. Faith and Repentance," because he was always insisting upon these two things. Philip Henry, remarking upon his name, writes somewhat to this effect—"As for Mr. Dodd's abundant preaching repentance and faith, I admire him for it; for if I die in the pulpit, I desire to die preaching repentance and faith; and if I die out of the pulpit, I desire to die practising repentance and faith." Some one remarked to Mr. Richard Cecil that he had preached very largely upon faith; but that good clergyman assured him that if he could rise from his dying bed, and preach again, he would dwell still more upon that subject. No themes can exceed in importance repentance and faith, and these need to be brought very frequently before the minds of our congregations.[2]

> He came to my desk with a quivering lip,
>   The lesson was done;
> "Dear teacher, I want a new leaf," he said,
>   "I have spoiled this one."
> In place of the leaf so stained and blotted,
> I gave him a new one, all unspotted,
>   And into his sad eyes smiled,
>   "Do better now, my child."
>
> I went to the throne with a sin-stained soul,
>   The old year was done;
> "Dear Father, hast Thou a new leaf for me?
>   I have spoiled this one."
> He took the old leaf, stained and blotted,
> And gave me a new one, all unspotted,
>   And into my sad heart smiled,
>   "Do better now, my child."

[1] Bishop Hall.
[2] C. H. Spurgeon, *Sermons*, No. 2073.

I know not where I'm going,
  But I do know my Guide;
And with child-like faith I give my hand
  To the Friend that's by my side;
And the only thing I ask of Him
  As He takes it, is hold it fast;
Suffer me not to lose my way,
  But bring me home at last.

IX.
Degrees of Faith.

LITERATURE.

Brooks, P., *Essays and Addresses* (1894).
Butler, H. M., *University and Other Sermons* (1899).
Clifford, J., *The Dawn of Manhood* (1887).
Clow, W. M., *The Secret of the Lord* (1910).
Dawson, W. J., *The Reproach of Christ* (1903).
Dick, G. H., *The Yoke and the Anointing* (1893).
Diggle, J. W., *Religious Doubt* (1895).
Dixon, A. C., *Through Night to Morning* (1913).
Forsyth, P. T., *The Principle of Authority*.
Garvie, A. E., *The Christian Personality* (1904).
Gibbon, J. M., in *The Miracles of Jesus* (1903).
Goodwin, H., *Parish Sermons*, iii. (1855).
Harris, J. R., *Memoranda Sacra* (1892).
Herman, E., *Christianity in the New Age* (1919).
Holden, J. S., *Guiding Thoughts*.
Illingworth, J. R., *Christian Character* (1904).
Inge, W. R., *Truth and Falsehood in Religion* (1906).
Ingram, A. F. W., *The Gospel in Action* (1906).
Jowett, J. H., *Things that Matter Most* (1913).
Krauskopf, J., in *Sermons by American Rabbis* (1896).
Lees, H. C., *The Sunshine of the Good News* (1912).
Lockyer, T. F., *The Inspirations of the Christian Life* (1894).
Mackay, W. M., *Bible Types of Modern Women* (1912).
Macmillan, H., *The Gate Beautiful* (1891).
Masterman, J. H. B., *The Challenge of Christ* (1913).
Meyer, F. B., *The Soul's Wrestle with Doubt* (1905).
Morison, J., *Saving Faith* (1886).
Reynolds, H. R., *Light and Peace* (1892).
Ritchie, A., *Spiritual Studies in St. Matthew's Gospel*, ii. (1902).
Selby, T. G., *The Commonwealth of the Redeemed* (1911).
Sheepshanks, J., *The Pastor and His Parish* (1908).
Skrine, J. H., *The Heart's Counsel* (1899).
Thorold, A. W., *Questions of Faith and Duty* (1892).
Watkinson, W. L., *The Ashes of Roses* (1906).
Woods, F. H., *For Faith and Science* (1906).
Experience, xxix. (1910) 228 (A. Shepherd).

DEGREES OF FAITH.

1. THERE are degrees of faith. This is due to the nature of man and to the nature of faith.

¶ I believe there are degrees in faith, and that a man may have some degree of it before all things in him are become new—before he has the full assurance of faith, the abiding witness of the Spirit, or the clear perception that Christ dwelleth in him.[1]

¶ That there are degrees I take for granted, tho' I shall afterwards have occasion to prove it in a Divine Faith; and these depend perfectly upon the capacity of the person that believes, or is persuaded. Now the capacity or incapacity of persons are infinitely various, and not to be reduced to theory; but supposing a competent capacity in the person, then the degrees of faith or persuasion take their difference from the arguments, or motives, or inducements which are used to persuade. Where sense is the argument, there is the highest and firmest degree of faith, or persuasion. Next to that is experience, which is beyond any argument or reason from the thing. The faith, or persuasion which is wrought in us by reasons drawn from the thing, the degrees of it are, as the reasons are: if they be necessary and concluding, it is firm and certain in its kind; if only probable, according to the degrees of probability, it hath more or less of doubting mixed with it. Lastly, the faith which is wrought in us by testimony or authority of a person, takes its degrees from the credit of the person, that is, his ability, and integrity. Now because *all men are liars*, that is, either may deceive, or be deceived, their testimony partakes of their infirmity, and so doth the degree of persuasion wrought by it: but God being both infallible, and true, and consequently it being impossible that he should either deceive, or be deceived, his testimony begets the firmest persuasion, and the highest degree of faith in its kind. But then it is to be considered, that there not

[1] *The Journal of the Rev. John Wesley, A.M.*, ii. 329.

being a revelation of a revelation *in infinitum*; that this is a Divine Testimony and Revelation, we can only have rational assurance; and the degree of the faith, or persuasion which is wrought by a Divine Testimony will be according to the strength of the arguments which we have to persuade us that such a testimony is Divine.[1]

(1) *It is due to the nature of man.*—The world of men is a world of variety. This inexhaustible variety it is which distinguishes God's workmanship from man's. And if there are not two blades of grass, no two faces, no two minds alike, would it not be wonderful if there should be so strange a departure from the general rule in spiritual things, and if, in the case of faith, there should be but one type and habitude of character and life, one measure and mode of confidence towards God? Observation teaches us exactly the reverse. For whatever our preconceived theories may be, it is certain that, in actual fact, all spiritual life is not fashioned alike, all souls are not cast in one mould. There is great faith; there is little faith; and there are all the grades between. And our Lord recognizes these differences when, while certainly not commending little faith for its littleness, He nevertheless declares that, though small, it has results; the little faith is not fruitless.

¶ What is the great gospel command? what is the Christian condition, of life and of service? "Believe." No measure of faith is prescribed, but only faith. If we believe, whether boldly or timidly, we obey the command, we fulfil the condition. Just as the soldier fights, whether his hand trembles as he grasps the sword, or he is served with a courage that makes him forget to fear; and just as a racer runs, whether he gasps for breath, or is full of freshness and vigour; so we keep the faith, whether timorously or boldly.[2]

(2) *It is due to the nature of faith.*—The mind in believing reaches its object, whatever that object may be, *mediately*, not immediately. There is, in other words, something *in the middle* between the mind and the object. This something in the middle may be more or less complex: whether simple or complex, it requires to be interrogated and interpreted. Hence it may be more or less thoroughly mastered: and thus the faith that reaches

---

[1] Tillotson, *Sermons*, xii. 23.
[2] T. F. Lockyer, *The Inspirations of the Christian Life*, 65.

DEGREES OF FAITH

its object through the intervening medium may be more or less coincident with absolute knowledge on the one hand, or mere opinion on the other.

If faith were founded on only a single passage of the Bible, it might stand indeed, but it could not be very secure. But if faith in the gospel, and in the Saviour as exhibited in the gospel, be grounded on a large induction of passages, carefully tested, sifted, and interpreted; and on a comprehensive consideration of the entire scope of the written revelation, there will belong to the faith a very different degree of stability and security. If there be added to this the experience in one's self, and the observation in the case of others, of the moral power of the object of faith then there will be great confirmation of the faith.

¶ If one's faith in the Trinity were founded solely on 1 John v. 7, "there are three that bear record in heaven, the Father, the Word, and the Holy Ghost, and these three are one," it would be very insecure. The verse is unauthentic. It is apocryphal, as has been admitted for long by all competent critics. It is not found in the critical editions of the New Testament. It was not found in the first and second editions of Erasmus's text. It is not found in any of the old manuscripts. It could not be found in any real revision of our Authorized English Version. It should never have been at all in any copy of the Bible. But what then? Is the doctrine of the Trinity in peril? Is it rendered uncertain, when this passage is withdrawn? Not in the least. But if any one's faith in the doctrine rested singly and exclusively on the testimony of this passage, it would falter and totter and collapse as soon as he found himself compelled to surrender the text.[1]

2. There is a difference in the range of faith as well as in its firmness. Very few persons either indiscriminately receive or indiscriminately reject each and every dogmatic assertion put forth in the name of the Christian religion. Even among acknowledged believers, there are doctrines—such, *e.g.*, as the doctrines of Baptismal Regeneration, Indefectible Grace, Verbal Inspiration, Final Perseverance—which are surely believed by some, and severely questioned by others.

This lack of unanimity in belief which is so conspicuous among individual Christians is equally conspicuous in collective Christian communities. The Christian Churches are by no means of one

[1] J. Morison, *Saving Faith*, 50.

mind in regard to Christian doctrine. The gulf between an orthodox Christian and a spiritually minded doubter is often less deep and fixed than the gulf between two Christian Churches both alike claiming to be orthodox. For the differences which divide the Churches styling themselves orthodox are by no means, or generally, mere differences of detail either in doctrine or in discipline. They are often differences lying at the very foundations of faith.

The Greek Church is not divided from the Latin Church merely by such questions as the marriage of the priesthood, and the worship of images, and the form of the tonsure, and the leavening of Sacramental Bread, and the time of keeping Easter; their differences reach down to the very nature of the Incarnation of the Son of God, and the Procession of the Holy Ghost. The questions on which the Reformed branches of the Latin Church are in conflict with the Papacy are questions not of words but of fundamental principles, such as the Canon of Scripture and its authority in relation to tradition: the powers of the priesthood and the operation of a Sacrament, the manner and condition of the forgiveness of sins, and the like. Nor even among the Reformed Churches can there be found anything like unanimity of religious opinion. The very conception of the Christian Church among Episcopalians is fundamentally different from that of Congregationalists; while the difference dividing Calvinistic Christians from Arminians is a difference reaching down to the roots of the religious responsibilities of men, and up to the summit of the predestinating sovereignty of the Eternal God.

The main thing is not to believe in many propositions faintly and doubtfully, but to get a fast grip upon the truths by which men live. All the great doctrines of salvation are related, and hang together by secret bonds; and if we once get hold of any of these, we may be sure that the Spirit of truth will in due season lead us into the whole truth. Having seen "His star," all fainter stars and nebulæ on the far horizon may be trusted in due time to resolve themselves into bright constellations. We have to be afraid only when we hold no one saving truth with any clearness or sincerity.

¶ The scientist is often content to study a single branch of knowledge, to apprehend and illustrate one great principle of nature. Ordinary men regard such extremely limited specialism as quite unworthy and of little value, but the thinker knows better. He knows that to really master a fragment is to get hold of universal truth. As Sir James Paget writes: "If the field of any speciality in science be narrow, it can be dug deeply. In science, as in mining, a very narrow shaft, if only it be carried deep enough, may reach the richest stores of wealth, and find use for all the appliances of scientific art."[1]

3. Such differences in the degree, as well as in the range, of faith, and, moreover, the difficulty of knowing what any one person really believes in the deeper sense, make it a very hazardous task to strike the average of intelligent Christian faith.

¶ Wordsworth's magnificent lines upon the sea-shell express the eternal idealism of countless minds which can frame to themselves no definite belief:—

> "I have seen
> A curious child, who dwelt upon a tract
> Of inland ground, applying to his ear
> The convolutions of a smooth-lipped shell;
> To which, in silence hushed, his very soul
> Listened intensely; and his countenance soon
> Brightened with joy; for from within were heard
> Murmurings, whereby the monitor expressed
> Mysterious union with its native sea.
> Even such a shell the universe itself
> Is to the ear of Faith; and there are times,
> I doubt not, when to you it doth impart
> Authentic tidings of invisible things;
> Of ebb and flow, and ever-during power;
> And central peace, subsisting at the heart
> Of endless agitation."

Yes, but listen to the reply from a more modern poet of less note—the very cry of unwilling belief:—

> "The hollow sea-shell which for years hath stood
> On dusty shelves, when held against the ear
> Proclaims its stormy parent; and we hear
> The faint, far murmur of the breaking flood.
> We hear the sea. The sea? It is the blood
> In our own veins, impetuous and near,

---

[1] W. L. Watkinson, *The Ashes of Roses*, 217.

And pulse keeping pace with hope and fear,
And with our feelings' ever-shifting mood.
Lo! in my heart I hear, as in a shell,
The murmur of a world beyond the grave,
Distinct, distinct, though faint and far it be.
Thou fool! this echo is a cheat as well—
The hum of earthly instincts; and we crave
A world unreal as the shell-heard sea."

Take either of these views, for either is intellectually tenable, and modern men will choose the majestic declaration, the despairing answer, according to the temperament they are born into or the happiness they have found. But both are sincere attempts to face the fundamental issue of belief.[1]

¶ *Weakness of faith* is partly constitutional, and partly the result of education and other circumstances; and this may go intellectually almost as far as scepticism; that is to say, a man may be perfectly unable to acquire a firm and undoubting belief of the great truths of religion, whether natural or revealed. He may be perplexed with doubts all his days, nay, his fears lest the Gospel should not be true may be stronger than his hopes that it will. And this is a state of great pain, and of most severe trial, to be pitied heartily, but not to be condemned. I am satisfied that a good man can never get further than this; for his goodness will save him from unbelief, though not from the misery of scanty faith. I call it unbelief, when a man deliberately renounces his obedience to God, and his sense of responsibility to Him: and this never can be without something of an evil heart rebelling against a yoke, which it does not like to bear.[2]

The sea of faith
Was once, too, at the full, and round earth's shore
Lay like the folds of a bright girdle furl'd.
But now I only hear
Its melancholy, long, withdrawing roar,
Retreating, to the breath
Of the night-wind, down the vast edges drear
And naked shingles of the world.[3]

4. While, then, we are to consider what Christian faith should be, and is, in its highest representatives, we must remember that

---

[1] "Oxoniensis," in *Do We Believe?* 31.
[2] *The Life and Correspondence of Thomas Arnold, D.D.*, i. 321.
[3] Matthew Arnold, "Dover Beach."

it may exist, and yet be real faith, at a lower level. For as long as faith is not sight, it will need not only to be acquired but to be maintained by an effort, whose strenuousness cannot but fluctuate in the majority of men; while the very method of its education is through trials and temptations that few can hope to surmount with their serenity entirely unscathed. Hence, while the secure faith of those whom we regard as saints must always be the Christian ideal, many lives which fall far short of this may yet be lives of faith, and bear fruit whereby they can be recognized as such.

> The more of doubt, the stronger faith, I say,
> If faith o'ercomes doubt. How I know it does?
> By life and man's free will, God gave for that!
> To mould life as we choose it, shows our choice.
> . . . . . .
> What matter though I doubt at every pore,
> Head-doubts, heart-doubts, doubts at my fingers' ends,
> Doubts in the trivial work of every day,
> Doubts at the very bases of my soul
> In the grand moments when she probes herself—
> If finally I have a life to show,
> The thing I did, brought out in evidence
> Against the thing done to me underground
> By hell and all its brood, for aught I know?
> I say, whence sprang this? shows it faith or doubt?
> . . . . . .
> With me, faith means perpetual unbelief
> Kept quiet like the snake 'neath Michael's foot
> Who stands calm just because he feels it writhe.

The condition thus described by Browning is hardly that of those who "declare plainly that they seek a country," "of whom the world was not worthy"; it is not the royal confidence that inspires martyrdom. But, in an age like our own, when men are often tried by intellectual distress as severely as were their forefathers by physical persecution, it is a state that must appeal to many Christians; and they need not doubt that it is a state of faith, and of very real faith, since it continues true throughout, at least to the aspiration for things hoped for; and out of that aspiration assurance ultimately comes, and satisfies the practical test of St. James, "Show me thy faith by thy works."

5. In harmony with these views, we find in Scripture a recognition of very different degrees of faith. Our Saviour said to His disciples, on the Sea of Galilee, when they were alarmed by the rising storm, "Why are ye fearful, O ye of little faith?" (Matt. viii. 26). He said to Peter at another time, "O thou of little faith, wherefore didst thou doubt?" (Matt. xiv. 31). He said, on the other side of things, to the Syrophenician woman, "O woman, great is thy faith" (Matt. xv. 28). He said too, in reference to the Roman centurion at Capernaum, "I have not found so great faith, no, not in Israel" (Luke vii. 9).

There may then be "little faith," and there may be "great faith." And hence there may not only be "assurance," there may likewise be "the full assurance of faith" (Heb. x. 22). The disciples had reason to say to the Lord, "Increase our faith" (Luke xvii. 5). And the Lord had good reason to say to the disciples, "If ye had faith as a grain of mustard seed, ye might say unto this sycamine tree, Be thou plucked up by the root, and be thou planted in the sea; and it should obey you" (Luke xvii. 6). The least real faith will do wonders. It will effect marvellous changes. It will root up and transplant. It will remove even "mountains" that would otherwise be immovable and obstructions for ever (Matt. xvii. 20).

I.

Little Faith.

So far as our evidence at present goes, the expression "little-faith" (it is only one word in the Greek) appears to come to us fresh minted from the heart and lips of our Lord Himself. Before Jesus Christ we have no evidence that any one ever used the word "little-faith."

¶ In these days when papyri are constantly reversing our judgments about rare words and proving them to have been of frequent usage, it is hazardous to say that Christ coined the term. Nevertheless there is at present no evidence of its use by any one before Him. And indeed since His day it has been little used. John Bunyan caught the echo of it in Bedford Jail and gave us a very vivid portrait of Little-faith and his troubles. It shows us a little man set upon by footpads, robbed of his ready money, though not of his jewels, which happily for him were too securely hid for their fingers to purloin. He had to beg his way, and went through life gloomy, yet came to the Heavenly City in the end. And though we may have some hard things to say of Little-faith, let us not forget that he is a hundred times better than No-faith, who is never found in the royal precincts at all. Yet Little-faith is plastic and plaintive and poverty-stricken at the best. The name is a coin from the Royal Mint. It is not only of Christ's coinage but of His currency, and we owe it largely to Matthew the professional penman who caught it from the Master's lips, that we can trace the occasions when the Lord used it. I cannot help feeling that it owed some of its weight to an inflexion of tone, serious and mocking all in one. His voice is loving yet reproachful, tender but troubled. There is a gentle banter, which was well calculated to make the disciples hang their heads. We can almost hear Him as He halts upon it, this five-syllabled bye-word, *oligopistos*. It is love's appeal to love for more trust. It indicates a spiritual side-slip in regard to His Person. He is not here talking of doubt as mere incredulity in regard to a fact, but as a moral surrender in which they have quailed before the adversary and failed in adversity.[1]

1. Little faith is better than no faith. The woman with an issue of blood, who could but summon courage to touch the hem of the Lord's garment, and who, when called into His presence, came fearing and trembling, was apparently not strong in faith. And yet her faith did a great thing for her. It availed for her immediate and thorough cure: "Thy faith hath made thee whole." So our Lord declares it to be with the believer whose faith is "as a grain of mustard seed." It is far from being a completed faculty or exercise, but the least in the Kingdom of God have in their actual, sympathetic, transforming confidence in a higher world a most precious source of vision and energy.

¶ I am always so afraid, as you come up to Oxford from the public schools to face, as you have often to face, doubts and difficulties you have never known before, lest you should despise that little mustard seed of faith which you bring with you. As I look over your future and see you going forth from Oxford and out into the battle of life, I know that the one thing you have brought here to church which is of ten times the value of your intellectual

[1] H. C. Lees, *The Sunshine of the Good News*, 169.

power and your social qualities is that mustard seed of faith; because as I see a world that is full of people dying every day and night, and full of temptations which perhaps are hard to realize, I know that your usefulness to that world all depends upon whether that mustard seed of faith is lost, or whether you are putting it to good use in this tempted, and suffering, and dying world.[1]

¶ I have read, that, when the first cable of the suspension-bridge that now spans the Niagara was about to be laid, a thin thread was attached to a kite and both sent, on a favouring wind, to the other side of the river. By means of that thread, a heavier string was pulled across, and by it a heavier one still, and then a rope, and then a tow, and then the cable, and the other parts of that mighty bridge that enables the people to pass in safety, from one side to the other, over the roaring cataract beneath. Let but those who doubt or disbelieve fasten the tiny thread of faith that lingers in them still to the spiritual side of life, and gradually it will become stronger and stronger until it will grow into a mighty bridge that will carry them safely, over the seething and hissing abyss of doubts and perplexities, unto the yonder peaceful shore.[2]

¶ He will not enter hell, who hath faith equal to a single grain of mustard seed in his heart: and he will not enter paradise, who hath a single grain of pride, equal to one of mustard seed, in his heart.[3]

2. Little faith can pray, if it cannot do more. We read in the Acts of the Apostles that when King Herod had put Peter into prison, after the death of James, "prayer was made without ceasing of the church unto God for him." That was clear evidence of the faith of the Church in God and in the power of prayer. Yet when their prayer was answered, and an angel had been sent and had delivered the apostle from prison, and brought him to the gate of the house where the assembled disciples were praying so earnestly, they would not believe that it was he. They told the damsel who kept the door that she was mad when she said that Peter was there; and when she insisted upon her tale, they said "It is his angel." They had faith, but it was accompanied by much doubt. They had faith enough to pray.

---

[1] A. F. W. Ingram, *The Gospel in Action*, 116.
[2] J. Krauskopf, in *Sermons by American Rabbis*, 302.
[3] *The Sayings of Muhammad*, 87.

DEGREES OF FAITH

And God responds with grace to help. If God made no response except to perfect faith, who could hope for help? But God has regard for beginnings, and His eye perceives greatness in the germ. The hand of the woman in the crowd trembled as it was stretched toward Jesus, and the faith behind it was superstitiously reverent, trusting in the virtue of the robe rather than in the One who wore it; yet the genuineness of that faith, feeble though it was, triumphed in God's loving sight. Real trust is real power, though the heart and hand both tremble.

To Nicodemus our Lord revealed the mystery of the Kingdom of God: the new life which marks the entrance into that Kingdom, and the uplifting on the cross—the pledge of the Divine love by which that life is secured (John iii.). To the Samaritan woman He revealed directly the secret of His Messiahship, but this was only after He had first claimed from her the acceptance of His statement that worship is to be no longer in Jerusalem or on Mount Gerizim, but wherever man shall worship in spirit and in truth (John iv.). That was not an easy statement for her to accept; but Christ claimed that she should do so on the basis of personal trust in Him. "Believe me" (John iv. 21). The case of the nobleman in Cana is still more remarkable. Our Lord treated him first just as He treated the Jews in Jerusalem. "Except ye see signs and wonders, ye will not believe" (John iv. 48). Yet as soon as the agonized cry broke from the father, "Sir, come down ere my child die," Christ granted him his heart's desire. We are left to conclude that between the first and the second appeal of the father something had broken down in the man's heart. He was now more dependent upon Christ than he had been at first. The venture of his soul upon the Christ was more complete than it had been; and He, who knew what was in man, found in that complete dependence an element of surrender to which He could respond, and the Christ was self-committed in that blend of power and love in which the sick child was restored to life.

¶ Whether it is a tree that will not bear or a devil that will not go, whether your life is dwarfed or dominated, the solution is always the same, the glorious grace of Jesus Christ. John Bunyan said that when the thieves were robbing Little-faith they saw Great Grace coming down the lane, and they ran away. So may He come to us even if it be upon the waves of the storm, and leave us in possession both of our spiritual jewels and ready money, that life may be not a toil but a triumph, a pilgrimage and a progress in one.[1]

3. But little-faith must not be content with its feebleness. Every time that it is mentioned by Christ it receives His rebuke. There are five occasions.

(1) The first is Matt. vi. 30: "But if God doth so clothe the grass of the field, which to-day is, and to-morrow is cast into the oven, shall he not much more clothe you, O ye of little faith?" It is a rebuke of *worry*, of needless anxiety. Mr. Harrington Lees agrees with Col. Mackinlay that the trouble probably arose from the fact that they were in the sabbatic year, in which they could not reap or harvest their corn, nor was the flax to be gathered in.

Christ points His warning finger saying, "Little-faith, who made the provision that gives the birds such a royal feast this year? Was it not your Heavenly Father? If He clothes the countless grass-blades in their flinty coat of mail, will He not find raiment for a few millions of His children? Does not your Heavenly Father know that your clothes wear out, and that your food runs short?"

¶ There is a charming legend which tells us how an angel was sent to comfort Eve when she was banished from the Garden of Eden and was mourning over the barren wilderness outside. No flower grew upon the soil cursed for man's sin, and the snow fell and covered the earth with a dreary shroud. It seemed as if it were the funeral of the world. But while the angel was speaking to Eve he caught a flake of falling snow, breathed upon it, and bade it take form and live. Ere it had reached the ground it had turned into a beautiful flower, which Eve prized more than all the fair blossoms she had left behind in Paradise; for the angel told her that it was the earnest of a happier time, when the lost joys should be restored and the summer that had vanished should come again.[2]

(2) The second occurrence is Matt. viii. 26: "And he saith unto them, Why are ye fearful, O ye of little faith? Then he arose, and rebuked the winds and the sea; and there was a great

---

[1] H. C. Lees, *The Sunshine of the Good News*, 188.
[2] H. Macmillan, *The Gate Beautiful*, 207.

calm." It is a rebuke of *fear*. The storm, says Dr. Morgan Gibbon, burst into the disciples' souls, and blew their faith away. They rushed in panic to the stern, and with clamours that rose above the howling of the wind, they cried, " Master! carest thou not that we perish?"

He rebuked their fear, yet He granted their prayer. For the Lord is full of pity and merciful. He will not always chide. To men who missed their chance He gave another. After Pentecost Jesus again went into a boat, and His disciples, great and small, followed Him. Tempests rose, the boat was often covered with waves, and He slept. But there was no panic. The sea rose higher. The boat filled. Still He slept; and still *they* trusted. Great seas of persecution broke over them, sweeping many away, but no cry of panic, no shriek of despair, greeted the world's ear. Rather a peace that passed all men's understanding possessed them in life and in death. A faith yet nobler than the Centurion's spoke; in their silence earth as well as heaven marvelled and said, "Great is your faith."

¶ " I was staying with some friends in Wilmington, Delaware. On my bed was a coverlet made of old brown linen spun in the old days. Over it were worked the lines:—

'God's greatness
Flows around our incompleteness,
Round our restlessness His rest.'

When I came down in the morning they asked me how I had slept, and my answer was, 'How could I have slept other than well with such a text as that on top of me.' The open sea was like the harbour that night. A voice through Mrs. Browning had said, 'Peace, be still. ' "[1]

(3) The third time we come upon little-faith is in Matt. xiv. 31: "And immediately Jesus stretched forth his hand, and took hold of him, and saith unto him, O thou of little faith, wherefore didst thou doubt?" The rebuke is of *cowardice*. There is another storm, but the same lake. There were crowds that had gathered round Him, and when it grew late in the day the disciples in their selfishness said, "Send them away." Now the Master stays with the multitude, and *sends away the disciples*. Then came the

[1] J. Rendel Harris, in *Experience*, July 1910, p. 229.

storm. But the Master had not forgotten them. He came across the water to them. Gradually there dawned upon their consciousness the fact of His presence. They feared it was a ghost, but they hoped it was Jesus. Peter asked for a sign. Little-faith is fond of signs. Christ said, Come; and Peter stepped out. It was an act of daring faith. Then he wished he were back in the boat; that was a piece of cowardice. But if he failed he sought the best means of recovery. If he had over-estimated himself, he did not make the mistake of under-estimating his Master. He cried, "Lord, save me!" Instantly the strong hand shot out and Peter was saved.

¶ After the deliverance the Lord spoke to him. We should have rebuked and then saved him. The Lord saved and then rebuked him. What was the cause of the fiasco? The old trouble, "Little-faith. Wherefore didst thou doubt?" Not "Wherefore didst thou come?" Christ never reproaches faith for being too audacious. Wherefore wast thou drawn in two directions? Peter's trouble was distraction. He tried to look both at the storm and the Saviour at one time. So distraction is a third source of trouble. Little-faith was robbed of his ready-money, says John Bunyan, but not of his jewels. Those were safe in a sure place. And many a soul to-day is secure in Christ, but has yet to learn how to be serene through Christ. Look not at wind or storm. Look to Jesus the author and finisher of faith, the antidote and foe of little-faith.[1]

(4) The next rebuke is of *materialism.* The passage is Matt. xvi. 8: "And Jesus perceiving it said, O ye of little faith, why reason ye among yourselves, because ye have no bread?" "If you are going to buy bread," says Christ, "do not buy it from the Pharisees or Sadducees. There is infection in it." They wonder what He means, and what is the reference of the saying. "It cannot be to the Pharisees, for there are no Pharisees here. It cannot be to the Sadducees, we are not tainted with 'modern thought.' It must be to the bread. He is annoyed because we have forgotten to bring bread." He looks up again, and says, "Little-faith, will you never understand? The very last thing you have to think about when you are with Me is bread. Have you not seen five thousand men and their families fed with only five loaves and two fishes; and do you not remember how much there

[1] H. C. Lees, *The Sunshine of the Good News*, 174.

DEGREES OF FAITH

was left over? Is it likely then that I would ask you to make sure that you have brought plenty of provisions? When will you learn that man does not live by bread alone, but by the word of God?" It is the *teaching* of the Pharisees and Sadducees that He is concerned about. They teach for doctrines, not the Word of God but the commandments of men, as Touch not, taste not, handle not.

(5) There is yet another occurrence of the word. It is in Matt. xvii. 20: "Then came the disciples to Jesus apart, and said, Why could not we cast it out? And he saith unto them, Because of your little faith." We owe it to the Revised Version. It is a direct rebuke of little-faith itself—simple *half-belief.*

¶ We are sometimes treated by the native Chinese evangelists to illustrations truly Eastern in character, as the following example will indicate. It was accepted by the audience as a solemn exhortation, as was the preacher's intention, the missionaries being the only ones present to whom the humorous side was evident. The subject was the importance of a wholehearted acceptance of the Gospel, and the foolishness and uselessness of a half-hearted belief. A man, we were told, was begging by the roadside; he was very ill, and a passing doctor had pity on him, and gave him some medicine which the man promised to take. Questionings, however, arose in his mind as to the reliability of the said doctor, and yet he could not but take the drug, as he felt so ill. A compromise was decided upon, and he took half the dose. For a few hours he felt wonderfully well, and rejoiced in his restored condition; towards night the pain was more acute than before, and he was at his wits' end. How he regretted his folly, for his illness was certainly more serious. A few months later the same doctor, travelling over the same road, met the same man now reduced to a bag of bones.

"What!" said he; "are you not the man to whom I gave medicine last time I came this way?"

"I am," he replied, "and I have been much worse ever since."

"Worse!" exclaimed the physician; "how is that?"

"I only took half the dose," said the man; "I did not venture to take the whole."

"Alas! alas!" he replied, "how terrible! Your illness is the result of parasites attacking your vitals. That medicine would have killed them all. Had you taken the full dose you would have been well; had you tasted none there would have been hope for you. You took a small dose, and the parasites were sent to sleep, and later, when the effect of the drug had gone over, they awoke more lively than ever. Having once tasted of the drug and experienced its effect, nothing will induce them to be trapped a second time. Return home, and prepare for a lingering death."

In the moral drawn, the folly of an endeavour to serve two masters was made clear—a truth which all present felt to have been powerfully interpreted.[1]

II.

Great Faith.

1. What is the difference between little faith and great faith? It is a difference of vitality. This is clearly shown by our Lord when He spoke of what faith could do if it were as a grain of mustard seed. "As a grain of mustard seed" (Matt. xvii. 20), small and insignificant but *alive*, faith grows in soul and society, till harmonies of living song find home and shelter therein. Such is the nature of faith as Jesus presents it.

(1) The mustard seed has *vitality*. It is only an annual, yet in Palestine it grows to the height of about twelve feet. One of the rabbis said that his mustard tree flourished so much in a certain year that he could climb into the branches of it. Whether that is true or not it illustrates the character of the mustard seed. It may begin small, but it cannot stay small; a grain of sand may, but not a mustard seed. Plant it and it takes hold of all the advantages of its environment; the tiny white tendrils shoot out and drain all the chemical powers that are stored in the ground, and draw the moisture from below, so that ere long it is on its way to become a fair tree.

So faith is represented by Christ as that which, if only possessed in the magnitude of a mustard seed, may be capable of great spiritual results; but it is to be possessed as a seed, and a seed is capable of becoming a tree, if only it is complete; it is not the size of the seed that determines its importance, a portion of a large seed is not the same as the whole of a small one; no, the seed contains a principle of *life*, and so faith in the heart, if it be but genuine, may grow and bear most wonderful fruits. The

[1] A. M. Cable, *The Fulfilment of a Dream*, 164.

DEGREES OF FAITH

question then for a man to ask himself is, What faith have I? am I believing in God, or am I believing in the world? am I walking through this life as one to whom this life is everything, as one whose highest end it is to enjoy the pleasures of sense for a season, and to allow all selfish passions and desires to run riot in excess; or am I walking through it in the fear of God, as one who knows that God's eye is upon his most secret thoughts, or still more as one who feels that having been redeemed by Christ from the dominion of Satan and sin, he is bound to yield himself up, body, soul, and spirit, to do Christ's will?

(2) Because it has vitality it has *power*. It is able to "remove mountains." That is literally true as a scientific statement. One of the most interesting features in denudation, as the geologists call it, is the way in which a little seed will fall into a fissure of rock, and begin to swell and grow, until in process of time the rock splits and breaks off, then crumbles and is borne by the rain into the nearest rivulet, which carries it down till it becomes sand on the sea-shore: the seed is moving the mountain into the sea. It is very slow, you say, but is it less certain? Imperceptible motion is no proof of immobility. The frozen glacier is really a flowing stream. Remember how in Mark xi. we read the story of the leafy but fruitless fig tree. Christ spoke a solemn ban, and apparently nothing happened. The fig tree looked none the worse. Next morning however the result was apparent. As Mark says (xi. 14, 20), the withering was from the roots, invisible but immediate.

¶ The mustard seed has that which the mountain has not. Emerson has a quaint little poem about a mountain and a squirrel quarrelling. The mountain taunted the squirrel with his insignificance, and the squirrel replied that though he could not bear a forest on his back, he could crack a nut as the mountain could not.[1]

(3) If faith has vitality as a grain of mustard seed it will have power to remove mountains. But not all at once. God gives us power for what He wants us to be; *i.e.* power for the next step; and all our future life is conditioned upon that. We say, "Increase our faith," and He says, "Exercise the faith you have." We must exercise the lower power before we attain to the higher. Suppose

---

[1] H. C. Lees, *The Sunshine of the Good News*, 182.

there is a powerful steam-engine which is able to do for you a year's work in a day: it is a reservoir of power, but the power is conditioned upon the exercise of a lower power; you must bring coals and fetch water and make up fire, and by and by the power becomes accessible to you. He that is faithful in least is faithful also in much; we must be faithful to the light already given us, faithful to our powers of love, thought, and obedience, if we are to be brought to the reception of the power in which saints have walked.

¶ I see a man with no very brilliant intellect, filled with faith, go down to some mission district where there is a perfect mountain of prejudice, paganism, and indifference. It seems a slight thing to go down—just this man with his faith. I go there five or ten years afterwards, and find the church crowded to the doors, and round him a warm-hearted, enthusiastic band of people, some of the public-houses shut up, and the moral tone of the whole place changed. How has it been done? Simply and solely by his faith. Faith has removed mountains; he has thrown himself upon GOD —GOD has answered to the call. He has gone in the name of JESUS CHRIST, and the LORD has been working with him, and therefore what has happened is that his faith has removed mountains, as was promised.[1]

2. Great faith is due not to the range of belief but to its reality. Faith, however limited or feeble, if only genuine and vital, is full of efficacy. A grain of genuine trust in the righteous God, in the supernatural universe, in the Divine government, in the virtue of the Cross, in the power of grace, in the life everlasting, contains within itself all virtue and promise. A hundred guineas were recently refused for a microscopic speck of the pollen of a rare orchid, so precious is the dust of beauty. The fact is, that microscopic speck of pollen would have enabled its purchaser to produce no one knows what abundance of hybrid and original orchids; to have adorned his own and a thousand other conservatories with new and delightful flowers. So our Lord teaches that out of a microscopic speck of genuine faith in God, in His most holy Word, in His eternal promise in Christ Jesus, will spring purity and peace, strength and victory, high character and heroic service—in this world all the graces of the

[1] A. F. W. Ingram, *The Gospel in Action*, 119.

Spirit, and in the next all the flowers and fruits of paradise. A vague, passive faith that is neither belief nor disbelief is worth little; a sterling faith, however weak and hesitating, holds the potency and promise of universal grace and glory.

¶ Some men seem to think they strengthen themselves against unbelief by multiplying the number of things they believe. They turn Romanists for fear of infidelity, as if a man should think that by filling the bottom of the boat with stones he keeps the sea further from him.[1]

3. The question is sometimes asked, What is the minimum of belief for the profession of Christianity? How little may a man believe and still call himself a follower of Christ? It is a mistaken question. The question never is how little or how much but *what* does a man believe, and *how*. There is at present a persistent demand for greater simplicity of doctrine, and that demand usually means fewer doctrines. But it is not a smaller amount of doctrine, it is a larger unity of doctrine. It is a more profound entrance into the heart of doctrine, in which its unity and simplicity reside, a more true grasp and enforcement of its spiritual meaning.

Take an example. There is none better for our purpose than that which is continually thrusting itself upon us in the discussion of the duration of future punishment. The condition of that question is one of the strangest of the phenomena of thought that ever have been seen. These two features in it impress us: first, it is being gravely and earnestly asserted that the principal question, at any rate a vital question, concerning the religion which teaches man that as the son of God it is his privilege and duty to love and obey his Father, is, What will become of him if he refuses to obey and love? and secondly, a multitude of men are found discussing whether punishment is to be temporary or eternal, who do not in their hearts believe that there is to be any punishment at all.

This state of things must have come from the loss or obscuration of the central truth, about which the whole problem of man's destiny must take its shape, which is the malignant and persistent character of human sin. Not as a question of what a few texts mean, not as a curious search after arbitrary enactments, but as a

[1] J. Ker, *Thoughts for Heart and Life*, 112.

deep study into the inevitable necessities of spiritual life, with a profound conviction that whatever comes to any man in the other life will come because it must come, because nothing else could come to such a man as he is, so ought the truth of future punishment to be investigated and enforced. For after all the preaching of rewards and punishments through all these centuries, the truth remains that no man in any century ever yet healthily and helpfully desired heaven who did not first desire holiness, and no man ever yet healthily and helpfully feared hell who did not first fear sin.

Men must be made to feel that the Christian religion is not a mass of separate questions having little connexion with one another, on all of which a man must have made up his mind before he can be counted a believer. The spiritual unity of the faith must be brought out and its simplicity asserted in the prominence given to the personal life and work of Jesus Christ and loyalty to Him as the test of all discipleship. There are excrescences upon the faith which puzzle and bewilder men and make them think themselves unbelievers when their hearts are really faithful. Such excrescences must be cast away, not by violent excision from without, but by the natural and healthy action of the system on which they have been fastened, which, as it grows stronger, will shed them, because they do not really belong to it. There are doctrinal statements which have done vast good though they were but the temporary aspects of truth as it struggled to its completest exhibition. They are doing vast good to-day, men are living by them still, but it is as men are seeing still the light of stars that were extinguished in the heavens years ago. Such partial, temporary statements men are still living by; but the time must come when they will disappear, and then it will be of all importance, when the star goes out, whether the men who have been looking at it and walking by it have known all along of the sun by whose light it shone, and which will shine on after this accidental and temporary point of its exhibition has disappeared for ever.

> God, if this were enough,
> That I see things bare to the buff
> And up to the buttocks in mire;
> That I ask nor hope nor hire,

DEGREES OF FAITH

Nut in the husk,
Nor dawn beyond the dusk,
Nor life beyond death:
God, if this were faith?

Having felt thy wind in my face
Spit sorrow and disgrace,
Having seen thine evil doom
In Golgotha and Khartoum,
And the brutes, the work of thine hands,
Fill with injustice lands
And stain with blood the sea:
If still in my veins the glee
Of the black night and the sun
And the lost battle, run:
If, an adept,
The iniquitous lists I still accept
With joy, and joy to endure and be withstood,
And still to battle and perish for a dream of good:
God, if that were enough?

If to feel in the ink of the slough,
And the sink of the mire,
Veins of glory and fire
Run through and transpierce and transpire,
And a secret purpose of glory in every part,
And the answering glory of battle fill my heart;
To thrill with the joy of girded men,
To go on for ever and fail and go on again,
And be mauled to the earth and arise,
And contend for the shade of a word and a thing not
    seen with the eyes:
With the half of a broken hope for a pillow at night
That somehow the right is the right
And the smooth shall bloom for the rough:
Lord, if that were enough?[1]

[1] R. L. Stevenson, "If this were Faith."

X.

THE GROWTH OF FAITH.

LITERATURE.

Alexander, A. B. D., *The Ethics of St. Paul* (1910).
Bamford, A. J., *Things that are Made* (1898).
Boyd, A. K. H., *Sermons and Stray Papers* (1907).
Bruce, A. B., *St. Paul's Conception of Christianity* (1894).
Calvin, J., *Institutes of the Christian Religion*.
Candole, H. L. C. V. de, *Christian Assurance* (1919).
Clarke, W. N., *An Outline of Christian Theology* (1898).
Dick, G. H., *The Yoke and the Anointing* (1893).
Ferries, G., *The Growth of Christian Faith* (1905).
Garvie, A. E., *The Christian Personality* (1904).
Harris, H., *Short Sermons* (1886).
Harris, J. R., *Memoranda Sacra* (1892).
Hatch, W. H. P., *The Pauline Idea of Faith* (1917).
Herman, E., *Christianity in the New Age* (1919).
Holdsworth, W. W., *The Life of Faith* (1911).
Hunter, J., *De Profundis Clamavi* (1908).
Inge, W. R., *Truth and Falsehood in Religion* (1906).
Lees, H. C., *The Sunshine of the Good News* (1912).
Mackay, W. M., *Bible Types of Modern Women* (1912).
Meyer, F. B., *The Soul's Wrestle with Doubt* (1905).
Morison, J., *Saving Faith* (1886).
Moule, H. C. G., *Faith* (1909).
Mursell, W. A., *Sermons on Special Occasions* (1912).
Parkhurst, C. H., *Three Gates on a Side* (1892).
Pulsford, J., *Quiet Hours*, ii. (1900).
Sidgwick, A., *School Homilies*, i. (1915).
Skrine, J. H., *The Heart's Counsel* (1899).
Smith, H. A., *Things New and Old* (1894).
Wallace, H., *Can we Know Jesus?* (1917).
Church Pulpit Year Book, vi. (1909) 111.

THE GROWTH OF FAITH.

ALTHOUGH faith is of Divine origin and a gift of God, nevertheless it is not at first perfect or complete. There is room for it to grow in strength and power, and apparently this growth may be indefinite. For after the Corinthians had been living the Christian life for some time, Paul expresses the hope that with the growth of their faith they may come to entertain a more just opinion of him, so that he may extend his missionary work to other fields. On the other hand, concerning the Thessalonians he feels that he ought to thank God continually for the exceedingly great growth of his converts' faith; for the Spirit's control over their lives has become greater, and in fellowship with Christ they have acquired a fuller and deeper knowledge of God. The "strong" brethren in the Roman community were also Christians of mature and robust faith. Faith might grow in depth and power, as it clearly had in the case of the Thessalonians and some of the believers in Rome.

Such growth indeed was the normal result of living in Christ, and is to be expected in the case of all Christians. For faith is a life, not simply a state or condition. And what is life but a constant moving and going forward? If our faith stands still, without any sign of improvement and increase in strength, it is a sure sign that there is something wrong in it. A child can no more remain always a child than faith can remain the same in a person year after year; there is but one thing that can stop the child's growth, and prevent it from becoming a man or woman, and that is the child's death. As long as it lives it must go on growing: and our faith, if it is a real living faith, must go on growing also.

Much of our faith, so-called, is only a beating of the air, and not really an advancement of the soul; we profess a great deal which has no practical bearing on our own lives. Yet all true believing is becoming, and a man cannot be a follower of the Lamb, in the real sense of the term, without his becoming moment by moment a different man; he alters his stature, not indeed by taking thought thereunto, but even as the lilies grow; and adding together the receiving and the becoming, we find that we are the children of God.

¶ If we take a stranger to view the Fitzwilliam Museum at Cambridge, it is possible that he will say that the outside is the finest part of it, and that it looks best from a distance; or he may say that the entrance-hall, with its display of coloured marbles and polished granite, is the best part of the museum. Certainly there are many that look at Christianity in this manner; thinking it perhaps a magnificent ideal of life, especially as seen in history; or perhaps as seen at some distance, as we view Sunday from the other days of the week. And others there are who think that the entrance of the Christian life is the best part of it, who say honestly from experience that the beginning of the life was the best for them. The reason being that they stopped there; otherwise people never could think that the happiest part of the life was that immediately consequent on conversion; for in reality the path of the just is a shining light, that shines more and more unto the perfect day. It is not like one of those ancient Egyptian temples of which one reads, in which we pass from daylight to shade as we enter, and into deeper gloom as we approach the secret shrine.[1]

I.

THE CONSCIOUSNESS OF PROGRESS.

1. In its first stage, faith may be compared to a seed. Christ Himself makes use of this very comparison, when, in answer to His disciples' prayer, "Lord, increase our faith," He says, "If ye had faith as a grain of mustard seed, ye might say unto this sycamine tree, Be thou plucked up by the root, and be thou planted in the sea; and it should obey you." And for the full meaning of this saying we have only to turn to His parable of the Mustard Seed, and we shall see that He points to the steady

[1] J. R. Harris, *Memoranda Sacra*, 20.

unfolding of faith. From being hid away in a corner of the heart, it springs up by degrees into a stately tree laden with fruit; and yet all along it is the same faith, the same in its first, almost invisible, beginning and in its final stateliness, as the oak is but the unfolded acorn, and the acorn contains within itself the future growth and strength of the oak.

¶ Is it not to be deplored, that faith should so often be accepted as an end, rather than a great beginning. Following a great beginning, there ought to be a *great progress*, that there may be a *great end*. In Christ, your character has a right and a real beginning. You will never have to repent of, nor to alter, this beginning. Your beginning is truly *for eternity*; for *Christ* is Eternal. He is "All and in all." "It hath pleased the Father that in Him *all fullness* should dwell." All creations and possibilities are in Him and from Him. "If you have received Christ Jesus the Lord," do not stand still,—"*walk in Him*." Faith is but the starting-post of your race: you must keep the racecourse, "forgetting those things which are behind and *reaching forth unto those things which are before*," if you mean to win "the prize." According to another figure; Faith is not your eternal house, but the first stone thereof on the Foundation, Jesus Christ: you must go on to build up your house, and you must take heed how you build thereupon.[1]

2. But the progress of faith is not a mere instinctive act or series of actions. It is our Lord's teaching that before beginning to build we must count the cost. The faith which, in the plant, goes forward in the absence of prudential considerations, will not go forward in us until the difficulties arising from such considerations have been solved. Our faith must count the cost before beginning to build, and be sure of being able to finish. If I, with power to count the cost, with the capacity of anticipating difficulty and disaster common to man, and perhaps with an inveterate tendency more special to myself of foreboding failure, can go forward as unhesitatingly as the mustard seed grows, it can be only because I have laid such firm hold on the fact of my relation to God that I know myself under His commandment—my feet in the way of obedience—and am, therefore, assured of His help. It is not that a delusion, which I am pleased to call "faith," has blinded my eyes to facts. I know the difficulties in my way to be

[1] J. Pulsford, *Quiet Hours*, ii. 16.

as serious as before, the obstacles as many; but I know also that the things that are impossible with men are possible with God. This consciousness of a Divine commission, which makes personally applicable to me every Divine promise, overcometh the world.

¶ If there be growth within us, we know it, for we are changed. Once, slaves to our passions—are we now the children of the will of God? Once, the opinion and the favour of the world were our guides and our goal—do we now suffer carelessly the loss of these things, so only we may approve ourselves to Him who judgeth righteously? Once, yielding readily to wrong, when wrong was pleasant and made life interesting—are we now resolute against temptation? Once, living wholly for this world, utterly wretched at the thought of death—are we now, while we bear the burdens of others here, pilgrims also of the invisible, and not ashamed to die? Once, careless or contemptuous of the thought of God, lightly or impertinently weary of any worship, any religion, do we now reverence the mighty realities of God and His Fatherhood, the reality of His life in the soul, of the love and communion of Christ Jesus, of our spiritual union with the race of man dead and alive, of eternal life, of duty, faith, self-sacrifice in and for God, and for man in God?[1]

3. In the prosecution of our own schemes, in following the devices and desires of our own hearts, we need to calculate very carefully what means we have at our disposal, to see what they are beforehand, and to test strictly their value. But when we are about our Father's business, when a Divine voice is calling us to service, we are justified in our expectation of rendering such service, not at our own charges, but supplied from Divine resources. We count the cost and estimate our means as accurately in the one case as in the other; but we have the faith of the grain of mustard seed in the latter case. Knowing ourselves servants of God, we know that the wealth of heaven and earth is ours in this service; and, therefore, though we count the cost we do it without anxiety.

¶ What men in their senses would tell four thousand or five thousand men to sit down on the grass and enter upon the task of feeding them with some half-dozen loaves and two or three fishes? The disciples never contemplated any such thing. Before they began to distribute their bread among the hungry ranks of men

[1] S. A. Brooke, *Sunshine and Shadow*, 107.

THE GROWTH OF FAITH

they believed they were entrusted with supplies other and more than the few paltry loaves they were handling. This was no philanthropic design of their own; it was the will of Him whose power they did not expect to see exhausted. Here at least they had the faith of the grain of mustard seed, and drew upon unseen resources.[1]

> In simple trust like theirs who heard,
>   Beside the Syrian sea,
> The gracious calling of the Lord,
> Let us, like them, without a word,
>   Rise up and follow Thee.

4. This conscious energetic life of faith should make progress steadily, uninterruptedly. It is motion in a straight line, and not in a closed curve. It is not like an Irish penance around a sacred well where we make progress with the final result of being where we started, and perhaps ready for another revolution, as indeed it must appear to some Christians whose circle is a week and whose starting-point a Sunday. Neither is it like the pilgrimage up Pilate's staircase at Rome, in which the pain of going up on our knees is varied only by the discomfort of coming down again and finding ourselves just about where we were before, as it must appear to some good people who live the up-and-down life. It is an upward and onward life; on our knees, if you will, but upward and upward and, like the stairs in Ezekiel's vision, still upward. And the Scriptures encourage us forward, bidding us leave the word of the beginning of Christ and go (not crawl) on unto perfection.

It is, however, a common experience that after the enthusiasm and joy of the beginning there comes a period of stagnation, sometimes even of backsliding. This has been attributed to the continued presence of legalism. History attests that it has ever been found a hard thing to remain standing on the platform of free grace. Descent from that high level to a lower, from grace to law, from faith to technical "good works," from liberty to bondage, seems to be a matter of course in religious experience, individual and collective. What happened in Galatia repeats itself from age to age, and in all churches. Legalism in some form recurs with the regularity of a law of nature.

[1] A. J. Bamford, *Things that are Made*, 139.

How, then, are we to reconcile this fact with the all-sufficiency of faith? We shall best do this by taking into account the law of growth in the Kingdom of God, enunciated by our Lord in the parable of the blade, the ear, and the ripe corn. Legalism is a characteristic of the stage of the green ear, in the spiritual life of the individual and of the community. The blossom and the ripe fruit, the beginning and the end of a normal Christian experience, exhibit the beauty of pure evangelic faith. The green fruit is a lapse from the simplicity of the beginning, a lapse which is at the same time a step in advance, as it prepares the way for a higher stage, in which evangelic faith shall reappear victorious over the legal spirit of fear, distrust, and self-reliance.

The cherry blossom was so proud, so gay,
    She told me yesterday
    That she would never die,
    That her white, exquisite, apparent immaturity
Would spread itself for ever,
    While the bee
Sucked, humming love songs, sweetness that would never
    Cease to be sweet
        From stamens rich amazingly
    And meet
            Eternally to furnish golden love dust
                For endless wooings meant.
She was so proud, so gay,
        So confident,
    I could not choose but trust
All that I heard her saying yesterday.

To-day a little lonely, fluttering,
Pale, fragile, frenzied thing
    Came panic strick'n and dumb;
    (Pathetically scared it seemed, poor leafling, so to come)
It settled on my shoulder
    Breathlessly,
And feeling it I felt the world grow older
        Until it shrank
            And shrivelled to nonentity,
        A blank
            Unmeaning world, annihilate, undivine.

THE GROWTH OF FAITH

> But in a flash there came
> Knowledge that swiftly grew,
> Spreading like flame.
> I have seen the sign, the sign!
> Have known her boast irrevocably true.[1]

5. What warning there for the soul which goes to sleep upon childhood's first beliefs! What encouragement to the honestly perplexed with difficulties! Belief is a growth: let it grow then, and, as man's stature outgrows its unsymmetries, let faith outgrow its disharmonies.

> O that I may grow!
> I see the leaves out-pushing hour by hour,
> With steady joy the buds burst out aflower
> Urged gladly on by Nature's waking power.
> O that I may grow.
>
> O that I may grow!
> What though Time cuts his furrows in my face,
> My heart may ever add grace unto grace,
> Graces with added days still keeping pace.
> O that I may grow.[2]

II.

THE ENCOURAGEMENT OF PROGRESS.

How is the growth of faith to be fostered? By increase of knowledge, by enlargement of experience, by the example of others, by prayer, and by the practice of the presence of God.

1. *Knowledge.*—The question of how much knowledge or intellectual understanding of Divine things is indispensable to an effective faith is one that we cannot answer. Experience shows that a very slight knowledge may often be a sufficient intellectual foundation for a strong and efficient faith. Discernment of truth is one thing, and willingness to accept truth is another; and strength of faith is governed more by willingness of heart than by intellectual discernment. Often we find clear perception with

---

[1] S. Miles, *Dunch*, 69.
[2] M. D. Babcock, *Thoughts for Every-Day Living*, 167.

little faith, and faint perception with strong faith. Since faith belongs more to the heart than to the intellect, intellectual understanding often avails less than we expect. Knowledge of theories concerning salvation helps but little, and explanations regarding Divine things often prove disappointing. Efforts to clear the way for personal faith by imparting such knowledge fail as often as they are successful. There is a simplicity in Divine things, by virtue of which the gospel of God's love needs little explanation; and the perception of this simplicity is the knowledge that is most helpful in the encouraging of faith. Faith is most helped at its beginning by seeing that God gives and man has but to receive. Even this may be intellectually apprehended without spiritual profit, but faith springs up as soon as the heart perceives this with its own peculiar insight.

¶ Is it faith to understand nothing, and merely submit your convictions implicitly to the Church? Faith consists not in ignorance, but in knowledge—knowledge not of God merely, but of the divine will. We do not obtain salvation either because we are prepared to embrace every dictate of the Church as true, or leave to the Church the province of inquiring and determining; but when we recognize God as a propitious Father through the reconciliation made by Christ, and Christ as given to us for righteousness, sanctification, and life. By this knowledge, I say, not by the submission of our understanding, we obtain an entrance into the kingdom of heaven. For when the Apostle says, "With the heart man believeth unto righteousness; and with the mouth confession is made unto salvation" (Rom. x. 10), he intimates, that it is not enough to believe implicitly without understanding, or even inquiring. The thing requisite is an explicit recognition of the divine goodness, in which our righteousness consists.[1]

2. *Experience.*—Faith grows as it is nourished by the events and crises of life. Anything that stirs us out of the monotonies of life and lifts us from grooves, throws us out more consciously upon the support of the Divine arms. Whenever we find ourselves suddenly confronting the unknown, faith is stirred within us. When we part with our friends for a season we say "goodbye," and perhaps think into the words all the meaning they properly contain—"God be with you." And when we bid our friends a long

---

[1] Calvin, *Institutes of the Christian Religion,* ii. 97.

farewell—how our hearts reach up unto God, and with what earnest looking unto Him we follow them as they move through the swinging gate and go to be with them that have gone on before and wait to bid us welcome when we shall follow.

May we who rest so cosily in the comforts and amenities of life, and who lean so heavily upon the enriching friendships of the good and the strong and the beloved, discover, when disappointments strike and bereavements overtake, that our leaning, even more than we suspected, was after all upon the arm of the Lord. As the light becomes paler and paler in the west may the stars glow with a steadier and cheerier splendour. And when we come at last to the night-fall of life, like Eliezer out amid the evening lights of Mesopotamia, may our faith assert itself in the gloaming, and may there be the revealing to us of the Divine arm mighty to save, the Divine hand gentle to shelter and to guide.

¶ If a man really love truth, if he be a disciple of progress, he will not permit himself to state his belief in the same terms year after year. As every year brings new experiences, so should it offer fresh interpretation of life. The genuine truth-seeker is more eager to keep the mind open than to arrive at some established conclusion. He hopes never to have any permanently settled beliefs, for he contemplates an eternity of intellectual progress. What a glorious prospect—the everlasting pursuit of truth![1]

> The words he uttered shall not pass away
> Dispersed, like music that the wind takes up
> By snatches, and lets fall, to be forgotten;
> No—they sank into me, the bounteous gift
> Of one whom time and nature had made wise,
> Gracing his doctrine with authority
> Which hostile spirits silently allow;
> Of one accustomed to desires that feed
> On fruitage gathered from the tree of life;
> To hopes on knowledge and experience built;
> Of one in whom persuasion and belief
> Had ripened into faith, and faith become
> A passionate intuition; whence the Soul,
> Though bound to earth by ties of pity and love,
> From all injurious servitude was free.[2]

[1] H. W. Dresser, in *Underneath the Bough*, 58.
[2] Wordsworth, "The Excursion," bk. iv.

3. *Example.*—If there is a duty to press forward there is also encouragement, a stimulating inducement, to do so. For other people are to be seen or known who have risen far towards the condition which man ought to exhibit, and the sight of them is invigorating. Their mind is clear and radiant; their faith, their principles and character are mature and settled; their step is firm and sure. They exert a powerful influence for good on the downcast spirit. Observation of them, or brief contact with them, restores to inward health and hope. They embody the nature we fondly desire; they show it to be attainable by beings of flesh and blood, living in the same times and amid the same surroundings as ourselves. By them the seeker for the highest good is convinced that he is on the right way; he is insensibly restored to hopefulness, and even enthusiasm. The truest, bravest, and most unselfish lives discovered in modern days call forth the sincere and delighted approbation of the person who has begun to keep close to God and to choose His will. He singles them out without difficulty from the general mass, accords them all honour for the worth which is exhibited, sees them to be guiding-stars for his own thought and practice. They stand high, so as to attract with power; they are not so eminent as to discourage by seeming to be of another order of being than oneself. They are what "every man in arms should wish to be." There is a common stamp impressed upon them, notwithstanding their individual characteristics. They have steadfast faith in God and His goodness, a faculty of self-control, a certain sense of superiority to the judgments that may be passed on them in the world, a passion for righteousness, a sincere love for mankind, and as the leading aim in life the purpose and endeavour to promote righteousness and charity on earth. And as a result, they give proof of a restfulness and a sunny serenity of soul in themselves, a clearness of conviction even in perplexing circumstances, weight of character, a fulness of the inner nature that is unfathomable, a mystery of the formed personality that exerts a ceaseless charm on others.

¶ It has been said that reverence of great names is the secular side of the ecclesiastical doctrine of the communion of saints, but it is necessary to remember that such reverence, if it is to elevate and ennoble us, must be directed aright, must be bestowed on what is really worthy of it. We must see that, when we let ourselves be inspired by the luminous idea of a great character, we take it in its purest form, free from the details, exaggerations, and prejudices of its historic setting. It would be as grossly unfair to judge Oliver Cromwell as merely or mainly the executioner of Charles I. as it would be to honour Nelson merely or mainly as the hero of Trafalgar. What we are morally bound to look for in a great man is, first, that he shall have worked for principles which we believe to be fruitful, and which are our own by virtue of that belief; and, next, that he shall have been the inspirer of his own action in virtue of character and therefore worthy of admiration and imitation. It is because Nelson answers these two conditions that we are able to accept him as a national hero. He worked for great principles—for fruitful principles, the value of which we realize even more now than they did a century ago. The great victory of Trafalgar, which secured for us the undisputed sovereignty of the sea, meant the liberty of our land, the extension of our empire, the development of our commerce, and the opportunity of moulding and building up our national character on nobler Christian lines, independent of continental corruptions. Captain Mahan writes of Nelson's " humble and sincere gratitude to God for rendering him the chief instrument of deliverance to his native land," and how, " by his devout recollection of his indebtedness to God, he sought continually to keep himself in hand." His last prayer, offered up on the morn of battle in sight of the opposing fleet, tells us why they buried him in the centre of St. Paul's, immediately under the very cross itself which surmounts the dome. " May the great God whom I worship grant to my country and for the benefit of Europe in general a great and glorious victory, and may no misconduct in any one tarnish it; may humanity after victory be the predominant feature in the British fleet. For myself, individually, I commit my life to Him who made me, and may His blessings alight on my endeavours to serve my country faithfully. To Him I resign myself and the just cause which is entrusted to me to defend. 'Amen! Amen! Amen!" Here is a prayer which breathes throughout the simplest, purest, highest faith of all—it is in truth that victory which overcometh the world.[1]

4. *Prayer.*—Prayer may very well come first, and stay last. And that not merely because it is a commonplace to say that prayer is the best way to get any blessing, notably any spiritual blessing; but because, in fact, a great many Christian people have found that, when by reading sceptical books, or associating much

[1] *Church Pulpit Year Book*, vi. 112.

with worldly society, or being greatly engrossed by worldly business, they have of a sudden discerned that their grasp of the truth they live by is weakened, there has come, God be thanked, through making it matter of prayer for several days, continually, a wonderful strengthening and brightening of their belief, a taking away of doubts, a setting firm upon the One Foundation.

Prayer does for faith what the soil does for the seed. The growth of a seed depends upon its response to its environment. It is the result of its acceptance of certain conditions. Some seeds are never put into conditions of growth; they may lie in a box or a packet, or as loose grain in a granary. But let the seed be put in the earth, and at once it is in its element. The chymic properties of the earth and the air co-operate with it; rain, dew, wind, sunshine all come to play upon it; by and by it appears in tender beauty above the ground and lives the life natural to its kind. It is not otherwise with the faith of men. It must be set in conditions of growth; it must respond to its environment. In many men faith lies hidden and dormant like the seed in the box; the capacity is there, the force is there, but it has never been used. It needs to be drawn out by a power akin to it. If we could endow a seed with personality and speech, we might imagine it to declare, "I believe in the sunshine; I believe in the great powers that cause the life to stir so mightily within me; I believe in the influence that draws me out of myself, changing the character of my whole life, giving me a new outlook, bringing me out of the dark ground into the sweet air and the living light of day: there is a force in me that moves towards the sun; I *feel* it; if I respond to it and yield myself to it I shall fulfil my proper function and realize my native destiny." And so, according to its faith, the seed yields itself up, pushes through the mould, and is rewarded by seeing the sunshine it believed in, and by being clothed upon in its native beauty.

¶ A young artist once complained to William Blake that the power of invention had forsaken him. To his astonishment, Blake turned to his wife suddenly, and said, " It is just so with us, is it not, for weeks together, when the visions forsake us ? What do we then do ? " asked he. " We kneel down and pray," said she.[1]

[1] G. H. Dick, *The Yoke and the Anointing*, 98.

King's Daughter!
Would'st thou be all fair,
Without—within—
Peerless and beautiful,
A very Queen?

Know then:—
Not as men build unto the Silent One,—
With clang and clamour,
Traffic of rude voices,
Clink of steel on stone,
And din of hammer;—
Not so the temple of thy grace is reared.
But,—in the inmost shrine
Must thou begin,
And build with care
A Holy Place,
A place unseen,
Each stone a prayer.
Then, having built,
Thy shrine sweep bare
Of self and sin,
And all that might demean;
And, with endeavour,
Watching ever, praying ever,
Keep it fragrant-sweet, and clean:
So, by God's grace, it be fit place,—
His Christ shall enter and shall dwell therein.
Not as in earthly fane—where chase
Of steel on stone may strive to win
Some outward grace,—
Thy temple face is chiselled from within.[1]

5. *Presence of God.*—Many know that memorable narrative, "The Practice of the Presence of God," the record of the experience of one Lawrence, the "lay-brother" of a French monastery in the seventeenth century, who developed to a noble degree and to great results of holiness the habit of recollection that "the Lord is near." Always, everywhere, as much in work-time as in the hour of prayer, as truly in the kitchen as in the chapel, he "remembered God" as present. His experience is for us also, if we also will seek it in humility and with practical resolution.

[1] J. Oxenham, "Everymaid."

Let that habit be formed, and we shall already be far on the way to a developed habit of faith exercised under the real needs of life. To recollect the neighbourhood of God, of our God, of the Father in the Son, the Son in the Father, brought to be not only near us but in our hearts by His Spirit—this is already to stand *habitually* ready to trust Him, and to speak to Him as those who trust. And this habituation of the soul to speak to Him, anywhere, at any moment, about anything, will be the natural process towards the habit of faith in its mature and beautiful fulness.

¶ Let us converse with God, till the habit to tell Him everything and to trust Him in everything becomes inveterate. Let us take the very next opportunity to begin; the difficult work, the troublesome letter, the apparent conflict of duties, the narrowness of means, the death of the beloved, the isolation, the growing old and tired. A hundred difficulties are around us; but Faith, that is to say, God trusted, is a master-key for the prison-doors of life. *Solvitur ambulando*, it was said of old—the problem is solved by walking. We will extend the saying by two words: *Solvitur ambulando cum Deo*—the problem is solved by the walk of Faith with God.[1]

> No, when the fight begins within himself,
> A man's worth something. God stoops o'er his head,
> Satan looks up between his feet—both tug—
> He's left, himself, i' the middle: the soul wakes
> And grows. Prolong that battle through his life!
> Never leave growing till the life to come![2]

III.

THE SIGNS OF PROGRESS.

How is progress in faith to be known? There are at least three good signs of it.

1. *A keener sense of sin.*—If there be genuine progress, while the power of sin will grow less, the sense of sinfulness will grow greater; for, as sin blinds and dulls the conscience, when sin

---

[1] H. C. G. Moule, *Faith*, 90.
[2] Browning, "Bishop Blougram's Apology."

THE GROWTH OF FAITH

grows weaker, conscience becomes more keen and tender. The deepest contrition of heart for sin is found, not in the newly-saved sinner, but in the fully-grown saint.

¶ Faith grows upon the soil of felt sin.[1]

2. *Greater dependence on Christ.*—Faith will seek and find an ever fuller measure—the inexhaustible grace of God in Christ. As the sense of need grows in the consciousness of the fulness that can meet it, the receptivity and responsiveness of the human personality to the Divine communion and communication will develop. The end of this growth is not self-sufficiency, but larger appropriation of and deeper satisfaction in the sufficiency which is of God in Christ.

> Thou knowest, Lord, the weariness and sorrow
>   Of the sad heart that comes to Thee for rest;
> Cares of to-day, and burdens for to-morrow,
>   Blessings implored, and sins to be confessed,—
> I come before Thee at Thy gracious word,
> And lay them at Thy feet: Thou knowest, Lord.
>
> Thou knowest all the past: how long and blindly
>   On the dark mountains the lost wanderer strayed;
> How the Good Shepherd followed, and how kindly
>   He bore it home, upon His shoulders laid,
> And healed the bleeding wounds, and soothed the pain,
> And brought back life and hope and strength again.
>
> Thou knowest all the present: each temptation,
>   Each toilsome duty, each foreboding fear;
> All to myself assigned of tribulation,
>   Or to belovèd ones than self more dear;
> All pensive memories, as I journey on,
> Longings for vanished smiles and voices gone.
>
> Thou knowest all the future: gleams of gladness
>   By stormy clouds too quickly overcast;
> Hours of sweet fellowship, and parting sadness,
>   And the dark river to be crossed at last;
> O what could confidence and hope afford
> To tread that path, but this: "Thou knowest, Lord"?[2]

---

[1] *Reminiscences of Andrew A. Bonar, D.D.*, 137.
[2] Jane L. Borthwick.

3. *Singleness of vision and of aim.*—It was the whole-hearted, unreserved, persistent, unfailing committal of themselves to the will of God that Jesus asked from the men around Him when He asked for faith in God. They were, though sentimentally religious, living a poor, broken, compromising life. They hoped for the Divine kingdom of their prophets' visions and prayers, but their eyes were also fixed on the glittering seductions of worldly and selfish ambition. They were eager for both the earthly and the heavenly things, but they had neither as ruling motive or purpose. They were divided against themselves, irresolute and unstable. Their confidence in the higher things was constantly yielding to fears, jealousies, and rivalries inspired by their love of the lower things. They tried to pursue a middle course, to serve two masters, to divide their allegiance between God and the world at war with the will of God. The call of Jesus was: " Have faith in God! Free yourselves from this dualism of the moral life! Break the tyranny of this double-mindedness! Do not conduct half of your life on one principle and the other half on a different principle! Let one great principle, one great affection, one great purpose, have full control of your life from centre to circumference in all its relations and parts! Deliver yourselves to follow the will of God! Let the will of God be your one all-comprehending allegiance!" It was this utter singleness of motive and aim, this sole devotion and service, this absolute surrender to the absolutely true and right, which Jesus called faith in God and to which He committed Himself and His cause.

¶ Whatever Lord Radstock thought right he did and said, and one noticed that he seemed to grow, as he grew older, in the graces of humility and liberality and to become one of the broadest Christians one ever met. He always reminded one of the words " This one thing I do "—his great and absorbing desire being to bring others to know Christ as a personal Saviour.[1]

[1] Mrs. E. Trotter, *Lord Radstock: An Interpretation and a Record*, 134.

XI.

THE FIGHT OF FAITH.

LITERATURE.

Brett, J., *The Cross* (1918).
Brooks, P., *The Mystery of Iniquity* (1893).
Burroughs, E. A., *The Valley of Decision* (1917).
Clifford, J., *Typical Christian Leaders* (1898).
Fosdick, H. E., *The Meaning of Faith* (1918).
Gurney, T. A., *The First Epistle to Timothy* (1907).
Horne, C. S., in *Sermons and Addresses* (1889).
Jenkins, E. E., *Life and Christ* (1896).
McNeile, A. P., *Letters on Faith* (1917).
Moule, H. C. G., *The Second Epistle to Timothy* (1905).
Nicoll, W. R., *The Garden of Nuts* (1905).
Oman, J., *Grace and Personality* (1917).
Oosterzee, J. J. van, *The Year of Salvation*, ii.
Porter, N., *Yale College Sermons* (1888).
Selby, T. G., *The Alienated Crown* (1904).
Christian World Pulpit, liv. (1898) 305 (F. W. Farrar).
Expositor, 7th Ser., ii. (1906) 284 (W. M. Ramsay).
Great Texts of the Bible: Genesis to Numbers (1911).

THE FIGHT OF FAITH.

1. THE phrase, "the fight of faith" is found in 1 Tim. vi. 12, "Fight the good fight of faith, lay hold on eternal life." The translation is an unfortunate one. The metaphor is not that of the battle but that of the ring. It is another example of the picture with which St. Paul makes us familiar, the picture of the wrestling or boxing match, with its strict conditions, its tense agony of struggle, its cloud of witnesses, its chaplet of reward to the victor (1 Cor. ix. 24; Phil. iii. 12; 1 Tim. iv. 10).

The expression in 2 Tim. iv. 7, "I have fought the good fight" is an instructive parallel. The old saint's mind goes back upon mental pictures dear in earlier days, and he sees again the struggling limbs and the swift feet of the Greek athletes. Life had long ago seemed to him to be vividly parabled by those scenes. In one great passage (1 Cor. ix. 24–27) he had developed the illustration in minute and powerful detail; the stern discipline of training, the strict rules, the rejection which must follow an infraction, the straight eager course of the runners, the terribly purposeful blows of the boxers, the wreath of leaves, "corruptible" shadow of the amaranthine crown of the victorious Christian. Again and again in other less conspicuous passages he had used those familiar and eloquent associations to animate himself and his disciples to live true to the Lord, true to present grace and to coming glory. Once more here, the *athlete of Christ* speaks the old dialect, but now with the accent of achievement and repose. He is so very near the end, so very much of the peculiar trial of his lot is for ever over, the "journeyings often," "the care of all the churches" (2 Cor. xi. 26, 28), and so certain is his Master to love him and to uphold him over those few difficult paces before the end that he speaks as if already off the field. Christ Jesus had enabled him so long for such a life that it was a relatively minor thing (may we not dare to say it?) to be sure that He would enable him, with a glorious adequacy, for the one last step of death.

¶ How often these farewell words have voiced the gratitude and courage, the calm and hope, of the saints of God, in the long course of the centuries, no tongue can tell; but assuredly no one in these later times had more authentic right to use them of himself than Charles Haddon Spurgeon, who repeated them as his last words at Mentone to his faithful secretary. It, too, was a pathetic scene. The worn warrior lays down his sword—a sword trusted in a thousand fights for God and right and truth, and says, "I have fought the good fight." One can hardly read it without a choking at the throat; but at once we feel the great utterances are as true of our nineteenth-century Paul as they were of the Apostle of the first century. They describe the entire purpose and distinctive temper of his life, and indicate the exhaustless sources of his boldness and fortitude, energy and valour. They are true of him as a lad and a man, as a preacher and writer, as a worker and builder. He was intrinsically a Crusader of massive strength and sterling character, imperturbable fearlessness and irresistible dash. Like Browning, he "was ever a fighter." The sword of the Lord was in his hands from his youth, and he attained to marvellous skill in the use of it. Sometimes, as with a battering-ram, he went against his foes, and overcame them. Verily he fought; he was always fighting, and his fight was a good one.[1]

2. But even if the metaphor in 1 Tim. vi. 12 were correctly reproduced, "fight the fight" is not idiomatic English. St. Paul's expression is literally "agonize the agony." Ellicott and Alford attempt to reproduce it with "strive the strife," which is no better English than "fight the fight." We must either accept the Greek idiom or be content with a paraphrase, such as "maintain the good contest of the faith."

¶ Weymouth's translation is: "Exert all your strength in the honourable struggle for the Faith"; the Twentieth Century New Testament: "Run the great race of the Faith"; Moffatt: "Fight in the good fight of the faith"; Way: "Wrestle in the glorious struggle of the Faith."

3. What is the meaning of "faith" in this place? In our

[1] J. Clifford, *Typical Christian Leaders*, 87.

modern speech we have come to use the word "faith" in two different senses. We describe by it that spirit of trust in God which is the key to salvation—the great principle informing and controlling genuine Christian life in all its stages. And this without doubt was the first meaning of the word. But the word "faith" is also used to denote the body of doctrine accepted in common by the disciples of Jesus Christ—those dogmatic interpretations of the New Testament teaching which have been built up in part by intellectual methods. In this secondary signification the word is a synonym for religion and formulated religious beliefs.

The following clause is decisive for the first of those meanings: "lay hold on the life eternal." Moreover "faith" here is obviously identified with the "good confession" borne "before many witnesses"; but the subject-matter of that confession is a personal experience, together with the gospel facts authenticated in that experience, and not a tradition. The faith for which he had to wage unresting warfare was a larger ramification of that which was the motive power of his conversion—a faith which united him not only to the Redeemer but also to the Redeemer's work, and was to be continuous through the successive acts of his vocation.

God in His wisdom has seen fit to determine that this root principle of the spiritual life shall be proved, strained, and perfected, by much buffeting and contradiction. He who has come into the possession of faith and would keep it to the end finds himself a combatant, whether he desires the part or not. A continuous faith is incompatible with quiescent moods and an unruffled career. Faith, whether we think of it as a life implanted within ourselves and our fellow-disciples, as the secret and the earnest of a character to be achieved, and of a providential work to be fulfilled, or whether we think of it as the burden of a testimony we must bear to our contemporaries, thrusts us into fierce and perhaps daily struggle. It marks out for us, clear as the lines drawn on a military map, an area within which our inward and outward strife must be passionate, if we are to guard that which is even more sacred than hearth and home.

In its attitude, towards both the present and the future, faith is meant to be an intense, sustained, valiant, pauseless advance, a pressing forward in face of much that would keep us back, a pressing upward through the down-driving clouds. The spirit of trust to which we are summoned is not all soothing poetry, gracious sentiment, uninterrupted and speckless sunshine. The temper of the disciple is prevented from settling down into drowsy religious affability. Faith is a receptive faculty of the new life opening the nature to all the gifts of God; but it needs effort to maintain the receptive habit, and if the habit is lost, whilst we are in moods of spiritual exhaustion produced by ingratitude, discouragement, human provocation, the bounties bestowed without money and without price cannot be freely conveyed to others. Faith itself is a gift of incalculable preciousness, but a gift bestowed to stimulate and embolden the wide ranging activities of the after life.

¶ Dante tells us that as soon as he essayed to climb the sunlit hill his way was challenged. It is a very ancient problem. The psalmist marvelled that, whilst the wicked around him enjoyed a most profound and unruffled tranquillity, his life was so full of perplexity and trouble. John Bunyan was arrested by the same inscrutable mystery. Why should he, in his pilgrim progress, be so storm-beaten and persecuted, whilst the people who abandoned themselves to folly enjoyed unbroken ease? Many a young and eager convert, fancying that the Christian life meant nothing but rapture, has been startled by the discovery of the beasts of prey awaiting him.[1]

> Shall I tell you about the battle
>   That was fought in the world to-day,
> Where thousands went down like heroes
>   To death in the pitiless fray?
>
> You may know some one of the wounded
>   And some of the fallen when
> I tell you this wonderful battle
>   Was fought in the hearts of men.
>
> Not with the sounding of trumpets
>   Nor clashing of sabres drawn,
> But silent as twilight in autumn,
>   All day the fight went on.
>
> And over against temptation
>   A mother's prayers were cast
> That had come by silent marches
>   From the lullaby land of the past.

[1] F. W. Boreham, *Faces in the Fire*, 189.

And over the field of battle
　　The force of ambition went,
Driving before it, like arrows,
　　The children of sweet content.

And memories odd and olden
　　Came up through the dust of years,
And hopes that were glad and golden
　　Were met by a host of fears.

And the hearts grew worn and weary,
　　And said, "Oh, can it be
That I am worth the struggle
　　You are making to-day for me?"

For the heart itself was the trophy
　　And prize of this wavering fight!
And tell me, O gentle reader,
　　Who camps on the field to-night?

4. Faith in God is the highest condition on earth of a human being. If faith in God is a reality, the realization of that faith is the highest conceivable state of men. How then is faith in God realized? In two ways—by growth in the knowledge of God and by fellowship with God.

(1) Now when faith unites me with God, there are two sources of growth: first, the natural effect upon my own mind of contemplating that which is infinitely higher than myself. By striving to know One who is too great for me ever to know perfectly, but whom I am invited and encouraged to know by the conscious progress I make in this knowledge, my faculties are in the condition of a constant and healthy strain, and necessarily expand. The second source of growth is not so easily defined, but, as a fact, it is equally distinct; there is the positive help communicated by the greater mind to the lesser. St. Paul expresses this truth perfectly: "The same Lord over all is rich unto all that call upon him" (Rom. x. 12). That is, if any man, be he Jew or Gentile, place himself by meditation and prayer under the sympathetic notice of the Divine presence, there will flow out to him immeasurable streams of sympathy, of love, and of revelation that shall act upon his strained faculties and upon his growth as a flood at the roots of a parched tree.

(2) Again, faith in God means friendship with God; and, whatever be the desirable aspects of human friendships, whether they take their origin in family life from the parent and the maturer offspring, or from the elder and the younger brother; or whether the affinities of taste, likeness, or pursuit, draw two minds together, the purest conditions and the noblest features of human intercourse are comprehended in indefinite capacity in our communion with the heavenly Father. If it be said that the idea of the Supreme Being is too vague from its vastness and its want of representation to awaken friendship in the worshipper, we reply that sympathy, trust, and love may flourish in a fellowship in which one of the parties is scarcely able to know anything of the other; as in the case of a young child whose affections thrive upon the simplest impressions and the mere touch of contact. But even supposing this objection could be made good as an abstract truth, it falls to the ground in the incarnation of Christianity, where the mystery of godliness is not in its obscurity but in its revelation: "manifested in the flesh" (1 Tim. iii. 16, RV). In Jesus Christ we love God when we love man; in the Maker of all men we behold the Brother of all men: and with the reverence, the trust, and the obedience inspired by the Godhead, we have the physical sympathy, the mutual suffering, and the common destiny which are the cords by which one man is drawn to another. Our friendship with God through Christ is not merely friendship with God, but is the model and inspiration of the entire circle of human relationships, without their frailties and their limitations. "Whosoever shall do the will of my Father which is in heaven, the same is my brother, and sister, and mother" (Matt. xii. 50).

I.

THE ENEMY.

Where is the enemy with whom the battle is fought? We do not need to go far to find him. The enemy is within. As Dr. Matheson wittily said, "The number of the Beast is No. 1." The battle is pitched where it always has been and always will be pitched—in the conquest of self for God. Now the conquest of

THE FIGHT OF FAITH

self for God is, first, to accept faith in God as the highest condition on earth of a human being; and, secondly, to subordinate in the pursuit of it, either for use or for temporary subjugation, every faculty, every passion, and every circumstance in life.

Here is the fight of faith: we do not contend here with metaphysical objections, or with the obscurities and imperfections of rational evidence; but with fleshly lusts, which war against the soul (1 Pet. ii. 11); with pride and undisciplined desire; with those idols which the mind makes for itself, and which gratify its covetousness, its sloth, its bigotry, its self-glory, and its hatred of subjection. Here the contest is with self. If in seeking faith in God "thy right eye offend thee," if that which belongs to thee, which was created by God Himself for thy use, is perverted from its use, and interferes with that within thee which is higher than itself, mortify it, even though its disuse mar the symmetry of thy life; it is more profitable for thee that thou shouldest do without it; it is for transcendent interests that these temporary losses and humiliations must be incurred. Every man must determine for himself which is the stumbling-block of his path. Our Lord, by suggesting three—the right eye, the right hand, and the foot—covers everything that is supposed to minister to pleasure and advancement; by rudely treating the most delicate and sensitive organ of the body, and disabling that which gives uprightness, support, and locomotion to the frame, the Divine Teacher shows that the finest and most cultured sentiments may be in our way, and the strongest and, considered in themselves, the noblest principles, principles which are intended to lead men on, may have a fatal bias, and make them step aside instead of marching forward.

Surely it always must be full of meaning that Christ Himself, before He began His struggles with the Pharisees and Scribes, went out into the desert and struggled with Himself. It must have been present with Him ever afterwards, that wrestling with the evil spirit and all the knowledge of Himself which it called out. Many a time the wilfulness, and narrowness, and selfishness which He saw in the faces which surrounded Him in some crowd in the temple must have been clearer to Him and easier to understand because they were just the passions which had tried to take possession of His own heart, and failed, during those long terrible days in the dark wilderness. There is no way in which whatever personal struggles with faithlessness and sin we may have gone through can be made to keep their freshness and power, and at the same time be kept from becoming a source of morbid wretchedness, no way that is half so efficient as that they should constantly be called on to light up for us the same sort of struggles in other men, and give us the power to help them with intelligence and sympathy. Demand that lofty service of every deep experience through which you pass. Demand that it shall help you to understand and aid the battles of your brethren, and then the devils of memory which haunt your life may be turned into strong angels, by whose help you may do the will of God, and be in some small way the Saviour of mankind.

¶ Inside of all the other battles we are fighting, there is the battle with ourselves. Inside of the battle with the world for the world, which the great champions of righteousness are fighting in their great way, and which you and I, I hope, are fighting in our little way, there lies the battle which every true man is always fighting with himself for himself—himself the hostile enemy, himself the precious prize. Oh, how real sometimes all that must become to the great workers for mankind! While Howard is travelling all over Europe, from prison to prison, while Clarkson has his hand upon the fetters of the slave, while Francke is gathering his orphans around him and struggling with their ignorance, while Garrison is striving to free the slave, sometimes the heart of each of them must have grown sick and faint with the freshly heard sound of its own inner conflict; sometimes each of them must have turned aside and shut the door upon all the tumult of the world and left the great cause for an hour to take care of itself, while he fought with himself for himself—with himself his own enemy, for himself his own prize. There are verses enough, you know, in St. Paul's Epistles which let us see that struggle with himself going on all the time underneath the other struggle with the men of Jerusalem and Athens. While the foreign war was raging, the home country also was all up in arms. How such men must have thought often within themselves that the foreign war would be as nothing, would be a very easy thing, if only there were peace at home. "I could convert the world easily," the missionary must often find himself saying, "if only I had a solid ground to stand upon, if only my own life were not all soft and weak with sin and doubt." And sometimes, too, the other thought must come, "What right have I to be busying myself with the world's miseries while all this unrest is tumultuous within me? Why is it not best to shut in myself upon myself and fight my own battle out before I meddle with the bigger battle?"

Such thoughts come naturally; but really it is good, no doubt, that the two strifes, the outer and the inner, the strife with self and the strife with the world's sin, should go on together. The man who knew no enemy within himself, who was so absorbed in fighting with the world's sin that he grew unconscious of his own inner life, by and by would become arrogant and superficial. Such men the world has often seen among its philanthropists. The man who is totally wrapped up in the war within him, the war with himself for his own life, grows selfish and grows morbid. The two must go on together. Each keeps the other healthy and true. Fight with your own sin, and let that fight keep you humble and full of sympathy when you go out into the world and strike at the sin of which the world is full. Fight with the world's sin, and let the needs of that fight make you aware of how much is wrong, and make you eager that everything shall be right within yourself. Here is the balance and mutual ministry of self-care and world-care which makes the truest man the healthiest philanthropist.[1]

"I search but cannot see
What purpose serves the soul that strives, or world it tries
Conclusions with, unless the fruit of victories
Stay, one and all, stored up and guaranteed its own
For ever, by some mode whereby shall be made known
The gain of every life. Death reads the title clear—
What each soul for itself conquered from out things here:
Since, in the seeing soul, all worth lies, I assert."

In this passage, Browning gives expression to an idea which continually reappears in his pages—the idea that human life, in its essence, is movement to moral goodness through opposition. His fundamental conception of the human spirit is that it is a process and not a fixed fact. "Man," he says, "was made to grow not stop."

"Getting increase of knowledge, since he learns
Because he lives, which is to be a man,
Set to instruct himself by his past self."

[1] P. Brooks, *The Mystery of Iniquity*, 82.

"By such confession straight he falls
Into man's place, a thing nor God nor beast,
Made to know that he can know and not more:
Lower than God who knows all and can all,
Higher than beasts which know and can so far
As each beast's limit, perfect to an end,
Nor conscious that they know, nor craving more;
While man knows partly but conceives beside,
Creeps ever on from fancies to the fact,
And in this striving, this converting air
Into a solid he may grasp and use,
Finds progress, man's distinctive mark alone,
Not God's and not the beasts': God is, they are,
Man partly is and wholly hopes to be."

It were easy to multiply passages which show that his ultimate deliverance regarding man is, not that he is, nor that he is not, but that he is ever becoming. Man is ever at the point of contradiction between the actual and ideal, and moving from the latter to the former. Strife constitutes him. He is a war of elements; "hurled from change to change unceasingly." But rest is death; for it is the cessation of the spiritual activity, whose essence is acquirement, not mere possession, whether in knowledge or in goodness.

"Man must pass from old to new,
From vain to real, from mistake to fact,
From what once seemed good, to what now proves best."

Were the movement to stop, and the contradiction between the actual and ideal reconciled, man would leave man's estate, and pass under "angel's law."

"Indulging every instinct of the soul
There, where law, life, joy, impulse are one thing."

But so long as he is man, he has

"Somewhat to cast off, somewhat to become."[1]

II.

THE PURPOSE.

What purpose is served by this conflict?

1. It is by wrestling in faith that the treasures of God's grace

[1] H. Jones, *Browning as a Philosophical and Religious Teacher*, 214.

THE FIGHT OF FAITH

are made ours. If He who inspires and safeguards our faith were to keep us in those smooth, stormless, well-sunned enclosures, where we should like to live our lives, He would limit His own opportunities of self-revelation to us. Faith is the faculty which apprehends the unseen; and whilst our faith is devoid of exercise and discipline, the unseen seems a very little part indeed of the real universe. The grace and the help that are hidden in its incalculable immensities can be touched only by the faith that has become dauntless and full-statured through many a sharp struggle. By continued wrestlings, this great God-created principle comes to a surer consciousness of its own power and the things it can achieve through Christ Jesus. If the scenes of trouble and conflict through which God's servants of old battled could be blotted from the pages of the Bible, how much of God's glory would be left there? It is the oft-contested and the much-exercised faith that wins the richest apprehension of God.

In the present half-believing age we are tempted to concentrate our strength upon work the benefits of which are immediate and visible. The man who loses some part of his faith often turns his back upon purely spiritual tasks, and sets himself to secular philanthropies which promise speedy and immediate transformation. Whilst we must never disparage gracious social enterprises, or think of them as of inferior sacredness, the highest tasks are those which demand the most gigantic faith, and force us into arduous conflict.

The sovereigns of earthly kingdoms reserve their highest honours for those who distinguish themselves in the hazards and hardships of war. Sometimes the old orders seem stale and insufficient, and new decorations have to be devised for the heroes who have surmounted difficulties which thwarted their predecessors. And God crowns with rare, fresh splendour the faith which persists and achieves through much buffeting and conflict. To awaken within us this saving and uplifting principle, and then to allocate our faith to spheres of congenial, unbroken quiet, would have been to circumscribe our opportunities of distinction, and to put a petty term to the promise of our destiny. Faith must be allowed to unfold itself to the uttermost, for it is the soul of every other virtue, and it finds its largest opportunities when events arise and issues are raised which tax its strength and incite it to feats winning the high praises of heaven.

"Faith," says the writer of the Hebrews, "is the proving of the things unseen." The dignity of the man of faith the very angels well may envy. The beings in the presence of God have never known the discipline of faith. They can never prove the things *unseen*: heaven may have lent to them its undimmed loveliness on which a stain has never rested. But earth can lend the nobler grandeur, when the spirit arises from its baptism of fire purified, exalted, and transfigured. To believe where all things are revealed and known—that is no virtue. But to believe where

> Faith and form
> Are sundered in the night of fear,

to have touched in the darkness the hand of God and followed His guiding "o'er moor and fen, o'er crag and torrent"; to have pierced the veil of sense and time and beheld the Unseen and Eternal; to have trusted when life was most a blank; to have hoped when earth seemed darkest, to have loved when God seemed cruellest, this is to have proved the empire of the spirit and its dominion over the world of sense. "Blessed are they that have not seen and yet have believed"—they are conquerors in the struggle—victors in the fight of faith.

> Say not, the struggle nought availeth,
>   The labour and the wounds are vain,
> The enemy faints not, nor faileth,
>   And as things have been they remain.
>
> If hopes were dupes, fears may be liars;
>   It may be, in yon smoke concealed,
> Your comrades chase e'en now the fliers,
>   And, but for you, possess the field.
>
> For while the tired waves, vainly breaking,
>   Seem here no painful inch to gain,
> Far back, through creeks and inlets making,
>   Comes silent, flooding in, the main.
>
> And not by eastern windows only,
>   When daylight comes, comes in the light,
> In front, the sun climbs slow, how slowly,
>   But westward, look, the land is bright.[1]

[1] Clough.

THE FIGHT OF FAITH

2. It is by wrestling that progress is made in the life of faith. The stress under which primitive man found himself was one of the causes which helped to convert him from a mere hunter into a founder of civilizations. We can never know our debt to those hot fierce pressures in our lives which we at first are tempted to resent as the work of a malign fate. Children of straitened circumstances are beginning to win the best prizes of scholastic life, and they well deserve them. The shrewdest inventors have often been struggling operatives. Dominant personalities do not grow where there are no difficulties, any more than the cedar of Lebanon will flourish side by side with the palm and the pomegranate in the hot plain. And what is true in common things applies to religious character, and to the life-principle out of which religious character grows.

¶ You remember what Christian saw in the Interpreter's house, where the meaning of Life was made clear to him by picture.

"And the Interpreter took him by the hand and led him into a pleasant place where was builded a stately palace, beautiful to behold; at the sight of which Christian was greatly delighted: he saw also upon the top thereof certain persons walking who were clothed in gold.

"Then said Christian, 'May we go in thither?'

"Then the Interpreter took him and led him up toward the palace, and behold at the door stood a great company of men, as desirous to go in but durst not. He saw also that in the doorway stood many men in armour to keep it, being resolved to do to the man who would enter what hurt and mischief they could. Now was Christian somewhat in amaze; at last when every man started back for fear of the armed men, Christian saw a man of very stout countenance come up to the man that sat there to write, saying, 'Set down my name, sir,' the which when he had done, he saw the man draw his sword and put a helmet on his head, and rush toward the door upon the armed men, who laid upon him with deadly force; but the man, not at all discouraged, fell to cutting and hacking most fiercely: so after he had received and given many wounds to those that attempted to keep him out, he cut his way through them all, and pressed forward into the palace: at which there was a pleasant voice heard from those that were within, saying,

'Come in, come in,
Eternal glory thou shalt win.'

So he went in and was clothed with such garments as they. Then Christian smiled, and said, 'I think verily I know the meaning of this.' "[1]

One who never turned his back but marched breast forward,
    Never doubted clouds would break,
Never dreamed, though right were worsted, wrong would triumph,
Held we fall to rise, are baffled to fight better,
    Sleep to wake.[2]

III.

The Method.

The fight of faith is no aimless affair. If we have to struggle, we struggle to win. To gain this end, then, some method must be pursued. How do we fight?

1. *By faith.*—The Christian life is not only a contest of faith, it is a contest by means of faith. It is inspired by faith as the spring of its activity, and the condition of its success. At first thought it seems a paradox to think or to speak of a fight by faith, or to connect a contest, which implies individuality and independence, with the idea of faith, which implies dependence and help. Perhaps we cannot state the problem, or solve it, better than by tracing its history in human experience. Before the times of Christ and of Paul, earnest men of many nations, and under a great variety of circumstances, had made an earnest business of the contest with passion and sin in their own souls and in the world about them. The need of this strife they saw and felt, with a clearness and strength of feeling to which the most of men in these easier times are utter strangers. They felt the burdens and sorrows of individual and collective human life. They experienced the impulses to evil as they were constantly revived within their own souls. They were appalled at the energy and strength with which sin organized itself afresh to resist and defy both the individual and the joint desires of those who would reform themselves and reform society.

---

[1] C. S. Horne, *Sermons and Addresses*, 93.
[2] Browning, Epilogue to "Asolando."

On a sudden, and yet as not wholly unexpected, a few of the race are confronted with a Person who overawes them by the mystery of His being, and attracts them by the strangeness of His condescension; who wins their confidence by the largeness of His invitations, and subdues their hearts by His love in death. The effect upon their character and springs of action is a new creation. The few who describe it, like Paul and Peter and John, declare that they were born by it into a new life; and their writings give jubilant expression to the new life of hope and victory which they began to live, through their joyful gratitude to the living Christ. What they say of themselves is observed of others. Scores and hundreds, thousands and tens of thousands, share in the new impulse which has come into human society. This new life is all comprehended in faith in the matchless personality of the dying and risen Christ. "This is the victory that overcometh the world, even our faith." "The life which I now live in the flesh I live by faith in the love of Christ, who loved me and gave himself for me."

¶ This good fight is a fight of *faith*; a fight which not alone is born from living faith in Christ, but to which faith supplies desire, courage, and strength, whilst it moreover assures us of the victory on the ground of God's own promise. "Through faith, through faith"; who shall reckon up all which, by the light of the history of God's kingdom, may be ascribed to this word? and what Christian has not earlier or later experienced the truth of this passage: "All things are possible to him that believeth"? Nay, we ourselves do not know what we might accomplish, if our faith were firm and unshaken. Faith has not only power to remove mountains, but to overcome the world. Faith is the first, faith is the most exalted, faith is the last requirement in the struggle of spiritual life. No one is overcome by sin, I boldly assert, till first the shield of faith has fallen from his enfeebled hand.[1]

(1) The faith by which we fight and win this battle is *personal*. It is the act or attitude of a person toward a person. We fight the battle of life under a leader and master and friend, whom we follow and love and obey, and in whom we trust and triumph and rejoice; in one word, in whom we *believe*. But though we fight the battle by Christ's help and by gratitude towards Him, we

[1] J. J. van Oosterzee, *The Year of Salvation*, ii. 224.

254   CHRISTIAN DOCTRINE OF FAITH

fight it out each man for himself. Subjectively, faith is an act, a disposition, a loving and obedient will; objectively, it rests on the living Christ, to whom all power is given in heaven and earth, and with whom is all sympathizing, all forgiving, and, therefore, all subduing love.

(2) And this fighting is *positive*. If faith is to help us against our adversaries, it must be confident and certain. If faith connects us with a person, we must know in whom we believe: *who he is*, so far as to be assured what he will be to us—what in our joys, what in our sorrows, what in our griefs, and what in our fears, what in our life, and what in our death. It follows that if we are to contend *by our faith*, we are to contend *for our faith*; simply because a man without positive convictions cannot contend at all, especially in an age which is shivering with doubt and uncertainty in every fibre of its intellectual life. At a time when every volume presents a novel theological theory or a new ethical speculation, either a new negation or a new sneer; when the foundations of all sorts of truth were never so confidently questioned, the best accredited facts so freely challenged, when the extremest needs of man's nature were never so boldly, or the most sacred of his hopes and aspirations so flippantly, disposed of—at a time when not a few believing souls are terrified with an undefined alarm, lest perhaps the foundations of their hopes and sacrifices shall sink into a yawning abyss—at this time the cry of distress is whispered from many lips, and the anguish is felt in many hearts: "Lord, I believe; help thou mine unbelief." At such a time love to others, as well as duty to ourselves, requires that every man who has a faith should make it positive, clear, and energetic. No man is worth much, in such a strife of opinion and of tongues as now prevails, who does not believe with positiveness, and believe with energy—the energy of that clear and calm conviction which is sustained by a life which is hid with Christ in God.

¶ The personal character of our conflict is strikingly exhibited in the letters which Christ dictated to the seven churches of Asia. He had something to allege against most of them: laxity in discipline, heresy in doctrine, abatement of zeal, all of which faults belong to a community. But from the manner in which He concludes the epistles, it is evident that these faults sprang from

THE FIGHT OF FAITH

individual declension in the vigour and courage of every man's inward fight. "He that overcometh" is blended with every salutation, not, they that overcome; and in the last letter He joins Himself with every bold and patient fighter of sin: "To him that overcometh will I grant to sit with me in my throne, even as I also overcame, and am set down with my Father in his throne."[1]

2. *By works.*—The battle is the Lord's, but His arm and shield never take from us the necessity of fighting.

(1) We use *diligence and determination*. No victory is possible, first of all, without will, without determination, resolve, absolute unwavering purpose by God's grace to subdue our evil passions. On this all depends. We must first give ourselves to our Saviour Christ, and to the influence of His Holy Spirit. We do not deceive ourselves with the silly notion that our personal temptations are abnormal, and exceptional; that it is more difficult for us than for others to escape from destruction. There has no temptation taken any one of us but such as is human, such as we are able to bear, such as is common to man. But with every temptation which besets us, even with those which, because of our yielding to them in past times, now attack us with tenfold force and fury, even for those God provides us not only with a way, but, as it is in the original, with the way, the very way, to escape.

¶ It is under the guise of warfare that morality always presents itself to Browning. It is not a mere equilibrium of qualities—the measured, self-contained, statuesque ethics of the Greeks, nor the asceticism and self-restraint of Puritanism, nor the peaceful evolution of Goethe's artistic morality: it is valour in the battle of life. His code contains no negative commandments, and no limitations; but he bids each man let out all the power that is within him, and throw himself upon life with the whole energy of his being. It is better even to seek evil with one's whole mind than to be lukewarm in goodness. Whether you seek good or evil, play for the counter or the coin, stake it boldly!

> Let a man contend to the uttermost
> For his life's set prize, be it what it will!

[1] E. E. Jenkins, *Life and Christ*, 98.

> The counter our lovers staked was lost
> As surely as if it were lawful coin:
> And the sin I impute to each frustrate ghost
> Is, the unlit lamp and the ungirt loin
> Though the end in sight was a vice, I say.
> You, of the virtue (we issue join),
> How strive you?—"*De te fabula!*"

Indifference and spiritual lassitude are, to the poet, the worst of sins. "Go!" says the Pope to Pompilia's pseudo-parents,

> "Never again elude the choice of tints!
> White shall not neutralize the black, nor good
> Compensate bad in man, absolve him so:
> Life's business being just the terrible choice."

In all the greater characters of *The Ring and the Book*, this intensity of vigour in good and evil flashes out upon us. Even Pompilia, the most gentle of all his creations, at the first prompting of the instinct of motherhood, rises to the law demanding resistance, and casts off the old passivity.

> Dutiful to the foolish parents first,
> Submissive next to the bad husband,—nay,
> Tolerant of those meaner miserable
> That did his hests, eked out the dole of pain,

she is found

> "Sublime in new impatience with the foe."

> "I did for once see right, do right, give tongue
> The adequate protest: for a worm must turn
> If it would have its wrong observed by God.
> I did spring up, attempt to thrust aside
> That ice-block 'twixt the sun and me, lay low
> The neutralizer of all good and truth.
>
> Yet, shame thus rank and patent, I struck, bare,
> At foe from head to foot in magic mail,
> And off it withered, cobweb armoury
> Against the lightning! 'Twas truth singed the lies
> And saved me."

THE FIGHT OF FAITH

Beneath the mature wisdom of the Pope, amidst the ashes of old age, there sleeps the same fire. He is as truly a warrior priest as Caponsacchi himself, and his matured experience only muffles his vigour. Wearied with his life-long labour, we see him gather himself together "in God's name," to do His will on earth once more with concentrated might:

> "I smite
> With my whole strength once more, ere end my part,
> Ending, so far as man may, this offence."[1]

(2) We use *prayer*.—The victory for ourselves cannot be won without prayer; for prayer—earnest, agonizing, heart-felt prayer—will make us leave off sinning, or else sinning will make us leave off praying. Real, passionate prayer—prayer like Jacob's wrestling with God by the midnight watch when he rose from being Jacob, the mean supplanter, into Israel, the prince of God—is inconsistent with any continued indulgence in any known sin, secret or open.

¶ It is possible so to be overborne by the pangs and losses and defeats of the Christian soldier as to lose faith in Divine love and providence. There is an awful possibility of giving over prayer, of coming to think that the Lord's ear is heavy that He cannot hear, and His arm shortened that He cannot save. There is a terrible significance in this passage, which we quote from a recent book: "Old Mr. Westfield, a preacher of the Independent persuasion in a certain Yorkshire town, was discoursing one Sunday with his utmost eloquence on the power of prayer. He suddenly stopped, passed his hands slowly over his head—a favourite gesture—and said in dazed tones: 'I do not know, my friends, whether you ever tried praying; for my part, I gave it up long ago as a bad job.' The poor old gentleman never preached again. They spoke of the strange seizure that he had in the pulpit and very cheerfully and kindly contributed to the pension which the authorities of the chapel allowed him. I knew him five-and-twenty years ago, a gentle old man addicted to botany, who talked of anything but spiritual experience. I have often wondered with what sudden flash of insight he looked into his own soul that day, and saw himself bowing down silent before an empty shrine."[2]

[1] H. Jones, *Browning as a Philosophical and Religious Teacher*, 104.
[2] W. Robertson Nicoll, *The Garden of Nuts*, 224.

> In the anguish of prayer
> It is well! it is well!
> Then only the victory of love is complete,
> When the soul on the cross
> Dies to all save its loss.
> When in utmost defeat
> The light that was fair
> And the friend who was sweet
> Flee away, then the truth of its love is laid bare
> In the anguish of prayer.[1]

(3) Another and most indispensable rule, for one who would have victory over sin, is *watchfulness over the thoughts of the heart*, without which they would only be evil continually. The heart must be kept pure, or the life will be impure. Let us not deceive ourselves with the pretence that thoughts are nothing; they are as real as deeds to that eye ten thousand times brighter than the sun which burns into the very secrets of our hearts. Out of the heart, said our Lord Jesus Christ, proceed evil thoughts, and then, as though the very flood-gates had been opened and the destroying waves let loose, the evil thought develops into the evil wish, and the evil wish into the evil purpose, and the evil purpose into the evil deed, and the evil deed into the evil reputation, and the evil reputation into the evil habit, into the deadly seeming of a tyrannous necessity. And so evil thoughts end in murders, adulteries, fornication, theft, deceit, false witness, covetousness. All these things come from within, and these defile a man. Never think lightly of an evil thought. Remember that there is a reverse process. Begin with faith; add to it virtue, and all the strands of Peter's rope, and you will not fear the tyranny of evil habit but will enjoy the liberties of the sons of God.

¶ Methought I saw a beautiful blind sister open the gates of Heaven; her name was Faith, and she just opened them wide enough for the soul to enter. But after her there came a brother, brave, a soldier, in arms; he opened them wider still—his name was Virtue-Bravery. Then after him there came another brother, pale, student-like, with a book in the one hand; his name was Knowledge—he opened them wider still. After him there came another sister, a nymph of ruddy, healthy hue; her name was Temperance—she opened them wider still. Another sister came,

[1] E. Underhill, *Theophanies*, 49.

THE FIGHT OF FAITH

with downcast eyes; her name was Patience—she opened them wider still. After her a brother, with prayerful lips and countenance; his name was Godliness—he opened them wider still; and was followed by another, called Brotherly-Kindness, who, with outstretched arms, opened them wider still. I wondered if there were any more; yes, there was one, a sister. Up she comes; she has been visiting in the huts where poor men dwell, with a basket on her arm and a bible in her hand, and she opens the gate widest of all—her name, they said, was Charity. And as I wondered what this might mean, I heard a voice saying, "Add to your faith virtue, and to virtue knowledge, and to knowledge temperance, and to temperance patience, and to patience godliness, and to godliness brotherly-kindness, and to brotherly-kindness charity. For if these things be in you, and abound, they make you that you shall neither be barren nor unfruitful in the knowledge of our Lord Jesus Christ," and, if so, a blessing shall be ministered to you abundantly in the everlasting kingdom of our Lord and Saviour.[1]

(4) Last of all the battle must be fought with *discrimination*. To let the battle against wickedness and cruelty pass over into a personal hatred of the wicked and cruel man, and exhaust itself in personal attacks on him for other things besides his wickedness—that is the constant peril. How often does the hot agitator need these calm, strong words: "Not against flesh and blood, but against principalities and powers, and the world-spirit of darkness, and the evil that is in the air"? We know the answer that will come: "Evil incorporates itself in man. How can you strike out the evil without beating down the men in whom it is embodied?" But surely no such statement as that, which is most absolutely true, can be stretched wide enough to cover the personal hatred, the wilful or careless misrepresentation, the petty spite, with which the earnest advocate of some cause which he thought indubitably right has very often followed up the man upon the other side, whom he believed of course to be indubitably wrong.

Just see what some of the personal disadvantages of such a disposition are. First, it puts it absolutely out of the angry partisan's power, in case he is not wholly right, to get any advantage or correction from the opposite light in which his opponent sees the same transaction which he thinks so wrong; second, it robs the furious hater of the chance to learn charity

Robertson of Irvine, Poet Preacher, 242.

and personal consideration, for of course the chance to think tolerantly of a man who differs from us comes to us when we differ from him, and if, the moment that we differ from him, we begin to hate him, it is as if we shut up the door of one of our best schoolrooms and turned the key of prejudice upon it; and yet again, it makes turbid and heavy and dull that stream of simple indignation against evil and love for righteousness which, when it is absolutely fresh and pure, is the most strong and persistent power in the world. These are the reasons why it is a sad loss when the fighter with wickedness turns his struggle against wickedness into angry attacks on men against whom perhaps their wickedness has first provoked him, but whom he has come now to hate for themselves.

¶ This was the spirit of our Lord's disciples when they wanted to call down fire on the village of Samaria. This was Luther's spirit when at Marburg he lost sight of the simple fight with error and plunged into a personal attack on Zwingle. It is the danger of all earnest men. It seems sometimes to be so inseparable from earnestness that the world thinks that it must not call it a vice or take any note of it in the earnest man. But no really earnest man can be so self-indulgent. Ever he must struggle to know who his true enemy is, and to fight finally with him alone. With wickedness we may be unmitigatedly indignant. We may hate it with all our hearts. Towards it there is no chance, there is no right, of indulgence or consideration. But with the wicked man, because he is both man and wickedness, we may be at once full of anger and full of love, and out of the spirit of the highest justice, both to him and to ourselves, insist always that it shall be the wickedness and not the man that we hate![1]

[1] Phillips Brooks, *The Mystery of Iniquity*, 81.

XII.

THE FULL ASSURANCE OF FAITH.

PART I.

LITERATURE.

Boutroux, E., *Philosophy and War* (1916).
Cairns, D. S., *The Reasonableness of the Christian Faith* (1918).
Candole, H. L. C. V. de, *Christian Assurance* (1919).
Clifford, J., *The Christian Certainties* (1893)
Curtis, O. A., *The Christian Faith* (1905).
Elmslie, W. A. L., *Studies in Life from Jewish Proverbs* (1917).
Forsyth, P. T., *The Principle of Authority.*
Garvie, A. E., *The Gospel for To-Day* (1904).
Gladden, W., *Where does the Sky Begin?* (1904).
Green, S. G., *The Christian Creed and the Creeds of Christendom* (1898).
Hodge, A. A., *A Commentary on the Confession of Faith* (1870).
Holden, J. S., *Supposition and Certainty* (1908).
James, W., *The Varieties of Religious Experience* (1902).
　,,　　,, *The Will to Believe* (1902).
Jones, J. D., *The Hope of the Gospel* (1911).
Lambert, J. C., *The Omnipotent Cross* (1899).
Moulton, J. H., *Religions and Religion* (1913).
Patton, W. J., *Pardon and Assurance* (1897).
Salmon, G., *The Reign of Law* (1873).
Selby, T. G., *The Holy Spirit and Christian Privilege* (1894).
Skrine, J. H., *What is Faith?* (1907).
Smith, G. B., *Social Idealism and the Changing Theology* (1913).
　,,　　,, in *A Guide to the Study of the Christian Religion* (1916).
Turner, F. S., *Knowledge, Belief and Certitude* (1900).
Vance, J. G., *Reality and Truth* (1917).
White, E., *On Certainty in Religion.*
American Journal of Theology, vii. (1903) 730 (F. H. Foster).
Biblical World, xxxi. (1908) 365 (H. S. Nash).
Christian World Pulpit, lix. (1901) 299 (J. Watson); lxv. (1904) 156 (R. Thomas).
Free Church Year Book, 1913, p. 58 (W. B. Selbie).
Harvard Theological Review, vi. (1913) 280 (L. P. Jacks).

THE FULL ASSURANCE OF FAITH.

1. WRITING about the year 1890, Dr. John Clifford spoke of the craving for certainty in religion as one of the most outstanding "notes" of our time. We rebel, he says, against the teaching which acquiesces in the fate expressed in the words "We have faith; we cannot know," and are satisfied only when we not merely know, but are sure that we know the thing as it is, the fact in itself, and the whole fact in its contour and its contents.

¶ Everything shapes itself as a question. Nothing escapes. God, Duty, and Immortality are the irremovable rocks on which the whole superstructure of religion rests; but men feel and speak as if gazing on a "seeming void" and ask, Are there any rocks beneath? Is there a God? Is duty a reality? Is eternity more than a wish, a dream, a vain, egoistic fancy? If God is, how can we be sure of His character, aims, will and disposition toward us? What is His attitude toward sin? Does He pardon it? If so, how? May we be sure of forgiveness, and that He and we are at peace? Has He spoken to us? Have we His actual words in our Testaments, Old and New? Is the whole content of the Testaments His "word"? If so, in what sense? Does God speak now? What is His part in the troubled, perplexed, mysterious, and awful life of to-day? Who will tell us and, telling us, make us sure that he tells us the fact as it is?[1]

2. Thirty years earlier this craving was much less felt, because assurance was a secure possession of the follower of Christ. "Fifty years ago," says Dr. Reuen Thomas (writing in 1904), "people used to know what the word meant. They knew it experimentally. They had conquered their doubts and had put their fears to sleep. They had quiet faces and sunny hearts. There were quite a few of this order. I have played all sorts of

---
[1] J. Clifford, *The Christian Certainties*, 11.

CHRISTIAN DOCTRINE OF FAITH

wicked experiments on them, but I could never ruffle their quietude."

¶ Sir Humphry Davy was no religious fanatic, and yet he said: "If I could choose what would be the most delightful and, I believe, the most useful thing to me, I prefer a firm religious belief to any other blessing; for it makes discipline of good, creates new hopes when earthly hopes vanish, and throws over the decay, the destruction of existence, the most gorgeous of all lights, awakens life in death, and from corruption and decay calls up beauty and divinity; makes an instrument of misfortune and of shame a ladder of ascent to Paradise; and far above all combinations of earthly hopes, calls up the most delightful visions of palms and of amaranth, the gardens of the blest and the security of everlasting joys, where the sensualist and the skeptic view only gloom, annihilation and despair."[1]

3. What had happened to disturb the sense of assurance was the progress of scientific exploration, and the notion, made familiar by Professor Huxley and others, that the scientific observer must be an agnostic in religion. "Science," says Dr. Clifford, "has entered life through every door, and broken up our peace in any conclusion that is not error-proof, and in any rules of life that have not borne the strain of all possible experience. The draughty houses of delusion, in which we have long dwelt, are pulled down, and most of us are hurrying to lodge ourselves in the soundly-built edifices of truth, if only we can find them."

> Mighty confidence!
> One pulse of Time makes the base hollow—sends
> The towering certainty we build so high
> Toppling in fragments meaningless.[2]

¶ There is nothing which is more resented and condemned in our time than an excess of certitude in religious belief. Society will readily forgive any measure of doubt or unbelief, but it will not forgive a measure of belief which exceeds its own. Men are angered not so much by the subject of your faith, as by its disproportionate degree. Whatever faith is stronger than their own is credulity, or bigotry, or presumption, or ignorant boldness. Whatever faith is less strong than their own is scepticism, or infidelity. There is nothing more firmly insisted on than that you ought to believe in the same things, and in about the same

---

[1] T. T. Eaton, *Faith and the Faith*, 29.   [2] George Eliot, *The Spanish Gipsy*.

THE FULL ASSURANCE OF FAITH

degree, that Society or the Church believes. And Society in our time believes very little in anything above sense. Suspense of judgment, open profession of ignorance, or of indifference, in religious matters especially, are reckoned by many the marks of knowledge and capacity. Life, it is said, can be carried on in its leading interests by sense perceptions; men's financial credit can be fixed by an easy rule of observation, or at least by an average of guesses, inquiries, and risks. And what more is needful? If you are in the dark—say so—and wait for death to end all doubts, by extinction, or admission into light beyond. Here the position that becomes us is that of the white marble effigy, in Père La Chaise,—of the man who lies on his tomb, with the shroud for his garment, and his forefinger placed upon his lips. We nothing know, the dead do not return to teach us—we must wait for death to solve the mystery.[1]

> Thou waitest for the spark from heaven! and we,
> Light half-believers of our casual creeds,
>   Who never deeply felt, nor clearly will'd,
> Whose insight never has borne fruit in deeds,
>   Whose vague resolves never have been fulfill'd;
>   For whom each year we see
> Breeds new beginnings, disappointments new;
>   Who hesitate and falter life away,
>   And lose to-morrow the ground won to-day—
> Ah! do not we, wanderer! await it too?[2]

4. Has the recognition of the limitations of science restored men's confidence in religion? Not altogether, and not directly. Writing some thirty years later than Dr. John Clifford, Dr. P. T. Forsyth says: "There are many people prepared to speak readily of Christian preaching, Christian personality, Christian work, Christian influence, or the Christian Church, for one who can or will speak freely of Christian certainty. Sympathy has taken the place of certainty. Many can say they love, or they labour, for one who can say 'I am sure.' Amid all our energy there is a deep aversion to asking what we really believe, where we really are with a creed which makes any love Divine, or anything worth doing at last. Which is as if a man of business refused to face the stock-taking, and never balanced his books."[3]

---

[1] Edward White, *On Certainty in Religion*, 19.
[2] Matthew Arnold, "The Scholar Gipsy."
[3] P. T. Forsyth, *The Principle of Authority*, 38.

Thus a theological task of incalculable importance is that of bringing to light the latent religious values of those aspects of modern life which hold us so strongly in their grasp, but which we have not been accustomed to interpret in a religious fashion. If this task is to be prosecuted in such a way as to construct a vital theology, primary attention must be given to the basis of religious assurance. For, as has been said, a theology which does not embody an appeal to the moral conscience of men is impotent.

From science itself we are likely to receive assistance in the recovery of religious assurance. It is to the assurance of faith that a modern writer on the psychology of religion would give the name of faith *par excellence*. "When the sense of estrangement," writes Professor Leuba, "fencing man about in a narrowly limited ego, breaks down, the individual finds himself 'at one with all creation.' He lives in the universal life; he and man, he and nature, he and God, are one. That state of confidence, trust, union with all things, following upon the achievement of moral unity, is the *Faith-state*. Various dogmatic beliefs suddenly, on the advent of the faith-state, acquire a character of certainty, assume a new reality, become an object of faith. As the ground of assurance here is not rational, argumentation is irrelevant. But such conviction being a mere casual offshoot of the faith-state, it is a gross error to imagine that the chief practical value of the faith-state is its power to stamp with the seal of reality certain particular theological conceptions. On the contrary, its value lies solely in the fact that it is the psychic correlate of a biological growth reducing contending desires to one direction; a growth which expresses itself in new affective states and new reactions; in larger, nobler, more Christ-like activities."

¶ Tolstoy's case was a good comment on those words. There was almost no theology in his conversion. His faith-state was the sense come back that life was infinite in its moral significance.[1]

I.

THE WORD.

The phrase "the full assurance of faith" occurs in Heb. x. 22. "Full assurance" is found also in Heb. vi. 11, "the full assurance

[1] W. James, *The Varieties of Religious Experience*, 247.

THE FULL ASSURANCE OF FAITH 267

of hope," and in Col. ii. 2, "the full assurance of understanding." The word rendered "full assurance" may mean no more than "fulness," as the Revised Version renders it in Hebrews. Lightfoot, however, decidedly holds to "full assurance," saying "for such seems to be the meaning of the substantive wherever it occurs in the New Testament." In 1 Thess. i. 5 the Greek word occurs with the adjective "much," so that "fulness" is an impossible translation there.

The word "assurance" has obtained a somewhat narrow theological use, if not even a controversial meaning. The more common word now is certainty, as in the Genevan Version of the Bible at 1 Thess. i. 5, "in much certaintie of persuasion." But a better equivalent is certitude. It is no longer possible, perhaps, to preserve the distinction between certitude or assurance and certainty, but it is at least worth while seeing what it is.

1. Certitude is a quality or aspect of a particular psychological state, or, as we say ordinarily, of a frame of mind. Certainty, on the other hand, is a quality of propositions; we speak of it currently as attaching to this or that statement. Though, of course, the "frame of mind" is induced by a "certain" proposition, the distinction between certitude and certainty is none the less real.

Certainty is an experience and not merely an impression, it is an assurance of something. We know, not that we feel somehow, but that we feel something. It connotes not only our certitude as its subjective side, but an objective worth. Certitude is valuable according to the certainty, the certain thing, it carries at its heart—which is in it but not of it.

¶ The introductory passage in St. Luke's Gospel contains in the original a little museum of Greek words, denoting the processes and results of proof in relation to Christianity, and they are substantially represented in our own version. The Evangelist distinguishes between what we now term *certitude*—or the belief of the mind—and *certainty*, or the solid reality of the facts or truths believed in;—the one an internal state, the other an external fact, fitted to be the basis of faith. He speaks of things which are "surely believed," and then of the "certainty" or safe reality of the things so believed in. He adds that with the object of causing Theophilus to know (or rather *thoroughly to know*) this certainty, he was about to write a fresh and orderly discourse founded on the testimony of eye-witnesses and ministers of the word of God, who could not be mistaken as to what they had seen or heard.[1]

2. Certitude, then, is a state of mind. Generally it is the repose that follows upon our assent to the truth of a statement. After much doubt and, it may be, many misgivings we acknowledge the certainty of a political programme, of an ethical or religious system, or of some philosophic code. The resultant state of mind while it lasts—it may be rudely shaken or it may terminate abruptly—excludes all denial, all doubt, and, at least, all the more harassing difficulties which tend to make our ordinary judgments rock and sway. The mind rests, calmly convinced of the "truth," undisturbed by the possibilities of criticism or future discovery.

¶ There was an old saint in far-away days—such a one, we can imagine, as was the Venerable Bede in the midst of his young students—who lived a life of such purity and serenity that his younger comrades marvelled. The wonder grew upon them so greatly, that at length they resolved to approach the master, and ask to be told the secret of this purity, this peace. They came one day, and said, "Father, we are harassed with many temptations, which appeal to us so often and so strongly, that they give us no rest. You seem to be untroubled by these things, and we would learn the secret. Do not the temptations that harass our souls appeal to you? Do they never come knocking at the door of your heart?" The old man listened, and smiled, and said, "My children, I do know something of the things of which you speak. The temptations that trouble you do come, making their appeal to me. But, when these temptations knock at the door of my heart, I answer, 'The place is occupied.'"[2]

3. The permanence of this state of mind depends ultimately upon the certainty of that which brings certitude. It is like hope. For hope, however deep its yearning, would be a poor friend of man were it not for the certainty to which it looks. For the certainty, however veiled, is there, and is the supreme justifier of every pure and holy hope that has ever dwelt in a human heart. Hope is not a blind and spectral figure in an empty world. It

---

[1] Edward White, *On Certainty in Religion*, 3.
[2] T. F. Lockyer, *Religious Experience*, 94.

THE FULL ASSURANCE OF FAITH

strains its eyes to see behind the clouds the glorious sun which is actually, eternally, there. And what that glorious sun is we know. The anchor of our hope entereth into that which is within the veil, whither the Forerunner is for us entered, even Jesus. That is the certainty. There is life at the heart of things because Christ is there; and we can say more. The certainty which justifies hope is not wholly veiled. He is here also; and hope has its facts beside it if only it always knew. For is this not the supremely memorable and historic fact with which our hopes and fears alike have all to do? "God so loved the world, that he gave his only-begotten Son, that whosoever believeth in him should not perish, but have everlasting life."

¶ The thing we are sure of will settle the nature of our certainty who are sure, and the thing we are most sure of will determine the nature of ourselves. The nature of certainty about the last things is not to be found by any amount of psychology, but by the nature of the revelation which emerges in the psychology—the sure word of prophecy. Psychology is a mere science of observation or experiment; and science can never give us reality, nor certainty about it.[1]

4. But as a rule no distinction is observed between certainty and certitude, either in theology or in Christian experience. Professor Olin Curtis in his manual of *The Christian Faith* defines certainty in this way: Christian certainty is that personal, moral assurance which a Christian man, in organic relation with the Christian brotherhood, has more and more profoundly, first and most vitally of the reality of his spiritual life in Christ, and then of the reality or truth of the objects and events and doctrines bound up with that life in Christ.

II.

THE CONDITIONS OF ASSURANCE.

1. We can never be absolutely certain of anything, in the sense of *intellectual* certainty, of which we do not fully know both the entire nature and the complete conditions.

[1] P. T. Forsyth, *The Principle of Authority*, 42.

¶ Where is absolute certainty to be found? The answer is, Nowhere. And the answer may be given with entire lightness of heart. There is no need to make a long face over it, as though some cherished ideal were being abandoned. Absolute certainty is, for beings constituted as we are, simply a meaningless phrase, —a phrase which expresses no human ideal, which represents nothing we cherish and nothing that we suffer by giving up. A truth so certain as to stand in need of no further witness; a truth so accurately stated that a finer accuracy is unattainable; a truth so utterly proved that no ingenuity of man can raise a doubt against it; a truth so indubitable as to defeat the perverseness which is determined to question it; a truth so rich that a fuller enrichment is impossible; a truth so self-sufficient as to call for no champions, no defenders, no prophets, apostles, and martyrs, —truth absolute in that sense never has had and never can have the slightest interest for any human being. Were truth of that kind to arrive upon the earth, the mind of man would simply be put out of commission, and the curtain would fall irrevocably on the drama of human life.[1]

2. All great questions of faith, when deeply considered, resolve themselves into moral issues; and therefore the question of religious certainty can never be rightly considered as merely an intellectual one. The certainty is moral; and such a moral certainty is the faith which is the basis of life as well as of its ideal constructions in religion, science, and philosophy. Knowledge is trustworthy only as held on faith.

Moral life rests on a foundation of faith—that righteousness is best and that right is good. It assumes the supremacy and adorableness of goodness and moral excellence, and the recognition of the highest goodness as the revelation of true Reality or God. The identity of moral goodness with ultimate reality is not indeed self-evident. But the adorableness of moral worth is essentially self-evident. It is a matter of moral recognition and appreciation, a moral determination, a movement of the moral and emotional nature. It is a faith which verifies itself in a coherent experience; for the man who believes that right is best has settled the question of the worth and goodness of life. If he can do right—and he always can—life is worth living. There is in man's moral nature that which satisfies him; and moral experience justifies an

[1] L. P. Jacks, in *Harvard Theological Review*, vi. 285.

THE FULL ASSURANCE OF FAITH

assumption of the value and significance of human life without which all argument about God is useless. It is an assumption that may still be made, a faith that may still be held, though the question of the goodness of the powers at work in nature be still unsettled.

> When the anchors that faith has cast
>   Are dragging in the gale,
> I am quietly holding fast
>   To the things that cannot fail.
>
> I know that right is right,
>   That it is not good to lie,
> That love is better than spite,
>   And a neighbour than a spy.
>
> I know that passion needs
>   The leash of sober mind,
> I know that generous deeds
>   Some sure reward will find;
>
> That the rulers must obey,
>   That the givers shall increase,
> That beauty lights the way
>   For the beautiful feet of Peace;
>
> In the darkest night of the year,
>   When the stars have all gone out,
> That courage is better than fear,
>   That faith is truer than doubt.
>
> And fierce though the fiends may fight,
>   And long though the angels hide,
> I know that Truth and Right
>   Have the universe on their side.

3. Assurance therefore depends not entirely on the certainty of things to be believed but also (and perhaps fundamentally) upon the believer's moral attitude. One cannot open the New Testament without seeing plainly on every page that both Christ and His messengers affirm on the one hand the revelation of certainty, and on the other fixed conditions of certitude in the learner; so that a man must *be* something, must place himself in

a certain posture, before he can stand in effective *rapport* with the revealed certainty. And failure in these conditions will nullify for him that certainty in the proportion of his failure.

¶ The Prophets Isaiah and Ezekiel dined with me, and I asked them how they dared so roundly to assert that God spoke to them; and whether they did not think at the time that they would be misunderstood, and so be the cause of imposition.

Isaiah answer'd: "I saw no God, nor heard any, in a finite organical perception; but my senses discover'd the infinite in everything, and as I was then persuaded, and remain confirm'd, that the voice of honest indignation is the voice of God, I cared not for consequences, but wrote."

Then I asked: "Does a firm persuasion that a thing is so, make it so?"

He replied: "All Poets believe that it does, and in ages of imagination this firm persuasion removed mountains; but many are not capable of a firm persuasion of anything."[1]

¶ There can be no absolute certitude about the impressions of the senses or the inferences drawn from them. There can be about moral and spiritual things. The knave may sincerely opine that it is best for his interests to lie and cheat; but the honest man knows that he is a being whose interests are above all external contingencies, and that under certain circumstances it would be madness to behave otherwise than in a way which would be directly opposed to every argument and persuasion of the senses. It is only the mind of the most highly "scientific" constitution that will have its confidence in knowledge of this kind tried by considerations of its moral and intellectual obligations to Hottentots and Australian aborigines. "We can live in houses without being architects"; and we can know, without knowing or caring to know how we came by our knowledge. The house of the gods has lasted intact since Abraham and Hesiod, and shows no sign yet of tumbling about our ears.[2]

4. It is true that faith is a venture, but it is only the first step of faith that is a leap in the dark:

> Nothing before, nothing behind;
> The steps of faith
> Fall on the seeming void—and find
> The rock beneath.

---

[1] William Blake, "A Memorable Fancy."
[2] Coventry Patmore, *Principle in Art*, 321.

The "whys" of logic become impertinences to him who knows. You will hold the Unseen, at times at least, more firmly than you ever held a scientific truth:

> The flesh I wear,
> The earth I tread, are not more clear to me
> Than my belief—explained to you or no.

¶ Patrick Walker has drawn the portrait of John Wellwood in *Some Remarkable Passages of the Life and Death of Mr. John Welwood*, and John Howie of Lochgoin has given him a place among the *Scots Worthies*. "I have no more doubt," he would say, "of my interest in Christ, than if I were in heaven already. I have oftentimes endeavoured to pick a hole in my interest, but cannot get it done." At length the end came. One sweet April morning, that time of the year when Perth is beginning to put on its loveliest robe, he said, as the joyful light of the dawning day began to flood the chamber where he lay: "Now eternal light, no more night nor darkness to me." Before nightfall he was gone.[1]

> I never saw a moor,
> I never saw the sea;
> Yet know I how the heather looks,
> And what a wave must be.
>
> I never spoke with God,
> Nor visited in heaven;
> Yet certain am I of the spot
> As if the chart were given.[2]

5. There are, then, certain conditions which must be observed if a man is to have personal assurance. They may be discovered in the New Testament.

(1) As a primary condition the writers of the New Testament insist on moral, rather than intellectual, qualifications. Every degree of mind above idiocy, they affirm, can be made to understand and enjoy something of the gospel and its certainties of truth and grace, if there be but an honest intention. It is a moral, much rather than an intellectual, revelation. Hence the first demand is that simplicity of purpose which Christ calls a "child-like" temper, truth-seeking, teachable, and honest.

---

[1] A. Philip, *The Evangel in Gowrie*, 105, 117.
[2] Emily Dickinson.

(2) Another condition of reaching assurance is that the study of the New Testament should be approached without prejudice. If we approach nature with a mind sincere and teachable, but holding some one erroneous thought which we persist in forcing in amidst her facts and phenomena, we shall thereby render it impossible to receive some other great truths in nature which are inconsistent with our theory. Thus also in interpreting apostolic certainty. If we carry to the school of Christ some preformed opinion respecting humanity, or the Deity, on some question respecting which the apostles *have been sent to instruct us*, we shall not only fail in reaching certainty on that subject, but we shall receive their instruction on other topics under perverting conditions which will hold our faith constantly tottering on the verge of scepticism.

¶ When the Cliffords tell us how sinful it is to be Christians on such "insufficient evidence," insufficiency is really the last thing they have in mind. For them the evidence is absolutely sufficient, only it makes the other way. They believe so completely in an anti-christian order of the universe that there is no living option: Christianity is a dead hypothesis from the start.[1]

(3) The last condition of assurance is secret and continued personal communion with God. And this means that the full assurance of faith is ours only when we are under the leading of the Holy Spirit of God. God's presence then gives at once assurance and power.

¶ It is by no natural faculty that man can hold communion with his Creator. His intellect may guide him to the conclusion that there is a First Cause, and his imagination may surround that First Cause with the fulness of all which is now seen in part; but in order to meet the living God in truth and reality, he must have something uncreated—he must have God's own Spirit. And that he might be thus provided, the Word, who was God, has come into the root of man's nature, that he might be there a fountain of the divine Spirit, from which a rill might run to every individual of the race, not compelling any one, but enabling every one, to know God and walk with him.[2]

¶ I remember once seeing in the streets of London a commonplace incident that filled my heart with gladness. I was feeling

---

[1] W. James, *The Will to Believe*, 14.
[2] T. Erskine, *The Doctrine of Election*, 112.

THE FULL ASSURANCE OF FAITH

very tired, and had to go across to the other side of London to preach. Somehow I thought I would rather do anything just then than go and face a church full of people, for I did not feel equal to speaking to them worthily or helpfully. My way led me up a hill—there are not many hills in London, but this was one of them—which was rather steep. Right at the foot of the hill I saw a boy on a bicycle. He was pedalling up the hill against the wind, and evidently found it tremendously hard work. I expect we all know how hard it can be to do just that thing. Well, just as he was working most strenuously and doing his best painfully, there came a trolley-car going in the same direction—up the hill. It was not going very fast, not too fast for the boy to get behind it, and with one hand to lay hold of the bar at the back. Then you know what happened. He went up the hill like a bird, and was up at the top of it long before I was, for I was on foot. Then it just flashed upon me, "Why, I am like that boy on the bicycle in my weariness and weakness. I am pedalling uphill against all kinds of opposition and am almost worn out by the task. But here at hand is a great available power—the strength of the Lord Jesus. I have only to get into touch with Him and to maintain communion with Him—though it may be as with only one little finger of faith, and that will be enough to make His power mine for the doing of this bit of service which just now seems too much for me."[1]

[1] J. S. Holden, *The Life of Fuller Purpose*, 89.

XIII.

THE FULL ASSURANCE OF FAITH.

PART II.

LITERATURE.

Boutroux, E., *Philosophy and War* (1916).
Cairns, D. S., *The Reasonableness of the Christian Faith* (1918).
Candole, H. L. C. V. de, *Christian Assurance* (1919).
Clifford, J., *The Christian Certainties* (1893).
Curtis, O. A., *The Christian Faith* (1905).
Elmslie, W. A. L., *Studies in Life from Jewish Proverbs* (1917).
Forsyth, P. T., *The Principle of Authority.*
Garvie, A. E., *The Gospel for To-Day* (1904).
Gladden, W., *Where does the Sky Begin?* (1904).
Green, S. G., *The Christian Creed and the Creeds of Christendom* (1898).
Hodge, A. A., *A Commentary on the Confession of Faith* (1870).
Holden, J. S., *Supposition and Certainty* (1908).
James, W., *The Varieties of Religious Experience* (1902).
,,   ,,   *The Will to Believe* (1902).
Jones, J. D., *The Hope of the Gospel* (1911).
Lambert, J. C., *The Omnipotent Cross* (1899).
Moulton, J. H., *Religions and Religion* (1913).
Patton, W. J., *Pardon and Assurance* (1897).
Salmon, G., *The Reign of Law* (1873).
Selby, T. G., *The Holy Spirit and Christian Privilege* (1894).
Skrine, J. H., *What is Faith?* (1907).
Smith, G. B., *Social Idealism and the Changing Theology* (1913).
,,   ,,   in *A Guide to the Study of the Christian Religion* (1916).
Turner, F. S., *Knowledge, Belief and Certitude* (1900).
Vance, J. G., *Reality and Truth* (1917).
White, E., *On Certainty in Religion.*
American Journal of Theology, vii. (1903) 730 (F. H. Foster).
Biblical World, xxxi. (1908) 365 (H. S. Nash).
Christian World Pulpit, lix. (1901) 299 (J. Watson); lxv. (1904) 156 (R. Thomas).
Free Church Year Book, 1913, p. 58 (W. B. Selbie).
Harvard Theological Review, vi. (1913) 280 (L. P. Jacks).

The Full Assurance of Faith.

I.

The Object of Assurance.

Of what are we assured? This question is important, because it is what we are sure of that enables us to say why we are sure of it. The object of certainty is a creative power which obliges us to say of our faith, when we would account for it, that it is not of ourselves, but is God's gift and His product in us. The object gives by its intrinsic and creative quality the ground of the certainty.

But this question, to answer it with any fulness, would demand a theological treatise to itself. We are concerned now only to note that to all of us who accept Christianity there are such certainties, assured by repeated and definite declarations of Holy Scripture, accepted by the general Christian consciousness, and attested by their influence upon our own souls. These connect themselves with the great threefold revelation, Father, Son, and Holy Spirit. That is to say, the Christian is one who owns the Fatherhood of God, the redemption which is by Christ Jesus, and the communication of light and life by the Eternal Spirit. How these thoughts are to be translated into dogma is not now the question. They are the powers of the new life; without them there is no Christianity. And the believer is one who has found them to be true. He receives them on the warrant of faith; but they have also passed into his consciousness and experience. He is sure of them; he has a right to be sure. No doubt, the testimony of consciousness and experience will be variously read by different minds. The certainty belongs not to the mode of apprehension, but to the fact itself; and the glad utterance of the soul will be, *I know.*

280 CHRISTIAN DOCTRINE OF FAITH

Connected with these central truths are many others upon which Christian thinkers often gravely differ. Such beliefs are sometimes termed the "non-essentials" of the faith—a term, however, which it seems on many accounts undesirable to employ. There is a certain faithlessness to truth in the very thought of such a distinction. The great questions of faith cannot bear to be put in duplicate form: What *must* I believe? and What *may* I believe? A man who desires to learn the whole counsel of God must be prepared to stand faithfully by all his convictions, on matters great and small, although indeed he may hold them with different degrees of assurance. To discriminate these several convictions, to ask which of them are fundamental, not to be denied without renouncing the Christian faith altogether and so rendering Christian fellowship impossible, is no doubt a delicate and difficult task—the more so, as we remember that the essentials of that fellowship as laid down in the New Testament are rather of the heart than of the head. Where there is true repentance, self-renunciation, trust in Christ as Saviour, love to God and man, there is essential Christianity.

What should be our attitude to the less essential things?

(1) We should seek distinct convictions respecting them. They belong to the revelation of God, and are not to be treated as indifferent. The fact that men have differently conceived of these truths does not invalidate them in themselves. Our own Christian life will be largely affected by our conceptions of them, and, as we have seen, we may be firmly convinced respecting them without being either dogmatic or exclusive. But to be thus firmly convinced, to know what we believe and why, is needful for the perfect man in Christ Jesus.

(2) Such beliefs will be held with very varying strength of conviction and sense of their relative value to the religious life. Certain of these beliefs will appear of more importance than others; and this comparative estimate, again, will vary in different minds. Thus it was said by Professor Duncan of Edinburgh (called Rabbi Duncan for his Hebrew lore), "I am first a Christian, next a Catholic, then a Calvinist, fourth a Paedobaptist, and fifth a Presbyterian. I cannot reverse this order." It would be interesting in like manner to have a similar testimony from other theologians, of different schools of thought, as to the order of their

convictions. Such a statement would perhaps be of as much value as their declarations of the beliefs themselves. It is not only what we hold, but how we hold it, and in what relation to other opinions, that indicates and determines our theology.

¶ My certainty that there is God is before my certainty that he requireth love and holiness of his creatures. My certainty of this is greater than my certainty of the life of rewards and punishments hereafter. My certainty of that is greater than my certainty of the endless duration of it, and the immortality of individual souls. My certainty of the Deity is greater than my certainty of the Christian faith. My certainty of the Christian faith, in its essentials, is greater than my certainty of the perfection and infallibility of the Holy Scriptures. And my certainty of that is greater than my certainty of many particular texts, and so of the truth of many particular doctrines, and of the canonicalness of some certain books.[1]

(3) On some of these questions Christian people are manifestly coming nearer to one another. It would be but a poor prospect for the Church if these secondary doctrines of the faith were to continue to the end the subject of endless debate and division. So long, however, as men are simply controversialists, it will probably remain so. They feel called to be champions of their respective creeds; there is the ever-present temptation to fight for victory rather than for truth; and even the vanquished in the wordy strife often love their cause all the more for the defeat—

Victrix causa Diis placuit sed victa Catoni.

But let the respective parties exchange their bellicose attitude for that of fellow-students of the Word and will of God, and approximation becomes possible.

¶ You used to say that comparatively few people really believed even in a God. On this and certain other fundamental questions I think I may dare to say that I believe—believe, I mean, in the deepest sense. But there are innumerable lesser points which must occur to any man who has to use the Bible and the Church services for other people besides himself, and for other people too sometimes on their deathbeds—points about which, if a man feels only the possibility of doubt, he can only work with half of himself. God knows, it is not pride of intellect that makes me say

[1] O. Dewey, *Works*, 361.

this. I believe in nothing more strongly than in the necessity at a certain point of belief without proof. But I cannot crush reason and remain a man. I see quite enough at Oxford of doubting for doubting's sake to make me abhor such a thing myself; but the abuse of some must not be allowed to stigmatize all. I cannot help believing myself that there is far more in common between men of different theological opinions than they themselves will allow; that the truth is far wider than any one man or school can comprehend. But until this is more recognized and the Church in some way or other made really Catholic, there must be many who long to go in but are obliged to stay out.[1]

1. We may begin at home—*I am sure of myself.*—In actual life nobody doubts the self. Naturally, whatever thing or event comes before us, the first thought is—how will it affect *me*? Human life indeed is a continuous succession of self-adjustments to varied circumstances, in which the motive is to obtain good and avoid harm to self. On occasions, we sacrifice self-interest for the welfare of others; but the existence of the self is then even more plainly in evidence, because of the strain we have to put upon it in order to curb its wonted instincts. In actual experience the self is indubitable. "As sure as I am of my own existence" is the expression of our strongest certainty.

¶ There is nothing of which I am so sure as I am of my personal identity, and yet there is nothing I am less able to prove if challenged for a proof. There is nothing, moreover, about which I could raise so many doubts myself, were I determined to raise them. How, for instance, can I make it absolutely certain that I, who am delivering this lecture am identically the same person as he who received the invitation to deliver it three months ago? I may be under an illusion. I may have been dreaming. An evil spirit may have deluded me. Perhaps I am the wrong man. "But no," you reply, "the committee who invited you are here to testify that you are the man they invited. And the audience is here to support their testimony." I answer, How do I know that the committee are not the wrong men? Before their testimony can make me absolutely sure of my identity, they must be absolutely sure of their own. Perhaps the committee is under an illusion. Perhaps the audience is composed of people who are not the people they think they are. Whatever reason I have for doubting my own identity, they have

[1] *Edward Thring*, i. 275.

THE FULL ASSURANCE OF FAITH 283

equal reasons for doubting theirs; and either party must beg the whole question before it can accept the testimony of the other. How then can we make sure that we are not all in Bedlam together? We cannot make it sure by any manner of means. But why? The answer is simple—we cannot make it sure, simply because it is sure already. No one who was really and utterly in Bedlam would ever raise the question whether he was there or not. Be that as it may, the instance is interesting because it shows how much easier it is to raise doubts concerning our primal certainties than to give proofs of them. Provided you *choose* to raise them, provided you are determined to raise them, the scope for doubt is simply limitless. But what difference do the doubts make to our certainty? Not one iota. Our inability to solve the conundrums I have just suggested leaves our belief in identity untouched. Nay, I go further. Were some heaven-born philosopher to appear on the instant and present us with an irrefragable proof that we are the men we think ourselves to be, we should tell that philosopher that he had brought coals to Newcastle, we should be unmoved by his logic, we should go away not one whit surer of our personal identity than we were before the proof was offered.[1]

2. *We are sure, next, of God.*—Not so immediately and perhaps never so fully certain as we are of self. We hear the name of God; it comes to us upon the lips of those who tell us that they know Him; generations and centuries of prophets and apostles and confessors and humble believers bear witness that He is, and that He is good—the Creator of the universe, the Father of our spirits, the source of all truth and love, and that we are made in His image to have fellowship with Him; that this is the highest possibility of the human soul, to receive, of His infinite fulness, the strength and the light and the peace which shall satisfy all our deepest wants. This is what they tell us, but we do not always easily verify their testimony. "Why," we are sometimes inclined to ask, "is not this truth more clearly revealed? Why, in a matter so great as this, is any room left for doubt? Why is not God as palpable as the earth, as demonstrable as the sun in the sky? Is not our need of Him our deepest need? Why should not the ministry to it be as direct and inevitable as that by which our physical natures are supplied? It is not so. We may have reasons for believing, but there are also many reasons

[1] L. P. Jacks, in *Harvard Theological Review*, vi. 283.

for doubt, and certainty is not attainable. And often we are forced to cry with Job:

> "O that I knew where I might find him!
> That I might come even to his seat!
> I would order my cause before him,
> And fill my mouth with arguments.
> . . . . . .
> Behold, I go forward, but he is not there;
> And backward, but I cannot perceive him:
> On the left hand, where he doth work, but I cannot behold him:
> He hideth himself on the right hand, that I cannot see him."

3. *We are sure of Christ.*—This is the secret of our certainty in God. Christ made God's faithfulness known by realizing the promises and revealed His love by dying for men. But what do we mean by being sure of Christ? No man ever believed more truly in Jesus Christ than Paul; no man was ever more sure that Christ had risen from the dead; no man was ever more firmly persuaded that Christ was keeping him, saving him, and that Christ would in eternity receive and crown him. On what did St. Paul rest? Was it upon the miracles of Christ? Except the miracle of the resurrection he never refers to Christ's miracles. Was it upon the life of Christ? It is a remarkable thing that Paul dwells very little on the life of the Lord. Was it upon his visions? No, they were only beautiful experiences and strengthening revelations. He rests upon his own individual and sustained experience of Jesus Christ. Once he met Christ and Christ revealed Himself to him. He committed himself into Christ's hands, and from that day he died with Christ, he rose with Christ, he lived with Christ, he suffered with Christ, he worked with Christ, he triumphed with Christ, and, as the years came and went, there was no person on earth so absolutely real to the apostle Paul as the Lord Jesus Christ. The whole world was as a dream to him compared with Christ, who loved him and gave Himself for him. It was by spiritual experience of Christ that he came to certainty and was able to say, "I know whom I have believed. I am persuaded."

¶ I have been steadily ploughing my way through the letters

THE FULL ASSURANCE OF FAITH 285

of Paul with a view to finding out the abiding essentials in Paul's teaching. What were the immovable certainties to him? What was the very heart of the whole matter? What was the blazing sun at the centre of his system? Now, whether we agree with a man or not, we ought not to misrepresent him. We ought to treat him honestly. If we are going to controvert him, all well and good. But if we are going to expound him, honesty demands faithfulness to the records. To explain a man away is to lie about him. St. Paul's assurance was founded in what, to him, was the central fact in his teaching—that central fact was what he called "Gospel." It was good news of such a kind that it deserved to be put in a place by itself and be called not culture, but "Gospel." The central truth was this—that in His death—which He accepted voluntarily, and without any compulsion—Christ had taken upon Himself the responsibility for the sins of the race. He so dealt with sin in that sacrifice of Himself, that the sinfulness of man no longer stood as a great impassable mountain between man and God. Christ's death interprets the love of God as nothing else does. In dying He was doing the will of His Father. Ask the apostle—How can I believe in the love of God? He has but one answer—The Son of God loved me and gave Himself for me.[1]

4. But when we speak of assurance we usually mean *assurance of one's own salvation*.—Now it is undeniable that a tone of confidence runs through the New Testament on the question of personal salvation. The apostles teach that the design of the gospel is to put an end to doubt on the most important problems of human life; to fix the soul on immovable foundations of truth; to lock it fast in the arms of Almighty love; to give it a directing pole-star amidst the billows of temptation, "so that we be no more children tossed on the waves, and driven about by every wind of doctrine"; and to enable it at last to confront death itself with a shout of victory.

Throughout the New Testament we find that the faith of the writers and their converts corresponds in force and clearness with the certainty on which it rests, and hope corresponds in its steadfastness with such a basis. They speak of "knowing" that they have a house not made with hands, eternal in the heavens; of "knowing God," who had taught them to call Him Father, by His own Spirit—they even boldly say that they "rejoice in tribula-

[1] R. Thomas, in *Christian World Pulpit*, lxv. 157.

tion" in "hope of the glory of God." They do not even wait to consider the modern notion that it is morally disreputable to look for any recompense of reward, but they press on straight ahead for the "city which hath foundations, whose builder and maker is God."

¶ The doctrine of "assurance" through the witness of the Spirit is an integral part of religion. Scripture teaches it; reason demands it; the creeds of all the Christian Churches assert it. It is incredible that, when God's love in Christ has established its empire in the believing heart, and sin is forgiven, and all the ties of the spiritual order are restored, this stupendous change should be unrealized. It is incredible that God should conceal His grace; that it can be His will that His pardoned child should live under the shadow of a lie.

But this gracious truth was, in Wesley's day, one of the lost doctrines of Christianity. It was in the Thirty-nine Articles, but it had faded out of human memory. It was no longer realized, nor even expected, in human experience. It had become a mere incredibility. Its rediscovery and reassertion are part of the great service Methodism has rendered to the general Christian faith. This is what Wesley says of it:

"I observed, many years ago, that it is hard to find words in the language of men to explain the deep things of God. Indeed, there are none that will adequately express what the Spirit of God works in His children. But perhaps one might say (desiring any who are taught of God to correct, soften, or strengthen the expression), by the 'testimony of the Spirit' I mean an inward impression on the soul, whereby the Spirit of God immediately and directly witnesses to my spirit that I am a child of God; that 'Jesus Christ hath loved me, and given Himself for me,' that all my sins are blotted out, and I, even I, am reconciled to God. After twenty years' further consideration, I see no cause to retract any part of this. Neither do I conceive how any of these expressions may be altered so as to make them more intelligible. Meantime, let it be observed, I do not mean hereby that the Spirit of God testifies this by any outward voice; no, nor always by an inward voice, although He may do this sometimes. Neither do I suppose that He always applies to the heart (though He often may) one or more texts of Scripture. But He so works upon the soul by His immediate influence, and 'by a strong, though inexplicable operation, that the stormy wind and troubled waves subside, and there is a sweet calm; the heart resting as in

THE FULL ASSURANCE OF FAITH 287

the arms of Jesus, and the sinner being clearly satisfied that all his 'iniquities are forgiven, and his sins covered.'"[1]

¶ It is very interesting to notice how, in times of awakening, the spiritual instincts imparted to the new-born soul by the Holy Ghost seek out the truth. One day, in a fisherman's house, we found two females sitting together with the Assembly's *Shorter Catechism* in their hands. They were talking over the questions on "Justification" and "Adoption," and were comparing these with some of the "benefits which accompany or flow from them," namely, "*assurance of God's love*, peace of conscience, and joy in the Holy Ghost." They were themselves happy in the calm assurance of the love of God; but a neighbour had somewhat perplexed them by insisting that they had no right to assurance until they could point to *sanctification* showing itself in their after-lives. On the other hand, those two souls could not see why they should wait till then; for if they had been "justified," and had a "right to all the privileges of the sons of God," they might at once have "assurance of God's love."[2]

¶ After describing the circumstances of a woman's conversion through the influence of Mrs. Price Hughes, Mr. Begbie gives the result of it in her own words: "A great tumult took place in my mind. It was like a crashing of masonry. There was no joy, and no peace, but an absolute *certainty*. I knew that my Redeemer lived. I knew that He desired to save me. I knew that I had only to trust Him and He *would* save me. I clutched Mrs. Hughes's arm, and clung to her with a kind of frantic terror. She told me afterwards that the clutch of my hand hurt her arm for many days; I was like one possessed—not outwardly, though I was trembling, but in my soul, where I was conscious of God. All I could do was to cling to Mrs. Hughes, and wait for the tempest in my soul to go. You see, the dawn had come not as it comes in England, tranquilly and slowly, but as it comes in the tropics, suddenly and at once, with a complete glory. I was *certain*. Afterwards there was joy and a great peace, but then, at that wonderful moment, everything in my soul and body centred in the single idea of absolute *certainty*. There was a God. There was a Christ. There was forgiveness for sin, and strength to withstand temptation. Like a flash the light had come. I saw how I was wronging my Lord, and piercing His loving heart, and at that moment the struggle and strife ended. I laid down my burden of sorrow and shame at His feet. I felt myself forgiven.

---

[1] W. H. Fitchett, *Wesley and His Century*, 428.
[2] *Reminiscences of Andrew A. Bonar*, 333.

I almost fainted under the revulsion of feeling, and what I really said or did I cannot tell."[1]

II.

THE NECESSITY OF ASSURANCE.

1. "The Reformers taught that assurance is of the essence of faith, and therefore that all believers have assurance. Luther and Melanchthon and Calvin taught this. It was taught also in the Augsburg Confession, and in the Heidelberg Catechism. It is not taught in any other of the Reformed confessions. This is now generally believed by Protestants to be an untenable position. There were two reasons which led the Reformers generally to take up this position—first, they were godly men themselves, constantly abounding in the work of the Lord, and God seems to have given them constant assurance of their salvation; second, they were contending with Romanists, who taught that no one could possibly know that he was a believer, without a special revelation from God, and they were naturally led to go to the opposite extreme, and to hold that no one could be a believer without knowing it. But almost all Protestants now agree that this position is an extreme and an untenable one, and that the doctrine taught in the Bible is that believers *may be,* and *should be,* assured of their salvation, but that persons may be believers without being assured of it."[2]

(1) The author of those words—an Irish Presbyterian—says further: Christians *may have* assurance, and *ought to have* assurance; but it is possible to be a Christian without having assurance. This is the doctrine of the Westminster Confession also. Except the Bible, there is nothing clearer on assurance than the 18th chapter of the Confession. It teaches that Christians "may, in this life, be certainly assured that they are in the state of grace"; and this certainty "is not a bare conjectural and probable persuasion, grounded upon a fallible hope, but an infallible assurance of faith"; yet that it "*doth not so belong to the essence of faith,* but that a true believer may wait long,

---

[1] H. Begbie, *In the Hand of the Potter,* 101.
[2] W. J. Patton, *Pardon and Assurance,* 209.

THE FULL ASSURANCE OF FAITH

and conflict with many difficulties, before he be partaker of it." The words, "doth not so belong," show that the Westminster divines considered *faith* and *assurance* to be very close to each other, though distinct.

The phrase in the Westminster Confession "infallible assurance" does not relate to the certainty of our faith or trust as to the truth of the object upon which the faith rests—that is, the Divine promise of salvation in Christ—but to the certainty of our hope or belief as to our own personal relation to Christ and eternal salvation. Hence it follows that while assurance, in some degree of it, does belong to the essence of all real faith in the sufficiency of Christ and the truth of the promises, it is not in any degree essential to a genuine faith that the believer should be persuaded of the truth of his own experience and the safety of his estate. Theologians consequently have distinguished between the assurance of faith (Heb. x. 22)—that is, a strong faith as to the truth of Christ—and the assurance of hope (Heb. vi. 11)—that is, a certain persuasion that we are true believers, and therefore safe. This latter is also called the assurance of sense, because it rests upon the inward sense the soul has of the reality of its own spiritual experiences. The former is of the essence of faith, and terminates directly upon Christ and His promise; hence it is called the *direct* act of faith. The latter is not of the essence of faith, but is its fruit; and is called the *reflex* act of faith, because it is drawn as an inference from the experience of the graces of the Spirit which the soul discerns when it reflects upon its own consciousness. God says that whosoever believes is saved—*that* is the object of direct faith: I believe—*that* is the matter of conscious experience: therefore I am saved—*that* is the matter of inference and the essence of full assurance.

¶ That this full assurance of our own gracious state is not of the essence of saving faith is proved—(1) From the form in which the offer of salvation in Christ—which is the object of saving faith—is set forth in the Scriptures: "Believe on the Lord Jesus Christ, and thou shalt be saved"; "Whosover will, let him take," etc.; "Him that cometh to me, I will in no wise cast out." Acts xvi. 31; Rev. xxii. 17; John vi. 37. The matter revealed, and therefore the truth accepted by faith, is, not that God is reconciled to *me* in Christ, but that Christ is presented to me as the foundation of truth, and will save me if I do truly trust. It

290 CHRISTIAN DOCTRINE OF FAITH

is evident that trust itself is something different from the certainty that we do trust, and that our trust is of the right kind. (2) All the promises of the Bible are made to classes—to believers, to saints, etc.—and not to individuals. (3) Paul appeared to doubt as to the genuineness of his faith long after he was a true believer. (4) As we saw above, the Bible contains many exhortations addressed to believers to go on to the grace of full assurance, as something beyond their present attainments. Heb. x. 22, vi. 11; 2 Pet. i. 10. (5) The experience of the great body of God's people in modern times proves the same thing.[1]

¶ This morning I went to call on M. Malan, without introduction, except that of many mutual acquaintances. I sat talking with him about two hours. The chief subject of discussion was that of assurance. He says that a Christian cannot be without assurance, except sinfully. This I agreed to, though not exactly on the same ground as that on which he puts it. The proof of adoption is a changed heart—2 Cor. v. 17. If a man see this change in himself, it is a proof to him that he has believed, because the work of regeneration is begun—the work which God performs in the heart of all whom He has chosen, conforming them to the image of His Son—Rom. viii. 29. If he does not see this change, it is evidently because of the predominance of sin, and therefore the want of assurance springs from sin. But Malan makes it sin, not indirectly, but directly. His argument, simply stated, is this: Whosoever believeth that Jesus is the Christ is born of God. You acknowledge that. Is He the Christ? Have you any doubt? You are sure He is? or do you mean to say you do not believe that He is? But if you tell me you do believe that He is, how can you doubt your safety? Would you make God a liar? for He says that "every one who believes is born of God." I do not think this satisfactory, because I believe many who never will be saved are convinced of it, and so in a certain sense believe it, as the devils do who tremble, or as Simon did—Acts viii. 13—who was yet in the bond of iniquity. And it is this possibility which can make a Christian doubt his own state even when he says, I believe. Still I admit that want of assurance is the mark of very low attainments in grace; because if sanctification were so bright as to be visible, there would be no doubt.[2]

(2) Take the Methodist position. There were many tragedies in the lives of Wesley's sisters, but with nearly all of them a strange peace lay on their dying beds. As an example, John

---

[1] A. A. Hodge, *A Commentary on the Confession of Faith*, 245.
[2] *Life and Letters of the Rev. F. W. Robertson*, 60.

THE FULL ASSURANCE OF FAITH

Wesley's account of the last moments of Patty, perhaps not the cleverest, but certainly the gayest, and perhaps the most ill-fated, of the Epworth girls, may be recalled. She died with a triumphant whisper on her lips : " I have the assurance I have so long wanted. Shout ! "

In his earlier days Wesley believed that such a conscious assurance was essential to salvation, but later he attained to a truer view—" When, fifty years ago, my brother Charles and I, in the simplicity of our hearts, taught the people that unless they *knew* their sins were forgiven they were under the wrath and curse of God, I marvel they did not stone us. The Methodists, I hope, know better now. We preach assurance, as we always did, as a common privilege of the children of God, but we do not enforce it under pain of damnation denounced on all who enjoy it not."

¶ There is no doubt Mrs. Wesley was puzzled. There was something infinitely perplexing to her in her sons' assurance : they were moving with every-day familiarity amongst those mysteries which all her life she had desired, yet feared, to look into. "For my part," she had written a few years before to her son John, "after many years' search and inquiry, I still continue to pay my Devotions to an Unknown God—I cannot know Him. I dare not say I Love Him—only this, I have chose Him for my only Happiness, my All, my only Good, in a Word, for my God— And when I sound my Will, I feel it adheres to its choice—tho' not so faithfully as it ought ; therfore I desire yr Prayers, wch I need much more than you do mine." [1]

(3) Take the Baptist position. Dr. B. H. Carroll asks : Is assurance necessary to being a Christian at all ? Is it such an essential element of saving faith that where it is lacking there is no saving faith ? Or, if you prefer it, is assurance such an instantaneous and continuous effect of saving faith that the one can never be, even for a moment, without the other ? So that where there is no such assurance you may positively know there is no faith.

He answers : " Such assurance is *not Baptist doctrine.* This is a question of fact to be settled by the evidence of history. And I am perfectly confident when you consider the evidence you will join me in saying that anything akin to this theory of

[1] M. R. Brailsford, *Susanna Wesley*, 115.

assurance is a vital and fundamental innovation on Baptist doctrine: 'This infallible assurance doth not so belong to the essence of faith but that a true believer may wait long, and conflict with many difficulties, before he be a partaker of it; yet, being enabled by the Spirit to know the things which are freely given him of God, He may, without extraordinary revelation in the right use of means, attain thereunto; and therefore it is the duty of every one to give all diligence to make their calling and election sure, that thereby his heart may be enlarged in peace and joy in the Holy Spirit, in love and thankfulness to God, and in strength and cheerfulness in the duties of obedience in the proper fruits of this assurance.'"[1]

2. There are three cautions to be given here.

(1) Men should not indulge in boasts of their religious assurance. False lives have no right, saintly lives have no need, and in ordinary lives it is out of place.

¶ Do I speak to you as one who has fully entered into this great inheritance? Nay, I am making no such claim. Often I am timid and despondent and more anxious than I ought to be; often small things vex me, and the judgment of men irks me, and I am afraid of losses and reverses; the whole trouble is that I am not nearly so sure of God as I ought to be. I am not standing on some eminence above you and calling down to you. I am standing with you, on the common plane of our humanity, but I am lifting my eyes to the hills from which our help must come, and trying to get you to look in the same direction. I have not yet attained, but I know, as well as I can know anything, that the life I am talking about is the right kind of life; that it would be worth to me more than everything else that I ever wish and strive for to be perfectly sure of God and to live, without flinching, right up to that assurance. I know that if that knowledge were in my heart all things would be mine,—the world, life, death, things present, things to come. I should never be a coward, I should never shrink from any sacrifice to which the truth summoned me. I should hold the prizes of pelf and praise for which men are wearing out their lives very cheap. I should not be bartering honor and integrity to get some little selfish advantage, and I should be as happy every day as the day is long. No; perhaps I could not be quite happy if those whom I loved were unhappy; I should have to carry their burdens, to

[1] B. H. Carroll, *Sermons*, 239.

THE FULL ASSURANCE OF FAITH   293

take upon my own soul something of their sorrow. But I should be able, so it seems to me, to help them far more than I help them now; to lead them, if they really loved me, out into the light of God.[1]

(2) No one should claim certainty on any subject if he does not possess it. The biographer of Cardinal Manning says: "As an accepted teacher in religion, the habit had grown upon him of speaking always on all points of faith with an absolute assurance of certitude. In a letter to Robert Wilberforce of this date, Manning confesses that 'people are rising up all over the country and appealing to me to solve doubts and difficulties which, as you know, perplex my own mind. But if I leave their appeals unanswered, they will think that I am as they are.' For him, a spiritual teacher, in whom his penitents put their trust, to whom they come for counsel and guidance, to confess to his doubts would give scandal and do grave harm. Hence it came to pass that he had to speak, considering it under the circumstances his duty to do so, with a double voice."[2]

¶ This arrogance is as unseemly as it is baseless. If the subject did not forbid it, yet the sense of imperfection ought to restrain a frail, fallible, erring human being from such presumption; presumption, too, which is commonly strong in proportion as the doctrine is dark and doubtful, and the mind is readier to decide than to examine. Such indeed was not the spirit of Newton, "child-like sage." Such was not the spirit of Socrates, who, against the all-knowing sophists of his day, was accustomed to say that he professed to know nothing; that he was only a seeker after knowledge. Such, in fine, has never been the spirit of deep study and patient thought. But assurance rises up to speak, where modesty is silent; and a rash judgment to pronounce, where patient inquiry hesitates; and ignorance to say "I know," where real knowledge can only say, "I believe."[3]

(3) Let not the assurance of salvation be the occasion for indolence or indifference to the call of the battle of life. Browning shows, from the experience of his own time, how religious certainty may stunt the soul's growth. For he finds that many of those who have received Christianity, who have

---
[1] W. Gladden, *Where does the Sky Begin?* 331.
[2] *The Life of Cardinal Manning*, i. 464.
[3] O. Dewey, *Works*, 361.

"found, and known and named" it, recognizing its beauty and its value, nevertheless live less worthy lives than the great men who died before it came. The Archbishop of Florence, that dignitary of the Church who refused to help Pompilia in her need, and "the Monastery called of Convertites," which attempted to dishonour her memory and plunder her child, ill bear comparison with the old pagan poet Euripides, who in that "tenebrific time, five hundred years ere Paul spoke, Felix heard," found reason for so much of temperance and righteousness, and attained so nearly to guess at what Paul knew. He passed before the coming of the sunrise, which, joining truth to truth, "shoots life and substance into death and void," yet though the skies were dark above him, he found a better path, and followed it more faithfully than many high-placed Christians, who "miss the plain way in the blaze of noon." It is the too easy assurance with which Christianity is accepted that enervates the moral fibre of its adherents. They have no longer any battles to fight, any Nero to brave, any doubts to overcome, and therefore they sink into a state of moral lethargy. There is no longer any fear of "sudden Roman faces, violent hands," such as set up a barrier to St. John; the days have passed when "imminent was the outcry, Save our Christ"; nor has the critic yet begun to ask, "Was John at all, and did he say he saw?"

> Is it not this ignoble confidence,
> Cowardly hardihood, that dulls and damps,
> Makes the old heroism impossible?

After this condemnation of his own time, the Pope sees, as it were in a vision, that the mission of the coming age will be

> To shake
> This torpor of assurance from our creed,
> Reintroduce the doubt discarded, bring
> That formidable danger back, we drove
> Long ago to the distance and the dark,

till doubt once more awakes the sleeping soul, rouses it to renewed activity,

> And man stand out again, pale, resolute,
> Prepared to die,—which means, alive at last.[1]

[1] A. C. Pigou, *Robert Browning as a Religious Teacher*, 84.

¶ I have often thought that the Christian life of many ministers has been too easy. Born and bred, taught and trained in a Christian home, they have gently and slowly grown in the knowledge and the grace of Christ, and have endured no terrible moral conflicts nor passed through any severe spiritual crises; consequently there is a wide range of the Christian salvation beyond their own experience. Only by greater intensity in their Christian living, and wider sympathy with other lives more sternly tested, can they transcend this disadvantageous limitation. For surely only he who has himself realized that the only help and hope of men perishing is in the cross of Christ can preach with such force and fervour as to arouse others to their danger and need, and to call forth their faith in Him who "is able to save to the uttermost all who come unto God by him." To be genuinely evangelical our message must be intensely experimental.[1]

III.

THE VALUE OF FULL ASSURANCE.

Let us "give diligence." Uncertainty, in matters of any moment, is anguish. If we would go forward with freedom in the way of life, we must be treading on firm ground. Is not this true of the things of common life? Continual uncertainty would be a harassment which we could not bear. It is true of business. For, though in business life there are manifold contingencies which cannot be calculated, yet, if the reasonable certainty of business did not far outweigh uncertainty, its anxieties would be intolerable. It is true of the higher realm of thought. Men have to move, indeed, with cautious steps amid all the mysteries of truth; but to think at all would be to suffer with an exquisite pain, if to discern between truth and untruth were impossible. It is true of the sacred relationships of human life: uncertainty here would be worse than death. And it is no less true of the life in God that, if we would have peace, joy, strength, we must have faith—a faith which brings certitude to the soul.

1. *It is of value for peace of conscience.*—To assure the conscience of pardon, to vanquish the fear of extinction in death, or the fear of awful judgment beyond, to reach the depth of man's

[1] A. E. Garvie, *The Gospel for To-Day*, 41.

spirit, the seat of his misery, by an effectual assurance of reconciliation, demands the direct and healing touch of a Divine life-giving hand, the direct voice of the Almighty Consoler. This requires a distinctly revealed "Covenant," not a guess, or a hope proceeding from man, but an "oath and a promise" of God; not a human peradventure, but a clear and distinct revelation of the redeeming love which apprehends us in Christ. It is this that the apostles say they bring us from heaven—"a good hope through grace" assured by many infallible proofs. They tell us that they bring glad tidings, definite enough to meet the necessity of every man, and make known a Saviour able to save to the uttermost all who come unto God by Him; so that God can be just, yet the justifier of him that believeth in Jesus.

2. *It is essential to thoroughness of character.*—If we would have fulness, thoroughness, beauty of spirit and life, we must have singleness of purpose, entire trust in the Master, and consecration to His service. If we love Him with all our strength, trust Him with all our heart, there will be no uncertainty about our experience, character, or destiny.

¶ Himself—his sensations and ideas—never fell again precisely into focus as on that day, yet he was the richer by its experience. But for once only to have come under the power of that peculiar mood, to have felt the train of reflections which belong to it really forcible and conclusive, to have been led by them to a conclusion, to have apprehended the *Great Ideal*, so palpably that it defined personal gratitude and the sense of a friendly hand laid upon him amid the shadows of the world, left this one particular hour a marked point in life never to be forgotten. It gave him a definitely ascertained measure of his moral or intellectual need, of the demand his soul must make upon the powers, whatsoever they might be, which had brought him, as he was, into the world at all. And again, would he be faithful to himself, to his own habits of mind, his leading suppositions, if he did but remain just there? Must not all that remained of life be but a search for the equivalent of that Ideal, among so-called actual things—a gathering together of every trace or token of it, which his actual experience might present?[1]

3. *It is essential for the best service.*—Who will burn for Christ

[1] Walter Pater, *Marius the Epicurean*, ii. 53.

except one who intensely believes in Him? Who will think it worth while even to attempt any distinctly Christian achievement in morals, unless on a basis of certainty that such conduct is "not in vain in the Lord"? Who can forgo retaliation, sensual indulgence, the pursuit of worldly aims or worldly praise, on the strength of a dim probability, or a vague dream of some just possible result in a dubious future? No—to practise the Christian morality in actual life we require to be filled with a certainty, and an overflowing gladness in the heart, which are capable of inciting to heroic deeds; to know that "these are the true sayings of God," that our faith rests on the rock of ages, and that nothing in the creation is more absolutely fixed than the connexion between a life or death of martyrdom for Christ, and an eternity of glory.

¶ To live to any purpose at all a man must have a certain amount of positive faith. The faith may be mean and squalid and base, but faith he must have if his life is to accomplish anything at all. His faith, his positives, his beliefs constitute the driving power of his life. No man can live on doubts and negations. The man who is sure of nothing will accomplish nothing, "He that doubteth is like the surge of the sea driven by the wind and tossed." He is the sport and plaything of circumstances—life for him is bound to be without meaning, purpose, or end. It is a man's positives that count, and if he has no positives he will count for nothing. This is true even of our secular life; it is still more true of the moral life; it is most true of all of the Christian life. If a man is to live the Christian life, there must be certain things which are not mere guesswork to him, but of which he is quite sure.[1]

4. *It is necessary if our message to others is to carry weight.*—If religion is to live in these days it must have a living message for these days. Such a message must be couched in language which the age can understand and must take account of its special defects and needs. If men have lost hold of religion and fail to find in it the old motives and sanctions and appeals, we may be sure that the fault is not altogether that of the men. We have to ask whether the religion itself has not changed, whether it still retains its soul, whether it stands as once it did for power and life, or has degenerated into empty forms. In other words, if men

[1] J. D. Jones, *The Hope of the Gospel*, 168.

have lost the old note of certainty, why is it, and how can it be restored?

¶ What is wanting in a good deal of preaching is personal certainty and urgency. Men preach a salvation the full value of which they have not themselves experimentally realized, and yet expect that they will persuade others of its supreme importance for them. They declare what the Bible and the Church teach about the cross of Christ, but they do not bear their own testimony to what the crucified has done for them in transporting them out of the shadow of death into God's marvellous light.[1]

¶ It is said that a certain eminent Doctor of Divinity once summed up a debate on some knotty theological problem in the following terms: "Well, gentlemen, speaking for myself, I think I may venture to say that I should feel inclined to favour a tendency in a positive direction, with reservations." It is easy to sneer at such an attitude; but in reality it is rather splendid. Here was an old man, who had spent the greater part of his life in studying the fundamental problems of metaphysics and history, and at the end of it all he had the courage to confess that he was still only at the threshold of the house of Knowledge. At least he had realized the magnitude of his subject, and if we compare him with the narrow dogmatists of other ages, we shall be forced to allow that in his exceeding humility there was some greatness, nobility of mind, and dignity. At the same time it must be confessed that such an attitude does not lend itself to expression in a terse, definite form; and that, unfortunately, is what is needed by the men who are busy doing the hard work of the world. The ordinary man wants something simple and applicable to the problems with which he has to deal. He wants a right point of view, so that he can see the hard facts which crowd his life in their proper perspective. He wants Power, that he may be able to master the circumstances which threaten to swamp him. For the nebulous views of modern theology he has little use.[2]

¶ The preachers who produce the deepest effects are those who, having fast hold of the elemental religious principles which their hearers already hold, but hold hesitatingly, or hold as in a dream, or hold without knowing what they hold, draw these out from the darkness in which they lie buried, and force them into activity, and vividly manifest the reality of their application to heart and conduct. That is what moves men so profoundly; they

---

[1] A. E. Garvie, *The Gospel for To-Day*, 41.
[2] D. Hankey, *A Student in Arms*, i. 185.

THE FULL ASSURANCE OF FAITH 299

come to church professing a creed, they hope that they believe it; but it slumbers, inoperative and inert, without practical force, without any direct or effectual significance. The preacher reads out the secret; he takes up this assumed creed; he gives it actual meaning; he spreads it out over the surface of life; he brings it to bear on the real facts of daily conduct with incision and with fire.[1]

¶ It was doubtless his evidently intense conviction of the absolute truth and the positive certainty of what he preached, that day after day drew crowds of the people of Boston to listen to the evangelist. We are given to understand that on the whole the intellectual atmosphere of Boston is not favourable to the growth of the full assurance of faith. Yet after all, notwithstanding Mrs. Humphry Ward's dictum that "the force of things is against the certain people," men do feel the magnetism of the preacher to whom the things he speaks of are obviously the supreme realities of life, which he himself unwaveringly believes and lives by, and which they also must unwaveringly believe and live by, or else incur incalculable spiritual loss. "For if the trumpet give an uncertain voice, who shall prepare himself for war?"[2]

¶ Some here present will remember that during the latter half of last century great things were expected in the interests of Christianity and the interests of religious truth from the influence of the Broad Church school of the Church of England. To-day where is that school? As the battle goes on and the armies are drawn up for conflict in that Church, one looks round for that distinguished school to exercise their influence, to make peace and to conciliate opposite views. Where are their associations? Where are their meetings? Where are their utterances? The school is non-existent for any practical purpose. It has virtually died out, and its wreck strews the shore. Is this because the Broad Churchmen were not learned? Is it because they were not pious? Is it because they were not earnest, fascinating, human, lovable? Let the names of Stanley, Maurice, and Kingsley, and, if you choose so to include him, who did not wish particularly so to be included himself, the greatest of them all, and the greatest preacher of last century, Robertson of Brighton, answer. What in younger days we expected from their influence on England, and their influence percolating through England, doubtless was correct. But they have no children to-day. There

---

[1] H. S. Holland, *Personal Studies*, 145.
[2] *Henry Varley's Life-Story*, 186.

is no organized body to-day representing their opinions and contributing their share to the great theological controversy.

And why not ? Because with all their excellences, and with all their sweetness, they did not sufficiently strike the note of dogmatic certainty, and did not, as the other schools have done, train up their children, their disciples after them, with crisp and clear forms of belief. Their creed was too nebulous a creed, and, however beautiful be the mist—the mist shot through by the sun, and with its glimpses, as it rolls away, of the sky—it is not by preference through the mist that one desires to climb the dangerous hills of faith.[1]

[1] John Watson, in *Christian World Pulpit*, lix. 299.

XIV.

THE FOUNDATION OF FAITH.

LITERATURE.

Barry, A., *Do We Believe?* (1908).
Bicknell, E. J., *A Theological Introduction to the Thirty-nine Articles* (1919).
Cairns, D. S., *The Reasonableness of the Christian Faith* (1918).
Carnegie, W. H., *Democracy and Christian Doctrine* (1914).
Drawbridge, C. L., *Is Religion Undermined?* (1906).
Drummond, J., *Spiritual Religion* (1870).
Ferries, G., *The Growth of Christian Faith* (1905).
Forsyth, P. T., *The Principle of Authority.*
Gardner, P., *The Religious Experience of Saint Paul* (1911).
Garvie, A. E., *The Gospel for To-Day* (1904).
„   „   in *Mansfield College Essays* (1909).
Gladden, W., *Where does the Sky Begin?* (1904).
Green, S. G., *The Christian Creed and the Creeds of Christendom* (1898).
Herrmann, W., *Faith and Morals* (1904).
Hill, R. A. P., *The Interregnum* (1913).
Inge, W. R., *Faith* (1909).
„   „   *The Philosophy of Plotinus* (1918).
James, W., *Some Problems of Philosophy* (1911).
Jowett, B., *The Epistles of St. Paul to the Thessalonians, Galatians and Romans,* ii. (1894).
Lecky, W. E. H., *The Map of Life* (1901).
Lockyer, T. F., *Religious Experience* (1913).
Mackenzie, W. D., *The Final Faith* (1910).
Mortimer, A. G., *Catholic Faith and Practice,* ii. (1898).
Mozley, J. K., *Ritschlianism* (1909).
Pringle-Pattison, A. S., *The Idea of God* (1917).
Raven, C. E., *What Think Ye of Christ?* (1916).
Rowntree, J. W., *Essays and Addresses* (1905).
Salmon, G., *The Reign of Law* (1873).
Skrine, J. H., *What is Faith?* (1907).
Thompson, S. P., *The Quest for Truth* (1915).
Watson, J., *The Doctrines of Grace* (1900).
Wilberforce, B., *Following On to Know the Lord* (1903).
Woods, F. H., *For Faith and Science* (1906).
Biblical World, xxxi. (1908) 365 (H. S. Nash)
Expositor, 6th Ser., vi. (1902) 334 (J. Stalker).
Hartford Seminary Record, xxiii. (1913) 280 (W. T. English).

The Foundation of Faith.

THE ground of certainty in religion is a subject which has of late received very close attention from the thinking minds of Europe; and in our own country more works than one of a high order have been devoted to its elucidation. In countries like Germany and France, where Protestantism is confronted by Roman Catholicism, the disposition to raise this question is stimulated by the challenge of the Romish Church to Protestanism to produce its credentials, but the necessity lies far deeper: thoughtful and earnest minds cannot but ask, How can we be sure that our religion is true? It is only shallowness or recklessness that can long refrain from asking this question. The more the issues, for time and eternity, involved in religion are realized, the more imperative must the desire become to be certain that we are building upon the rock and not upon the sand.

It is indeed a tremendous question; to be asked and answered, not as an abstract question, but in its practical application to ourselves and to the various conditions of our actual life in this twentieth century of Christianity.

1. Now, in the first place, it is always to be remembered that we inherit our Christianity, as we inherit our knowledge, our institutions, our civilization in all its forms, from the ages of the past. It comes to us "time honoured" in the true sense of the word, as a great living reality, which has proved itself the leading force, moulding and directing human progress—intellectual, social, moral, spiritual—and creating (so to speak) the very atmosphere of our higher life. In spite of all imperfections, internal corruptions, external antagonisms, it has shown through all the ages a transcendent vitality; if these could be taken away, or even

diminished, it is clear that this beneficent vitality has in itself capacity for infinitely higher development. It is, indeed, the highest example of that inheritance from the past on which, under the great law of evolution, the whole, or nearly the whole, of human progress depends. We cannot stand aloof from it. Whether we will or not, it presents itself as a dominant force of influence, and it claims from us an "obedience of faith." We must recognize that reality; we must examine and test that claim. We may accept or reject it; but we cannot ignore it. Its Divine Founder has Himself said, "He that is not with me is against me; and he that gathereth not with me scattereth."

2. Nor is this all. The individual soul is not left to itself to investigate and estimate this great spiritual force and this transcendent claim. It is from the beginning taught and educated on this all-important subject by those who profess to speak in the name and by the inspiration of God Himself. To the child that religious education comes from parents, teachers, pastors; to the manhood of the world from a Church of Christ, of which these are the representatives. So, we read, Christ Himself ordained; while He claimed as supreme the witness of the Holy Spirit, He added to all His disciples "ye also shall bear witness of me." In this we have the highest exemplification of the general law of the progress of all human knowledge, which generally comes to mankind not by original thought and discovery, but by the teaching of those who have, or claim to have, superior knowledge and wisdom, both from individual teachers and from the accumulated knowledge and collective wisdom of human society.

3. But on this great question above all others, no man can divest himself of his unalienable moral responsibility of judgment. For faith is the free adhesion of the individual soul face to face with the supreme spiritual realities of its life. Naturally, therefore, it is the express command of the Apostolic teaching itself that men are to "prove all things" and to "hold fast to that which they find to be good." True faith is not simple credulity, it must "try the spirits whether they be of God." But for men generally this proof is not so much theoretical as practical. If by practical experience they find that Christianity has a real spiritual

efficacy; if they find that a living Christian faith is a light of guidance in the perplexities and mysteries of life; if they find in it a moral inspiration, victorious alike over weakness and sinfulness within and over the antagonism of evil without; if they find in it an unfailing comfort in sorrow and disappointment, and an undying hope of future victory and happiness; if, above all, they realize through it a true spiritual communion with the Divine—then they seek no further. In the words of Holy Scripture they "have tasted that the Lord is gracious," and it is enough, and more than enough, for them. How His grace works in the soul and why it was needful that it should work in the way which the gospel proclaims, they may not clearly see. But for this knowledge they can well afford to wait. There may be for them still many unsolved mysteries of God and man, and many perplexities which are severe trials of their faith. But if in spite of these they have what they find to be "a lantern to their feet and a light to their path," they are rightly content to follow it. There is a true insight in those well-known words:

> I looked to Jesus, and I found
> In Him my Star, my Sun;
> And in that light of life I'll walk
> Till travelling days are done.

4. But while this is the wisdom and the happiness of the great mass of men, yet it may be necessary to look on the great question, so to speak, from without, and to see what, so considered, is the "defence of the hope that is in us"—what are (to use the common term) the evidences on which our faith rests, and through which we "know him in whom we believe." It must be so always for the Church of Christ in its unceasing witness to the world and its bold claim of the world's allegiance to its Master. It may be so for the more thoughtful and more inquiring minds of the leaders of human thought, who cannot help longing to look into the deeper things of God, that they may apprehend them for themselves and may teach them to their brethren. It will certainly be so for those whose faith is actually so troubled and even bewildered by the denials and doubts of which in these days of inquiry the air is full, that they must seek to think out for themselves, or seek to learn through the guidance of others, the

grounds on which the faith of Christendom rests. In all these cases the great inquiry cannot be put aside without prejudice to the vitality of faith itself. When our spiritual inheritance is undisturbed, we are content to enjoy it and strive to use it rightly, but when it is seriously questioned, we must study its title-deeds.

I.

The Church.

1. The religious certainty of a large majority of Christian believers rests, nominally at least, upon the authority of the Church. Conceiving of religion as a gift to us from God in the sense of a sacred deposit handed down for man's guidance perfect and complete in all of its appointments and arrangements, it is perfectly reasonable to believe that its explanation will be rigidly immutable. There will be great doctrines to be accepted with unquestioning faith and definite duties to be performed with undeviating loyalty. The infallible Church and the infallible Pope are a natural and logical necessity in this view of the situation. Indeed if an infallible authority, outside the individual soul, is absolutely necessary to the religious life for the development of certainty, the Roman Church has the only logical and rational doctrine of such infallibility.

¶ This infallible claim is made for example by Cardinal Manning, who asserts: "That God has not only revealed His Truth, but has made a divine and imperishable provision for the custody, perpetuity, and promulgation of His Truth to the world; that is to say, through the channel of His Church, divinely founded, divinely preserved from error, and divinely assisted in the declaration of Truth."[1]

2. The conception of faith as a body of doctrine, supernaturally accredited and therefore to be accepted in its entirety, is primitive. The guiding idea of Catholicism began to establish itself as soon as there was a Church for it to grow in. "The Catholic theory of apostolic tradition," says Sabatier, who writes from a Protestant standpoint, "is found clearly defined and established as an infallible and sovereign law in the times of Irenæus,

[1] *Contemporary Review*, xxiv. 153.

THE FOUNDATION OF FAITH

Tertullian, and Hippolytus." The concentration of power in the hands of the Roman Church, as the authoritative interpreter of this tradition, advanced as if by an automatic process. To quote Sabatier again: "The future centre of the Catholic Church appeared from the commencement of the second century," and in the year 194, "for the first time a bishop of Rome, Victor, speaks as master to the other bishops, presents himself as interpreter and arbiter of the universal Church, acts as universal bishop, and proclaims heretical the churches that would resist his authority." In Cyprian's time the bishops were all theoretically equal. Yet such is the interior logic of the system that Cyprian himself laid the foundation of a new evolution which was to produce from the body of bishops that *episcopus episcoporum* against whom he had tried to guard himself. The trend of the Catholic polity towards a centralized despotism went on irresistibly and inexorably.

When once the Roman primacy is recognized, all later developments of the papal prerogative, down to our own times, are only the logical conclusion of the Catholic conception of the Church. The infallibility which was the attribute of the universal Church was gradually concentrated in the Roman Church, and thence passed to the Roman bishop. When the Pope was held to be the head and voice of the Church, the infallibility of the Church could not express itself through another mouth.

¶ Roman Catholicism is a religion of authority. When a man who has been a Protestant becomes a Roman Catholic, he must learn a kind of submission that we in England, or America, know nothing of in any other relation of life, unless we are soldiers on a campaign. Where the Church has spoken, the loyal Catholic must obey without question. Nor is this authority confined to religious matters. "That authority," says Cardinal Newman, "has the prerogative of an indirect jurisdiction on subject-matters which lie beyond its own proper limits, and it most reasonably has such a jurisdiction. It could not properly defend religious truth without claiming for that truth what may be called its *pomoeria*, or, to take another illustration, without acting as we act, as a nation, in claiming as our own not only the land on which we live, but what are called British waters. The Catholic Church claims, not only to judge infallibly on religious questions, but to animadvert on opinions in secular matters which bear upon religion, on matters of philosophy, of science, of literature, of history, and it demands our submission to her claim. It claims to censure books, to silence authors, and to forbid discussions. It must, of course, be obeyed without a word, and perhaps, in process of time, it will tacitly recede from its own injunctions."[1]

¶ The following words, written by Father Morris in his last retreat, and quoted in his Life by Father J. H. Pollen, S.J., will cast further light on his character, and confirm the impression left by the description in the Autobiography:

"In all my life as a Catholic, now fully forty-seven years, I cannot remember a single temptation against faith that seemed to me to have any force. The Church's teaching is before me, as a glorious series of splendid certainties. My mind is absolutely satisfied. Faith is an unmixed pleasure to me, without any pain, any difficulty, any drawback.... I have no private judgment to overcome, and no desire to exercise my private judgment. It is a greater pleasure to receive and possess truth with certainty, than to go in search of it and to be in uncertainty whether it has been found. The teaching of the Church is perfectly worthy of God, and it makes me happy. A declaration or definition of the Holy See is a real joy to me. So much more of certain and safe possession of truth."[2]

3. But the testimony of the Church is not to be set aside because the Roman Church claims infallibility. By the testimony of the Church ought to be understood the voice of believing men throughout all the ages. In Romanism the testimony of the Church has been limited to her authoritative teaching of doctrine, when she is really working in an intellectual sphere, and is demanding an intellectual faith. The testimony of the Church should be extended to include her witness to the salvation of the human soul, through the grace of Jesus Christ, and here she is speaking within a spiritual sphere, and is making her appeal to the heart. Her witness is of incalculable value, and comes short only of the testimony of Holy Scripture. Should any one hesitate to believe the gospel declared by the prophets and apostles in the Bible, because it is too good to be true, or should any one desire some human evidence from those who have made the great experiment of faith, then the Church comes in and supplements the contents of Holy Scripture. An innumerable company of saints of all ages and various intellectual creeds

---

[1] W. R. Inge, *Faith*, 92.
[2] M. D. Petre, *Autobiography and Life of George Tyrrell*, i. 229.

THE FOUNDATION OF FAITH

declare that they have heard the voice of God, and have gone forth like Abraham at His command, risking their whole spiritual position and an unknown future upon the Word of God and the Person of Jesus Christ. They have run this risk, and they have not been put to confusion; they have rather discovered, and are prepared to declare, that the half had not been told them of the goodly land into which they have already come, and whose fulness stretches before them into Eternity. It is as if a sinful man, penitent for his past and longing to see the salvation of God, should stand at the door of God's Kingdom holding in his hand one of the great invitations of the Evangel, such as "Him that cometh unto me I will in no wise cast out." "Is this to be read," he says, "in the fulness of its meaning? and is it possible that such a person as I am embraced in its intention?" Unto this wistful soul comes one witness after another from the gates of the Kingdom, prophets, apostles, saints, martyrs. Each one comes now as an individual believer, and each one as he comes sets his seal upon the invitation, declaring that he has trusted, and that God has been true. And at the sound of this Amen the fearful soul plucks up heart to believe.

¶ When we come to religious maturity *our only authority must be faith's object itself in some direct self-revelation of it.* Our authority is what takes the initiative with our faith. Only so is the authority really religious, only as creative. *Our only final religious authority is the creative object of our religion, to whom we owe ourselves.* Every statement about God is challengeable till God states Himself, in His own way, by His own Son, His own Spirit, His own Word, His own Church, to our soul, which He remakes in the process. And the challenge, coming at the right place (alas, for the heartlessness of those who force it!), is God's ordinance, to drive us onward and inward upon the soul's centre and King there.[1]

4. Ruskin has written in his picturesque way: "There is therefore, in matter of doctrine, *no such thing* as the Authority of the Church. We might as well talk of the authority of a morning cloud. There may be light *in* it, but the light is not of it; and it diminishes the light that it gets; and lets less of it through than it receives, Christ being its sun. Or, we might as well talk of the

[1] P. T. Forsyth, *The Principle of Authority*, 22.

authority of a flock of sheep—for the Church is a body to be taught and fed, not to teach and feed; and of all sheep that are fed on earth, Christ's sheep are the most simple (the children of this generation are wiser), always losing themselves; doing little else in the world *but* lose themselves; never finding themselves; always found by Some One else; getting perpetually into sloughs, and snows, and bramble thickets; like to die there, but for their Shepherd, who is for ever finding them and bearing them back, with torn fleeces and eyes full of fear."[1]

The half-truth thus eloquently expressed needs, no doubt, to be supplemented by another view of the Church's mission. *Ecclesia docens* is still a reality. The Church, as part of its high calling, is set to teach. It is a pillar and support of the truth, although it is not, as both the Authorized and Revised Versions make it in 1 Tim. iii. 15, "*the* pillar and foundation."

There are few passages of the New Testament (writes Dr. Hort[2]) in which the reckless disregard of the presence or absence of the Article has made wilder havoc of the sense than this. To speak of either an Ecclesia or the Ecclesia as being *the* pillar of the truth is to represent the truth as a building, standing in the air supported on a single column. Again, there is no clear evidence that the rare word $ἑδραίωμα$ ever means "ground" = "foundation." It is rather, in accordance with the almost universal Latin rendering, *firmamentum*, a "stay" or "bulwark." St. Paul's idea, then, is that each living society of Christian men is a pillar or stay of "the Truth," as an object of belief and a guide of life for mankind; each such Christian society bearing its part in sustaining and supporting the one truth common to all.

While, then, we reverently listen to the voice of the Christian Congregation, whether in the smaller societies of the faithful or in their aggregated numbers, so far as their collective utterance can be heard, we still claim the right to hear and to interpret for ourselves, as far as in us lies, the Oracles of God. For we are personally responsible.

¶ It would be difficult to over-estimate the harm done by the claim of any organization to exclusive Authority in matters of faith. For when a claim to infallibility is coupled with the

---

[1] *Notes on the Construction of Sheepfolds.*
[2] *The Christian Ecclesia*, 174.

prohibition of all independent inquiry two results follow—bigotry and scepticism: bigotry in those who cannot think, and scepticism in those who can.[1]

¶ Let every man who is engaged in persecuting any opinion ponder it; these two things must follow: you make fanatics, and you make sceptics; believers you cannot make.[2]

¶ Archbishop Temple says: "The study of Theology and Criticism imperatively demands freedom for its conditions. To tell a man to study and yet bid him, under heavy penalties, to come to the same conclusion with those who have not studied is to mock him. If the conclusions are prescribed, the study is precluded."

Westcott, late Bishop of Durham, writes: "The life of man is the knowledge of God. But this knowledge lives and moves. It is not a dead thing embalmed once for all in phrases."

Compare the above with a recent Roman Catholic episcopal utterance, part of a pastoral address: "If the Abbé Loisy has followers within the Church, as we are informed he has, it cannot be doubted that the danger for Catholics is by no means imaginary. . . . In his view our present knowledge of the Universe should suggest to the Church a new examination of the dogma of Creation. . . . But," says the Bishop, "if the formulas of modern science contradict the science of Catholic dogma, it is the former that must be altered, not the latter" (Extract from "The Tablet," 27 August 1904. Address by the Bishop of Newport).[3]

II.

The Bible.

1. The certainty of Christian faith is often built upon the Bible. It is there that we discover the personality of God, and the historical truth about Jesus Christ, and the reality of the supernatural world. And, although the Bible has passed, and is still passing, through the fires of criticism, it is coming out unscathed in everything that concerns its essential testimony. Nor can we read that wonderful book, and think of its wonderful history, without seeing and knowing that Christianity is not a

---

[1] S. P. Thompson, *The Quest for Truth*, 102.
[2] F. W. Robertson, *Sermons*, 1st series.
[3] C. L. Drawbridge, *Is Religion Undermined?* 7.

thing of "cunningly devised fables," but a religion that is built upon the everlasting rock.

Yet there are multitudes of persons whose hearts have been filled with the Christian certainty, although they never possessed the Bible, and never read the Bible. It was so in the early years of Christianity; for the first triumphs of the gospel were won before the New Testament was written. It is so still, in heathen lands, where men who have no Bibles, men who could not read the Bible even if they had it, believe in Christ because they have heard the word of the preacher. And, on the other hand, we must remember that there are men who read the Bible, and study it with care, and yet are not persuaded. And all this goes to show that the Bible, by itself, is neither necessary nor sufficient as the ground of Christian assurance.

2. Although the Bible is not *necessary* as a foundation for the assurance of faith, yet it is true always that faith comes by hearing, and undoubtedly "hearing" comes usually from the Bible. What one hears is the gospel of God. Holy Scripture teaches us the greatness and the hopelessness of our sin, the tender mercy and loving compassion of God, His purpose of salvation, and the gift of Jesus Christ. Holy Scripture also declares to us the arrival of the Son of God within our race by the Incarnation, His life of perfect obedience and law-keeping, His passion and His death. Holy Scripture also explains to us that in His life and death Jesus was a representative of the human race, and that by His resurrection and ascension and endless intercession He has become our Saviour, and Holy Scripture lays down with the utmost clearness, and with overflowing grace, the excellence of Jesus as the Friend and Lord and Redeemer of the human soul. Finally, the voice of God through Holy Scripture appeals to each man that he should make no delay and have no hesitation, but should make haste and instantly commit himself into the hands of Christ. We are commanded and encouraged to believe throughout the length and breadth of the Bible, and therefore every man is justified in this trust, and any one refusing to trust is condemned.

3. But the Bible is not always used fairly. It is treated as an authoritative manual of theology, a text-book of doctrine. Proof-

THE FOUNDATION OF FAITH 313

texts are collected from any and every part of the Bible in support of the doctrine which has been accepted; and no matter in what connexion they appear in Scripture they are supposed to be fully authoritative for the purpose, as being the word of God, which is eternal, above the circumstances of time and place, and of the individuals who were chosen to utter it. There is no idea, or at least no adequate idea, of a development of revelation in the olden time, or of a real growth of faith in the man of to-day. It is assumed as a matter of course that any proposed mode of pleasing God and gaining peace with Him must be grievously defective if it does not take account of the fulness of the remedy understood to be afforded in Scripture, and apply that necessary remedy forthwith in its entirety. The rejection of the theology in question is usually declared to be the result of negative or destructive criticism, and of man's refusal of God's word and law, and of his resolution to be a law to himself. In truth, it is only a narrow and imperfect interpretation of Scripture that is rejected; and revelation which proves to be infinite in its scope may be upheld and emphasized instead.

If the Bible is an infallible authority it must be historically inerrant. If that is true and its truth is to be demonstrated, it must come down to us through some medium which also of necessity must be infallible. There must also be some definite and authoritative interpretation of the book which must be infallible as well. The only possible medium and authority would be the Church, and unless the Church itself is infallible, we could never be certain that it had given to us unchanged the infallible word of the eternal God. We all know that the very books to be incorporated as authorities were determined by Church councils. Unless they were guided infallibly how could the results of their deliberations be infallible?

¶ The theory of the inerrancy of the original documents, developed in the higher criticism controversy some years ago, reminds one of the declaration of the infallible Pope by the Catholic Church a few years earlier in the stress of their conflict with the scientific spirit of the age. Calvin's doctrine was probably the next necessary step in the evolution of the Christian faith. Still we cannot help regretting, however necessary and inevitable it may have been, that the Reformation, having escaped the tyranny of the infallible Church, should have erected in its place that of an infallible and historically inerrant Bible. For this latter authority, though in many respects preferable to the former, is equally futile in the region of religious certainty. We are glad to remember that among the early reformers Luther and Zwingli substituted the theology of experience for that of authority.[1]

¶ Luther had not based the truth of Christianity on the infallibility of the Bible at all in the same way as later Protestantism, which has, in practice, made this the foremost dogma of theology. Luther had found redemption in the Holy Scriptures because in them he had heard the Word of God, and in them had appeared to him with overwhelming might the redeeming, liberating Person of Jesus. The infallibility of the Bible can never be a fact of experience, but it was as nearly such for Luther as it has ever been for any man: the whole situation was changed when the infallibility of Scripture was made the basis of a systematic theology, being itself a dogma to which, from most men at least, a purely formal assent is all that can be expected.[2]

4. Is the Bible inspired? Are not the Gospels challenged as historical records? And if we are to give up the infallibility of Scripture how can we rely upon the historicity of Jesus? The trouble with such questions is that people continually forget that the real basis of faith is not, never has been, and never will be, an infallible book. The Bible is the gathered literature of a people, intensely human, wide in its range and variety, unequal in its spiritual value. Its inspiration is to be judged by the simple test of its ability to inspire, and its value lies not in its supposed infallibility, but in its record of phenomena unique in human experience, illustrating the working of God in the human heart, and, above all, the message, life, and death of Jesus Christ, and the beginnings of the Christian Church. The theory of an infallible text is purely mechanical, not spiritual, and inasmuch as the theory dehumanizes the Bible, while distorting its really Divine quality into a parody of the fact, it has worked untold mischief, destroying the sense of reality and lowering the Bible to the level of an idol or a fetish. We may indeed welcome in the higher

---

[1] W. F. English, in *Hartford Seminary Record*, xxiii. 282.
[2] J. K. Mozley, *Ritschlianism*, 119.

critic and all that he signifies a return to an intelligent belief in the Divine worth of the Scriptures, confident that scholarly and reverent study of material so rich in spiritual teaching must be increasingly fruitful. Truth can never be destroyed; in the fiercest light of criticism it can never suffer.

"So long," says Erskine of Linlathen, "as a man receives his Christianity merely on the authority of a church or a book—so long as it has not commended itself to his higher reason and moral sense, or reached his inner consciousness—he has no real hold of Christianity; he is believing only in his church or in his book."

¶ Biblical criticism has decomposed and analysed the Jewish writings, assigning to them dates and degrees of authority very different from those recognized by the Church. It has certainly not impaired their significance as records of successive developments of religious and moral progress, nor has it diminished their value as expressions of the loftiest and most enduring religious sentiments of mankind.[1]

5. The Westminster Confession thus states the grounds for believing in the authority of Scripture: "We may be moved and induced by the testimony of the Church to a high and reverent esteem of Holy Scripture, and the heavenliness of the matter, the efficacy of the doctrine, the majesty of the style, the consent of all the parts, the scope of the whole (which is to give glory to God), the full discovery it makes of the only way of man's salvation, the many other incomparable excellences, and the entire perfection thereof, are arguments whereby it doth abundantly evidence itself to be the Word of God; yet notwithstanding, our full persuasion and assurance of the infallible truth and divine authority thereof is from the inward work of the Holy Spirit, bearing witness by and with the word in our hearts."

"Now," says Dean Inge, "this is an admirable statement of what revelation through the Bible really is. The 'testimony of the Holy Spirit' is the response of our inmost personality to the external stimulus supplied by the inspired literature. This testimony is the primary ground of Faith. It is 'God working in us,' and working through concrete experiences of various kinds, as it appears that He always does work. But this is not a theory

[1] W. E. H. Lecky, *The Map of Life*, 202.

of inspiration which can either erect Scripture into an oracle for determining off-hand difficult matters of conduct, or which can cut the knot of critical problems. The Holy Spirit testifies that the character and teaching of Jesus Christ are divine, and that we may follow Him and believe in Him with perfect confidence. It certainly does not testify that the Mosaic account of creation is scientifically correct, or that the book of Daniel was written in the sixth century B.C."

¶ The Bible nowhere lays claim to be regarded as *the* Word, *the* Way, *the* Truth. The Bible leads us to Jesus, the inexhaustible, the ever unfolding Revelation of God. It is Christ "in whom are hid all the treasures of wisdom and knowledge," not the Bible, save as leading to Him.[1]

6. The current maxim which tells us that "the Church is to teach and the Bible to prove" is largely but not wholly sound. Certainly the Church has a vastly important teaching function; the most conspicuous example of its work in that field is the "Nicene" Creed; and what thoughtful Christian would give anything but an attention most reverent and humble to that great didactic voice of Christendom? No mind not altogether careless and self-confident would ignore the affirmations concerning revealed truth collected and embodied there.

But then other and balancing considerations have also to be remembered. The Church, however defined, is not a co-ordinate oracle beside the Bible. Still less is the Church a teacher such that the Bible is, as it were, its attendant, following it everywhere with "proofs" dutifully furnished to teachings assumed to be always correct. History shows the Church, the Jewish Church in our Lord's time and the Christian Church since then, greatly needing now and again to have its teaching not proved but corrected by the Bible. The reverent Christian will reverence the Church. But he will also ask, reverently and on his knees, "How readest thou? What saith the Scripture?"

¶ Brownlow North had an intense veneration and love for the Bible, as the word of the living God. It was inwoven with his whole spiritual experience. From that day in Elgin, when, striking his hand upon his open Bible, as his eye rested on the text Rom. iii. 22, he exclaimed, starting to his feet, "If that

---

[1] G. Macdonald, *Unspoken Sermons*, 1st ser., p. 53.

THE FOUNDATION OF FAITH 317

scripture is true I am a saved man," till the day twenty years afterwards, when on his dying bed in the house of a stranger he turned to a young officer, and said, with his fast ebbing breath, "You are young, in good health, and with the prospect of rising in the army : I am dying ; but if the Bible is true, and I know it is, I would not change places with you for the whole world," that Bible was the daily food of his soul, his lamp in the night, his teacher, his counsellor, his trust, and his treasure. Never for an hour did he swerve from his childlike faith in these Scriptures of truth, or from his manly allegiance to all the doctrines, precepts, and promises of the Divine Word. And he spent his whole time, talents, and toil in preaching to the people, wherever they would come to listen, all the words of this life.[1]

¶ At the last, during the long communings of the night when he lay sleepless, happy to be free, if only for a few moments, from pain, the simple old faith came back to him. He had arrived long before, as we have seen, at the grand discovery : that the perfect soul wants the perfect body, and that the perfect body must be inhabited by the perfect soul. To this conclusion he was led by Nature herself. Now he beheld clearly—perhaps more clearly than ever—the way from this imperfect and fragmentary life to a fuller, happier life beyond the grave. He had no need of priest ; he wanted no other assurance than the voice and words of Him who swept away all priests. The man who wrote *The Story of my Heart* ; the man who was filled to overflowing with the beauty and order of God's handiwork ; the man who felt so deeply the shortness, and imperfections, and disappointments of life that he was fain to cry aloud that all happens by chance ; the man who had the vision of the Fuller Soul, died listening with faith and love to the words contained in the Old Book.[2]

7. Both the Bible and the Church point to Christ, and therein lies their value for faith and assurance.

(1) The history of the Bible has its centre in the Gospel record of His manifestation on earth ; all that goes before it in the Old Testament is the preparation for His coming as the Messiah of the expectation of Israel ; all that follows it is the proclamation to the world of the first Advent and the foretelling of the second. The law of the older times is "the schoolmaster

---

[1] K. Moody-Stuart, *Brownlow North*, 237.
[2] W. Besant, *The Eulogy of Richard Jefferies*, 355.

to bring men to the righteousness of God in Christ"; in His teaching it is perfected; by His Spirit it is to be written on the heart in the fulness of the Gospel dispensation. The prophecy of Israel with ever-increasing clearness reveals Him as the Seed of Abraham, the Prophet of prophets, the Son of David and his Lord, the Emmanuel of the Presence of God with man. The Apostolic prophecy of the New Testament sets Him forth as the Son of God and man, in whose humanity dwells all the fulness of Godhead. The Psalmic element of response to the Divine revelation realizes in aspiration and devotion the communion with God in Him, in foresight in the Old Testament, in thanksgiving and adoration in the New. Every way we are taught to pass through God's revelation of Himself "in divers times and measures" to One who is "the effulgence of his glory and the very image of his substance." We sin against that scriptural teaching if we fail to pass beyond it to rest on Christ Himself, as in His Gospel and His Person the Word which is from the beginning was and is God.

(2) So also it is in the parallel witness of the Church. In every metaphor as in full utterance of express teaching, He is set forth as all in all—the foundation and corner stone on which the Church is built, and by which its fabric is built up—the Vine of which we are the branches—the Head in whom as a body it has its light and life, the extension (as it has been called) of the Incarnation of the Divine in the human. The word which the Church sets forth in authoritative teaching and exhortation is the word of Eternal life, which is directly and indirectly, implicitly or explicitly, the word of Christ Himself. The Sacrament of entrance into the Church is the "putting on the Lord Jesus Christ," and the regeneration in Him. The worship of the Church is simply the representation on earth of His Intercession in Heaven, offered, whether in Confession and Prayer or in Thanksgiving and Adoration, through Christ and in Christ. Of the whole spiritual life of the Church collectively and of its members individually it is said that "to love is Christ." "I live; yet not I, it is Christ that dwelleth in me"; of its future life the one secret is that Christ is in you, the hope of glory.

THE FOUNDATION OF FAITH

III.

ARGUMENT OR INTUITION.

1. We may base our faith, then, upon the authority of the Church or upon the authority of the Bible, or upon both. But these are not the only possible foundations. For we may trust to argument or to intuition. Both are possible, though only one seems to receive the blessing of full assurance.

(1) The apostle Thomas may be taken as an example of the first; he desired to possess a faith. To possess a faith is to find God, and His relation to man, and His self-revelation in the Incarnation, and the sonship of the race, as Leverrier found the planet Neptune, by inference; through the exercise of the faculties which are purely intellectual. Such a man says: "I desire to find God; but whoever made me gave me my brain. I am so constituted that logic stands as a gate-keeper at the door of my emotional nature, and will let nothing pass that cannot be framed into a syllogism." This was the mental attitude of Thomas. In the well-known statue of this apostle, at Copenhagen, he is represented with a measuring rod in his hand, as though he would measure, by the capacity of the human mind, any theory of God offered for the acceptance of his faith. He has been blamed; reverent inquiry has been stigmatized as rationalistic doubt; obedience to the injunction "prove all things" has been condemned as unjustifiable scepticism.

(2) The other alternative, "being possessed by a faith," is perhaps best illustrated by the apostle Peter. It is less easy of definition, for its action is outside the terms of our experience; but it is the providential opening of the spiritual sense, the awakening of an intuitive faculty, the quickening into activity of an inward vision. It is an endowment bestowed by the Spirit of God; no man is responsible for not possessing it. When, under its influence, Peter made his brilliant confession of the nature of the Christ, the Lord turned round upon him with a gesture of surprise, "Flesh and blood did not tell you that; you have not received that through your intellect. Blessed art thou, Simon Barjona, for this has been revealed to thee by the Father in heaven." Robertson describes this inward vision as "the some-

thing within which makes a thing seem to be true because it is loved." Tennyson etherializes it in the words:

> Her faith is fixt and cannot move,
>   She darkly feels him great and wise,
>   She dwells on him with faithful eyes,
> "I cannot understand: I love."

Neither of these definitions is exhaustive, because to the soul possessed by a faith things do not "seem" to be true, they "are" true; and Tennyson's words, "cannot understand," are inappropriate, because the intense conviction of the truth arrived at by awakened intuition is far above what we call "understanding."

2. A man follows the method of argument when he holds that his Christian belief is to be proved, like his belief in the truths of politics or nature, by the processes of reason; as when he says that the resurrection of Jesus is made certain by evidence which would convince a court of law. Or when he says that the religion of Christ is based on historic facts which are verified as all history is, that is, by inductive reasoning, or on the personal experiences of believers, which again is an induction. Or yet again, when he holds the articles of the faith contained in the Creeds because they may be proved by most certain warrants of Holy Scripture, which is another logical process, that of deduction.

Suppose we set out to prove that Jesus of Nazareth was the Son of God. We should first examine the source of this hypothesis, the Christian tradition, by inquiry into the authorship and date of the Gospels, the purity of their text, the character, moral and intellectual, of the witnesses from whose record the tradition started; not forgetting to consider the value of the witness which exists outside the canonical writings, that, namely, of the continuous Christian consciousness of Churchmen, as expressed in the writings of theologians or in institutions of the society. We should examine too the practical results upon conduct and mind of the Christian creed, and decide whether these could be accounted for only by that creed's being a record of fact. Further, we should compare the Christian theory of man and his destiny with what observation tells us of other reality—physical, intellectual, moral

THE FOUNDATION OF FAITH

nature—and decide whether this reality and our own theory were in disagreement or in harmony.

What is likely to be the result? The result might be a verification of our hypothesis or it might be a falsification; likelier yet it would be an open verdict. To the question, "What think ye of Christ—is He of heaven or of men?" the answer would be, "We cannot tell."

¶ Of other things which are popularly called religion, I have my opinion positive and negative. But religion to me is not opinion—it is certainty. I cannot govern my actions or guide my deepest convictions by probabilities. The laws which we are to obey and the obligations to obey them are part of my being of which I am as sure as that I am alive. The things to argue about are by their nature uncertain, and therefore it is to me inconceivable that in them can lie *Religion*.[1]

3. We follow the method of intuition when we find the root of religious certainty in the immediate and intuitive perception or consciousness of God. Not mere intellectual certainty—for, as Bergson has so well shown, the intellect is only a special faculty or adaptation of the mind or soul, a kind of whittling down of the whole consciousness to serve immediate and limited purposes—but the certainty of that intuition which is the vision of the whole soul in consciousness. As the soul recognizes the spiritual world and appropriates it to himself there awakens within the soul an inward certitude. This certitude is not gained once for all, any more than human freedom is so gained; it must be sought ever anew and obtained by the highest activity of the whole man, be he small or great, ignorant or learned, as we divide and estimate individuals. "He that willeth to do his will shall know." Certainty is dependent not upon our capacity, but upon the completeness of our response to the Divine. A man must sell all that he has to obtain this pearl of great price. It broadens and deepens with the growth of the consciousness and experience of God.

¶ It seems to me that Bishop Wilkinson's strength lay in the fact that the core and centre of his faith was an exquisitely simple one—an intuition, for which "certainty" is but a halting word, of the Fatherhood of God and of His hourly care for men, made

[1] *Life of Froude*, 431.

manifest in the Life and Love of Jesus Christ. His whole purpose was to realize this presence at every moment of his life, and to lead others to realize it.[1]

¶ It was this private certainty in regard to truth and all things that Blake shared with the greatest minds of the world, and men doubted him partly because he was content to possess that certainty and had no desire to use it for any practical purpose, least of all to convince others. He asked to be believed when he spoke, told the truth, and was not concerned with argument or experiment, which seemed to him ways of evasion. He said:

"It is easy to acknowledge a man to be great and good, while we
Derogate from him in the trifles and small articles of that goodness,
Those alone are his friends who admire his minutest powers."[2]

¶ That there is no knowing, in the sense of written reasons, whether the soul lives on or not, I am fully aware. I did not hope or fear. At least while I am living I have enjoyed the idea of immortality, and the idea of my own soul. If then, after death, I am resolved without exception into earth, air, and water, and the spirit goes out like a flame, still I shall have had the glory of that thought.

It happened once that a man was drowned while bathing, and his body was placed in an outhouse near the garden. I passed the outhouse continually, sometimes on purpose to think about it, and it always seemed to me that the man was still living. Separation is not to be comprehended; the spirit of the man did not appear to have gone to an inconceivable distance. As my thought flashes itself back through the centuries to the luxury of Canopus, and can see the gilded couches of a city extinct, so it slips through the future, and immeasurable time in front is no boundary to it. Certainly the man was not dead to me.[3]

4. Yet there is a place for reason and argument. Again and again has the awakening of the intuitive been the direct result of the cultivation of the intellectual. This was the experience of Kingsley; it all comes out in the conversations in *Hypatia*. He hungered to find God; he drank deep of the cup of scientific

---

[1] A. C. Benson, *The Leaves of the Tree*, 127.
[2] A. Symons, *William Blake*, 245.
[3] R. Jefferies, *The Story of my Heart*, 28.

research; he convinced himself that logically there was but one substance, and that one substance was God. When he arrived at that point "he possessed a faith." He wanted more; the hunger of his human heart was not satisfied; he followed sequences logically. If all phenomena were expressions of the one substance, God, and if humanity were the highest of these expressions, then the noblest specimen of humanity was the most perfect expression of God, and by consequence wholly Divine. Therefore Jesus was God. And though Jesus was God under a limitation, still God was at the same time in all things. And as his mind ascended this sequence step by step, the Spirit of God within him glowed brighter and brighter, because, with Thomas, he proved all things. And his dying words, so calm, and true, and trusting, witnessed that he was passing to the endless life with God, not as the "possessor of a faith," but as one whose faith, pure, simple, and intense, had now "possessed him."

¶ The church must find room for the individual thinker in his attempts to work out into more and more logical expression the belief of the church. We have said some hard things about the logician. We have had in mind the type of thinker who imagines that strict logical procedure is everything and who fancies that the correct rule is logic first and life afterward. We now insist that in her attempts to meet the religious demands of men in her seizures of thought-positions the church must make provision for the satisfaction of intelligent logical needs. The logician does not discover, but he can do a great deal to straighten out and put in order what has been discovered. The church has seized the great highways of the truth, the highways which lead to the kingdom, but the logician can straighten the curves and reduce the grades. He may even upon occasion put up a sign of "No thoroughfare" to the right hand or to the left. The great highways across the mountains of our land were not discovered by the scientific surveyors. The hunters and traders had found the passes before the surveyors, and the savages had travelled them before the traders, and the wild beasts before the savages. Civilization, however, needed the fine work of the surveyor in levelling and straightening a way for the later comers. Mankind has from the beginning been travelling along the line of certain instincts and aspirations and assumptions. The trained thinker, who recognizes the limitations of his craft, can do immense help in straightening and broadening the church's right of way.[1]

[1] F. J. McConnell, in *Methodist Review*, xc. 230.

IV.

Experience.

1. We are now able to make the important statement that the ultimate ground of Christian certainty lies in the positive facts of Christian experience. Is it the assurance of salvation that we desire? The only valid ground for the certainty of salvation is the consciousness of present life in Christ. There is no evidence so indubitable as this. I do not ask external testimony. I do not need intellectual reasonings to convince me that I live. All the reasons that philosophy or science can adduce are powerless against my simple consciousness of life.

So it was with St. Paul. His letters and sermons are full of arguments, no doubt, full of pleadings and persuasion, but they all start from and rest upon his vision of the living, risen Saviour. His last word is always, " When it pleased God to reveal his Son in me "; that was the elemental fact which he proclaimed and which summed up everything, the personal experience from which he started on his career as an apostle. The place of Athanasius as a great religious leader has been obscured by his position as a theologian; but when we turn to his writings, where do we find less of what is commonly called dogmatic theology? There is argument, reasoning, searching for proofs and their statement; but all that belongs to the outworks in his teaching. The central citadel is a spiritual intuition—I *know* that *my* Saviour is the God who made heaven and earth. He took his stand firmly and unflinchingly on that personal experience, and all else mattered little compared with the fundamental spiritual fact. It was not his arguments, but his unflinching faith, that convinced his generation.

So it was with Augustine, Bernard, Francis; so it has been with every great religious leader of the Christian people. His strength, whether of knowledge, or of conviction, or of sympathy —his driving power, if the phrase may be used—has always come from direct communion with the unseen, and rests upon the fact, felt and known by himself and communicated to others by a mysterious sympathy, that it has pleased God to reveal Christ in him in some way or other.

THE FOUNDATION OF FAITH

So it was with Luther and the Reformation, in which he was the leader. Its driving power was a great religious experience, old, for it has come to the people of God in all generations, and yet new and fresh as it is the nature of all such experiences to be. He *knew* that his life was hid with Christ in God in spite of all evil, in spite of sin and sense of guilt. His old dread of God had vanished, and instead of it there had arisen in his heart a love to God in answer to the love which came from the vision of the Father revealing Himself. He had experienced this, and he had proclaimed what he had gone through; and the experience and its proclamation were the foundation on which the Reformation was built. Its beginnings were not doctrinal but experimental.

¶ To those who impugn our faith in the Son of God, we have the answer ready with which the man to whom He had given sight met the cavils of Jewish rationalism. "Why herein is a marvellous thing, that ye know not from whence He is, and yet He hath opened mine eyes." So in moments when we are tempted to doubt or to distrust:

> If e'er when faith had fall'n asleep,
>   I heard a voice "believe no more"
>   And heard an ever-breaking shore
> That tumbled in the Godless deep;
>
> A warmth within the breast would melt
>   The freezing reason's colder part,
>   And like a man in wrath the heart
> Stood up and answer'd "I have felt." [1]

2. It is sometimes said that the Reformers made too much of feeling. Thus Osborne: "For most people, this continual centring of religion in their own feelings or experiences is as impossible, unwholesome, and unreal as is the secular ignoring of religion at the other extreme. A healthy religion, like a healthy body, is not always consciously dwelling on its own existence. In the case of minds in which sentiment predominates, this becomes pietism, often no doubt consistent with a deep and tender devotion to our Lord, but always in danger of assuming the hothouse plant attitude to life, of losing the healthy objectivity in doctrine and virility in practice of the Catholic faith. Is there not a real

[1] S. G. Green, *The Christian Creed and the Creeds of Christendom*, 20.

truth in Newman's remark in one of his Anglican sermons, that 'Luther found men enslaved to their works, and he left them enslaved to their feelings'? Or at least, if not directly true, it is certainly true of many tendencies of that powerful mind, robust in itself, but over-subjective in the type of religion which it made prevalent."[1]

But this is simply to misunderstand what is meant by feeling. Listen to Bowne: "The oft-repeated dictum 'feeling proves nothing' is one of those which, from frequency and vehemence of utterance, have been mistaken for self-evident. It is true only for individual, isolated, and transitory feelings; the great, fundamental, and abiding feelings of the race may prove much. Those who appeal to this dictum are seldom aware to what an extent feeling and sentiment enter into our intellectual life, and even into their own theories. The deepest propositions concerning life, and duty, and character, have no other proof than the moral recoil which attends their denial. At the same time the only disproof possible is the absence of that recoil. It is an attempt to prove a negative on the strength of negative evidence. Every one in whom the moral nature is active needs no proof of the beauty of holiness; and he regards a denial as we regard a blind man's protest against the absurd doctrine of vision. In Fénelon's *Télémaque*, Ulysses tries to convince one of his crew who has been changed into a hog by Circe, that it is shameful for a man to be a pig, but without success. Here is a point where argument is impossible. If there be no sense of dignity in man nothing can appear degrading. Both in ethics and in esthetics the ultimate fact upon which all theory is built is a movement of the sensibility, which thus founds the distinction of good and bad, beautiful and ugly. The most rigorous rationalist in morals cannot escape the ultimate appeal to feeling to sanction his theories. The whole mental life, also, springs out of feeling. It is extremely doubtful if a purely perceptive being, without any subjective interests, could attain to rationality, even if its physical existence were secured. Indeed, it is demonstrable that our sentiments outline and control all mental development. Before mental growth can begin, there must be an awakened interest, and when the interest is awakened, the leaden chaos of sense-experience begins to take

[1] C. E. Osborne, *Religion in Europe and the World Crisis*, 136.

THE FOUNDATION OF FAITH

on intelligible forms. The love of truth, which is the mainspring of science, is only one phase of religious feeling and worship. Truth, as simple correspondence of thought with fact, cannot arouse enthusiasm. It has, indeed, a low value of utility, but nothing on which a soul may live."[1]

¶ Whatever I feel, I feel beyond all doubt. If I see blue sky, I may be quite sure that I do experience the sensation of blueness. We are very likely to confuse what we feel with what we associate with it or infer from it; but the whole of our consciousness, so far as it is the result of pure intuition and free from inference, is certain knowledge beyond all doubt."[2]

3. To Christian experience all other grounds of certainty at last arrive and find their value there. The modern proof of the truth of the Bible is its worth for and in Christian experience, and the modern argument for the value of the thought of past ages is that it has expressed and ministered to Christian experience. The Bible itself is a record and interpretation of man's experience of God; and Church dogma is an attempt to formulate in terms of thought what has seemed essential for man's experience in God's revelation. The experience of prophets, apostles, even of Christ Himself, of Fathers and Reformers of the Church, must be verified and vitalized in the soul's experience of God's grace.

There is a kind of certainty arising from having oneself "tasted and seen" which on all the levels of knowledge, from the lowest physical one upwards, is felt to be of a superior order to that due to hearsay. Every one recognizes the difference between the man who has merely acquired the theory of any art and the man who has mastered the same by years of practice. It is one thing to learn what love is by the reading of romances and another to learn it by loving and being loved. Not less different is the knowledge of religion due to personal contact with the objects of religion from that due to the testimony of others; and the true aim of all testimony on the subject is to lead us to acquire that knowledge for ourselves. Both the Bible and the Church have been far too often represented as making demands on the individual—demands to believe what they teach on pain

---

[1] B. P. Bowne, *Studies in Theism*, 65.
[2] F. B. Jevons, *Principles of Science*, i. 271.

of perdition. It is a far juster view of both to regard them as approaching the individual with promises that, if he seek God, he shall find Him. From prophets and apostles, from fathers and doctors comes the testimony that, when in their sin and misery they stretched forth their hands, they encountered not vacancy but a living God and Saviour; and the intention of their testimony is not that we should adopt as our creed that which they regarded as true, but that, when in the stress of our own life and the consciousness of our own misery we lift our eyes to the hills, we should be able to do so with hope of finding what they found. And, if we have found it, our impressions of its reality and blessedness will be of the same nature as theirs. It may be mediated through their testimony, yet it will be immediate, the soul and God, the sinner and the Saviour, coming into direct contact; and, when we are experiencing the blessedness of this union with the actual objects of the spiritual world, we can say to every witness, including even the Bible, "Now we believe, not because of thy saying: for we have heard him ourselves, and know that this is indeed the Christ, the Saviour of the world."

¶ In a true sense the Church is authoritative and the Scriptures are authoritative. It is, however, not an authority of compulsion, but the authority of inspiration. It is the authority of conviction, and there is no spiritual value in any other. It is an authority which makes its way, not by forcing assent, but by winning it through an appeal to that which is "likest God within the soul." Every attainment in religion is the result, not of submission to some outward law or external authority, but of obedience to a law which has become the very essence and principle of our own being.[1]

4. The faith of experience is at once firm and fearless. It is confident of the ground under its feet and, therefore, it cordially welcomes all investigation and all new light. It is so in any realm of life, in every field of science.

Here is that mysterious something, that tremendous force whose essential nature we can probably never penetrate, called electricity. Many are the hypotheses and speculations which the theoretical scientists construct to explain and interpret it. What is our attitude of mind toward those various theories? Probably

[1] R. M. Jones, *A Dynamic Faith*, 20.

THE FOUNDATION OF FAITH 329

it is an attitude which is at once fearless and expectant. We know what this great force has done for us and is doing for us every day; how it runs our machinery, drives our vehicles, lights our houses, flashes our messages over the wires or through the viewless air; how it performs a thousand services for us daily. We are confident, absolutely confident, that it is all that it has proved itself to be in our own experience and the experience of mankind. How much more it shall prove itself to be on deeper study and larger application, we cannot tell. Therefore we leave investigation and inquiry absolutely free, confident that they cannot take from us anything that we already have, sure that they will reveal to us greater wonders yet undreamed of.

Even so in the realm of religion. It is just as sure and certain ground as the realm of natural science. For the objects and facts of spiritual experience are surely as real as the objects and facts of physical experience. Only in both cases the hypotheses and interpretations shift and vary. For example, we know that the Bible is inspired, because it inspires us. We are, therefore, ready to give Biblical criticism a free hand, confident that a reverent, searching scholarship will bring to us yet larger utterances of the Word of God, for we know, with the old Puritan Divine, that "God hath yet more light to break forth from His Holy Word."

5. Since the certainty of individual salvation in Christ comes solely out of the personal consciousness of Christian life it is capable of growth. The certainty of a saintly man like St. Paul —the certainty which is produced by a long Christian experience that rests upon what Christ has been, in the manifold necessities of a strenuous life, in its arduous duties, fierce temptations, sore conflicts, depressions, and sorrows—becomes an absolute feeling, as indubitable as life itself.

It ought to be a constantly growing experience, for there is always more in God than any one has made his own, and no one has ever exhausted the unsearchable riches of Christ. These attainments of Christian experience are the equivalents of the statements of the Bible and the propositions of the creed; but they are the Bible and the creed transmuted into meat and drink, so that they may become bone of a man's bone and flesh of his flesh. This is the certainty of which Luther used to say that on a dying bed it is not enough to be assured by even the angel Gabriel that our religion is true; we must be as sure of it as that three and two are five or that an ell is longer than half-an-ell; we must be so sure of it that, if the whole world declared it to be false, we could quietly and joyfully rest on our own conviction.

¶ There are only two provinces of absolutely sure knowledge; one is pure mathematics and the other is the experience of the soul. When we say "The whole is greater than the part" we are stating an axiom which is embedded in our constitutions, and in order to contradict it you would have to reconstitute the mind, and for that matter the universe. This axiom belongs to the nature of things, and the Almighty Himself could not make the part greater than the whole. When St. Paul says "I know" in religion he is falling back upon his spiritual consciousness. First, he realized Christ in Heaven at the right hand of God, next he observed Christ doing great wonders in his own life, and finally he found Christ in his own soul. He was now united to the Lord after so close a fashion that for him to live was Christ, and his life was hid with Christ in God. None could shake his faith, for he carried Christ within him, none could separate him from the Lord, for he was with Christ in the heavenly places.[1]

[1] J. Watson, *The Inspiration of our Faith*, 223.

XV.

THE CONFIRMATION OF FAITH.

LITERATURE.

Bell, G. K. A., in *The Meaning of the Creed* (1917).
Benson, M., *The Venture of Rational Faith* (1908).
Chandler, A., *Faith and Experience* (1911).
Cremer, H., *A Reply to Harnack on the Essence of Christianity* (1903).
Curtis, O. A., *The Christian Faith* (1905).
Dixon, H. T., *The Life of the Spirit* (1919).
Forsyth, P. T., *The Principle of Authority*.
Gardner, P., *The Religious Experience of Saint Paul* (1911).
Garvie, A. E., in *Mansfield College Essays* (1909).
Green, S. G., *The Christian Creed and the Creeds of Christendom* (1898).
Grubb, E., *The Personality of God* (1911).
Holland, H. S., *Pleas and Claims for Christ* (1892).
Hughes, H. M., *The Theology of Experience* (1915).
Jones, R. M., *A Dynamic Faith* (1901).
Little, P., *The Pacific Northwest Pulpit* (1915).
Macgregor, W. M., *Christian Freedom* (1914).
Moule, H. C. G., *Faith* (1909).
Muir, G. G., *Shoulder to Shoulder*.
Nicholson, W. T., *The Mysteries of God* (1916).
Pearson, A., *The Claims of the Faith* (1905).
Rees, T., *The Holy Spirit* (1915).
Shore, T. T., *Some Difficulties of Belief* (1877).
Simpson, J. G., *Great Ideas of Religion* (1912).
Spens, W., *Belief and Practice* (1915).
Thompson, S. P., *The Quest for Truth* (1915).
Warfield, B. B., *Faith and Life* (1916).

THE CONFIRMATION OF FAITH.

ROBERT BROWNING once wrote to a friend, "I want you to give my conviction a clinch." The two words, conviction and clinch, suggest the philosophy of certainty in belief. First there is a personal element, the person himself gets a conviction; then there is a social element, the personal conviction is clinched, or confirmed, by other men. You believe in your country, in her history, in her constitution, in her institutions, in her people, in her significance among the nations. Your belief amounts to such a conviction that you could gladly die to express it; and yet every other patriot makes you a little more certain that your country is worth dying for.

But faith is confirmed in many ways. The chief means of confirmation are (1) the testimony of others, (2) its own fruits, and (3) the witness of the Spirit.

I.

THE TESTIMONY OF OTHERS.

1. When a man comes to the knowledge of Jesus Christ as Paul did, not by any laborious process of argument but by a swifter operation of the mind, he does not need to seek about for confirmations. So far as he himself is concerned, and so long as the power of the vision holds him, he is possessed by a certainty which is complete. In Emerson's phrase, "the contradiction of all mankind cannot shake it, and the consent of all mankind cannot confirm it." And yet to every man there come changes of mood. Courage flags and the mists come down; and, specially, the burden of the surrounding indifference may press upon him.

He is convinced that he did see, but why is he alone in seeing? It is very well for Luther to compare the simplicity of his own conviction to the straightforward sense that 3 and 7 make 10, as if there were no possible room for debate. But one uncomfortable difference obtrudes itself; for in the arithmetical case, everybody who is not an imbecile or a savage arrives at the same result, whilst in the spiritual a man may make the damping discovery that he is quite alone in his conclusion.

Dr. Dale confesses that he sometimes wondered whether he should be sure that his own perception of the sun and stars was trustworthy, if he were alone in seeing them. "For myself, when I actually saw the sun rising morning after morning, and ascending the meridian, and when I actually saw the constellations glittering in the heavens at night, the conviction of their reality would be irresistible; and yet side by side with this conviction there would be doubt—doubt mastered and suppressed but with life in it still, and certain to grow large and strong if for many weeks brooding clouds concealed the celestial glories. But if, here and there, another man came to see what I saw, and by degrees, groups of men; if, by a surprising discovery of a lost literature, it became certain that the poets of a vanished people had sung of the stars and the sunrise and the sunset, and their sailors had steered their course by them, I should become sure of myself, and all doubt would vanish. So the knowledge that other men, as the result of their appeal to Christ, have passed into a diviner world, have received accessions of strength, . . . have seen evil passions wither, while it adds nothing to the distinction or power of similar experiences of my own, relieves me from the doubt which would worry my faith, if my experience were solitary and unique." Paul was little troubled by such fantastic bewilderments, for he knew whom he had believed; and yet he did welcome confirmation when it came, because it served to enrich his thought of Jesus Christ, and thus might make his ministry more widely efficacious.

2. A man might sometimes doubt his own experience, if it stood perfectly alone. But what if he sees it multiplied from a thousand different quarters? Scientific men have sometimes arrived at results of which they felt pretty confident; but their confidence grew into an absolute certainty when other scientists,

THE CONFIRMATION OF FAITH 335

living in other parts of the world, and working by different methods, arrived at results precisely similar. Here is a Christian man who has had his own experience—that wonderful experience which follows the entrance of Christ into the heart. But suppose it seems to him almost too wonderful to be true. Suppose the greatness of the wonder should itself beget a doubt. He goes out, and seeks the confidence of a brother Christian; and, lo, he finds heart answering to heart.

For a Christian is not a hermit. He is not alone either in his experience or in the expression of his experience. He has a community, he lives in a testing and supplementing and confirming community. In every crisis of his life, in every new turn of public opinion, in every phase of self-knowledge, in every look at his moral ideal, before and during and after every self-decision, he is bounded by a brotherhood. And this brotherhood is singularly adapted to the needs of the Christian man. It is made up of moral persons, all trying to complete their life in truth and reality; all these moral persons have had the initial moral and Christian experiences; all have now the same profound relation to Jesus Christ and His death for their salvation; and still all these redeemed moral persons come together with countless differences in individuality, in mental training, in position and occupation, in influence over men, and in present religious attainment. Thus, this brotherhood has mighty resources in social service and confirmation. It is too much to say that this confirmation is coercive, turning conviction into knowledge; but it is not too much to say that it gives to personal assurance such ratification that the Christian consciousness is full of certainty.

¶ Emerson reports that in some New England towns before the Civil War, "every man was an Abolitionist by conviction, but he did not believe that his neighbour was. The opinions of masses of men, which the tactics of primary caucuses and the proverbial timidity of trade had concealed, were discovered by the War, and it was found, contrary to all popular belief, that the country was at heart Abolitionist, and for the Union was ready to die." The discovery of such agreement in opinion does not change belief, but it may give it a different quality. Galileo, with every one against him, might doggedly mutter, "And yet it does move," for his conviction was independent of the crowd; but if people whose judgment he valued had one by one come to his side, and if each new convert had arrived at his conclusion by observations and reflections of his own, the conviction would at least have been more triumphantly entertained.[1]

3. If the consent of others is to have legitimate influence over us it must be a free consent. If you put, by means of ecclesiastical authority, a high premium on some particular opinion, then the evidential value of a consensus of thought in favour of that opinion is greatly weakened. In enforcing particular opinions by ecclesiastical discipline, you destroy the rational authority for that particular opinion which you are seeking to foster. Such a use of ecclesiastical discipline is not merely something which might not command our assent, but something as to which we might be comparatively indifferent if we agreed with the doctrine in question. The measure of our belief in the doctrine in question must be the measure of our objection to a process which cuts at the root of rational authority for that doctrine.

What confirms our faith is therefore never the mere voice of the multitude. Augustine's famous dictum, *Securus judicat orbis terrarum*, is often quoted as though it signified much the same thing as the pagan proposition, *Vox populi vox Dei*. But truth cannot be determined by any majority vote, whether in the House of Commons or in the Council of Nicæa. "The longest Sword, the strongest Lungs, the most Voices, are false measures of Truth." Certainty is not to be attained by conformity to the vote of the majority, by shouting with the crowd. The philosophy of By-ends is a virtual denial that there is any quest for truth.

¶ Weak minds find confirmation of their beliefs in the discovery of the same beliefs in other people. They do not take the trouble to find out how their neighbours obtained these beliefs. If they are current at the time, the probability is that the coincidence is worthless as any evidence of validity.[2]

4. In accepting testimony we prefer that of those who have made themselves masters of the subject. The words of Livingstone concerning Africa, and of Nansen concerning the icy North, are accepted at once. We do not demand evidence of their credibility before we receive their reports. Then why do we not with the

---

[1] W. M. Macgregor, *Christian Freedom*, 140.
[2] Mark Rutherford, *More Pages from a Journal*, 220.

same readiness accept the testimonies of those who have explored "the unsearchable riches of Christ" when the power of our own verification by experience is at our hand?

¶ We have no hesitation in accepting the words of Darwin on such a subject as worms, because he spent forty years of his life in making their acquaintance, and in studying their ways. If he had spent the same time and energy in studying angels, we would have acknowledged him as an authority on that subject also; but, as he did not, we cannot. We are quite prepared to accept Huxley as an authority on natural science, for he has studied the subject, but we are not prepared to accept his verdict upon the Lordship of Jesus Christ and the joys of His service, for on such matters even Huxley is no authority whatever.[1]

II.

Its Fruits.

1. There can be no mistake as to whether a man is possessed of faith. "By their fruits ye shall know them." It is not easy—it is, in fact, often impossible—to tell what a man believes, in the ordinary sense of the word; for he may say he believes one thing, when all the time he knows he believes another; he may even think he believes something, when in reality he does not. But, just as it would be absurd for us to make asseverations of bravery, when we were visibly trembling at the very smell of powder, so is it ridiculous to profess a confidence that God will render to every man according to his works, when we are acting as if this were, to say the least, unlikely. He who is confident cannot act as if he were in doubt. Faith made Moses refuse to be called the son of Pharaoh's daughter; it led him to despise the treasure in Egypt, and to set at naught the wrath of the king. It inspired men with such courage and strength that they subdued kingdoms, escaped the edge of the sword, turned to flight the armies of the aliens; or, if it were otherwise ordained—if they were tortured, stoned, sawn asunder—it helped them to bear their agony without a murmur. It enabled the Hebrew Christians originally to endure their great conflict of sufferings, and to take joyfully the spoiling of their goods; it would help them, in the future, says the

[1] G. G. Muir, *Shoulder to Shoulder*, 161.

writer, to run with patience the race set before them, and, in their striving against sin, to resist unto blood—that is, to the extent even of laying down their lives.

We believe Christ because we can test the power of His life in our lives and because we can see whether His highest claim is true. He professes to be able to take a man who has lived in sin, who has been self-centred and absorbed in self, who has borne all the marks of the earthly, and given no promise of the heavenly life, and to transform him into a being of the spiritual order, glowing with love, forgetful of self, dying to live, and living to do the will of another, and with a life in parallelism with the Divine purpose. In short, He claims to be able to impart the Divine life to men, to spiritualize and transform their lives.

It is a claim which can be as carefully tested as the law of gravitation. How do you know there is such a law? You see every particle of matter in the universe obey it. It swings satellites and planets and by it you can calculate their motions and positions. It draws the whole ocean and dashes it twice a day high up the beach and you can announce weeks before the exact moment of flood-tide.

How do we know that Jesus Christ is the power of God unto salvation and that God's love comes through Him to us? There is one sure test. Try Him. Turn your face to Christ, obey every call from Him, make an experiment of following Him completely, trust Him as you trust the laws of nature, throw yourself upon Him in absolute confidence, act as though you saw Him standing by you. The result will be—the testimony is universal—that you will find a new creation going on within. The old nature will go as the ghostly leaves of winter go when the new buds open. The new nature will come as " noiselessly as the spring-time her crown of verdure weaves." New avenues of activity will open, life will become richer, the reality of God will stand no more in theory, heaven will not seem some far-off terminus, and God's will will cease to be some stubborn objective law; it will become an inward choice and pleasure.

Such a Christianity has a three-fold demonstration: its effect on other individuals, its effect on our own personal lives, and its transforming effect on society. No one who has ever seen a saint made by the power of God in Jesus Christ can doubt that there is

THE CONFIRMATION OF FAITH

something dynamic in such a religion. One may doubt the truth of transubstantiation, or question the value of outward baptism, but he knows that only a spiritual power can change hate to love, sullenness to sweetness, harshness to gentleness, impulsiveness to calm patience, and fretful discouragement to confidence and victory.

Then comes the first-hand evidence in one's own life. There can be no proof so convincing as the fact that He has drawn *me* out of the horrible pit and the miry clay. He has established *my* goings and put a new song in *my* mouth. We know that we are of God because we love, because we have the witness, because we overcome, because God has brought us up into His life. Then there is that slow but steady coming of the Kingdom, going on before the eyes of those who can see—the propagation of the Divine life through the world. "The dial plate marks centuries with the minute finger." It seems like the slow swing of the globe in the precession of the equinoxes which in a thousand years gives us a new pole star. But though slow, like the motion of the glacier, the movement of God in history toward "one far off divine event" is unmistakable and irresistible. The old corrupt order does change, the relics of a pagan age are weeded out, the entrenched evils of centuries finally do yield. New revelations come, prophets appear, the horizon of light enlarges. Men become more civilized, more humanized, more spiritualized, more Christlike. The New Jerusalem is something more than a dream, because God is at work in His world, and when we take long perspectives we trace His hand.

¶ I could cite many instances where faith in Christ has very apparently altered a man's whole outlook and action. Naturally, most of my observation has been among fishermen, and it has included men of almost every kind of temperament. One was a man with whom I afterwards made several voyages. A man of exceptionable physique, he had been the victim of uncontrollable temper, and various of his drinking sprees had ended in the police station as the result of violent assaults on others. He had destroyed his home and his wife had left him. He was rapidly ruining his own splendid physique, and the lives of all those with whom he came in contact. Suddenly he became sober and peaceful, built up his home again and took back his wife, and developed an absolutely unselfish passion to try to save his fellows from the slavery that had been his. He always claimed that his faith in Christ was the secret of the change. He was so cheerful and so uniformly optimistic that his very face became transparent with happiness, and I have never had a more delightful shipmate. I once asked him to say a word to encourage other men. He stood up to try, and unaccustomed tears coursed down his cheeks. At last he said, "To think of the like of me talking to them men," and sat down. This class of men has been well illustrated by Mr. Harold Begbie in his *Twice-born Men* and *Broken Earthenware*. In my own experience it has been multiplied many times. Indeed, I have often wondered why so many clergy and other workers have asked me whether I have read these books, as if the results they describe were rare experiences. It is only the recording of them that is rare. There is a reticence always on the part of all good workers to draw deductions from their own work prematurely. There can be no question of their occurrence, however, though my own experience shows me that these more emotionally susceptible men are most liable to temporary retrogression. But even so, I am devoutly thankful for such changes as may occur to change their life and environment, changes which I can attribute to nothing else but their faith. I am certain that any one who, even though without faith himself, though also without prejudice, would seek to record such cases in the way we record cures of disease—which only affect part of men's lives—would be surprised at the extent and value of suddenly acquired faith in the Christ.[1]

¶ When St. Teresa's superiors tried to persuade her that her early visions were delusive, she allowed that she might mistake one person for another. "But if this person left behind him jewels as pledges of his love, and I found myself rich having before been poor, I could not believe, even if I wished, that I had been mistaken. And these jewels I could show them; for all who knew me saw clearly that my soul was changed; the difference was great and palpable."[2]

2. Of the fruits of faith we may name—

(1) HUMILITY.—As necessary as the root to the plant, as necessary as the foundation to the structure, so is humility to the organism of the Christian character. It is humility at the basis of all other characteristics that gives its peculiar quality to strictly *Christian* virtue; to the courage, for example, to the

[1] W. T. Grenfell, *The Adventure of Life*, 21.
[2] W. M. Macgregor, *Christian Freedom*, 148.

endurance, to the purity of principle, to the hatred of evil in every form, which is shown by the true disciple. And the true secret for the presence and growth of true humility resides just here, in the felt and cherished fact of an entire dependence upon Another, and that Other—Jesus Christ. It is no product of an artificial and studied self-abasement, an elaborate practice of certain definite humiliations. Such things, especially when they take shape in acts and practices which in the least degree tend to make a *display* of "voluntary humility" (Col. ii. 18), can very easily slide into a subtle but dangerous form of self-exaltation, hard, cold, ambitious, untrue, tainted with a pharisaic readiness to compare self favourably, however secretly, with others.

But the humility "which is from above" is a very different thing. It rises out of a close contact between the disciple and the Master, the vassal and his Lord. That contact keeps the man always *and naturally* low and little in his own esteem, yet in a manner which has not the slightest connexion with debasement. It means the habitual consciousness of an immeasurable difference, an infinite superiority in the glorious other Person. But this consciousness is so vitally penetrated with a concurrent certainty of connexion, of affinity, that there is nothing in it of repulsion. Rather it involves an indescribable attraction, and the reception into the whole humbled being of the uplifting and ennobling "power of Christ."

(2) LOVE.—The real Christian is the man who has got, and is using, a new power to love. Any one who calls himself a Christian, and is not practising love in his dealings with others, is simply deceiving himself. Let none say that "love," so frequent and so much insisted upon in the First Epistle of John, has some technical and sublimated meaning, such as "love for souls." The writer knows nothing of a love for souls which is not also a love for bodies. He takes pains to show exactly what he is talking about; the love that seeks to supply a brother's physical needs (iii. 17); the love that stops at nothing short of "laying down our lives for the brethren" (iii. 16).

There is, of course, all the difference in the world between the selfish and the unselfish varieties of love. The love of the drunkard and the sensualist is not here in question. It is not the love that seeks to get, but the love that seeks to give; that finds its satisfaction, not in clutching at the loved object, but in pouring self out for its welfare. It is the love that Jesus showed for the leper and the lunatic; the love that won the heart of Zacchæus, that made children feel happy when His arms were round them, that forgave His tormentors on the Cross.

To be a Christian, says the apostle, is to possess and to use this power of loving men : to have one's nature filled with love, that is to say, with God (iv. 7, 8). And this is only developing the teaching which in the Gospels is attributed to the Master Himself. It is those who share the universal spirit of the Father, and love even their enemies, who "become" His children (Matt. v. 44-48); it is only as we forgive others that we ourselves can be forgiven (vi. 14, 15); it is those who minister to the needs of their fellow-men who will inherit the Kingdom (xxv. 40); it is by love to one another that the disciples of Jesus are to be recognized (John xiii. 35).

¶ The Christian loves; therefore he has the truth. His proof is not of a nature to be communicated by words; but neither can words take it away. You cannot prove to him that he does not love God; and if he loves God, will you dare to insist that he does not know Him ? I have already asked it once, and I ask it again : Can he who loves God be deceived; is he not in the truth ? And if Christianity alone gives him power to love God, is not Christianity exclusively the truth ? Such is the certainty in which the faithful rejoice. I do not add that it is cherished and quickened by the Holy Spirit. I only speak of obvious facts, facts respecting which the unbelieving as well as the believing can satisfy themselves. And I limit myself to saying that the faith of the true Christian has for its peculiar characteristics a certainty which elevates it above that of any other belief.[1]

¶ Where was the recognition of the solidarity of the race before the parable of the Good Samaritan ? Where was the urging of the obligations of us all to provide for the survival, not of the fittest, but of the unfittest, before the "inasmuch" of the 25th of St. Matthew ? Where were the altruistic virtues before the Divine self-devotion of Calvary ? Are a Curtius and a Regulus cited in reply ? The faith of a Christian requires the like at the hands of all its children, and the Word of Truth has begotten hundreds of thousands, since, in the earliest of its progeny, it

---

[1] A. Vinet, *Vital Christianity*, 114.

"begat the first fruits of its creatures." Where was philanthropy before Barnabas, and Dorcas, and St. Martin of Tours? Where were the sick poor before God in Christ "bare our sicknesses and carried our sorrows"? Who founded hospitals before a Christian Valens or Fabiola? Does our classical friend, dipping into his Grote, hint at Epidaurus and its temple-hospital? Let him dip a trifle deeper, until he sees every dying patient ruthlessly turned out, to die a little sooner of exposure and neglect lest a death within doors should discredit the institution and pollute the precincts of the God. Where is your non-Christian Elizabeth of Hungary, Wilberforce, Howard, Nightingale, Baroness Burdett-Coutts, Shaftesbury, Father Damien? Did all these, and hundreds more, bind as a phylactery between their eyes, and as a sign upon their right hands, the 13th of the 1st of Corinthians, after binding in a bundle and burning the 15th and the four Gospels?[1]

III.

THE WITNESS OF THE SPIRIT.

The personal experience which becomes a test of faith is full of energies and activities in the soul which are not self-derived, but which mark the entrance of a Stronger than the Strong Man. "If the Tempter should persuade a man to doubt whether the Gospel be true," says Richard Baxter, "he may have recourse into his soul for a testimony of it, for thence he can tell the Tempter by experience that he hath found the promises of the Gospel made good to him. Christ hath there promised to send His Spirit into the souls of His people, and so hath He done to me; He hath promised to give light to them that sit in darkness, to bind up the broken-hearted and set at liberty the captives, and all this He hath fulfilled upon me. . . . The helps which He hath promised in temptations, the hearing of prayer, the relief in distress, all these I have found performed, and thus I know that the Gospel is true." These sentences, in concrete and moving phrase, embody the Reformation doctrine of "the testimony of the Holy Spirit."

¶ For as God alone can properly bear witness to His own words, so these words will not obtain full credit in the hearts of

---

[1] A. Pearson, *The Claims of the Faith*, 107.

men until they are sealed by the inward testimony of the Spirit.[1]

¶ By the Testimony of the Spirit I mean an inward impression of the soul whereby the Spirit of God directly witnesses to my spirit that I am a child of God; that Jesus Christ hath loved me and given Himself for me, that all my sins are blotted out, and I, even I, am reconciled to God.[2]

¶ Little is said by Roman Catholics upon the grace of assurance and the other works wrought in us by the Holy Spirit. That indeed is not to be wondered at; for the lay member of the Church is treated as though he were a mere minor or infant, and had no need to pry into the stamps and signatures and title-deeds which concern his settlements, but must accept implicitly the oral asseverations of executors and trustees. The assurance of the Spirit and the sponsorship of the priest inevitably conflict with each other, and the one or the other must be more or less depreciated by the competition. If the priest is in truth a surety for the absolution of the penitent who unreservedly commits his cause into official hands, and the sacrament of the body and blood of Christ is an unconditional pledge and an indestructible substratum of salvation, the importance of this witness is sensibly minimized. Why should I be jealous over my inner life, and cherish tempers of fine spirituality, so that I may be in a condition to enjoy this witness, if I may have a rough and ready assurance upon much easier terms? And, on the other hand, if God Himself becomes a witness of salvation within me, why should I not be free to think of an official priesthood as of comparatively limited and subordinate importance? As we possess this inward witness, the needlessness and impertinence of all sacerdotal pledges and guarantees will become more and more obvious.[3]

1. The chief passage of Scripture to which the doctrine of the Holy Spirit's witness refers is Rom. viii. 16: "The Spirit himself beareth witness with our spirit, that we are children of God."

(1) This text is so clear that (even if it were the only text) we can assert that the testimony of the Holy Spirit that we are God's children is a reality. That the Spirit witnesses with or to our spirits that we are children of God is just as certain as that there is such a state as sonship to which we may be introduced or that

---

[1] Calvin, *Institutes* I. vii. 4.   [2] Wesley, *Sermons*, x., xi.
[3] T. G. Selby, *The Holy Spirit and Christian Privilege*, 107.

THE CONFIRMATION OF FAITH 345

there is such a being as the Spirit of God to bear witness of it. These great facts all stand or fall together. And that is as much as to say that no Christian man can doubt the fact of the testimony of the Spirit that we are children of God. It is accredited to him by the same authority which accredits all that enters into the very essence of Christianity. It is in fact one of the elements of a full system of Christian truth that must be acknowledged by all who accept the system of Christian truth.

(2) It is just as clear from the text that the testimony of the Spirit is not to be confounded with the testimony of our own consciousness. However the text be read, the "Spirit of God" and "our spirit" are brought into pointed contrast in it, and are emphatically distinguished from one another. Accordingly, not only does Meyer, who understands the text of the joint testimony of the Divine and human spirits, say: "Paul distinguishes from the subjective self-consciousness, I am the child of God, the therewith accordant testimony of the objective Holy Spirit, Thou art the child of God"; but Alford also, who understands the text to speak solely of the testimony of the Spirit, borne not with but to our spirit, remarks: "All are agreed, and indeed the verse is decisive for it, that it is something separate from and higher than all subjective conclusions"—language which seems, indeed, scarcely exact, but which is certainly to the present point. It is of no importance for this whether Paul says that the Spirit bears witness with or to our spirit; in either case he distinctly distinguishes the Spirit of God from our spirit along with which or to which it bears its witness. And not only so, but this distinction is the very nerve of the whole statement, the scope of which is nothing other than to give the Christian, along with his human conclusions, also a Divine witness.

¶ The witness of the Holy Ghost is something other than, additional to, and more than the witness of our own spirit; and it is adduced here, just because it is something other than, additional to, and more than the witness of our own spirit. The whole sense of Paul's declaration is that we have over and beyond our own authority a Divine witness to our childship to God, on which we may rest without fear that we shall be put to shame.[1]

[1] B. B. Warfield, *Faith and Life*, 183.

(3) The witness of the Spirit is thus a witness which is not to be identified with that Divine life which is said to be present in the universe and in the soul of man. It is distinct and personal. The apostle is apparently carrying on the analogy of the legal process of adoption, and he summons, as it were, two separate witnesses to establish the mighty fact that the alien has been received into the family of God. The independence of their testimony is essential to the idea which he endeavours to express. And this becomes apparent when we remember what it is for which the Spirit stands in the thought of the Apostolic Church. To them the Holy Spirit was not simply the universal Life which breathes in all creation and stirs in the personalities of men. No doubt they would have assented to the words of the Book of Wisdom, which declares that God's "deathless spirit is in all things." But as Christians—and this is the important point for us to remember—it was through Jesus Christ that they had been brought into contact with Him. The Spirit of which St. Paul speaks is the Spirit of Jesus, whose relationship with the Giver of life was so intimate that the apostle could even say, "The Lord is the Spirit." So interchangeable do the terms become that to speak of being filled with the Spirit and of being found in Christ is to use two different modes of expressing a single experience.

If you ask what it is that makes the essential difference between the catholic gospel and all mystical methods of approaching God, it is here that you will find it. The Spirit bears this witness to the Father in the great public universal fact of Christ. There is no aristocracy, intellectual or spiritual, in the Christian apprehension of the eternal world. Faith is the one condition, and faith is as democratic as conscience, as popular as Nature itself. The heavens declare God's glory. His law converts the soul. And in Jesus of Nazareth the Word hath breath. He works with human hands, yet with the Divine finger, casting out demons and establishing the Kingdom by the Spirit. Christ is the pledge that we are God's children. His voice is the testimony of the Spirit. His mighty working, not only in the history of the past, but in the preaching of His messengers, the ministration of His Sacraments, the lives of His followers, the continuance of His society, is the assurance that God has not left Himself without witness. A world which includes Christ is no treeless Sahara. An environment which embraces Christ's Cross is no dry and sandy tract. A land where He builds His Church is a home for the lonely. The wilderness and the solitary place have become glad for us; the desert has rejoiced and blossoms as the rose.

¶ Rainy agreed with Pfleiderer, as with Martineau, that the inward spiritual witness is the true revelation. Still this is by no means always clear and conclusive. How do I know I am not misled by my own feelings and confusing God's revelation with my own way of thinking? It is here, said Principal Rainy, "that the concurrence of the outward and the inward has a peculiar effect of assurance." "The divine within me and the non-divine are inextricably mixed, perhaps; but the finger of God without is wholly independent of me."[1]

2. How is the witness of the Holy Spirit conveyed to the human spirit? The question recalls a long history of controversy. It is enough now to notice that God fulfils Himself in many ways. The Spirit will bear its witness to each spirit of man or woman according to their individuality. The risen Lord Himself, during the forty days of His resurrection life, came under great variety of circumstances, and with every differing kind of evidence of His presence, to each and all of His disciples. First He came to the loving hearts of women, whose words—the first Easter-Day sermon —seemed only "idle tales" to the apostles themselves; and then with logical demonstration to the cold reasoning intellect of Thomas; now to individual disciples walking on the common highway, who saw Him only when He broke and blessed the bread, and it revealed to them why their hearts had so burned within them on the way; and then to the assembled Church with words of benediction and of peace. And thus still the Holy Spirit's witness comes—now to some tender soul who cannot reason, but can only love, with simply an angel's message, which not only the world but the Church may for a moment think but an "idle tale"; and again to some consummate, lordly intellect, which is at last convinced by touching the nail-print and the riven side. Now He comes to solitary individuals on the dusty highway of life, who know not whence sprang every earnest pulsation of their burning hearts, till some day, perhaps in the

---

[1] P. C. Simpson, *The Life of Principal Rainy*, ii. 136.

breaking of the Eucharistic bread, they see at last that it must have been He that was with them; and again He is present to the assembled Church when in some hour of danger it has shut the door, and then found that He is with them in the midst.

(1) The Quaker doctrine of the Inner Light, in its customary form, lays stress more on the giving of a message than on the confirmation of faith, but it never fails in its acknowledgment that the primary activity is of Christ. "I knew not God but by revelation," says Fox himself, " as He who hath the key did open." "I came to my knowledge of Eternal Life," says William Dewsbury, " not by the letter of Scripture, nor from hearing men speak of God, but by the inspiration of the Spirit of Jesus Christ, who is worthy to open the seals."

¶ Thirteenth fifth month, 1757.—Being in good health, and abroad with Friends visiting families, I lodged at a Friend's house in Burlington. Going to bed about the time usual with me, I awoke in the night, and my meditations, as I lay, were on the goodness and mercy of the Lord, in a sense whereof my heart was contrited. After this I went to sleep again; in a short time I awoke; it was yet dark, and no appearance of day or moonshine, and as I opened mine eyes I saw a light in my chamber, at the apparent distance of five feet, about nine inches in diameter, of a clear, easy brightness, and near its centre the most radiant. As I lay still looking upon it without any surprise, words were spoken to my inward ear, which filled my whole inward man. They were not the effect of thought, nor any conclusion in relation to the appearance, but as the language of the Holy One spoken in my mind. The words were, CERTAIN EVIDENCE OF DIVINE TRUTH. They were again repeated exactly in the same manner, and then the light disappeared.[1]

(2) But there is a more common way of witness than that of the Inner Light. The Spirit witnesses to our spirit by His work of faith in us and by His work of joy.

(a) *His work of faith.*—His work of faith is the tidings which He imparts, the matter of those tidings is forgiveness. This is good cheer, "Son, be of good cheer, thy sins be forgiven thee" (Matt. ix. 2). "In whom we have redemption through his blood, even the forgiveness of sins" (Col. i. 14). "Through this man is

[1] *The Journal of John Woolman*, 84.

THE CONFIRMATION OF FAITH 349

preached unto you forgiveness of sins" (Acts xiii. 38). "Being justified by faith, we have peace with God" (Rom. v. 1). "Agree with thine adversary," said Christ. God is the adversary to all impenitent sinners, but He is a placable adversary, "we are in the way with him." That way is the Lord Jesus. He has put us in that way, He "hath laid on him the iniquity of us all." But to be at peace with Him we must agree with Him, that is, fall in with His conditions. These are confession of our sins, hearty repentance, and also a true and sincere faith to believe in that living "way" and that all that God has said thereof is true. This is enough to give us peace *with* God, but it is not enough to give us the peace *of* God. There is such a thing as believing in the truth of God's Word and not believing in it in its relation to ourselves. There is such a thing as believing in God's salvation as a complete salvation, but though it is so for others it is not so for me. Now such a frame of mind, though it is not inconsistent with faith is inconsistent with peace. But until faith can appropriate God's promises, there may be salvation, but not present peace. If I will have peace I must believe that Christ's salvation is my salvation, that my sins are forgiven.

(*b*) *His work of joy*, which is His seal. To be sure of a general offer is one thing, to be sure you have closed with it is another; the two things are carefully distinguished in Scripture. "After ye believed, ye were sealed with that holy Spirit of promise" (Eph. i. 13); and what is the consequence of that seal, or what does it consist in? A living realization of the objective of the proposed believing, "the eyes of your understanding being enlightened; that ye may know what is the hope of his calling, and what the riches of the glory of his inheritance in the saints" (ver. 18). This is "the earnest of the inheritance," the Pisgah view of the landscape, the breadth, the width, the grasp and the appreciation, the delight in the opened landscape, the complacence and joy and satisfaction in it, this makes up the assurance.

¶ Here take notice that the soul of a Saint consists of sacred riddles, and holy contradictions: "Rejoice (saith David) before him with trembling": if rejoicing, how can he tremble? if trembling, how can he rejoice? Oh, that is an unhappy soul which cannot find an expedient betwixt these extremities! that cannot accommodate these seeming contrarieties: *Rejoicing*, when he looks on a gracious God; *trembling*, when he beholds a sinful self: *Rejoicing*, when looking upward on God's promises; *trembling*, when looking downwards on his deserts. Ever *triumphing* that he shall be saved; and ever *trembling* lest he should be damned: ever certain that he shall stand; and ever careful lest he should fall.[1]

[1] *The Collected Sermons of Thomas Fuller, D.D., 1631–1659*, i. 485.

XVI.

JUSTIFICATION BY FAITH.

LITERATURE.

Bartlet, J. V. and Carlyle, A. J., *Christianity in History* (1917).
Bicknell, E. J., *A Theological Introduction to the Thirty-nine Articles* (1919).
Birks, T. R., *Justification and Imputed Righteousness* (1887).
Body, G., *The Life of Justification* (1871).
Bowne, B. P., *The Essence of Religion* (1911).
Bruce, A. B., *St. Paul's Conception of Christianity* (1894).
Buchanan, J., *The Doctrine of Justification* (1867).
Bushnell, H., *Forgiveness and Law* (1874).
„ „ *The Vicarious Sacrifice* (1866).
Denney, J., *The Christian Doctrine of Reconciliation* (1918).
Diggle, J. W., *The Foundations of Duty* (1913).
Drummond, J., *Studies in Christian Doctrine* (1908).
Drummond, R. J., *The Relation of the Apostolic Teaching to the Teaching of Christ* (1900).
Forsyth, P. T., *The Principle of Authority*.
Garvie, A. E., *The Gospel for To-Day* (1904).
Gibson, E. C. S., *The Thirty-Nine Articles*, ii. (1897).
Jones, E. Griffith, *Faith and Verification* (1907).
Jones, W. B., *The Peace of God* (1869).
Knox, E. A., in *Christian Faith and Practice Papers*, No. 209.
Lindsay, T. M., *A History of the Reformation*, i. (1906).
Litton, E. A., *Introduction to Dogmatic Theology*^{2} (1902).
Lock, W., in *Oxford University Sermons* (1901).
McLaren, W. D., *Our Growing Creed* (1912).
Morgan, W., *The Religion and Theology of Paul* (1917).
Moule, H. C. G., in *The Fundamentals*, ii.
Moulton, J. H., *Religions and Religion* (1913).
Newman, J. H., *Lectures on the Doctrine of Justification*^{3} (1874).
Nichols, J. B., *Evangelical Belief* (1899).
Oman, J., *Grace and Personality* (1917).
Quick, O. C., *Essays in Orthodoxy* (1916).
Rhinelander, P. M., *The Faith of the Cross* (1916).
Ritschl, A., *The Christian Doctrine of Justification and Reconciliation* (1900).
Sanday, W. and Headlam, A. C., *The Epistle to the Romans* (1902).
Simpson, J. G., *What is the Gospel?* (1914).
Stevens, G. B., *The Theology of the New Testament* (1899).
Tymms, T. V., *The Christian Idea of Atonement* (1904).
Westcott, F. B., *St. Paul and Justification* (1913).
Williams, E. J. W., *A Plea for a Re-consideration of St. Paul's Doctrine of Justification* (1912).
Woods, C. E., *The Gospel of Rightness* (1909).

JUSTIFICATION BY FAITH.

1. THERE are many to whom the doctrine of Justification by Faith makes but little appeal nowadays. They regard it at best as an abstruse dogma which does not particularly interest them, and they are sometimes more than half inclined to pronounce it obsolete. Theological doctrines vary in attractiveness at different periods: they have their times of predominance and their times of comparative neglect. At the present day the attention of theologians is being largely concentrated on the problems that surround our Lord's life, and one result is that the doctrinal teaching of St. Paul has, for the moment at any rate, receded into the background.

¶ Has it ever occurred to you that Justification has lost its great place among us? Depend upon it, Luther was right in insisting on its supreme importance. It appears to me that I rarely use the word; and although it is quite true, as I think I have said in my lectures on the Ephesians, that Paul could make a great statement of the breadth and power of the Christian Redemption without using it, he had the conception for which the word stands wrought into the substance of his life and thought: I fear that I have been sparing of the word because I have not grasped the thing. It has come to me of late, with much vividness and force; I wonder whether it will remain and grow. It lies in immediate and vital contact with the Atonement.[1]

2. The truth of justification by faith is something more than the watchword of an extinct controversy emblazoned on the banners of the conquerors, but no longer able to wake echoes in the hearts of men. "The just by faith shall live." That is still the law of life for all of us, and it will not fail. Still those who

[1] *The Life of R. W. Dale of Birmingham* 526.

stand upon their watchtower and watch the signs of the heavens, will see the vision of that truth gleaming through the darkness, and will "write it on tables so that he that runs may read it." Still without that faith there is no true righteousness, and without the righteousness there is no true life. We need it in all its width and power, in all its variety of application, in its bearing upon our personal salvation, upon our growth in holiness, upon our hopes for others, upon the mysteries of the world's evil. We must go back from the faith which, in the teaching of the Lutheran Reformers, assumed, in the very heat of their warfare against scholasticism, something of a scholastic character, to the wider teaching of St. Paul. We must unite with the experience and the faith of the apostle the experience and the faith of the prophet who was his forerunner.

¶ We have met people who could get up no enthusiasm about justification by faith. It was a dogma to be accepted, but they saw in it nothing to exult about. That is because our theologians have been such bad teachers of theology. They smother us with words which they fail to make alive. For this is a doctrine to stir us when we do understand it. It made Luther's blood leap in his veins. It meant for him that, after all the torture of ceremonial, fast and vigil to get himself right with God, he found the whole business centred in just trusting God. The formidable Being whose wrath he had been labouring to propitiate needed no efforts of that kind. He was already his friend. God meant good to him, had done so from the first. He was to do his best as a man in the world because God loved him and believed in him; believed in his possibility of being and doing something. That, for Luther and the rest of us, is the true saving faith. The life of faith means a faith on both sides. We believe in God, and God believes in us; believes in us as worth saving, as worth doing His best with, as having possibilities that make us worth all His care.[1]

I.

THE NECESSITY.

1. Of all questions that can occupy the mind of man none is more important than this: "How do I stand with God?" To dismiss it as unimportant and unpractical, is to dismiss as unreal

[1] J. Brierley, *Life and the Ideal*. 47.

the one great Reality to which our personality, as distinct from our senses, responds. To evade it by vague statements about an All-loving Father, who will put things right in the end, is to dishonour God. A generation brought up on these statements is now groping painfully to restore its sense of "the Majesty and Mastership of God." If "the modern man does not worry about his sins," this is a proof not of his progress, but of retrogression. With all its faults and mistakes the sixteenth century was alive to the reality of God, and it is our wisdom to discover the great truths which underlay its scholastic terminology, and to state them afresh to ourselves in terms of modern thought. This appears to be all the more necessary now that the Church is attempting through the influence of the war to discharge its duty of witness to the world. If God is real, and I am real, every other inquiry is in fact secondary to the inquiry, "How do I stand with God?"

¶ What does a man mean then who says he feels his sin and wants relief? I think the analysis is very clear, though it leads us to the brink of unfathomable things and unutterable agonies and longings. Such a man means, to begin with, that he is awake to the reality of God, and that he has at least in some degree the feeling that nothing really matters save a right relationship to Him. The sense of sin, that is to say, has its whole root from first to last in an awakened desire for God and goodness.

God may be little known and vaguely realized. His name may be hardly more than a symbol for the spiritual and the unseen, for what is permanent and perfect. But none the less He is desirable and desired, not for His gifts or favours but for Himself. The psalmist's cry, "My soul is athirst for God, yea, even for the living God," may be, at this first stage, far beyond the power of the awakened sinner, but at least it is no longer alien to him. It has become intelligible and congenial. God is the true end; goodness the true life; and sin has come to block the way and cheat him of the prize.[1]

2. By universal consent of all who have tried to think it out, the answer to the question "How do I stand with God?" can only be "I am a sinner and need forgiveness of my sin." But it is also clear that this is a very insufficient answer. There are many kinds of forgiveness. There is forgiveness of the rebel who

[1] P. M. Rhinelander, *The Faith of the Cross*, 39.

obtains an amnesty, but retains rebellion in his heart. There is forgiveness of a friend, who is warned at the same time that friendship on its old footing can never be restored. There is forgiveness of a child, who is told that any repetition of his fault will bring down immediate punishment. In each of these cases forgiveness leaves a sting in the heart of the forgiven. He is not punished, but he is not reconciled. If the Divine forgiveness is on these lines, the question "How do I stand with God?" is very far from being a message of peace. It is a message of remission of punishment, which rests on no true conception of the nature of God; and only in an age of slipshod thinking could it obtain any currency.

(1) Notice two things: First, a simple pardon, bestowed without any accompanying circumstances, must have drawn some degree of gratitude from the criminal, if he knew his danger; and this would have been all. But when he views the perfect and holy obedience of a great benefactor as the ground of his pardon, he is induced to look with love and admiration towards that obedience which gained the Divine favour, as well as towards the friend who paid it.

(2) Again, the sinner does not want God without God's goodness. No passing over, no good-natured tolerance, no kind indulgence will suffice; it is real godliness, real fellowship he wants. And how can he be in fellowship with God unless he is identified with goodness? unless God can look on him, with all the rest of His dependent creatures, and see that he, the sinner, is actually very good?

3. There is a better answer, known commonly as the doctrine of Justification by Faith, which teaches that God has provided for sinners not only a full forgiveness, not only the power to overcome sin, but also a complete, a Divine righteousness. In that righteousness man has no share but that of accepting it by faith. "Therefore it is of faith, that it might be by grace" (Rom. iv. 16). So, accepting it, he makes it his own, and is able to answer the question "How do I stand with God?" with the simple reply: "I am at peace, entirely at peace, with Him. By faith I am one with Christ, and Christ with me, and all that is His is mine." This is the doctrine of Justification by Faith.

JUSTIFICATION BY FAITH

¶ To St. Paul the question presented itself *at the first* (in pre-Christian days) in the "Jewish" form. For he was born "privileged," even beyond the common run of his countrymen. He possessed advantages innumerable. "Philippians" tells us how (in his regenerate days) he regarded these advantages. By a vigorous oxymoron he counted them "*less than nothing.*" Like the character in Hans Andersen who asks contemptuously, "Do you call that a *hill*? We should call it a *hole,*" St. Paul declares he reckoned his "gain" as mere "dung." No more would he go about (as he did in these old days) to keep himself "right with God," by doing and doing and doing. He would not even assume that he started "right with God," and only had to keep so, by loyalty to the Covenant. His point of view was transformed. All was merged in one great question, How shall I *become* right with God—right once for all? And the answer came, "Through Christ." Here was the new way, the God-appointed way. Henceforth he never wavered in heart and soul conviction that "justification" for him was an accomplished fact. He had "become right" with God, "in Christ Jesus," as a result of "faith." It was the wholly new beginning of a wholly new existence.[1]

II.

The Meaning.

1. It is often said, and not without some reason, that the very word "justification" has to-day become repugnant to English congregations, and it is certain that in countless pulpits it is seldom if ever used. As a reaction from the passionate discussions and the wearisome technical disquisitions which once abounded, this disuse of the term is not unnatural. It must also be confessed that the Latinized term is itself repellent, and serves to hide the sequence of thought in Paul's great argument, because it conceals the affinity of the word *dikaioun* (to justify) with the words *dikaios* (righteous) and *dikaiosune* (righteousness). It would have been a great blessing to English readers if all these terms had been rendered in Anglo-Saxon, so preserving their relationship and avoiding the harshness and coldness of the Latin term. But, however strongly we may regret the original and now irreparable mistake of early translators, the word justify stands

---
[1] F. B. Westcott, *St. Paul and Justification*, 15.

for an aspect of truth which cannot be neglected without loss, and whatever our feeling about its ecclesiastical misuse, the teaching of the New Testament on the subject will commend itself as simple, beautiful, and evidently true, and as a potent instrument for the furtherance of faith and righteousness.

¶ We presume that there will be not a few who very seldom, indeed, think of themselves as justified, or as needing justification. In meditating on our spiritual necessities, or on our spiritual condition in general, the word *justify*, or *justified*, or *justification* rarely comes up. The word *Christ* comes up always. The word *Saviour*, too, and the word *save*, or *saved*, or *salvation*. And the word *pardon*, too, or *pardoned*, and the words *peace* and *hope* and *holiness* and *joy* and *rest* and *heaven* and the *heavenly home*. These words, and others somewhat akin, come up in troops before our minds when we think of our spiritual necessities and prospects. But it is, we presume, very different indeed as regards the words *justify, justified, justification*.[1]

2. To discover the meaning of justification it is necessary to examine and determine the sense in which the verb *dikaioun* and its passive *dikaiousthai* are used in Scripture.

(1) In the Old Testament the active voice is used by the LXX as the translation of the Hebrew *hizdik* in a judicial or "forensic" sense: to "do right to a person," *i.e.* to do justice to his cause, and so to acquit (see Ex. xxiii. 7; Deut. xxv. 1; 2 Sam. xv. 4; 1 Kings viii. 32; 2 Chron. vi. 23; Ps. lxxxii. (lxxxi.) 3; Isa. v. 23, l. 8, liii. 11; Jer. iii. 11; Ezek. xvi. 51, 52); in other words, its meaning is not to "make a person righteous," but to "make him out righteous," or to "treat him as righteous." But in itself the word indicates nothing as to whether he is or is not righteous. So in the passive, a person is said to be "justified" when he is regarded as righteous, held "not guilty," or acquitted (see Gen. xliv. 16; Job xxxiii. 32; Ps. li. (l.) 5, cxliii. (cxlii.) 2; Isa. xliii. 9, 26, xlv. 25).

(2) In the New Testament outside the Epistles of St. Paul the word is not of frequent occurrence, but wherever it is found (eleven times in all) its meaning is just the same. "Wisdom is *justified* by her works" (Matt. xi. 19; cf. Luke vii. 35), *i.e.* not "made righteous," but *vindicated, proved* to be righteous. In Matt. xii. 37

[1] J. Morison, *Sheaves of Ministry*, 306.

JUSTIFICATION BY FAITH 359

it is opposed to "condemned," and thus is equivalent to "acquitted." "By thy words thou shalt be *justified*, and by thy words thou shalt be condemned." The lawyer, willing to *justify* himself, says: "And who is my neighbour?" where the meaning evidently is to vindicate himself, or make himself out to be righteous (Luke x. 29; cf. xvi. 15). The publican "went down to his house *justified* rather than" the Pharisee (Luke xviii. 14).

These are representative instances, and establish the meaning of the word outside St. Paul's writings. But as the ph.ase "to be justified by faith" is due to him, it becomes necessary to examine further into his usage of the word. It is employed in his Epistles altogether twenty-five times; and while in some cases it is unambiguous and *must* mean *treat as righteous*, and so (in the case of the guilty) pardon and acquit, in no single instance can the meaning of "*make* righteous" be established for it. This statement is one that can easily be verified, and therefore only a few examples need be cited. "To him that worketh, the reward is not reckoned as of grace, but as of debt. But to him that worketh not, but believeth on him that *justifieth* the ungodly, his faith is reckoned for righteousness" (Rom. iv. 4, 5). "All have sinned, and fall short of the glory of God; being *justified* freely by his grace through the redemption that is in Christ Jesus" (Rom. iii. 23, 24). "With me it is a very small thing that I should be judged of you, or of man's judgement: yea, I judge not mine own self. For I know nothing against myself; yet am I not hereby *justified*: but he that judgeth me is the Lord" (1 Cor. iv. 3, 4). In 1 Tim. iii. 16 the word is used of Christ, who was "manifested in the flesh, *justified* in the spirit."

From these examples the meaning of the word may be ascertained without difficulty. It is regularly employed of the sentence or verdict pronounced on a man by God, and does not in itself tell us whether the person over whom the sentence is pronounced is really righteous or not. When a man is justified he is "accounted righteous," or regarded as righteous.

¶ Justification is always the *opposite, and exactly the opposite of condemnation*. When we justify the conduct of any person, we do the opposite of condemning it; and when we condemn it, we do the opposite of justifying it. When we justify a *person* for his conduct, we do the opposite of condemning him. When we condemn him, we do the opposite of justifying him. When justifying or condemning a person's conduct, we compare it with some rule or standard of right or wrong; and having made the comparison, we judge. If we judge it to be right, we justify it. If we judge it to be wrong, we condemn it. When justifying or condemning a person himself, we compare him with some ideal of a person in our mind, and having made the comparison, we judge accordingly, and hence either justify or condemn. We must either justify him or condemn him, or stand in doubt regarding him. We must judge him to be right and righteous, or judge him to be wrong and unrighteous; or else we must remain in doubt whether he is right and righteous on the one hand, or wrong and unrighteous on the other.[1]

3. Justification, then, is a verdict of acquittal. But a caveat must be entered against understanding this metaphor of the modern law court as though there were some legal reality corresponding to it in God's dealings with men. To justify means to account or reckon as righteous. So far as the term goes, nothing is implied as to the reasons for which this takes place. A man may be actually righteous, or he may only be regarded for the purpose in hand as though he were righteous. In either case he is accepted as righteous.

The word "acceptance" may perhaps lead us better than any other to see how the term "justification" really does express the characteristic Christian experience. We speak of one person as being accepted by another. The members, for example, of an exclusive social circle agree to "accept" new recruits for their fellowship in consequence of their possession of certain qualifications, their *cachet*, as the phrase is. But in this instance or in that they may for reasons which are deemed sufficient tacitly forgo these qualifications. The man or woman in question is accepted in the particular coterie and admitted to whatever rights and privileges spring out of relationship with it. And the Epistle to the Ephesians speaks of Christians as "accepted in the beloved." In virtue simply of their trust in Christ, their acceptance of what He has accomplished on their behalf, they find themselves "accepted" by God, admitted in one fellowship to those personal relations with the Father which carry with them the consecrating

[1] J. Morison, *Sheaves of Ministry*, 307.

power of the indwelling Spirit. Now this acceptance is what St. Paul means in the earlier Epistles by justification.

¶ The fact of justification is just as real whether it is a definite pronouncement on the part of God or whether it is implied in those new relations in which the believer finds himself as a consequence of his faith in Jesus. St. Paul believed, took it for true, was convinced that he had been brought into living, saving contact with God through the exalted Nazarene. He had obeyed the heavenly vision. He had been baptized into the fellowship of the Spirit, and was daily experiencing His power in reproducing in him the Divine holiness. Here was the assurance that he was risen to a new life in Christ. He was justified by faith.[1]

4. But what is the faith that justifies? An important light is thrown on this question by Rom. iii. 21–26, which may in one aspect be viewed as a definition or description of justifying faith. There faith is in the first place defined with reference to its personal object as the "faith of Christ," which means not the faith that Jesus is the Christ, but rather faith in Christ as the embodiment of Divine grace. It is further indicated that that in Christ on which the eye of faith is chiefly fixed is the redemption achieved by His death, wherein the grace of God to the sinful manifests itself. According to this passage, therefore, the faith that justifies is not simply faith in God, or faith in God's grace, or faith in the truth that Jesus is the Christ, but faith in Jesus as one who gave Himself to death for man's redemption, and so became the channel through which God's grace flows to sinners. Following out this idea of faith, justification might be defined as a judicial act, *whereby God regards as righteous those who trust in His grace as manifested in the atoning death of Christ.*

¶ The righteousness of God is through faith in Jesus Christ. It is for all who believe. God set forth Christ in His blood, as a propitiation, through faith. The man for whom the propitiation avails, the man who is justified by God, is he who can be characterized by his faith in Jesus. But what is faith? There is nowhere any definition of it in Paul, and it is idle to look for its meaning in the lexicon. It is obviously, in this passage, correlative to the propitiation; it is that which Christ in His character of propitiation appeals for and is designed to evoke in the hearts of sinful

[1] J. G. Simpson, *What is the Gospel?* 158.

men. When the sinner stands before Christ on His cross, Christ a propitiation, bearing the sin of the world, what is he to do? What he sees there is the astounding truth that the last reality in the world is not, as he might have feared, sin, condemnation, estrangement, death, but a love which bears sin, taking it in all its dreadful reality upon itself, and, out of the very passion in which it does so, appealing to him. How is he to respond to this appeal? Paul has no difficulty in answering: he must respond by faith. He must trust himself to such love instantly, unreservedly, for ever. He cannot negotiate with God about it. He cannot suggest that perhaps upon reconsideration something else might be found which would suit all parties better than sin-bearing love on the one side and the unconditional acceptance of it and surrender to it on the other. He cannot suggest that less than the propitiation might meet the demands of his case, and that he might be saved in a way which did not make him so deeply Christ's debtor. He cannot qualify his indebtedness by the idea that a life of good works in future will enable him, at least to some extent, to clear scores with Christ, and to stand upon his own feet. There is a disproportion which makes them absurd and impious between all such ideas and Christ the propitiation, Christ in the love of God bearing the sin of the world. Once we see what that is, we see there is only one right thing to do with it: to trust it instantly, and to the uttermost. Of course we can turn away from it, and live—and die—in our sins. We can ignore it and harden our hearts against it, as we can against any appeal of any love. But that is wrong. The only right thing to do is to trust it, to let go, to abandon ourselves to it, keeping nothing back. This is what Paul means by faith. And it is the whole of religion on the inner side, just as Christ the propitiation, or the sin-bearing love of God, is the whole of religion on the outer side—the whole, at all events, of the gospel, that is, of Christianity as the religion of redemption from sin. When a man believes in this sense, he does the only thing which it is right to do in the presence of Christ, and it puts him right with God. It really puts him right. There is nothing imaginary or fictitious about it. Sinner as he is, his whole being comes into a new relation to God through his faith, a relation in which there is no more condemnation. God justifies the ungodly man on the basis of his faith in Jesus, and there is nothing unreal about the justification. He proclaims and treats him as one who is right with Himself. And he *is* right with Himself. As long as he maintains the attitude of faith he remains right, nor is there any other attitude in which he can ever be right. Christ makes for ever the same appeal, which demands for ever the same response, and in that appeal and response Christianity, including the gospel message and the Christian life, is exhausted.[1]

¶ St. Paul's language is the product of his age and training; his meaning is catholic in its application and eternal in its truth. Let us take an illustration which will bring out this fact by the force of a complete external contrast. Generations of mothers, nurses and governesses, since the world began, have learned and verified the lesson that the wavering self-control of a child, which suffers complete breakdown if he is told "not to be a baby," may be stimulated to further effort if he is told "to be a man." Why? Because the mention of manhood makes appeal to the child's faith, which is for him the substance of things hoped for. It is his proud belief that he is capable of manhood, and, when that faith is stirred, there is at least some chance that forgetting those things that are behind and reaching out to those things that are before, he will press toward the mark for the prize of that high calling (to him how pathetically high!) which he feels dimly to be his. All those who have had any experience of dealing with the young know well the need of responding to such faith. No method of treating a child is more effective for good, when wisely used, than the method of trusting him, or putting him on his honour—in other words, the method of treating him as the trustworthy man which he feels he has it in him to be. To a superficial view this method may seem to involve an element of fiction and make-believe born of a profounder insight into the truth. Even the weak-willed child has the germs of honour and manliness within him, and by giving him credit for his possibilities we make them actual; we do not, of course, put into him any alien virtue from without, but we elicit something which was really his, but needed our trust to draw it forth. Now in thus treating a child we do essentially justify him by his faith. He believes in his capacity for manliness, and therefore we treat him as a man in order that he may become one.

Not wholly otherwise, according to St. Paul's doctrine, does the Heavenly Father justify all His human children. True, there is one important difference. The child's faith, in the illustration we are taking, is a faith mainly in a power or capacity of his own, the Christian's faith is a faith in Christ's power to make His followers like to Himself. Yet ideally at least Christ's manhood is ours also—at any rate, Christ has put it into our manhood to become one with His; and if we have the faith to reach out after that union, the Love of God, which knows our possibilities no less

[1] J. Denney, *The Christian Doctrine of Reconciliation*, 162.

than our shortcomings, has no need of fiction in order to treat us as what in Christ we may become. For in Christ manhood has died to sin and for sin, and therefore the highest and strongest of all appeals can be made at once to any man whose faith will claim membership in Him—" Ye are dead; your life is hid with Christ in God; *therefore* seek those things which are above." As St. Paul clearly perceived, the Law was powerless, because it made appeal to man on the ground of what he was not. It told him that he was a sinner in the same breath that it exhorted him to be a saint; just as our more modern ethics of evolution tell man that he is an ape, while they may, or may not, exhort him to be an angel. But the Gospel of the Atonement appeals to man on the ground of what he is: "You are in Christ, you are God's adopted child, you are restored to fellowship; therefore behave yourself worthily of that gift." Thus, in the old words of the woman of Tekoa, has God devised means whereby His banished be not outcast from Him.[1]

5. Justification may be looked at as an experience within the believer; and the meaning of the experience is simply this: the believer, who because he has faith—the faith which is the gift of God, which is our life and which regenerates—is regenerate and a member of the Christian fellowship, and is able to do good works and actually does them, does not find his standing as a person justified in the sight of God, his righteousness, his assurance of pardon and salvation, in those good works which he really can do, but only in the mediatorial and perfectly righteous work of Christ which he has learned to appropriate in faith. His good works, however really good, are necessarily imperfect, and in this experience which we call Justification by Faith the believer compares his own imperfect good works with the perfect work of Christ, and recognizes that his pardon and salvation depend on that alone. This comparison quiets souls anxious about their salvation, and soothes pious consciences; and the sense of forgiveness which comes in this way is always experienced as a revelation of wonderful love.

This justification is called an act, and is contrasted with a work; but the contrast, though true, is apt to mislead through human analogies which will intrude. It is an act, but an act of God; and Divine acts are never done and done with, they are

[1] O. C. Quick, *Essays in Orthodoxy*, 106.

JUSTIFICATION BY FAITH

always continuous. Luther rings the changes upon this. He warns us against thinking that the act of forgiveness is all done in a single moment. The priestly absolution was the work of a moment, and had to be done over and over again; but the Divine pronouncement of pardon is continuous simply because it is God who makes it. He says: "For just as the sun shines and enlightens none the less brightly when I close my eyes, so this throne of grace, this forgiveness of sins, is always there, even though I fall. Just as I see the sun again when I open my eyes, so I have forgiveness and the sense of it once more when I look up and return to Christ. We are not to measure forgiveness as narrowly as fools dream."

6. In the Protestant polemic with Roman Catholic doctrine, the conception of Justification by Faith is contrasted with that of Justification by Works; but the contrast is somewhat misleading. For the word "justification" is used in different meanings in the two phrases. The direct counterpart in Roman Catholic usage to the Reformation thought of Justification by Faith is the absolution pronounced by a priest; and here as always the Reformer appeals from man to God. The two conceptions belong to separate spheres of thought. The justification of which the mediæval Christian had experience was the descending of an outward stream of forces upon him from the supersensible world, through the Incarnation, in the channels of ecclesiastical institutions, priestly consecration, sacraments, confession, and good works; it was something which came from his connexion with a supersensible organization which surrounded him. The justification by faith which Luther experienced within his soul was the personal experience of the believer standing in the continuous line of the Christian fellowship, who receives the assurance of the grace of God in his exercise of a personal faith—an experience which comes from appropriating the work of Christ which he is able to do by that faith which is the gift of God.

In the one case, the Protestant, justification is a personal experience which is complete in itself, and does not depend on any external machinery; in the other, the Mediæval, it is a prolonged action of usages, sacraments, external machinery of all kinds, which by their combined effect are supposed to change a sinner gradually into a saint, righteous in the eyes of God. With the former, it is a continuous experience; with the latter, it cannot fail to be intermittent as the external means are actually employed or for a time laid aside.

7. There is a danger of laying too much stress on individual experience. This emphasis was a natural reaction against the dangerously mechanical and materialistic view of the Church and its Sacraments against which the Reformers protested. Personal salvation, personal and intimate relation with God, were truths which needed to be emphasized at a time when masses, pardons, and indulgences were freely bought and sold. The official Church had made light of living faith in a living God. It was natural that stress should be laid on the share that each individual soul must take in establishing its own relation with God. But the fact remains that Christ loved the Church and gave Himself for the Church, and that the Church is His Spouse and His Body. That the Church as a whole should be justified freely and only by faith in the merits of Jesus Christ, or that the Church should put off her filthy garments, and be clothed in the righteousness of Christ, is language which hardly presents any suggestion of difficulty to a devout mind familiar with Holy Scripture. Nor is there any real difficulty when the metaphors are translated into simple prose. That God should accept the whole body of His redeemed, not for any merit of its individual members, but simply for the perfect merits of Jesus Christ, is only natural when we think how sinful and imperfect is each several member of that great company.

From the same point of view is apparent the necessity of the sacraments which the doctrine of Justification by Faith is supposed to overlook. In the sacrament of initiation, in the sacrament of communion, it has pleased God to minister to each member of the Body all that belongs to the Body as a whole, sealing to each one those promises of life and grace without which there could be no Body of Christ at all. Nor is it conceivable that any single member can receive spiritual gifts mechanically, or otherwise than by a living faith in God and His Word. The sacraments are not substitutes for faith, or steps towards Justification, but a Divine provision for quickening, strengthening, and confirming faith.

¶ It is in the restoration of a spiritual for a mechanical conception of the Church of Christ that the hope of better understanding of all Christian truth lies. The faith will not be seen in its true proportions, but will continue to be distorted, so long as individualism loses sight of the Body of Christ, or externalism magnifies the claims of the visible Church at the expense of personal faith in the living Christ, without which there is no membership of His Body.[1]

III.

THE CHANNEL.

One of the historians of the Council of Trent, of great repute [Pallavicini], tells us that the assembled fathers were much exercised in attempting to explain the apostle's statement, "We conclude that a man is justified by faith without the deeds of the law" (Rom. iii. 28). We cannot wonder at their perplexity when we remember the scholastic training which they had received, particularly as regards the theory of an infused justifying righteousness. In what sense were they to understand the faith which St. Paul apparently makes the instrument, or condition, of justification? How reconcile his words with the prevalent teaching of the Church? It is obvious that faith, for some reason and in some sense, occupies a very prominent position in his reasoning on justification; it cannot be overlooked; it must be explained, or explained away. The difficulty was obvious, and was met as best it might. "With few exceptions," says Pallavicini, "they all agreed that when a man is said to be justified by faith, faith must be taken, not as the whole and the immediate cause of justification, but as the first preparation, and the first necessary root, to the actions whereby the gift is obtained; or if we may, in some sense, assign it the function of an immediate cause, yet it must not then be thought of as alone, but in conjunction with penitence and baptism."

This description of justifying faith was adopted by the Council

[1] E. A. Knox, in *Christian Faith and Practice Papers*, i.–iv., 209d.

and appears in its decree. "Whereas," it says, "the Apostle declares that we are justified by faith, and gratuitously, he must be understood in the sense which the Catholic Church has always assigned to his words, namely, that faith is the commencement, the root, and the foundation, of all justification; since without it it is impossible to please God. And as to the gratuitous nature of justification, it means that none of those things which precede justification, whether faith or works, deserve the grace of justification itself. Faith is thus classed with the preparatory antecedents to justification, such as conviction of sin, alarms of conscience, and a general hope of God's mercy. In itself it is assent to the truths of revelation, especially as interpreted by the Church; as such it places the sinner on the road to justification, but it is not the direct instrument, still less the only one, of receiving that gift, or of retaining it when received."

This amounts merely to saying that a man must be a professed believer in Christianity before we can enter into the question of his justification; which, however true, does not throw much light upon the matter. The only office of faith, then, is to lead up to the sacrament of baptism, in which the special grace of justification is infused, and in which faith itself is transformed from acquiescence in the truth of revelation into a faith informed by love (*fides formata*). In this state it may be allowed to take its place among other graces as a means of justification; and so St. Paul is to be understood. The Council, however, does not explain why, of all graces, faith should be singled out so remarkably by the apostle for the office of justifying.

1. "We are justified by faith." If a man believes, he is saved. Why so? Not as some people sometimes seem to fancy—not as if in faith itself there were any merit. There is a very strange and subtle resurrection of the whole doctrine of works in reference to this matter; and we often hear belief in the gospel of Christ spoken about as if *it*, the work of the man believing, was, in a certain way and to some extent, that which God rewarded by giving him salvation. What is that but the whole doctrine of works come up again in a new form? What difference is there between what a man does with his hands and what a man feels in his heart? If the one merits salvation, or if the other merits

salvation, equally we are shut up to this: Men get heaven by what they do; and it does not matter a bit what they do it with, whether it be body or soul. When we say we are saved by faith, we mean, accurately, *through* faith. It is God that saves. It is Christ's life, Christ's blood, Christ's sacrifice, Christ's intercession, that saves. Faith is simply the channel through which there flows over into my emptiness the Divine fulness; or, to use the good old illustration, it is the hand which is held up to receive the benefit which Christ lays in it. A living trust in Jesus has power unto salvation only because it is the means by which the power of God unto salvation may come into my heart. On that side is the great ocean, Christ's love, Christ's abundance, Christ's merits, Christ's righteousness; or, rather, that which includes them all, there is the great ocean, Christ Himself; and on this is the empty vessel of my soul, and the little narrow pipe that has nothing to do but to bring across the refreshing water—that is the act of faith in Him. There is no merit in the dead lead, no virtue in the mere emotion. It is not faith that saves us; it is Christ that saves us, and saves us through faith.

¶ Faith is nothing in itself. It is its object which is everything. It is just the opening of the soul which lets in God.[1]

2. It may be said without irreverence that the reason why, in God's method of salvation, faith is selected as the channel of God's grace is not because there is any special virtue in it, or because it is the greatest of all Christian graces, for charity is greater (1 Cor. xiii. 2, 13), but because faith is peculiarly fit for this particular office, since there is in it that element of self-surrender, of trust, confidence, and reliance on another, which necessarily excludes all reliance on self and our own merits. Had we been justified by something else, as love, there would have been the possibility of reliance on self, and the notion of *earning* salvation would not have been in the same way shut out. Further, it is faith that enables us to realize the unseen. It is "the assurance of things hoped for, the proving of things not seen" (Heb. xi. 1); and thus it makes things distant become near, and admits them to close embrace.

Faith is indeed the only conceivable channel through which

[1] R. W. Barbour, *Thoughts*, 77.

the sanctifying, ennobling, and joy-giving riches of God's goodness can be conveyed into man's nature. Paul everywhere regards God's grace as the primal source of all blessings, but points out that God can give effect to His spontaneous liberality only through human faith. Giving and receiving are correlative and cannot be disjoined. Without a receiver there can be no transmission of a gift, nor can the giver enjoy the highest blessedness which love can know. The love I do not trust is as no love to me. The spiritual gifts and inspiring truths which, being imbibed, would come to the soul as rain and dew and sunshine to the earth, are as non-existent to the unbeliever. Forgiveness may be ready; God may be waiting to be gracious; He may be stretching forth His hands for days and years, but only faith can take His favour as a little child receives a gift.

¶ It is a popular fallacy that faith is an arbitrary condition of salvation imposed by God, but which might be dispensed with or exchanged for something else. There is no substitute for faith. Without faith no social intercourse is possible, and personal beings stand apart, isolated, hostile, suspicious, and all commerce of the affections is arrested. Not because God would impose a needless condition of salvation, but because He desires to make no condition, to withhold no good thing, because to Him it is more blessed to give than to receive, or to retain, He freely offers all that man can need. Because He wills to give liberally, and without upbraiding, He seeks to awaken our receptive trust. It is therefore "of faith that it may be according to grace."[1]

3. Faith is our response to the grace of God in Christ. The glory of the gospel of Jesus Christ is that it has revealed the generous, undeserved love of God to us. The essence of it is that He does not treat us as we have dealt with Him. His love has survived our rebellion and evil ways. "He hath not dealt with us after our sins; nor rewarded us according to our iniquities." However ill men treat Him, He treats them kindly and well; causing His sun to rise on the evil and the good, and sending rain on the just and the unjust; and more than this, sounding the call of pardon and reconciliation to the whole world in spite of its long-continued iniquities and bitter alienation. This is the

[1] T. V. Tymms, *The Christian Idea of Atonement*, 379.

essence of the gospel of Jesus Christ. And it seems to suggest that God in His relation to us acts with a benevolence and grace which work irrespective of our attitude towards Him.

This is all divinely true. None the less is the issue of the gospel, its power to bless and enrich us, dependent on our response to it. The offer is free, "we are saved by grace." But it is "through faith," and faith on man's side corresponds to grace on God's side—it is the response of the soul to the appeal of love. According to our faith, so shall it be unto us. If we have no faith, there is no grace available for us, however freely and gladly it may be offered; if we have little faith, we shall have little grace; if we have great faith, we shall have large and royal grace to help, to bless and save us. If we do much for Christ, He can do much for us; if we give ourselves freely and fully to Him, He can give Himself freely and fully to us.

¶ The virtue of Faith lies in the virtue of its Object. That Object, in this matter of Justification, so the Scriptures assure us abundantly and with the utmost clearness, is our Lord Jesus Christ Himself, who died for us and rose again. Here the simplest reliance, so it be sincere, is our point of contact with infinite resources. When the vast dam of the Nile was completed, with all its giant sluices, there needed but the touch of a finger on an electric button to swing majestically open the gates of the barrier and so to let through the Nile in all its mass and might. There was the simplest possible contact. But it was contact with forces and appliances adequate to control or liberate at pleasure the great river. So Faith, in reliance of the soul, the soul perhaps of the child, perhaps of the peasant, perhaps of the outcast, is only a reliant look, a reliant touch. But it sets up contact with JESUS CHRIST, in all His greatness, in His grace, merit, saving power, eternal love.[1]

¶ We must not be blind to the depth and richness of Paul's conception of faith. It is not the mere recognition that a certain set of historical facts is true, that Jesus of Nazareth died on the Cross and rose again from the dead. Nor is it the acceptance of a theological interpretation of these facts, that they released energies for the salvation of mankind. This coldly intellectual way of regarding them is alien altogether from the evangelical idea of faith. There is intended by it rather a temper and attitude of the soul. It implies as its necessary condition the

[1] H. C. G. Moule, in *The Fundamentals*, ii. 115.

sinner's consciousness of his condition, of his guilt and moral helplessness, and the impossibility of releasing himself from either one or the other. In this state of condemnation and impotence, finding in himself and in the world about him no relief for his condition, he is prepared to respond to the message of salvation in Christ. Casting away all thought of his own merit as commending him to God, for he feels himself to be a sinner in God's sight, renouncing all efforts at self-reformation as superficial and ineffective, his whole being turns with a glad sense of confidence to Him that is mighty to save, with the deep gratitude of one who has been saved from despair. Cutting himself loose from all the supports on which he has hitherto rested, he takes the supreme risk of faith and launches himself into the void, but he makes his venture in the confidence that he will not be left to his fate, but be caught and held fast by the everlasting arms. And this faith, in which self-surrender, love, gratitude, and implicit trust are mingled, effects the mystical union between the soul and its Saviour. The intellectual element is presupposed in it, the believer must recognize the existence of God, his own sin, and God's reaction against it, his inability to attain the moral ideal which God demands from him, the truth of the great redemptive facts proclaimed in the Gospel. This is the indispensable foundation of faith. But faith is something which embraces also the emotions and the will, it is the movement of the whole personality, the soul's flight for refuge to Christ. Its inmost mystery, indeed, baffles analysis; how it effects the mystical union is God's secret and not ours. But its mystical effect must be closely allied to its emotional element.[1]

IV.

THE BLESSINGS.

Justification by Faith involves Salvation, Righteousness, and Eternal Life. Being justified implies being saved from sin and from the wrath of God, it signifies being endowed with the opportunity and ability to become righteous, and it involves the enjoyment of an eternal life consequent on righteousness being attained. It appears to be a true, and perhaps a sufficient, account of the meaning of justification, as the term is used by St. Paul, to say that it is the being accounted righteous and

[1] A. S. Peake. *Christianity: Its Nature and Its Truth.* 292.

destined to eternal life by reason of being saved from sin and put in the way of becoming actually and truly righteous. Or, since eternal life is through righteousness, and salvation from sin is a necessary antecedent to the becoming righteous, justification may be defined more briefly as the being accounted righteous by reason of being endowed with a gift of righteousness.

¶ Justification is no mere fiat of God, no mere arbitrary pronouncement. God reckons the true perfection of life as already ours, because in identifying ourselves with Christ we have entered upon the way of its increasing realization. In the union of the soul with Christ and the consequent participation of His life, there is the pledge and promise of the completion in the believer's life of the righteousness which is already by anticipation accorded to him. Man is in a sense already what he aspires to be. What we believe in we are. There must be something in us of that moral beauty which we admire in another, and to declare that we believe in Christ and accept Him as the ideal of our faith and endeavour is already to have something of the Christlike in our soul. The implanted seed contains within it the potency of the completed life. There is an element of Pauline truth in Lowell's poem:

> The thing we long for, that we are
> ˙ For one transcendent moment,
> Before the Present poor and bare
> Can make its sneering comment.
>
> . . . .
>
> To let the new life in, we know,
> Desire must ope the portal;
> Perhaps the longing to be so
> Helps make the soul immortal.[1]

1. *Salvation.* — How does justification involve salvation? Because it means not only the acquittal of the sinner but also his restoration to God's favour. For justification is not merely forgiveness. It differs from forgiveness by transcending it. It does not contradict it; it includes it, being a kindred but greater thing. Forgiveness remits penalty; it allows the offender to depart; at least it need imply no more than this. God's acceptance of sinful man does this—and very much more. It welcomes him to draw near, it beckons him in, it casts arms of love around him, it bids him be at home. In Christ's great parable the

[1] A. B. D. Alexander, *The Ethics of St. Paul*, 149.

prodigal was indeed forgiven the gross sin of his vicious and heartless prodigality. But that was not all. He might have been forgiven, and yet kept at a certain distance from his father, at least for a while. But not so; he was accepted. He was met with an embrace and led into a festival. He was bidden to be much more at home than ever.

We do indeed as sinners most urgently need forgiveness, the remission of our sins, the putting away of the holy vengeance of God upon our rebellion. But we need more. We need the voice which says, not merely, you may go; you are let off your penalty; but, you may come; you are welcomed into My presence and fellowship.

¶ Wesley spent a couple of days at Oxford, where he preached at the Castle on Sunday to a numerous and serious congregation. Then he returned to London. Ten days later he saw his mother once more at Salisbury. He was just ready to start for Tiverton to visit his eldest brother, when he received a message that Charles was dying at Oxford. He set out without delay, but found, to his great relief, that the danger was past. By this means he renewed his intercourse with Böhler, who was still at Oxford, and had been at Charles Wesley's side in his illness. "By him," he says "(in the hand of the great God), I was, on Sunday, the 5th" (March, 1738), "clearly convinced of unbelief, of the want of that faith whereby alone we are saved." Wesley immediately concluded that he was unfit to preach. He consulted Böhler, who urged him to go on. "But what can I preach?" said Wesley. "Preach faith *till* you have it," said his friend; "and then, *because* you have it, you *will* preach faith." This sound advice Wesley followed. It is interesting to know that the first person to whom he offered salvation by faith was a prisoner who lay under sentence of death at the Castle. Here, in the place to which his friend Morgan had introduced him more than seven years before, he began his work as a preacher of the righteousness of faith. The incident is the more remarkable because Böhler had many times asked Wesley to speak to this man, but he had refused because he was a zealous assertor of the impossibility of a death-bed repentance. Wesley's prejudices were yielding at last.[1]

2. *Righteousness.*—When a man is justified he is accounted righteous. "Abraham believed God, and it was accounted to him for righteousness." Now righteousness does not mean one thing

[1] J. Telford, *The Life of John Wesley*, 96.

in the Old Testament and another in the New. Righteousness is nothing less than conformity to the law of holiest manhood, which is the law of God; and hence, whenever and wherever achieved, it is one righteousness, just as God is one and manhood one. Its requirements are as great for Christian as for Jew, nay, greater, because its standard is more completely and searchingly defined. Among the earliest declarations of Christ's ministry was the solemn word, "Till heaven and earth pass, one jot or one tittle shall in no wise pass from the law, till all be fulfilled." Then He took up the old legislation point by point, and showed how much more inward and genuine obedience must thenceforth be than ever before.

When St. Paul contrasts the righteousness which is of the law and the righteousness which is of faith, he designates not two different righteousnesses, but two different means of attaining the same righteousness. His sole purpose is to show how faith accomplishes "what the law could not do, in that it was weak through the flesh."

Righteousness is called the righteousness of God. For it belongs to the believer yet is not his personal righteousness. It is a thing revealed, to which a man submits. It also belongs to God, yet is not His personal righteousness. It is a "gift" from God to men. It is Divine credit for being righteous bestowed on a man when he believes in, or trusts, God. God accounts one who believes in His grace righteous; He reckons his faith for righteousness.

(1) The righteousness which is by faith is the righteousness of a new relationship to God. The relationship of man to God by nature is one of alienation which passes into enmity. "The carnal mind is enmity against God." But when, each one in his own way, we come to see God in His truth and goodness and mercy, we change our minds toward Him. We stand in a new relationship to Him, a relationship of trust to the Maker of our bodies and the Father of our spirits. Our faith may be no more than a grain of mustard seed, but it is potent to alter our relationship, and to reshape our lives. Now, next to being loved, to be trusted is the most satisfying attitude that one spirit can take up toward another. It brings us into a relationship which quenches all enmity and alienation.

¶ A child may have been wilful and petulant until its mother's anger has been roused, but when the little arms are clasped in a sobbing confidence round the mother's neck, the trust confessed in the clinging pressure banishes all alienation. The man who has erred in his word or deed, and wronged us to our wounding, comes to us trusting in our magnanimity and kindness, and his trust brings him at once into a new relationship. In a similar manner, when a human soul, hitherto cherishing base thoughts of God and rebellious in will against His demands, turns to trust in God, he enters into a new relationship. In that new relationship he is forgiven. His sins are not imputed to him, and his faith is counted to him as righteousness.[1]

(2) The righteousness which is by faith is a righteousness of a new principle of life. In the moment in which a man trusts in God and takes up a new relationship to Him he is born again. In that new birth he is endued with a new principle and energy of life. The germ of the holy character is implanted in his soul. But it is only the promise and the potency of righteousness. It is the dream of an attainment, a devotion to something afar, the will and purpose of a strength and beauty yet to be. Yet that principle within him determines what he is. Not his emotions, not the expression of his convictions, not the grace of his prayers, and not even the tenor of his commonplace day, but this inward and secret passion of his will marks the man's true quality. Not only has he been forgiven and accepted, but God has wrought in him the root and rudiment of righteousness, and he stands before God's all-seeing eye in a righteousness imputed to him in his act of faith.

¶ The gardener plants an acorn in the loam, and soon the green shoot appears. He names that little, tender, almost formless green stem an oak. It bears no resemblance to the oak in the meadow, with its gnarled and knotted trunk, its stubborn arms, and its spread of branch and leaf. But to that frail, little, upspringing thing the gardener imputes the perfection it will one day attain. A painter takes his brush and draws upon the canvas a few initial strokes in an hour of clear conception and fresh inspiration. There may be no more than a rough and hasty sketch of what will yet be a finished masterpiece. The visitor to the studio may be struck more by the crudeness of the colouring and the startling contrast of the light and shade. But to the painter

[1] W. M. Clow, *The Evangel of the Strait Gate*, 143.

JUSTIFICATION BY FAITH

it is a picture, with a name, and when he has spent his thought and time upon it the face will stand out in its beauty. He imputes a perfection it does not yet possess. So the human spirit, at present compassed about with infirmity, whose hours are strangely mingled with effort and aspiration, lapse and indulgence, flushings of joy and tears of remorse, may seem to have no claim to be counted as righteous. But he has believed in God. He has yielded himself to the will and the power of God. The Divine One who knows the hour of self-surrender, and marks the true bent of the soul, accords to him a righteousness not yet achieved —a righteousness which is of faith. The cry of penitence, the craving of the heart for holiness, the girding of the loins to walk in the way of a stricter truth and purity, the throb of a true devotion to Christ, all are yet imperfect, but they are the promise and potency of a perfection yet to be, and the principle behind them is counted by God as righteousness.

> All instincts immature,
> All purposes unsure,
> . . . . .
> All I could never be,
> All, men ignored in me,
> This, I was worth to God, whose wheel the pitcher shaped.[1]

(3) *The righteousness which is by faith is the acceptance of the righteousness of Christ, in a faith which makes us one with Him.* There comes a moment when not only the things we have done in the flesh, the foul procession of thoughts within the soul, the whirl and dance of feeling which stir the blood in our veins, but even our generous deeds, gentle moods, kindly impulses, yes, and even our sob of penitence and our hour of far-visioned faith, are seen to be all flawed and faulty in God's sight. There comes an hour when we are too conscious that, were God's great light to be cast upon our souls and our lives, men would hide their faces from us ashamed. In that hour a man cannot trust in the new relationship, or the new principle of life. He comes to see his sin as Christ saw it. He shares, in his measure, in Christ's grief and burden for it. He consents to Christ's sacrifice as the means of his reconciliation and the source of his forgiveness. In an act of faith he identifies himself with Christ, and becomes one of that great company, and a member of that body, of which Christ

[1] W. M. Clow, *The Evangel of the Strait Gate*, 145.

is the Head. He believes not only in the marvel but in the miracle of forgiveness, and he rises to know himself not only forgiven but redeemed, and to stand for ever within the righteousness of Christ.

3. *Eternal life.*—Eternal life is in Christ Jesus. To have the righteousness of Christ is to have the life that is eternal. Eternal life may be said to be the Johannine phrase that is equivalent to the Pauline justification by faith. And so the faith which is the channel of justifying grace is also the assurance of a life that is to come.

There is nothing in man, no gift of genius, no force of will so marvellous as this faith in God and the Life Eternal which Christ inspires. When we think what men and women of common clay like ourselves have done and suffered for the sake of a God they have never seen and a heaven beyond the clouds—how they have patiently suffered the loss of all things, and have mounted the fiery pile with joy, clasping their faith to their hearts, as a king the crown which is his glory, or a miser the gold which is his treasure—this surely is the most marvellous spectacle earth has to show. We do not half feel the wonderfulness of it. We are conscious chiefly of the flaws and imperfections of our faith. We feel how weak and struggling and ineffective it is. We do not see the glory, or feel the grandeur of it. But one day we shall. What looks mean and meagre under the grey skies of earth will shine out in its proper splendour in the sunshine of Christ's manifested presence. To have such faith in God, in the eternal life of righteousness and love, is the highest of which the human soul is capable. It is the triumph of the Divine in man. Christ Himself marvels at it.

> The winds that o'er my ocean run,
> Reach through all worlds beyond the sun;
> Through life and death, thro' faith, through time,
> Grand breaths of God, they sweep sublime.
>
> Eternal trades, they can not veer,
> And blowing teach us how to steer,
> And well for him whose joy, whose care
> Is but to keep before them fair.

O thou, God's mariner, heart of mine!
Spread canvas to the airs divine;
Spread sail and let thy fortune be
Forgotten in thy destiny.[1]

[1] D. A. Wasson.

XVII.

Sanctification by Faith.

LITERATURE.

Abbott, L., *The Christian Ministry* (1905).
Alexander, A. B. D., *The Ethics of St. Paul* (1910).
Beet, J. A., *The New Life in Christ* (1895).
  „   „ *Holiness Symbolic and Real* (1910).
Bicknell, E. J., *A Theological Introduction to the Thirty-nine Articles* (1919).
Brown, W. A., *Christian Theology in Outline* (1907).
Bruce, A. B., *St. Paul's Conception of Christianity* (1894).
Denney, J., *The Christian Doctrine of Reconciliation* (1917).
Ferries, G., *The Growth of Christian Faith* (1905).
Fletcher, M. S., *The Psychology of the New Testament* (1912).
Forsyth, P. T., *Christian Perfection* (1899).
  „   „ *The Principle of Authority.*
Gore, C., *St. Paul's Epistle to the Romans*, i. (1899).
Griffiths, W., *Onward and Upward.*
Harris, H., *Short Sermons* (1886).
Hughes, H. M., *The Theology of Experience* (1915).
Marshall, Walter, *The Gospel Mystery of Sanctification.*
Moule, H. C. G., *Faith* (1909).
Mozley, J. K., *Ritschlianism* (1909).
Sidgwick, A., *School Homilies*, i. (1915).
Smellie, A., *Lift Up Your Heart* (1915).
Stevens, G. B., *The Pauline Theology* (1892).
Strong, A. H., *Systematic Theology*, iii. (1909).
Woods, E. S., "*On Service.*"
Expository Times, xiv. (1902–03) 490 (J. M. Hodgson).

SANCTIFICATION BY FAITH.

WHILE specially associated in Christian thought with justification, that initial act of consecration to God with which the Christian life in its higher forms commonly begins, faith is by no means confined to it. On the contrary, it abides as a permanent element in the religious life. It is the instrument not only of justification, but of sanctification as well. It is the presupposition of all the higher religious virtues, and enters so indissolubly into the making of the Christian life that the words of the apostle are literally true: "Whatsoever is not of faith is sin."

Faith is not the only means of sanctification. The Cross of Christ sanctifies, the Holy Spirit sanctifies, prayer sanctifies. But that faith also is an instrument of sanctification there is no doubt. "According to your faith be it unto you," Jesus used to say to the sick and impotent folk who sought His healing when He was on earth. The exalted Christ had a similar message for Saul the persecutor, when He changed him into Paul the apostle. "I send thee unto the Gentiles," He told His new-found bondman and freeman, "that they may receive an inheritance among them that are sanctified by faith in me." And in the last word of Peter which the Book of Acts records, that spoken to the Jerusalem Council, we listen to the same note. God, Peter declared, "made no distinction" between us Jews and those strangers and foreigners who had been drawn to Him from heathendom, "purifying" or "cleansing their hearts by faith," just as He did and does our own. According to our faith is our spiritual health. We are sanctified by faith in Christ. God cleanses and purifies the heart by faith. The teaching of the New Testament seems consistent and clear.

¶ There is an old book that rings with the music to which

some of us are never tired of hearkening—the book which Walter Marshall wrote more than two hundred years ago, and which he called *The Gospel Mystery of Sanctification*. Ebenezer and Ralph Erskine, and that redoubtable swordsman Adam Gib, recommended it, in the century after its publication, to Scottish saints; and so the most cautious and conservative theologian among us need not look askance at its doctrine. The book sprang, as the best books do, out of a personal experience. Walter Marshall was a Presbyterian minister in England in the times of the Commonwealth and the Restoration. But for many years he was exercised with troubled thoughts, and by his own mortifying efforts he sought for peace of conscience. The peace did not come; his trials still increased. Whereupon he consulted others, and particularly Mr. Baxter, whose writings had been his daily counsellors; and Richard Baxter, as wise as he was humble, told him that these writings were harming instead of helping him, for he was taking them too legally. Afterwards, still hungering after the hidden treasure, he sought out "an eminent divine, Dr. T. G.," as the prefatory note to *The Gospel Mystery* designates him—that is, Dr. Thomas Goodwin. He gave him an account of the state of his soul. He went minutely over the sins which lay on him like a weighty burden. But Goodwin replied that he had forgotten to mention the greatest sin of all, that of unbelief, in not believing on the Lord Jesus Christ both for the remission of his guilt and for the sanctifying of his nature. Goodwin was a true spiritual surgeon that day; he diagnosed the malady, and his scalpel laid bare the mischief; his word was a word in season. Walter Marshall saw at last the truth which Francis Quarles preaches, and which not a few Christians are culpably slow to learn, that

> It is an error ev'n as foul to call
> Our sins too great for pardon as too small.

He set himself to the studying of Christ as he had not studied Him before; and he attained to eminent holiness, much peace of conscience, and joy in the Holy Ghost. When King Charles came home, they put him, the quaint Preface says, "under the Bartholomew Bushel, with near two thousand more lights, whose illuminations made the land a Goshen." But the Bartholomew Bushel distressed him exceedingly little; for he had received his baptism of assurance and strength; and out of his own history he spun for you and me his golden book. What is the Gospel Mystery of Sanctification? It is, Walter Marshall answers, the simplicity and the continuance of a faith which is always waiting on Christ, and taking from Christ, and rejoicing in Christ.[1]

¶ The work which the Lord had assigned her [Madame Guyon] was wholly different from what she had anticipated. God often works thus. Thus, at the foot of the Alps, when she thought her great business was to make ointments, and cut linen, and bind up wounds, and tend the sick, and teach poor children the alphabet and the catechism (important vocations to those whom Providence calls to them), she uttered a word from her burdened heart, in her *simplicity* without knowing or thinking how widely it would affect the interests of humanity, or through how many distant ages it would be re-echoed. And that word was, Sanctification by Faith. Both the thing and the manner of the thing struck those who heard her with astonishment. Sanctification itself was repugnant; and sanctification by *faith* inexplicable. In the Protestant Church, it would have been hardly tolerable; but in the Roman Catholic Church, which is characterized by ceremonial observances, the toleration of a sentiment which ascribes the highest results of inward experience *to faith alone*, was impossible. So that, instead of being regarded as an humble and devout Catholic, as she supposed herself to be, she found herself suddenly denounced as a heretic. But the Word was in her heart, formed there by infinite wisdom; and in obedience to that deep and sanctified conviction which constitutes the soul's inward voice, she uttered it; uttered it *now*, and uttered it *always*, "though bonds and imprisonments awaited her."[2]

I.

Faith Justifying and Sanctifying.

From the forensic aspect of justification, as pardon in harmony with law, we pass now to its ethical outcome in righteousness of life. The former predominates in Paul's Epistles, but the latter is not omitted. Faith not only puts man right with God through the appropriation of the saving benefits of Christ's death, but it brings him into vital relation with God, whereby he actually attains inward and outward conformity to the moral law. Faith works by love (Gal. v. 6), and self-surrendering faith is the condition of the Holy Spirit's indwelling whereby alone "the

---

[1] A. Smellie, *Lift Up Your Heart*, 73.
[2] T. C. Upham, *The Life of Madame Guyon*, 155.

requirements of the law are fulfilled" in those "who walk not after the flesh, but after the Spirit" (Rom. viii. 4).

1. The first justification or acceptance is therefore a preliminary step: it is acceptance for admission into the Divine household, or city of God, or life in Christ. It is a means to an end, and that end is the fellowship of Christ and continually developing assimilation to Him.

The close connexion between these two elements of experience is shown by the ease with which Paul transmutes the objective facts which were the basis of his assurance of pardon into symbols of the process of moral renewal through which he had passed. "If we have become united with him by the likeness of his death, we shall be also by the likeness of his resurrection; knowing this, that our old man was crucified with him, that the body of sin might be done away, that so we should no longer be in bondage to sin; for he that hath died is justified from sin." The objective facts both produce and typify the inward process. The act of faith, which apprehends God's grace in Christ, involves so complete an acceptance of Him that we share His crucifixion, and burial, and resurrection. Our old self is crucified and buried with Him, and we rise with Him to newness of life. In other words, the consciousness of acceptance with God and that of moral renewal are the crown of the same venture of faith and of the same operation of the Divine grace.

2. Does this mean, then, that justification and sanctification are processes following the one on the other, of which the former is over before the latter begins? Such a statement must be repudiated so far as its latter clause is concerned. You cannot thus logically sever a vital process. They are two parts of one vital process; and the man who is not *on the way* to being made like Christ (however far off it he may be at the moment) is by that very fact shown to be not in a state of justification or acceptance with God. The two experiences must necessarily be treated by theology in order, and sometimes they are regarded as successive stages; but in reality they are synchronous, whether gradual or instantaneous. The doctrine of Justification by Faith is thus the expression, not of a legal fiction, but of a reality of experience.

3. No doubt the faith that justifies precedes the faith that sanctifies. The religion of the Bible is the religion of a sinner. The book comes to man first of all as *such*. Its *immediate* object is not the regulation of conduct, the formation of character, the production of practical excellence, and so on. This, indeed, is its grand and ultimate aim, the end which it incessantly pursues, and without accomplishing which it accomplishes nothing; but its first, immediate, direct object, is not this. *That* is the pardon of the guilty, their reconciliation to God; then comes the regulation of external behaviour, the promotion of that holiness "which becometh saints."

The having our "heart set at liberty" is a preliminary to "running the way of God's commandments." Yet even so we must recognize that Paul never exactly uses this language. When he describes the stages of God's dealings with the soul he passes from justification to glorification, or (final) deliverance from sin and wrath. Or, on one occasion, he mentions sanctification before justification. This is in part accounted for by the fact that the word translated "sanctify" or "sanctification" means rather "consecrate" (as to priesthood) or "consecration." And though this consecration involves "sanctity" (in our sense) because of the character of God to whom we are dedicated, yet it may precede it; and we are in fact consecrated and hallowed at the moment when we are accepted into the "priestly body" and anointed with the Divine unction. This exact meaning of the term "sanctification" in part accounts for Paul's not speaking of sanctification and justification as successive stages of the spiritual life. When he is speaking about justification he is answering the question, What is the attitude of the human soul towards God which sets God free, so to speak, to accept it and work upon it? And the answer is, The attitude of faith. When he speaks of sanctification, or rather consecration, he is answering the implied question, How is the individual to be thought of when he has been admitted to baptism into the Christian community? And the answer is, He is to be thought of as consecrated, or as sharing the life of a consecrated people.

¶ In the Bible, Christianity is given us as a whole; but men are apt to take confined and partial views of it. Faith is connected in Scripture, both with the pardon of sin and with the deliverance from the power of sin; or, in other words, with justification and sanctification, according to common language. In its connexion with justification, it is opposed to merit, and desert, and work of every description; "It was by faith that it might be by grace, or gratuitous, or for nothing," Rom. iv. 16. Some exclusively take this view, which in itself is correct, but which does not embrace the *whole* truth. Faith, as connected with sanctification, "purifieth the heart," "worketh by love," and "overcometh the world," and produces every thing which is excellent and holy, as may be seen in that bright roll which is given in Heb. xi. Some again are so engrossed with this view of the subject, that they lose sight of the former. This is a fruitful source of error.[1]

II.

NEW LIFE.

There is a remarkable consensus among apostolic writers in looking upon the Christian life as a new state of being.

1. So new is it that they speak of it unhesitatingly as resulting from a new creation or new birth. In evidence of this the following passages may be quoted. "Jesus answered and said unto him, Verily, verily, I say unto thee, Except a man be born anew, he cannot see the kingdom of God. . . . Except a man be born of water and the Spirit, he cannot enter into the kingdom of God" (John iii. 3, 5). "As many as received him, to them gave he the right to become children of God, even to them that believe on his name: which were born, not of blood, nor of the will of the flesh, nor of the will of man, but of God" (John i. 12, 13). "Lie not one to another; seeing that ye have put off the old man with his doings, and have put on the new man, which is being renewed unto knowledge after the image of him that created him" (Col. iii. 9, 10). "Of his own will he brought us forth by the word of truth, that we should be a kind of firstfruits of his creatures" (Jas. i. 18). "Seeing ye have purified your souls in your obedience to the truth unto unfeigned love of the brethren, love one another from the heart fervently: having been begotten again,

SANCTIFICATION BY FAITH

not of corruptible seed, but of incorruptible, through the word of God, which liveth and abideth" (1 Pet. i. 22, 23).

2. It has often been said that Christianity is summed up in the two commands—" Thou shalt love the Lord thy God with all thy heart, and with all thy soul, and with all thy mind," and " Thou shalt love thy neighbour as thyself." In fact, this is not Christianity at all; this is Christ's summary of Judaism, His summary of the law which defines man's obligation to God. But this definition of man's obligation to God is not distinctively Christian; it is hardly even distinctively Jewish. Christianity is the statement of what God has done and is doing for man; and what it affirms God has done and is doing for man is this: God has come into life and filled one human life full of Himself that He may fill all human lives full of Himself, and in doing this He has brought the world deliverance from its sins, and transformed its sorrows into sources of a joy deeper than any sorrowless joy.

¶ When Ernest Wilberforce was appointed to the See of Newcastle he received a letter from Wilkinson of St. Peter's, Eaton Square, who was himself to be raised to the Episcopate before many months had elapsed: "May God bless you, my dear Ernest, in this great work. Mrs. Wilberforce remembers what I have more than once said to her as to the gifts which God has given you. You remember a walk we once had in the Park when we talked of faith in its wider sense as expressing the power which is given to man of opening his heart to receive what God has already given us in Christ Jesus our Lord. Dear Ernest, open wide your heart and receive the fulness of the Power of the Holy Ghost, and let that Divine Spirit bring out for the use of the Church all the gifts which are only waiting for His touch to be developed. Believe that God has chosen you to be His instrument —to be the channel through which His life may flow out to your diocese. The more you feel your natural weakness so much the more do you dwell on the Divine Power which only requires for its manifestation the comprehension of our own nothingness and faith in the reality of His in-dwelling Presence.[1]

3. How is it that we can have such unbounded confidence in faith as the principle of this new life ? By what means does it make the new life in Christ a life of sanctity ? St. Paul gives an

---

[1] *Life of the Right Reverend Ernest Roland Wilberforce*, 98.

answer. There are two ways in which faith produces holiness of life—it brings the believer into fellowship with Christ, and it is energetic through love.

(1) *Fellowship.*—We know what we mean by communion or intercourse with our fellow-men. By the written word, by word of mouth, even by the silent touch or look, a man enters into relations with his fellow. The one mind acts and reacts upon the other; it gives and receives; it is influenced much or little: the whole personality may be changed by contact with another, whether for better or for worse.

Fellowship with Christ is not essentially different. However mystic and transcendental this fellowship may appear to some minds, it will not be denied that in proportion as it is realized in any Christian experience it must prove a powerful stimulus to Christlike living. No man can, like the apostle, think of himself as dying, rising, and ascending with Christ without being stirred up to strenuous effort after moral heroism. No man, be his temperament what it may, can understand and believe in the lovingkindness of God, as proclaimed in the gospel, without being put under constraint of conscience by his faith. The man who earnestly believes himself to be a son of God must needs try to be Godlike. Even if in spiritual character he be of the unimaginative, unpoetic, matter-of-fact type, he will feel his obligation none the less; it will appear to him a plain question of sincerity, common honesty, and practical consistency. In comparison with the mystic, he may have to plod on his way without aid of the eagle wings of a fervid religious imagination; nevertheless observe him, and you shall see him walk on persistently without fainting. He knows little of devotee raptures; Paul's way of thinking concerning co-dying and co-rising is too high for him. He does not presume to criticize it, or depreciate its characteristic utterances as the extravagant language of an inflated enthusiasm; he simply leaves it on one side and, renouncing all thought of flying, is content with the pedestrian rate of movement. But the steadiness of his advance approves him also to be a true son of faith.

There thus grows up a mystic union with Christ, an identification of the believer and his Redeemer, so that Christ's acts become his acts. There is a beautiful reciprocity and interchange of giving and receiving, love answering to love, and life to life. In

SANCTIFICATION BY FAITH

this self-forgetful surrender of the whole man to Christ, the old ego with its inner strife and trembling vanishes, and a new selfless personality, a new spiritual manhood, takes its place, of which we can give no other explanation than that which Paul offers us, as the secret of his own experience—" I live; and yet no longer I, but Christ liveth in me." "Faith in Christ" means "life in Christ." And this complete yielding of self and vital union with the Saviour, this dying and rising again, is at once man's supreme ideal and the source of all moral greatness.

¶ In all human history and experience have men ever discovered a more uplifting moral force than the companionship of Jesus Christ? Think of the transforming influence that He exerted, in the days of His earthly life, upon the characters of that little band of men and women who companied with Him among the hills of Galilee. Business men and tax-gatherers, fishermen and soldiers, women in their homes and women on the streets—all climbed to heights of which they had never dreamed, and this simply through the influence of this strange Man they had come to love. They may not have been able to analyse, perhaps hardly even realize, what had happened to them; all they knew was that *He* had come into their lives, and that that had made all the difference. And, after He had left the earth as a visible presence, this kind of thing went on happening. Indeed, the magic of His presence was even more potent than before. Those who needed Him, and longed for Him, found Him entirely available, even though not visible to their earthly eyes. And this discovery was always as sunlight flooding into darkened lives. Here is, indeed, the very heart and core of Christian experience; and from generation to generation it has never failed. Into lives wearied by failure, bruised by pain and sorrow, barren of hope, empty of meaning and purpose, *He comes*, when the door is open, and His coming always turns the scale. "Jesus Christ came into my cell last night," wrote Samuel Rutherford, in prison in Aberdeen, "and every stone of it glowed like a ruby." "Beauty for ashes, the oil of joy for mourning, the garment of praise for the spirit of heaviness"—these are some of Christ's exchanges. Is there a man or woman among us who does not need this transfiguring touch on character and circumstance? Is there one of us who can afford to do without the proffered friendship of Jesus Christ?[1]

(2) *Love.*—In Gal. v. 6 Paul speaks of faith "energizing

[1] E. S. Woods, "*On Service,*" 18.

through love." Now if faith be really an energetic principle, and if it do indeed work from love as its motive, then we may expect from its presence in the soul right conduct of the highest order. Out of the energy of faith will spring all sorts of right works, and those works will not be vitiated by base motives, as in religions of fear, in connexion with which superstitious dread of God proves itself not less mighty than faith, but mighty to malign effects, making men even give of the very fruit of their body for the sin of their soul. The only question therefore remaining is: Are the apostle's statements concerning faith true? is faith an energetic force? does it work from love as its motive?

There should be no hesitation in admitting the truth of both statements. That faith is an energetic principle all human experience attests. Faith, no matter what its object, ever shows itself mighty as a propeller to action. If a man believes a certain enterprise to be possible and worthy, his faith will stir him up to persistent effort for its achievement. The eleventh chapter of the Epistle to the Hebrews settles the question as to the might inherent in faith. In this might all faith shares, therefore the faith of Christians in God.

But why should the faith of Christians work by *love*? Why not by some other motive, say fear, which has been such a potent factor in the religious history of mankind? Is there any intrinsic necessary connexion between Christian faith and love? There is, and it is due to the Christian idea of God. *All turns on that.* The God of our faith is a God of *grace*. He is our Father in heaven, and we, however unworthy, are His children. Therefore our faith inevitably works by love. First and obviously by the love of gratitude for mercy received. For, whereas the question of a religion of fear is: "Wherewithal shall I come before the Lord that I may appease his wrath," faith speaks in this wise: "What shall I render unto the Lord for all his benefits?" But not through the love of gratitude alone; also through the love of adoration for the highest conceivable ethical ideal realized in the Divine nature. God is love, benignant, self-communicating, self-sacrificing. To believe in such a God is to make love, similar in spirit if limited in capacity, the law of life.

III.

GROWTH.

1. "The kingdom of heaven is like unto leaven, which a woman took, and hid in three measures of meal, till the whole was leavened." If the parable of the mustard seed bids us look upon the growth of faith, considered simply in itself, that of leaven bids us look upon it in its effect and influence upon what lies outside it. We know how leaven or barm works; place it in the middle of a lump of dough, and leave it, and very soon it begins to make the dough heave and swell; little by little it penetrates the whole of it and leavens the whole mass. And in just the same way faith acts upon the heart; it stirs it all up, and little by little it changes its whole nature. It never lies idle, from the first moment of its beginning to work, but keeps spreading, first in one direction, and then in another, and never leaves off till it has leavened the whole lump, and brought it all into the same nature with itself. It cannot rest whilst there is a single bad passion remaining in the heart. Wherever faith and sin meet, they meet as deadly enemies, one of which must subdue and drive out the other; and there can be no rest or peace in the heart till that is accomplished.

(1) Think first of what may be faith's possibilities in the mastery of evil, its negative achievements. Through the faith of Christ we are to overcome, it is said, the lust of the flesh, the lust of the eye, and the pride of life. We master carnal appetite; we master envy, jealousy, and resentment; we master pride, vanity, and ambition. Faith conquers in other directions also; we refrain from indulgence in fretfulness, anxiety, and care. In a word, those who are begotten of God sin not, writes John. The world, the devil, and the natural self are overcome. We enjoy marked freedom from the invasions of conscious iniquity.

(2) Faith's possibilities appear also on the positive side of spiritual life, to be seen in the graces with which the new nature is adorned. The beauties of holiness become increasingly visible in conduct and character. The love of God and the love of one's neighbour gain the mastery within, manifesting themselves as the ruling powers; we obey the first and second great commandments.

The patience and gentleness of the Lord Jesus show themselves in temper and behaviour. Being quickened by the Holy Spirit we tread in the steps of the Master. A growing measure of Christ-likeness gets to be the dominant feature in life. We are the pure in heart, and see God.

¶ Do not think that faith is something above and beyond you; there is none here that has not done a deed of faith as well as the noblest servant of God. Whenever you have resisted temptation to idleness, and done your work; whenever you have shrunk from a lie which would have made things more pleasant; whenever you have by prayer or struggle banished a mean or angry or impure thought; whenever you have forgiven an injury; whenever you have sided with the right against the wrong, you have shown Faith. There is none here who has not known what it is.[1]

(3) Besides the usual and quieter modes of growth, faith is not without its occasional and extraordinary forms of advancement, in which progress is made as with leaps and bounds. We read of such in the apostolic age, happening now and then; and the like occur still, happening now and then.

Was Stephen favoured with a glowing rapture just before his martyrdom? Fletcher of Madeley, on the eve of his departure, may be said to have had a similar transport; visited with such a disclosure of the Divine goodness as filled his soul with an overpowering ecstasy of delight. "God is love!" he exclaimed. "Shout! Shout aloud! Oh, it so fills me that I want a gust of praise to go to the ends of the earth!"

Was the hostile career of Saul of Tarsus suddenly closed by a manifestation from on high? So was that of Colonel Gardiner; the man's old and reprobate course instantly stopped by a vision from the unseen, and his new career of pious devotion soon entered on for the rest of his days. And the like has to be affirmed of Jacob Parsons; who, returning from his usual haunts of vice, retired to bed a drunken sot, but arose in the morning a changed character; after which, as one that knew him well could testify, "for thirty-five years he lived a perfectly blameless life, beloved by everybody." In explanation of this wondrous transformation of being, the man himself ever insisted that, during this the most memorable night of his life, the Lord Jesus had appeared to him;

[1] J. M. Wilson, *School Homilies*, i. 3.

SANCTIFICATION BY FAITH

and to his dying day he remained what may be called a miracle of Divine grace.

Again, was Paul caught up to the third heaven, there to hear unspeakable words which no man could utter? So was William Tennant, the American friend of George Whitefield. And most devoted was the active spiritual life which followed, the force of the rapture holding the good man for long as if in another world. And, as the little ones have a place in the ministries of Divine love, the incident may be told of the young girl, merriest of her circle, who, after a heavy fall on ice, was grieved beyond measure to learn, from the medical verdict on her case, that she was never to walk again. "Oh, that I could but die!" she exclaimed. But a vision of the night came to her relief. She dreamed of heaven and its happy tenants. Some of the celestials came to her. She even saw the Lord Jesus. And in her eyes tokens of lasting joy took the place of tears. "Mother," said she, "I am not going to fret, even though I shall not be able to run about any more. Oh! the King is so lovely, so lovely; and if He wants me to lie still for Him, why, I can do it." And the child kept her word. In spite of pain and weariness, the room in which the young invalid lay came to be the spot around which all the sunshine of the house seemed to gather.

(4) But these epochs and critical moments in the spiritual life just referred to will nearly always be found to stand related to something habitual which went before them as preparation. St. Paul's habit of prayer, for example, his formed instinct to turn to Christ under crushing need instead of letting the need merely paralyse him, led up in an organic order to the Divine answer which suddenly glorified his misery into victory. Our immediate business in the spiritual life is to bring our spirit to meet the Divine Spirit, however true it is that He all the while divideth "to every man severally as he will." Therefore let us form the habit of faith amidst "all the changing scenes of life," under the conditions of the common day as they come not to others but to us.

How shall we do so best? On the whole, in very simple ways. First of all, let us form the spiritual habit of "setting the Lord always before us." We can never too often remember, nor too simply, that the true power of true faith lies in its Object.

Therefore let us recollect the Object. Let us habitually say within the soul the creed of life: "I believe in God, in God in Christ, in the Christ of God."

> He lives, He loves, He knows;
> Nothing that thought can dim;
> He gives the very best to those
> Who leave the choice to Him.

It is possible so to think that truth, and so to confess it, if only to ourselves, that it shall grow out of an act into a habit, and become the attitude and not merely a motion of the soul. We may contribute to the process in many ways. We may foster it by fresh thought, with prayer, upon the vast ranges of reason that gather round the certainty; by recalling and treasuring up the innumerable testimonies to the fact of God borne to us by the experiences of the saints; by definite acts of devotion; by persistent companionship with the Bible; by use in spirit and in truth of the sacrament of the body and the blood of the Son of God.

2. Growth in holiness is not always steady and unwavering. The bright spring-time of faith, when all is as if bathed in sunlight, is not lasting in the experience of any person. The days of struggle, weariness, and comparative gloom soon recur. Not that faith has vanished, or that its benefits prove to be hollow; the faith is fixed, and the choice is made, and there is profound peace and lasting confidence as the effect. The course of life is established, not wavering: the feet are planted as on a rock. Yet there comes to be a sense of remaining want; the experience of exquisite and unmixed joy passes away; many questions are raised. There is a descent from the heights to the rude common world. There is an advance through conflict within and without, and as the result of faithfulness and patient waiting.

In the region of faith and personality this must always be so. Our material goods, the results of our civilization, we can lock up and pass on. We consolidate and transmit them. We transmit our improvements. But our spiritual goods we must daily regain, daily adjust, and daily fecundate. The certainty of yesterday will not do for to-day. It must be recertified to-day. Always we must go back to adjust our compass at the inexhaustible Cross.

SANCTIFICATION BY FAITH

We must return to our living authority for our obedience and reassurance. What we are so sure of is a positive Word, with features changeless and always recognizable for what it is; but it is also a living and waxing Word, as living for to-day as for yesterday and for ever, which, the more it changes, is the more the same. It is a Word, and not a scheme. It is a personal power, and not an intellectual palladium which we snatch up, throw on our shoulders, and carry out of the fire. And therefore it is that moral progress is so slow—because we cannot make a *thing* of it, and transmit it, as we do material gain. Each man has to verify for himself, and to acquire his legacy. He may accept gravitation, but he has to acquire sanctification, and win his soul.

¶ Faith is no mere charter for comfort. It has no *rentiers*. And the experience of salvation's ripening power is the only real way to continued certainty of its truth. Apologetic is not so valuable to convert the world as to confirm the Church which does convert, to give faith a foundation in the world's reality, and to unify its knowledge of the Son of God. The same Apostle of the first Epistle to the Corinthians, who insisted in the second chapter that faith did not come by the arguments of men, but by the power of the Spirit, goes on in the fifteenth chapter to confirm the Church's wavering faith in the resurrection of Christ by many infallible proofs.[1]

3. Is it possible to reach perfection by faith? Yes, if faith is never separate from perfection. Christianity is the perfect religion because it is the religion of perfection. It holds up a perfect ideal, it calls us incessantly to this ideal, and it calls *all* to this ideal. *Each* man is called, and each man is *always* called, to it. It is a religion that issues from the perfect One, and returns to His perfection. But it returns through a far country and a dread. It returns by way of redemption, so that the means of reaching this perfection for us sinners is not achievement but faith.

¶ There are two notions of perfection which are wrong, and a third which is right. The first idea is Pietist; the second is Popish; the third is Protestant, Apostolic, Christian.

(1) The Pietist idea pursues perfection as mere quietist sinlessness with a tendency to ecstasy. Its advocates are people sometimes of great grace and beauty; but it represents a one-sided, narrow, and negative spirituality. Its religion is largely emotional,

[1] P. T. Forsyth, *The Principle of Authority*, 37.

mystical, and introspective. Its adherents are apt to be the victims of visions and moods. They seek perfection in a state of sinlessness. It is a condition largely subjective, ascetic, anæmic, feminine. It prescribes an *arbitrary* withdrawal from the interests, pursuits, and passions of life. It is a cloistered virtue. It is *distrait*, not actual. There is an absence of true humility.

(2) The Popish idea of perfection has much in common with the Pietist. It is unworldly in the negative sense; it flees from the world, it does not master it. It is embodied in the monk and the nun. In the Roman system the monk is the ideal man, the nun the ideal woman. The whole Roman system rests on the double morality involved in this distinction. It is a religion by double entry. It teaches that only some are called to perfection, while for the majority the demands made are much more ordinary. Rome succeeds, like certain governments, by lowering the educational standard for the masses, by not being too hard on the natural man. But it canonizes a starved and non-natural man, on whom it is very exacting. It compounds for its laxity with its adherents by its severity with its devotees. There are *precepts*, it says, which all must obey, and there are *counsels* which are only for those few destined to perfection.

(3) These Pietist and Papist ideas of perfection are Catholic more than Evangelical, and thus are destroyed by the vital, free, final, sufficient, and perfect principle of Christian *faith*. The true perfection is the perfection which is of God in *faith*. The perfect obedience is not the obedience which is *associated with* faith or flows from it, but the obedience of the soul which *is* faith and which is the saving power and perfection for all. To be perfect is to be in Christ Jesus by faith. It is the right relation to God in Christ, not the complete achievement of Christian character.[1]

¶ The error at the root of all false ideas of perfection is this: it is rating our behaviour *before* God higher than our relation *to* God—putting conduct before faith, deeds before trust, work before worship. That is the root of all pharisaism, Romanism, paganism, and natural and worldly morality. It is the same tendency at bottom which puts the sacraments above simple faith, which neglects the worship of the sanctuary for work in a mission, or replaces the gospel by ethical culture.

Christian perfection is not a perfection of culture. It is not a thing of ideas or of finish. Such perfection is for the select few, for a natural elect. It is the perfection of the *élite*. This is so even with ethical culture. Its fine programme is yet no gospel. The soul's true and universal perfection is of faith. It is a perfec-

---

[1] P. T. Forsyth, *Christian Perfection*, 63.

tion of attitude rather than of achievement, of relation more than of realization, of trust more than of behaviour. Conduct may occupy three-fourths of our time, but it is not three-fourths of life. To say that it is, is to return from the qualitative to the quantitative way of thinking, from which culture was expected to deliver us. The greatest element in life is not what occupies most of its time, else sleep would stand high in the scale. Nor is it even what engrosses most of its thought, else money would be very high. It is what exerts intrinsically the most power over life. The two or three hours of worship and preaching weekly has perhaps been the greatest single influence on English life. Half an hour of prayer, morning or evening, every day, may be a greater element in shaping our course than all our conduct and all our thought; for it guides them both. And a touch or a blow which falls on the heart in a moment may affect the whole of life in a way that no amount of business or of design can do.[1]

[1] P. T. Forsyth, *Christian Perfection*, 76.

XVIII.

Personality in Faith.

LITERATURE.

Alexander, A. B. D., *The Ethics of St. Paul* (1910).
Bacon, L. W., *The Simplicity that is in Christ* (1892).
Benson, M., *The Venture of Rational Faith* (1908).
Chandler, A., *Faith and Experience* (1911).
Diggle, J. W., *Religious Doubt* (1895).
Dorner, I. A., *A System of Christian Doctrine*, i. (1880).
Douglas, L., *The Christian Doctrine of Health* (1916).
Fletcher, M. S., *The Psychology of the New Testament* (1912).
Forsyth, P. T., *Positive Preaching and Modern Mind* (1907).
Greenwell, D., *The Patience of Hope* (1894).
Hare, J. C., *The Victory of Faith* (1874).
Holdsworth, W. W., *The Life of Faith* (1911).
Holland, H. S., in *Lux Mundi* (1891).
Inge, W. R., *Faith* (1909).
Kilpatrick, T. B., *New Testament Evangelism* (1911).
Knight, G. H., *The Master's Questions to His Disciples* (1903).
Liddon, H. P., *Sermons on Some Words of St. Paul* (1898).
Morgan, H. T., *Port Royal* (1914).
Morrison, G. H., *The Afterglow of God* (1912).
Mozley, J. K., *Ritschlianism* (1909).
Patmore, C., *Principle in Art* (1913).
Porter, N., *Yale College Sermons* (1888).
Salmon, G., *The Reign of Law* (1873).
Selby, T. G., *The Holy Spirit and Christian Privilege* (1894).
Sheldon, H. C., *New Testament Theology* (1911).
Skrine, J. H., *Pastor Agnorum* (1903).
„   „   *What is Faith?* (1907).
Speer, R. E., *The Master of the Heart* (1908).
Thompson, S. P., *The Quest for Truth* (1915).
Tyrrell, G., *Hard Sayings* (1899).
„   „   *Oil and Wine* (1907).
Westcott, B. F., *The Historic Faith* (1883).
Expository Times, v. (1894) 261 (F. Relton).

Personality in Faith.

1. Faith is a personal relationship. It is between persons; it is not between things. Nor is it between persons and things. We can trust ourselves to a ladder, a bridge, or a boat; but it is evident that confidence in the uniformity of natural law and in the adaptability of any such inanimate instrument as a ladder or a boat to our purpose, is not faith but knowledge founded on inference, and certain in proportion to the validity of the reasoning on which it is founded.

We might say that we have faith in a fact or a truth, but only when we have some personal interest in it. It might be demonstrated to us that the planets are inhabited; but we should not say that we had faith in that fact until we could feel ourselves personally concerned in it. Many things may be affirmed or proved respecting the Divine nature (purely speculative theories), which, for the same reason, stand in no connexion with our faith. So, too, the truth that appeals to our faith must be about some other person. We may be convinced of abstract principles; but before they can elicit faith, they must be clothed in personality. We know that goodness exists, but we have faith in a good man. All can recognize the wisdom and love that pervade a beautiful universe; but faith must feel them as the wisdom and love of an ever-present God. Faith contemplates the truth it receives as a precious golden link, binding in some sort of fellowship the believer and some higher spiritual being. It is this peculiarly personal character of faith that gives to it that warm glow of emotion which we feel always belonging to it, which enables us to say that we believe with the heart, and which accounts for faith so essentially and profoundly governing the springs of character and of life.

¶ Faith which is the foundation of our spiritual life is before all things a personal relation between ourselves and Christ; it is an affection of our whole soul in regard to Him; and by no means a merely intellectual relation of our mind to a truth or a system of truths. It is true, in a sense, to say that the "object" of our faith is the Apostles' Creed, which is a bundle of propositions set forth, commented on, and considerably amplified by the Catholic Church. But faith in the teacher comes before faith in the teaching. We must believe in Christ and in the Church before we believe in what they teach us.[1]

2. There are very few passages in the Gospels where Christ uses the word "faith" or the word "believe" to describe an intellectual attitude toward certain truth. Christ constantly uses "faith" as a term that is not applicable to the relation of a man to an opinion, or of a man to a thing. He uses "faith" as a term that is applicable only to the relation of a person to a person. I believe not things that people tell me, I believe the people themselves, and my belief in them is faith. A little child, knowing very little of life, sits on the father's knee learning its first lessons of life, and believes what the father tells it. Now its belief in what the father says is not an act of faith, it is a fruit of faith. It is the relationship of confidence between the child and the father that makes the child believe anything the father says, and its belief in what the father tells is simply one of the accessory sequences of its faith in the father. Faith, with Jesus, is personal confidence in Himself. Faith, with Jesus, is the answer of a man's soul to His soul, the touch of a man's personality upon His personality, the surrender of a willing life to Jesus Christ as its Lord and its King.

That is the explanation of the healing of the man with the withered hand. There stands before the Christ a man with a withered arm. The limb hangs perfectly useless by his side. The nerves have ceased to act in the shrunken limb. Its muscles have atrophied; they no longer obey the command of the will. Movement has long since ceased to be possible. And Christ says, "Stretch forth thy hand." We should find it easy to excuse the man if he had burst into the laugh that declares an embittered spirit. "Stretch it out? Why, that is the very thing I have

[1] G. Tyrrell. *Oil and Wine.* 41.

PERSONALITY IN FAITH

wanted to do all these years. If I could do it at all, would I have waited for your instructions? You are making what I need as a gift the condition of your giving. You must give me first some other power, and then there will be some chance of my doing what you say. Don't tell me to do what I want you to give me the power of doing." Just for one moment the man stands looking into the quiet eyes of Him who knows both the innate powers and the sad paralysis of the human heart. Just for one moment; and then something stirred within the man. *It was faith in Christ.* Only that; but how much it was! The nerves that had long since been utterly irresponsive, dead fibres of a useless limb, began to tingle, as once again there flowed along them the almost forgotten vibration. The feeble muscles obeyed, grew full and round again, and slowly the long palsied limb was lifted up, and into all its dry and desolate channels there came once more the blessed tide of life. That power to use his arm, was it a product or a cause? Did he not obey the initial impulse? Did he not receive the fuller power? His power sprang from his faith; it issued in power. It was from faith; it was to faith. The final issue was life.

3. When we realize that the central feature of Christian discipleship is a relation to a Person, the word "faith" assumes that meaning of trust which is really the highest meaning it is capable of bearing. The first and last meaning of faith for the Christian must be trust in a Person. All other meanings of faith are subordinate to this one. The Christian ought to be able to think of his life entirely in the terms of trust. His conduct ought to be the practical issue of that trust, his theology ought to be the formulated statement of it, and as a member of Christ's Church he is, ideally speaking, one of the company of the faithful. Directly we allow abstract and artificial ideas to govern and determine our conceptions of Christian conduct, knowledge, and organization, we are bound to lower the meaning of faith and take away from it its rich personal significance.

The insistence of the New Testament on the feeling of trust as the root of true faith is clear enough in the original Greek, but is obscured in the English version through the lack of a simple verb to express in one word the phrase "to-have-faith-in." The translators of the New Testament have had to fall back upon the word "believe," which quite obscures the original meaning of the writers, and seems to lay the chief stress on the intellectual element in faith. But in numberless places where the phrase "believe-*in*" or "believe-*on*" occurs, it is not belief that is emphasized but, in reality, confidence or the feeling of trust. A reference to such passages will show that the object of this faith is a person, "God" or "Christ," so that the phrase "to-believe-in," or "to-believe-on," or "faith-toward" connotes trustful reliance upon the personal object mentioned. This appears in such representative passages as, "Believe-on the Lord Jesus Christ, and thou shalt be saved" (Acts xvi. 31); "Ye believe-in God, believe also in me" (John xiv. 1); "To him that worketh not, but believeth on him that justifieth the ungodly, his faith is reckoned for righteousness" (Rom. iv. 5).

¶ When the birds one day—in a beautiful story of Mr. Warde Fowler's—were discussing the nature and character of man, they were much puzzled by him. They thought him harsh and difficult to understand—all but one bird. At the end of the debate the swallow, spreading its wings to fly up into the boundless air, said, "We live by love and trust. As for understanding, that will come afterwards."[1]

¶ There is a very curious illustration of how completely the traditional theological idea of faith, now so rarely met with outside of the theological systems, had, almost to our own day, occupied the mind of the church to the exclusion of the New Testament idea. Never was an honest sermon so searched for heresies as Albert Barnes's sermon on "The Way of Salvation"; and yet of all its gainsayers, no one thought of objecting to the mistake that lay patent on the surface of it. The preacher, drawing out in ample argument his views of the method of the divine government, of atonement, and of regeneration, exclaims with impassioned earnestness, "Fly to this scheme!" "Commit your eternal interests to this plan!" Upon which Drs. Junkin and Breckenridge reply, with equal earnestness, "Don't do anything of the kind! Don't fly to Mr. Barnes's scheme—to the New England plan! Fly to our scheme—commit yourself to the Scotch system, or the Dutch!"—and never saw that the gospel "Way of Salvation" was, not to commit oneself to anybody's

[1] A. F. W. Ingram, *Banners of the Christian Faith*, 17.

"scheme," but to "commit oneself, in well-doing, to a faithful Creator."[1]

> What is the point where himself lays stress?
> Does the precept run "Believe in good,
> In justice, truth, now understood
> For the first time?"—or, "Believe in me,
> Who lived and died, yet essentially
> Am Lord of Life?" Whoever can take
> The same to his heart and for mere love's sake
> Conceive of the love,—that man obtains
> A new truth; no conviction gains
> Of an old one only, made intense
> By a fresh appeal to his faded sense.[2]

I.

THE PERSON OF CHRIST.

1. The object of Christian faith is Christ. Says Dorner, Faith can be called Christian faith in the full sense of the word only when, as regards its contents, it has united itself with the central fact of the Christian religion, with Jesus Christ as the personal unity of Divine life and human in whom the powers of redemption and perfection are included.

Faith in the Person of Christ is everywhere central in St. John's Gospel. Nathanael "believes" that Christ is the Son of God and King of Israel, through a sign: Christ promises him a more spiritual basis for a higher kind of belief. In John iii. 16-21, the evangelist's comment on the discourse with Nicodemus, we have faith opposed to rebellion or disloyalty, and thus we get a nearer determination of faith as including obedience and loyalty. In the discourse about the Bread of Life, in ch. vi. the persistent demands of the Jews for a sign are rebuked by our Lord: "Ye have seen me, and yet believe not"; and their question, "What must we *do*, that we may work the works of God?" is met by the remarkable declaration, "This is the work of God, that ye believe on him whom he hath sent." Personal devotion includes the

---

[1] L. W. Bacon, *The Simplicity that is in Christ*, 35.
[2] Browning, *Christmas-Eve*, xvii.

"works of God," and these works will never be done without it. In xii. 44 Christ says, "He that believeth on me, believeth not on me, but on him that sent me." Faith in Christ and faith in God are identical; but the former is the way to the latter.

What is true of the Fourth Gospel is true of every book of the New Testament. The apostles of the Lord have many and varied descriptions of religious experience; but they unite in teaching that the object of faith is Christ, and that the act of faith is personal commitment to Him. This experience, identical among all Christians, is the *differentia* of Christianity, not from the religion of the Old Testament, for it too was a religion of grace and of faith, but from legalism in one extreme, and Neo-Platonic mysticism in the other. Faith, in the New Testament sense, saves, not because *it* does anything, not because of the moral quality it possesses as an act of obedience, not even because it is directed to Christ, but because it is the condition under which Christ can do His saving work. In the act in which the soul, discerning the sufficiency of Christ, commits itself to Him, Christ lays hold of it, delivers it, brings it to God, and saves it by Divine redemptive energy. The indispensableness of faith is a commonplace of New Testament evangelism. The evangelist, like his Lord, is powerless where it is absent, and he rejoices with exceeding gladness when he notes its presence, often most conspicuous in the least likely quarters. While, therefore, the evangelist cannot create faith, he labours for it, prays for it, waits for it, as the triumphant issue of what God is doing through his instrumentality.

The New Testament knows no means of producing faith, save "preaching Christ." Preach Christ in the significance and value He has in the New Testament. Make Him manifest in the completeness of His salvation, the glory of His Person, and the supremacy of His Place and Power.

The New Testament prescribes nothing else than such a witness to the sufficiency and the sovereignty of Christ. But it does prescribe this. It knows no other means to the end. The modern Church cannot refuse the testing question: What is the outcome of its preaching, and its many activities? Is it faith in Christ? If not, it has failed of the vocation which has called it into being.

2. The great danger at present is to be content with faith in an ideal of our own conceiving, an ideal which is short of the Divine ideal of personality and love embodied in Jesus Christ. The great philosophers of the ancient world believed in love, truth, justice, and purity. They aspired to reach them and retain them, but they swept away from their embrace like phantom forms of cloud before a rushing wind. For, beautiful as their ideal was, it had no heart, no life, no human reality. No human love could be given to it. It was not bound up with social or domestic life. Faith in it produced little, for it was not a faith which worked by human love. Hence the life of the noblest heathen was a desperate effort to realize the mighty dreams and longings of the heart.

¶ I have often fancied with delight the rapture of Socrates, Plato, Zeno, when the truth and the light they had been toiling all their lives to find burst upon them in the revelation of the Word made flesh; but here, on earth, there ever came after their brightest vision an encroaching shadow of doubt in which aspiration sank down, trembling with cold and palsy-stricken. They had nothing absolutely perfect in human nature on which to build their faith, no ground for assurance of human attainment in a human life which had attained and triumphed. But *we* have, and it is shame and sorrow if we do not walk worthy of our knowledge.[1]

¶ "God so loved the world, that he gave his only-begotten Son, that whosoever believeth *in him* should not perish, but have everlasting life." The Evangelist, we see, has no difficulty in stripping off the non-essentials and reaching at once the heart of belief. To him the belief of the saints is the belief in a Divine Person—not even the belief in the fact of the Incarnation, but, beyond that, the personal trust which leads us to accept the Person of Jesus Christ as the Lord of our life and the Master of our soul. For such belief is not merely part of a dogmatic creed, it is part of life itself. It is only apprehended and interpreted by being lived. When Dr. Liddon was described as a man who "seemed as one who was often thinking of the gaze of Christ lighting on him, the hand of Christ pointing to some act of service, the voice of Christ prompting some witness to the Faith," we were brought very near to the thought of that belief in a living Person which is the belief of the saints.[2]

[1] Stopford A. Brooke, *Sermons*, 11.
[2] S. A. Alexander, *The Saints' Appeal*, 21.

3. We return again, therefore, to the fundamental fact that Christian faith is trust in Christ. If the object of faith were certain truths, the assent of the understanding would be enough. If the object of faith were unseen things, the confident persuasion of them would be sufficient. If the object of faith were promises of future good, the hope rising to certainty of the possession of these would be sufficient. But if the object be more than truths, more than unseen realities, more than promises; if the object be a living Person—then there follows inseparably this, that faith is not merely the assent of the understanding, that faith is not merely the persuasion of the reality of unseen things, that faith is not merely the confident expectation of future good; but that faith is the personal relation of him that believes to the living Person its object—the relation which is expressed not more clearly, but perhaps a little more forcibly to us, by substituting another word, and saying, faith is *trust*.

By laying hold of that simple principle, "Because Christ is the object of faith, therefore faith must be trust," we get bright and beautiful light upon the grandest truths of the gospel of God. If we will only take that as our explanation, we have not indeed defined faith by substituting the other word for it, but we have made it a little more clear to our apprehensions by using a non-theological word with which our daily acts teach us to connect an intelligible meaning. If we will only take that as our explanation, how simple, how grand, how familiar too it sounds—to *trust* Him! It is the very same kind of feeling, though different in degree, and glorified by the majesty and glory of its object, as that which we all know how to put forth in our relations with one another. We trust each other. That is faith. We have confidence in the love that has been around us, breathing benedictions and bringing blessings ever since we were little children. When the child looks up into the mother's face, the symbol to it of all protection; or into the father's eye, the symbol to it of all authority—that emotion by which the little one hangs upon the loving hand and trusts the loving heart that towers above it in order to bend over it and scatter good is the same as the one which, glorified and made Divine, rises strong and immortal in its power, when fixed and fastened on Christ, and saves the soul. The gospel rests upon a mystery, but the practical part of it is no mystery.

¶ When we come and preach to you, Trust in Christ and thou shalt be saved, we are not asking you to put into exercise some mysterious power. We are only asking you to give to Him that which you give to others, to transfer the old emotions, the blessed emotions, the exercise of which makes gladness in life here below, to transfer them to Him, and to rest safe in the Lord. Faith is trust. The living Person as its object rises before us there, in His majesty, in His power, in His gentleness; and He says, I shall be contented if thou wilt give to Me these emotions which thou dost fix now, to thy death and loss, on the creatures of a day. Faith is mighty, Divine, the gift of God; but oh! it is the exercise of a familiar habit, only fixed upon a Divine and eternal Person.[1]

II.

Our Own Personality.

1. Faith is *in* the Person of Christ: it is also *with* our own personality. Now the personality of man is usually regarded as made up of three elements—intellect, emotion, will. The faith of the New Testament can be readily analysed into these three elements. Sometimes the intellectual factor (as belief) operates most prominently, at other times the emotional (as a feeling of trust) bears sway, and yet again the moral side (as purposeful surrender) at times appears in the forefront. Faith is a complex state of mind in which all these elements are present within the personality. But one or other, according to the temperament and disposition of the subject, takes the lead and gives character to the whole state.

The mind of man is a unity, consisting of intellect, emotion, and will, blending inextricably and with incessant variations in every life. No one can keep these in perfect balance; every one is constitutionally biassed to one or other of them. The man of intellect will emphasize thought in his religion; his brother will find his religious nature most fully satisfied in emotion; while a third will realize himself in (it may be) social service. All three —intellect, emotion, will—are present in every act of the mind, but present in varying degrees, and in the practical work of the Church this variation is clearly exhibited.

[1] A. Maclaren, *Sermons Preached at Manchester*, i. 170.

(1) The man whose bias is intellectual inclines to lay emphasis on doctrine, which is the intellectual interpretation of religious experience. He would probably argue that there is nothing more likely to lead to a spiritual experience than a statement of spiritual truth. In every other sphere, systematic thinking is considered necessary; why should any one try to minimize its importance in the most vital of human interests? Sooner or later we must ask whether religion is a reality: "Is it true?" we demand; and the wisdom of a man will be seen in his laying hold of what the most experienced believe to be the truth. Our man of intellect therefore lays stress on creeds and confessions, suspects innovations in doctrine, and has no patience with heresy in Church or school. He will also show an aversion to stirring up feelings in the minds of the young, or attempting to test men's Christianity by their feelings and by the experiences through which they have passed.

(2) The man of emotions, on the other hand, contends that you may believe all the creeds and remain unchanged in heart and will. He calls the intellect cold, critical, hard, while he holds that what is needed to make a Christian is a tender, broken, and contrite heart. He is glad, therefore, to see that men are moved, and only when they are moved in a meeting does he say it was living, and obviously under the power of the Spirit. When a revival is manifesting itself in a community, the men of emotion work to gather crowds together; they expect excitement and approve of contrivances by which it is increased—the outbursts of singing, public confession of sin, sudden surprises by shouting or movement. There are plans by which a mass of men and women can be rendered pliable, or "suggestible," *i.e.* easily moved by an address. These men argue that the main difficulty in saving men from the power of sin is the first step, the surmounting of a barrier which custom, habit, or the fear of men's judgment has placed in their way, and that it is most easily surmounted in a great wave of emotion. After that has been done, it is easy to instruct the beginner in doctrine and to lead him to Christian work.

(3) The third type is the man of will, who believes that the deepest thing in life is neither an intellectual proposition concerning God nor an emotion, but an action. Intellect and emotion may have a work of their own, but the essential matter is that

we *do* something. He does not much care whether people think for themselves or not, if only they act aright. The thinking of most men is of little avail; let them obey, for it is by obedience that they come to the knowledge of doctrine. Accordingly men of this type come to insist on law and order. They point to the commandments, and regulations, and methodical ways of God.

2. Each of these elements of our personality finds its appropriate expression.

(1) The intellect is the instrument of knowledge. Faith, says Scripture, cometh by hearing. John the Baptist, we are told, came for a witness, that all men might believe through him. And St. Paul asks, "What then is Apollos? and what is Paul? Ministers through whom ye believed."

(2) Feeling expresses itself in affection between one person and another. The knowledge of "the Name of Christ," of the revelation, that is, of the Father and of the Son, involves and issues in love. "Beloved, let us love one another; for love is of God; and every one that loveth is begotten of God, and knoweth God. He that loveth not knoweth not God; for God is love."

(3) The will finds its expression in action. Love must, if it be real, prove itself in action. "Hereby know we love, because he laid down his life for us: and we ought to lay down our lives for the brethren. But whoso hath the world's goods, and beholdeth his brother in need, and shutteth up his compassion from him, how doth the love of God abide in him?" "If a man say, I love God, and hateth his brother, he is a liar: for he that loveth not his brother whom he hath seen, cannot love God whom he hath not seen."

¶ Christian faith is an operation of the whole nature, into which the practical powers enter as surely as the intellectual, and an article of the Christian creed is not really believed, until there is in the practical life of the believer a movement corresponding to the movement in the intelligent life. When he believes that the Father creates or the Spirit sanctifies, he not only thinks something—he feels something and he does something; there is an emotion that corresponds to the conception, and there is, so far as opportunity for it is present, an action too. If these fail, he has not believed the thing: his act is not faith.[1]

[1] J. H. Skrine, *Pastor Agnorum*, 239.

3. As each of these elements of our personality has its own expression, so one is not to be fostered or commended at the expense of another. There is nothing more futile than the attempt to offer to God something we do not possess—to whip up emotions when we were meant to reflect, to waste our life in public work when our gift is for seclusion, or to labour vainly at erudition when we have a genius for the reclaiming of our outcast fellow-men.

The charity of Christian men is widening, for they see that souls may be redeemed in many ways, and may reach the presence of the Father along paths that lie far apart. It matters little which we travel, if we come home at last.

¶ My conviction is that we can do nothing—not even remain passive—without the consent of the image (sometimes perverted) of God which is in us. I mean that mysterious Trinity—the Intellect, the Will, and Affections. The Will is, I think, incapable of producing belief without the concurrence of the other two—but they in their turn are equally so without the Will. This doctrine is most precious to me. About this time last year, my faith was fearfully shaken, because, upon one day honestly examining it, I found that it was not based upon pure intellectual conviction. Not knowing the true nature of belief, I thought I was wrong in believing any longer; so, to my infinite anguish, I suspended my belief till such time as I should see better reason for holding it. Several months of inexpressible misery were spent by me. I could arrive at nothing beyond the strongest *probability* in favour of Christianity. At length it seemed to me that Bishop Butler had taught that mere *probability* is the foundation of all our belief. Set in the right train of thought by this recollection, I soon arrived at what to me is an inestimable truth, and my faith has never been in the slightest degree shaken since. Directly a doubt suggests itself, I say, "Is all probability in favour of Christianity?" My intellect answers in the affirmative. My heart loves that of whose existence my intellect allows the probability, and my will puts the seal to the blessed compact which produces faith. What is there that we should believe if we insisted upon absolute proof of the intellect?[1]

4. Faith is not a matter of thinking, feeling, or willing separately, but an act in which the whole personality is involved. "Every genuine act of faith," says Julius Hare, "is the act of the whole

[1] *Memoirs and Correspondence of Coventry Patmore*, ii. 146.

man, not of his Understanding alone, not of his Affections alone, not of his Will alone, but of all three in their central aboriginal unity. It proceeds from the inmost depths of the soul, from beyond that firmament of Consciousness, whereby the waters under the firmament are divided from the waters above the firmament. It is the act of that living principle which constitutes each man's individual, continuous, immortal personality."[1]

Faith is not an activity of the intellect only; for studying a railway time-table, and believing that a train starts for London at a certain hour, will not bring a man into that great city. Nor is faith an activity of the affections only; for your feeling gratefully confident in the safety of travel by your favourite railway company, while you remain at home seated in your cosiest arm-chair, will not remove you from one place to another. Nor yet is faith an activity of the will only; for the will, unless urged by desire and enlightened by the intellect, would act aimlessly and uselessly. When, in faith, you make a venture, and when, in doubt, you hesitate, all the parts of your soul are active; your intellect thinks, your heart desires or feels averse, and your will decides or remains in suspense.

¶ Faith is not a matter of the head alone, nor of the heart alone, nor of any part of the spiritual man taken by itself. It is something which belongs to the whole spiritual character, and which affects every part of it. Sometimes it is intellectual, and then it embodies itself in the formation of or the assent to creeds. Sometimes it is emotional, and then it shows itself in strong love and loyalty towards God. Sometimes it is volitional, and shows itself by active deeds of charity and self-sacrifice. But in each case it is the act of the whole man, and not of any separate part of him, which is, let me say in passing, good philosophy as well as sound theology and sound practice.[2]

5. When we recognize faith as an act of the whole person we are able to give it its widest significance. We see that, in the words of Canon Scott Holland, it is "an elemental energy of basal self," that is, something that is perfectly natural to the best nature we have. It rises spontaneously from our deepest being,

---

[1] J. C. Hare, *The Victory of Faith*, 46.
[2] F. Relton, in *The Expository Times*, v. 262.

and is as natural as a child's faith and trust in its father and mother.

The best illustrations of faith are those drawn from our everyday life. By faith a child is enabled to live, to draw its very breath and food of daily existence from those by whom it came into the world; to look at them with deep, clear, trusting eyes, believing all they say, and believing them utterly and completely good. By faith the child, grown older, lives its intellectual life, sitting at the feet of master and teacher and pastor, and books and nature, and its own intuitive perceptions of things, and learning thence first to believe and to obey, in order that hereafter it may be able to obtain self-mastery, and to subdue all knowledge under its feet. By faith the lover looking into his mistress's face learns the secret of her soul, and in the glory of his "maiden passion for a maid" gains oftentimes his first glance at the glory of the Divine Love, a glory which first makes him tremble and then stand firm. By faith the man, battling with the world within and the world without, learns to discern a Power higher than himself and yet within himself, fighting on his side against all unreality and unrighteousness and error, and, by the consciousness of his daily victory, becomes one with that which thus he learns to know, until the faith of God becomes his faith, and he cries in the rapture and exultation of triumph, "I have fought a good fight, I have kept the faith." By faith the man when his work is done is content to know this world but a shadow, its prizes but illusions, its hopes but phantoms, its gains but losses, and to trust himself to his unseen Pilot to cross the Bar into the unknown land "where beyond these voices there is peace." In a word, faith is the sustaining and uplifting power that enables us to see Him who is invisible, and seeing to endure. It is the eye of the spiritual man to which is vouchsafed a vision of the eternal realities lying behind and beneath all temporal and passing phenomena. It is the ear of the soul catching the sound of the celestial harmonies heard often faintly but surely above the discord and wailing of the threnodies of earth. It is the spiritual hand stretching upward into the darkness, until, caught by the hand of the Unseen, it holds It and is held by It. It is the spiritual tongue singing the song of Zion in a strange land, and praising God even when His face is hidden, as we think, from us. Such is faith, a spiritual power, a spiritual force, a spiritual reality.

¶ Faith addresses itself to Man's whole being—it sounds every depth; it touches every spring; it calls back the soul from its weary search within itself, full of doubt and contradiction; it presents it with an object, implicit, absolute, greater than itself —" One that knoweth all things." It provides for every affection, every want and aspiration. Faith stretches itself over humanity as the prophet stretched himself above the child—eye to eye, mouth to mouth, heart to heart; and to work a kindred miracle, to bring back life to the dead, by restoring the One to the One— *the whole nature of Man to the whole nature of God.*[1]

6. But in giving faith its widest significance we must see that we do not rob it of its saving force. Certainly to St. Paul the word meant more than intellectual assent. He thought of faith as issuing from the centre of man's personality and expressing his volitional and affectional nature, in that he says with the heart man believeth unto righteousness. The same applies to the description of the specifically Christian principle as a faith that works by love. To the same effect also is the representation that faith is a means of vital union with Christ, so uniting its subject to Him that it becomes appropriate to speak of a mutual indwelling. In short, it is manifest that the faith which Paul exalts as the condition of salvation signifies nothing less than a thorough self-committal to God in Christ. It stands for this great ethical deed, and so contains implicitly not a little that might be designated by other names. By virtue of necessary connexions thorough self-committal to God in Christ involves a penitent forsaking of sin, a loyal confession of Christ, and a sincere espousal of the path of obedience to the known will of God.

Paul did not suppose that faith saves in its own virtue as a work or personal performance. The antithesis which he makes between salvation by works and salvation by the free gift of God in Christ emphatically negatives a supposition of that sort. The method of faith, he distinctly affirms, is the method according to grace. He conceives, therefore, of faith as the graciously appointed condition of salvation rather than its meritorious ground. It is not necessary, however, to imagine that he rated it

[1] Dora Greenwell, *The Patience of Hope*, 56.

as a mere indifferent instrument, serving by appointment a useful purpose, but having no ethical worth in itself. Without doubt he considered it to be intrinsically a noble and ennobling activity of the human spirit, and he has indicated as much by placing it alongside of hope and love among the things that have abiding worth.

¶ Jesus Christ is making His appeal to the whole of our life; He is offering us the whole of Himself to be appropriated by the whole of ourselves. He is offering us His life in exchange for ours. He is offering us Himself in exchange for ourselves, His divinity for our humanity; and all that He asks of us is not that we should adjust ourselves to a certain opinionative attitude toward Him—we shall do that all right in time if we do this other—but that we should bring ourselves, as He Himself put it, into the temperament and atmosphere of a little child. "Except ye be converted and become as little children, ye shall never enter, ye shall not even recognize, the kingdom of Heaven."[1]

¶ When a man sees the glory of God in the face of Jesus Christ he sees with his whole being. In *mind* he lets the Incarnate enter him; he *thinks* the Incarnation. He clears away from his mental retina false images, as an "early disciple" had to clear from his prejudice of his false Messianism, or Paul his Pharisaism, and receives upon it the image of a Jesus who is God; fastens his attention on the spiritual order of things behind the visible; ventures the intellectual venture by which we trust our conclusion that the spiritual is there indeed; searches the scriptures of the Book and of Nature, to know whether these things are so, with the dry light of a pure intention, seeking not himself but truth; in brief, makes that surrender of mind to fact which is in lesser matters the virtue of philosopher and scientist.

In the affections he admits the Incarnate. He turns from the desired things, in which a man is seeking only himself—from the gold, the wine, the food, the passion, sensuality, and that "last infirmity"—and fills the hunger of the heart with Christ, made of a woman, that he might be sought and found by the mortal's love; sought and found, as by an à Kempis rapturing in his cloister, or by a Catharine doing mercies in the street for the brethren, in whom she does it unto Him.

And in his action he receives the Incarnate. For his willing is the willing away of the self to let the Father's will, discovered in Jesus of Nazareth, be done by an *imitatio Christi*. An imitation, not as that cloistered one has planned it, not a Christ-

[1] R. E. Speer, *The Master of the Heart*, 68.

like submissiveness only, but also a Christlike forcefulness, of striving, toiling, getting and spending, of war, adventure, conquest, rule.

This then is the Response; thus the soul adjusts itself to the fact in its environment, the Son of God become incarnate in Jesus born at Bethlehem.[1]

> The law of faith
> Working through love, such conquest shall it gain,
> Such triumph over sin and guilt achieve?
> Almighty Lord, thy further grace impart!
> And with that help the wonder shall be seen
> Fulfilled, the hope accomplished; and thy praise
> Be sung with transport and unceasing joy.[2]

[1] J. H. Skrine, *What is Faith?* 157.
[2] Wordsworth, "The Excursion," bk. ix.

www.ingramcontent.com/pod-product-compliance
Lightning Source LLC
Chambersburg PA
CBHW070058020526
44112CB00034B/1432